T0340619

that shaped it. Students who read carefully will be rewarded with not only a profoundly enriched understanding of the Gospel but also a solid introduction to Greco-Roman literary, rhetorical, and dramatic traditions."

—**Colleen M. Conway**, professor of religious studies,
Seton Hall University

"Jo-Ann Brant has written a commentary on the Fourth Gospel that is ideal for the classroom and the pastor's study, while also proving useful to the scholar. She serves as an authoritative guide to the world of ancient literature and makes two major contributions. First, by paying close attention to the intricacies of the Johannine narrative, she demonstrates in considerable detail the sophistication with which the Fourth Gospel was constructed. Second, she gives attention to both the Jewish and Hellenistic backgrounds of the Fourth Gospel without overemphasizing one at the expense of the other. I recommend this commentary highly."

—**Chris Keith**, assistant professor of New Testament and
Christian origins, Lincoln Christian University

"Brant engages extensively with both ancient and modern sources in such a way that the student receives an introduction to major figures and currents in both the ancient world and modern scholarship on John. Her special focus on ancient rhetoric includes explanation of the terms and techniques, providing the student with a lively working introduction to this field of study. Her commentary is clear, concise, and engaging, with many insights that provide an important supplement to the more conventional and comprehensive commentaries."

—**Rodney A. Whitacre**, professor of biblical studies,
Trinity School for Ministry

John

John

JO-ANN A. BRANT

Baker Academic
a division of Baker Publishing Group
Grand Rapids, Michigan

© 2011 by Jo-Ann A. Brant

Published by Baker Academic
a division of Baker Publishing Group
PO Box 6287, Grand Rapids, MI 49516–6287
www.bakeracademic.com

Printed in the United States of America

Library of Congress Cataloging-in-Publication Data

Brant, Jo-Ann A., 1956–
     John / Jo-Ann A. Brant.
        p.   cm. — (Paideia: commentaries on the New Testament)
     Includes bibliographical references and index.
     ISBN 978-0-8010-3454-1 (pbk.)
     1. Bible. N.T. John—Commentaries. I. Title.
BS2615.53.B73 2011
226.5′07—dc22   2011012330

Contents

Figures and Tables

◫

Figures

Tables

Foreword

Paideia: Commentaries on the New Testament is a series that sets out to comment on the final form of the New Testament text in a way that pays due attention both to the cultural, literary, and theological settings in which the text took form and to the interests of the contemporary readers to whom the commentaries are addressed. This series is aimed squarely at students—including MA students in religious and theological studies programs, seminarians, and upper-division undergraduates—who have theological interests in the biblical text. Thus, the didactic aim of the series is to enable students to understand each book of the New Testament as a literary whole rooted in a particular ancient setting and related to its context within the New Testament.

The name "Paideia" (Greek for "education") reflects (1) the instructional aim of the series—giving contemporary students a basic grounding in academic New Testament studies by guiding their engagement with New Testament texts; (2) the fact that the New Testament texts as literary unities are shaped by the educational categories and ideas (rhetorical, narratological, etc.) of their ancient writers and readers; and (3) the pedagogical aims of the texts themselves—their central aim being not simply to impart information but to form the theological convictions and moral habits of their readers.

Each commentary deals with the text in terms of larger rhetorical units; these are not verse-by-verse commentaries. This series thus stands within the stream of recent commentaries that attend to the final form of the text. Such reader-centered literary approaches are inherently more accessible to liberal arts students without extensive linguistic and historical-critical preparation than older exegetical approaches, but within the reader-centered world the sanest practitioners have paid careful attention to the extratext of the original readers, including not only these readers' knowledge of the geography, history, and other contextual elements reflected in the text but also their ability to respond correctly to the literary and rhetorical conventions used in the text. Paideia commentaries pay deliberate attention to this extratextual repertoire in order to highlight the ways in which the text is designed to persuade and move its readers. Each rhetorical unit is explored from three angles: (1) introductory matters; (2) tracing the train of thought or narrative or rhetorical flow of the argument; and (3) theological issues raised by the text that are of interest to the contemporary Christian. Thus, the primary focus remains on the text and not its historical context or its interpretation in the secondary literature.

Our authors represent a variety of confessional points of view: Protestant, Catholic, and Orthodox. What they share, beyond being New Testament scholars of national and international repute, is a commitment to reading the biblical text as theological documents within their ancient contexts. Working within the broad parameters described here, each author brings his or her own considerable exegetical talents and deep theological commitments to the task of laying bare the interpretation of Scripture for the faith and practice of God's people everywhere.

Mikeal C. Parsons
Charles H. Talbert

Preface

When my students complain that the problem with the Bible is that no one can agree on its meaning, I counter with the suggestion that when people cease to discuss and debate its meaning, Scripture will have become a dead rather than a living tradition. Commentary is a vital part of a religious tradition that brings those who live in the present into dialogue with the community that received the text and the communities that have handed down the text to us. While some older commentaries are so insightful that they continue to deserve a place in a seminary reference room or on the open stacks, none provides the final word. Archaeological discoveries, observations about both the nature of human societies and the physical world, new methodologies, and, though sometimes regrettably, prevailing ideologies—these call for continuous reengagement and fresh commentary. This commentary belongs to the Paideia series and makes its contribution by intentionally instructing its reader about such things as ancient argumentation and narrative conventions in order to prepare the next generation of readers to enter into the commentary tradition.

A file in my office marked "graduate papers" contains a paper dated March 1985 on Jesus's "cleansing" of the temple, in which one can find my first attempt to comment on the Gospel of John. I wrote, "John's depiction of the event reads like the script of a play by blocking out a character's movements." At the time, my interest in the Gospel of John was limited to the requirements of my doctoral comprehensive exams. I went on to write a dissertation on "oaths and vows: how to make them, how to break them" in Second Temple Judaism, but when I began to teach the New Testament, I found that John was the Gospel I most enjoyed pondering with my students and that my interest in its dramatic structures grew stronger with each reading. Twenty years later, a complete monograph on John's use of theatrical conventions finally appeared (Brant 2004). My interest in ancient drama continues to inform my work, but this commentary allows my broad interest in how language does things to come into play.

While this commentary is the product of many hours of solitary labor, a wide circle of people made it possible for me to devote my time to this work. I wish first of all to thank James Ernest, editor of the Paideia series, who proposed that my name be added to the list of contributors to the series and provided significant suggestions about the content of the manuscript. I thank R. Alan Culpepper for giving his vote of confidence and the general editors Mikeal C. Parsons and Charles H. Talbert for extending the invitation to write the John volume. I am grateful to Wells Turner, senior editor, and to Rachel Klompmaker, editorial assistant, for bringing the project to completion. I owe many thanks to Dave Garber, who served as copyeditor and spared me much embarrassment by catching many errors.

I am indebted to the support provided to me by all my colleagues at Goshen College. A few must be named for particular reasons. President James Brenneman believed that this was an important project that I should accept. Dean Anita Stalter approved of my sabbatical to complete it. Professor Paul Keim never failed to show interest when I answered his question, "What are you working on now?" Librarian Laura Hostetler kept me continuously supplied with books and articles from other libraries. Nine brave students—Saron Ayele, Michael Dicken, Dusty Diller, Ashley Ervin, Dara Joy Jaworowicz, Kaleem Kheshgi, Dirk Miller, Breanna Nickel, and Matthew Plummer—participated in a seminar course on the Gospel of John and provided valuable feedback on the first draft of the commentary. I am especially grateful to Dara Joy Jaworowicz, who served as my assistant for several years and whose growing passion for biblical studies reinvigorates my own. I thank my circle of friends in the Ancient Fiction and Early Christian and Jewish Narrative section of the Society of Biblical Literature for keeping my work grounded in a broad context. Above all, I am thankful for my husband, Joe Springer, who always anticipates my needs and has added organization and delight to my life.

Commentary on ancient texts requires translation or working from translations. Translations of Greek and Latin texts are my own unless stated otherwise. Quotations from the Hebrew Bible are from the NRSV. My translation of the Gospel of John is not intended for liturgical use. It follows the syntax and replicates the grammar of the Greek as closely as possible. As a result the English translation is not always grammatically sound and frequently less elegant than the original Greek. Occasionally the choice of English words seeks first to reproduce Johannine figurative language rather than provide the best literal translation. John, like other ancient classical Greek authors, uses the subjunctive mood much more than modern English authors. Most contemporary translations use indicative rather than subjunctive verbs whenever possible. I have translated the subjunctive with either an infinitive or subjunctive verb form in order to preserve the mood appropriate to the context. John switches back and forth in his use of past tenses and the historical present, and some translations mute this by consistently using the past tense. With the exception of the verb *oida* (the perfect form of *eidomai*, "I see," that has the present sense of "I know"), this translation preserves the tense of the Greek verbs, especially the historical present. John seems to use the historical present as part of a rhetorical strategy to create a sense that narrated past action is unfolding before one's eyes. John uses *oun* instead of *de* or *kai* at the beginning of sentences with unusual frequency. Conjunctions normally appear at the beginning of sentences in ancient Greek expository discourse (speeches/dialogues embedded in the narrative). Because we do not use conjunctions at the beginning of sentences in English, it is difficult to draw attention to John's asyndeton (the absence of an explicit conjunction) in translation. Therefore I comment when seemingly significant cases of asyndeton occur or insert a word, such as "immediately," in square brackets to signal the effect of the asyndeton.

Translation and written composition is a process of selection and reduction. Alternate wording, digressions, additional illustrations, and supporting quotations now sit in files labeled deleted material. I hope that what is left, this commentary, does justice to the care with which the author we know as John selected the content of his Gospel.

Jo-Ann A. Brant

Abbreviations

General

†	year of death	Gk.	Greek
acc.	accusative	Heb.	Hebrew
AT	author's translation	i.e.	*id est*, that is
b.	Babylonian Talmud	Lat.	Latin
ca.	*circa*	lit.	literally
cent(s).	century/centuries	*m.*	Mishnah
cf.	compare	nom.	nominative
chap(s).	chapter(s)	NT	New Testament
col(s).	column(s)	OT	Old Testament
dir.	director	par.	parallel
ed.	edited by, edition	pl.	plural
e.g.	*exempli gratia*, for example	rev.	revised
		t.	Tosefta
Eng.	English	trans.	translator, translated by
esp.	especially	vol(s).	volume(s)
ET	English translation	x	following a numeral = times, number of occurrences
et al.	*et alii*, and others		
fig.	figure, figurative	*y.*	Jerusalem Talmud

Bible Texts and Versions

ASV	American Standard Version	KJV	King James Version
ISV	International Standard Version	LXX	Septuagint
		MT	Masoretic Text

NA[27]	*Novum Testamentum Graece*. Edited by [E. and E. Nestle and] B. Aland et al. 27th rev. ed. Stuttgart: Deutsche Bibelgesellschaft, 1993.

NIV	New International Version
NRSV	New Revised Standard Version

Ancient Corpora

OLD TESTAMENT

Gen.	Genesis
Exod.	Exodus
Lev.	Leviticus
Num.	Numbers
Deut.	Deuteronomy
Josh.	Joshua
Judg.	Judges
Ruth	Ruth
1–2 Sam.	1–2 Samuel
1–2 Kings	1–2 Kings
1–2 Chron.	1–2 Chronicles
Ezra	Ezra
Neh.	Nehemiah
Esth.	Esther
Job	Job
Ps(s).	Psalm(s)
Prov.	Proverbs
Eccles.	Ecclesiastes
Song	Song of Songs
Isa.	Isaiah
Jer.	Jeremiah
Lam.	Lamentations
Ezek.	Ezekiel
Dan.	Daniel
Hosea	Hosea
Joel	Joel
Amos	Amos
Obad.	Obadiah
Jon.	Jonah
Mic.	Micah
Nah.	Nahum
Hab.	Habakkuk
Zeph.	Zephaniah
Hag.	Haggai
Zech.	Zechariah
Mal.	Malachi

DEUTEROCANONICAL BOOKS

1–4 Macc.	1–4 Maccabees
Sir.	Sirach
Tob.	Tobit
Wis.	Wisdom of Solomon

NEW TESTAMENT

Matt.	Matthew
Mark	Mark
Luke	Luke
John	John
Acts	Acts
Rom.	Romans
1–2 Cor.	1–2 Corinthians
Gal.	Galatians
Eph.	Ephesians
Phil.	Philippians
Col.	Colossians
1–2 Thess.	1–2 Thessalonians
1–2 Tim.	1–2 Timothy
Titus	Titus
Philem.	Philemon
Heb.	Hebrews
James	James
1–2 Pet.	1–2 Peter
1–3 John	1–3 John
Jude	Jude
Rev.	Revelation

DEAD SEA SCROLLS AND RELATED WRITINGS

CD	*Damascus Document*
1QS	*Rule of the Community*
1QSa	*Rule of the Congregation*
4QTest	*Testimonia* (4Q175)

TARGUMIC TEXTS

Tg. Ps-J.   Targum Pseudo-Jonathan

RABBINIC LITERATURE

B. Qam.   Baba Qamma
Ber.   Berakot
Eccles. Rab.   Ecclesiastes Rabbah
Exod. Rab.   Exodus Rabbah
Gen. Rab.   Genesis Rabbah
Ḥag.   Ḥagigah
Meg.   Megillah
Mek.   Mekilta
Menaḥ.   Menaḥot
Miqw.   Miqwa'ot
Neg.   Nega'im
Nid.   Niddah
Num. Rab.   Numbers Rabbah
Pesaḥ.   Pesaḥim
Pesiq. Rab Kah.   Pesiqta de Rab Kahana
Ruth Rab.   Ruth Rabbah
Šabb.   Šabbat
Sanh.   Sanhedrin
Šeb.   Šebi'it
Ta'an.   Ta'anit
Yad.   Yadayim
Yebam.   Yebamot

OLD TESTAMENT PSEUDEPIGRAPHA

Apoc. Ab.   Apocalypse of Abraham
2 Bar.   2 Baruch (Syriac Apocalypse)
1 En.   1 Enoch (Ethiopic Apocalypse)
Jos. Asen.   Joseph and Aseneth
Jub.   Jubilees
L.A.E.   Life of Adam and Eve
Let. Aris.   Letter of Aristeas
Sib. Or.   Sibylline Oracles
T. Ab.   Testament of Abraham

APOSTOLIC FATHERS

1 Clem.   1 Clement
Did.   Didache

NEW TESTAMENT APOCRYPHA AND PSEUDEPIGRAPHA

Acts Pet.   Acts of Peter
Gos. Pet.   Gospel of Peter

NAG HAMMADI CODICES

Gos. Thom.   II,2 Gospel of Thomas
Thom. Cont.   II,7 Book of Thomas the Contender

Ancient Authors

ACHILLES TATIUS

Leuc. Clit.   Leucippe et Clitophon

AELIUS THEON

Progymn.   Progymnasmata

APHTHONIUS THE SOPHIST

Progymn.   Progymnasmata

AQUINAS. See THOMAS AQUINAS

ARISTOPHANES

Ach.   Archarnenses
Vesp.   Vespae

ARISTOTLE

Eth. nic.   Ethica nicomachea
Phys.   Physica
Poet.   Poetica
Pol.   Politica
Rhet.   Rhetorica
Soph. elench.   Sophistici elenchi

AUGUSTINE OF HIPPO

Tract. Ev. Jo.   In Evangelium Johannis tractatus

AULUS GELLIUS

Noct. att.   Noctes atticae

CASSIUS DIO

Hist.	Historia romana

CHARITON

Chaer.	De Chaerea et Callirhoe

CICERO

Amic.	De amicitia
Att.	Epistulae ad Atticum
Fam.	Epistulae ad familiares
Inv.	De inventione rhetorica
Off.	De officiis
De or.	De oratore
Or. Brut.	Orator ad M. Brutum
Phil.	Orationes philippicae
Sest.	Pro Sestio
Tusc.	Tusculanae disputationes

CLEMENT OF ALEXANDRIA

Paed.	Paedagogus
Strom.	Stromata

CYPRIAN

Test.	Ad Quirinum testimonia adversus Judaeos
Unit. eccl.	De catholicae ecclesiae unitate

DEMOSTHENES

Fals. leg.	De falsa legatione
Halon.	De Halonneso

DIO CHRYSOSTOM

3 Regn.	De regno iii (Or. 3)

DIONYSIUS OF HALICARNASSUS

Ant. rom.	Antiquitates romanae

EPICTETUS

Diatr.	Diatribai (Dissertationes)

EPICURUS

Gnom. vat.	Gnomologium vaticanum

EURIPIDES

Alc.	Alcestis
Andr.	Andromache
Bacch.	Bacchae
Hel.	Helena
Herc. fur.	Hercules furens
Iph. aul.	Iphigenia aulidensis
Iph. taur.	Iphigenia taurica
Med.	Medea
Phoen.	Phoenissae
Tro.	Troades

EUSEBIUS

Hist. eccl.	Historia ecclesiastica

HELIODORUS

Aeth.	Aethiopica

HERMOGENES

Progymn.	Progymnasmata

HERODOTUS

Hist.	Historiae

HESIOD

Theog.	Theogonia

HIPPOLYTUS

Haer.	Refutatio omnium haeresium

HOMER

Il.	Ilias
Od.	Odyssea

IRENAEUS

Haer.	Adversus haereses

ISOCRATES

Demon.	Ad Demonicum (Or. 1)

JEROME

Comm. Ezech.	Commentariorum in Eze-chielem libri XVI
Comm. Ps.	Commentarioli in Psalmos

JOHN CHRYSOSTOM

Hom. Act.	Homiliae in Acta apostolorum

Hom. Jo.	Homiliae in Joannem		**PHILO OF ALEXANDRIA**	
Quatr. Laz.	In quatriduanum Lazarum		Cher.	De cherubim
			Flacc.	In Flaccum
JOHN OF SARDIS			Fug.	De fuga et inventione
Progymn.	Progymnasmata		Leg.	Legum allegoriae
			Legat.	Legatio ad Gaium
JOSEPHUS			Mos.	De vita Mosis
Ag. Ap.	Against Apion		Mut.	De mutatione nominum
Ant.	Antiquitates judaicae		Opif.	De opificio mundi
J.W.	Jewish War		Spec.	De specialibus legibus
Life	The Life			
			PHILOSTRATUS	
JULIANUS AEGYPTIUS			Ep.	Epistulae
Ep.	Epigrammaticus			
			PLATO	
JUSTIN MARTYR			Apol.	Apologia
1 Apol.	Apologia i		Phaed.	Phaedo
Dial.	Dialogus cum Tryphone		Symp.	Symposium
JUVENAL			**PLAUTUS**	
Sat.	Satirae		Capt.	Captivi
			Mil. glor.	Miles gloriosus
LIVY			Pers.	Persae
Hist.	Historiae (Ab urbe condita)		Stic.	Sticus
			Trin.	Trinummus
LONGUS				
Daphn.	Daphnis and Chloe		**PLINY THE ELDER**	
			Nat.	Naturalis historia
LUCIAN				
Sat.	Saturnalia		**PLINY THE YOUNGER**	
			Pan.	Panegyricus
MARTIAL				
Epig.	Epigrammata		**PLUTARCH**	
			Adul. amic.	Quomodo adulator ab amico internoscatur
NICOLAUS THE SOPHIST				
Progymn.	Progymnasmata		Alex.	Alexander
			Ant.	Antonius
ORIGEN			Cor.	Marcius Coriolanus
Comm. Jo.	Commentarii in evangelium Joannis		Dem.	Demosthenes
			Demetr.	Demetrius
Hom. Job	Homiliae in Job		Phoc.	Phocion
			Pomp.	Pompeius
PETRONIUS			Quaest. conv.	Quaestiones conviviales libri IX
Satyr.	Satyricon			
			Ti. C. Gracch.	Tiberius et Caius Gracchus
PHILODEMUS OF GADARA				
Lib.	De libertate dicendi			
Vit.	De vitiis			

POLLUX
  Onom.   Onomasticon

POLYBIUS
  Hist.   Historia

QUINTILIAN
  Inst.   Institutio oratoria

SENECA (THE YOUNGER)
  Clem.   De clementia
  Ep.   Epistulae morales
  Vit. beat.   De vita beata

SOPHOCLES
  Ant.   Antigone
  El.   Elektra
  Oed. col.   Oedipus coloneus
  Oed. tyr.   Oedipus tyrannus

SUETONIUS
  Aug.   Divus Augustus
  Cal.   Gaius Caligula
  Claud.   Divus Claudius
  Dom.   Domitianus
  Jul.   Divus Julius
  Tib.   Tiberius

TACITUS
  Ann.   Annales

TERTULLIAN
  Apol.   Apologeticus
  Cor.   De corona militis
  Marc.   Adversus Marcionem
  Praescr.   De praescriptione
               haereticorum
  Scap.   Ad Scapulam
  Spect.   De spectaculis

THEOPHRASTUS
  Char.   Characteres

THOMAS AQUINAS
  Joh.   Expositio in evangelium
               Joannis

THUCYDIDES
  Hist.   Historia

VALERIUS MAXIMUS
  Fact.   Facta et dicta memorabilia

XENOPHON OF EPHESUS
  Ephes.   Ephesiaca

XENOPHON THE HISTORIAN
  Cyr.   Cyropaedia

Ancient Collections and Anonymous Works

Dig.	Digesta	Rhet. Her.	Rhetorica ad Herennium
Res gest. divi Aug.	Res gestae divi Augusti (funeral inscription)		

Modern Works, Series, and Collections

NPNF[1]	Nicene and Post-Nicene Fathers. 1st series. Edited by P. Schaff. 14 vols. 1886–89. Repr., Peabody, MA: Hendrickson, 1994.	OTP	The Old Testament Pseudepigrapha. Edited by J. H. Charlesworth. 2 vols. Garden City, NY: Doubleday, 1983–85.
		P.Herc.	Herculaneum papyrus

John

Introduction

Beginning in the late Middle Ages, the lecterns in European cathedrals from which Scripture was read often took the form of an eagle, the symbol for John the Evangelist, with the result that the Latin word for eagle, *aquila*, became a synonym for lectern. The eagle's widespread wings provided a desk upon which to rest a cumbersome medieval Bible. While the symbol for the Fourth Evangelist may have been more suited to this function than Mark's lion or Luke's ox, Matthew's angel might have worked equally well. Art historians and congregations that continue to install eagle lecterns look to the association of the image with the Gospel of John and not just the shape of the symbol to account for its popularity. How appropriate to read "the Word of God" from a symbol for the evangelist whose soaring rhetoric proclaims, "In the beginning was the Word."

The Gospel of John is fraught with familiar symbolism and imagery, and readers often treat it as a compendium of sayings from which one can lift out a passage or image here or there for spiritual or artistic inspiration. In contrast, reading the Gospel of John as a single literary work can be a disorienting experience. The Gospel introduces Jesus with

Figure 1. The eagle lectern from the fourteenth-century Buckland Church of St. Andrew.

Johannine scholars borrow the Greek rhetorical term *aporia* (difficulty, or puzzle) to indicate places where the text seems to contradict itself or its structure unravels (see, e.g., the abrupt jump in location from Jerusalem to the Galilee in John 6:1). In rhetoric, an *aporia* occurs when a speaker argues both sides of an issue. Perhaps the most famous instance of an *aporia* in a literary work is Hamlet's soliloquy, "To be or not to be: that is the question."

an ambiguous signifier, the *Logos*, and then proceeds through a select number of episodes that, for a modern audience, provoke one persistent question: why is this Gospel so different from the Synoptic Gospels? Lines that Christians commonly cite as foundational to their faith, such as "I am the way, and the truth, and the life" (14:6), begin to perplex when read within their narrative setting, in which Jesus antagonizes rather than inspires his audience. This commentary brings into view subtleties and complexities in the text, as well as the coherence that may evade modern readers, by identifying the rhetorical and narrative strategies and key theological themes that make the Gospel a unified work.

To prepare for a sustained reading of the Gospel, this introduction addresses some of the traditional questions of authorship and provenance, but the principal focus is on introducing features of the Gospel's rhetoric and narrative structure that facilitate a synchronic versus a diachronic reading. A diachronic reading is concerned with identifying stages in the development of the text: the appropriation of literary sources by its author and revision by various editors. A synchronic reading focuses on the extant text (a text based on careful discernment of the best manuscript traditions by an international and ecumenical committee of lower critics). While many aporias in the Gospel of John can be explained away by presupposing multiple editors with different priorities, the synchronic approach demonstrates that the Gospel's interlocking and sustained themes and rhetorical strategies render it a unified literary work and that, in many cases, aporias may either serve a literary purpose or simply be a feature of human thought.

Date, Authorship, and Provenance

The earliest extant NT fragment, $\mathfrak{P}^{52}$ (Rylands Library Papyrus 457), contains John 18:31–33 and 37–38 and is dated to ca. AD 130. Hippolytus of Rome (ca. 170–236) quotes an Alexandrian gnostic named Basilides, who quoted John 1:9 around AD 130 (*Haer.* 7.10). Justin Martyr, writing in about AD 155, knew the dialogue with Nicodemus in John 3:1–5 (*1 Apol.* 61). Together these references indicate that the latest possible date for the composition was in the early first half of the second century. The apparent lack of acknowledgment of the Synoptic Gospels or explicit reference to the destruction of the temple in the Gospel provides support for an argument for composition before AD 70. The emphasis on exclusion from the synagogue rather than the temple (9:22; 12:42; 16:2), however, suggests to most scholars a date after the destruction of the temple, in a period when Christians and Jews began to define themselves in mutually exclusive terms. Many contend that a lengthy time period is required for the development of the Gospel's Christology. Some suggest that, by the time the Gospel is written, sufficient time has passed for the rise of a Johannine sectarian community that intentionally disregarded the synoptic material. Both the criteria of developed Christology and sectarian status are contestable, and many scholars are now pushing the date for the development of both Christian and Jewish orthodoxies into the third or even fourth century. Nevertheless, a date a decade or so after AD 70 seems to be warranted. Though the Gospel does not refer to the destruction of the temple, the question of how to worship without a temple seems to inform the dialogues and action of the Gospel.

In this commentary, the name "John" is used to refer to the author of the Fourth Gospel. This habit reflects the historical attribution of the Gospel to the disciple John and is not an assertion of the validity of the attribution. The Gospel itself names "the disciple whom Jesus loved," popularly known as the Beloved Disciple, as its authority. The earliest attestation that John the son of Zebedee is the author of the Fourth Gospel comes from Irenaeus († ca. AD 180; *Haer.* 3.1.1; quoted in Eusebius, *Hist. eccl.* 5.8.4), who recalls hearing the elderly Polycarp († ca. AD 155) say that he had it directly from John. Irenaeus is not consistent; he also attributes his source to Papias († ca. AD 163). Moreover, Eusebius questions whether this might be a reference to John the Elder, the author of 2 and 3 John. What is significant about these early attributions is that by the second century, tying the author to a known and authoritative first-person witness had become important. Modern arguments about authorship have been less concerned with lining the author up with one of the twelve disciples and more interested in broadening the scope of discipleship and leadership in the early church by including as candidates for authorship Mary Magdalene (de Boer 1996), Lazarus (Waetjen 2005, 18), Thomas Didymus (Charlesworth 1995), and Nathanael (Catchpole 1998). While these possibilities are intriguing, evidence is thin and has not persuaded many scholars to adopt any particular identifiable individual. Many find themselves returning again to the hypothesis that either John the son of Zebedee, perhaps in collaboration with John the Elder, is the authoritative witness who informs the Gospel (Hengel 1993). What is noteworthy is how identification of authorship is tied to trends within the church: first to centralize authority, and then to decentralize it.

Several scholars have argued that the Beloved Disciple is an idealized figure (e.g., Loisy 1903) or that the phrase "the disciple whom Jesus loved" is a circumscription for a number of witnesses (e.g., Casey 1996, 160–64). Jesus loved all his disciples and friends. There is, nevertheless, sufficient evidence pointing to an individual who had a significant teaching career and died, perhaps unexpectedly (see 21:20–24), to treat the Beloved Disciple as a particular disciple, but within the Gospel he does fulfill a special role. His identity is carefully veiled, suggesting that he serves an important literary or exemplary function that stands apart from any authority that one might ascribe to him by virtue of his role as a leader or performer of heroic acts. Unlike Simon Peter, he has access to privileged conversations with the high priest, and he does not blurt out what he thinks, sparing him the scrutiny subjected to the confessions of other characters or the test of loyalty that Simon Peter at first fails. In the narrative, what he knows, he keeps to himself (20:8). He stands in a dialectical relationship with Simon Peter. The two are frequently paired (1:35, 40; 13:23–24). Simon Peter is the traditional martyr who witnesses to his faith through his obedient death, whereas the Beloved Disciple witnesses by watching attentively, recognizing or making sense of what he sees in light of Jesus's teaching or actions and Hebrew Scripture, and then eventually sharing it with others. While he may be more astute than Peter, he is not represented as prescient (13:28); he like others is enlightened by Jesus's resurrection. Moreover, he plays no significant role in the action. He is like many other anonymous witnesses who have faithfully handed on what they have seen and heard in order to sustain a tradition of belief and practice.

In the final verses of the Gospel, the narrator states with reference to the Beloved Disciple, "This is the disciple, the witness concerning these things, and the one who has caused these things to be written" (21:24). While the narrator tells us that the Beloved Disciple is the authority for the truth of what has been written, the action is not focalized through the eyes of the disciple. The narrator recounts scenes at which no disciple is present. Moreover, the narrator refers to the Beloved Disciple in the third person, and 21:23 seems to imply that he has died. In antiquity, authors often referred to themselves in the third person. Thucydides begins his history with these words: "Thucydides, an Athenian, composed the history of the war between the Peloponnesians and the Athenians" (*Hist.* 1.1.1). In this case, however, the use of the third person points to a complicated process of publication.

To speak of the author of the Gospel requires clarification. The Beloved Disciple seems to stand in the position of a teacher from whom the composer or author learned the story. The word "author" connotes the source for the words on the page but not necessarily the person who wrote the words. In antiquity, one did not have to be literate to be the author of a piece of writing, especially a letter. Composers of letters and literature often dictated to a secretary who may have had strong literary skills and who might have, therefore, been free to finesse the grammar and vocabulary of a composition. In his study of Greco-Roman letter writing, E. Randolph Richards (2004, 64) finds that a secretary's role fell somewhere between transcriber, contributor, and

Gnosticism

Gnosticism refers to various movements (Jewish, Christian, and pagan) in antiquity claiming that a malevolent demiurge created the material world to entrap divine sparks (souls) in mortal flesh. Esoteric knowledge (*gnōsis*) of the soul's true nature then liberated humans from the material world. Some early twentieth-century scholars in the history-of-religions school reconstructed a gnostic redeemer myth about a heavenly being who comes to earth to control demonic forces and impart wisdom. They treated this myth as foundational to the Gospel's Christology, but manuscript evidence suggests that the redeemer myth developed *after* the canonical Gospels were composed. Debates continue within the academy regarding the date of gnostic thought and whether gnostic Christian movements should be treated as heretical and marginal or alternate and significant expressions of early Christianity.

composer. In personal letters to his secretary Tiro, Cicero thanks him for his invaluable service in Cicero's "studies and literary work" (*in studiis, in litteris nostris*; *Fam.* 16.4.3; see also 16.11.1) and on one occasion describes how Tiro "loved to be the standard [*kanōn*]" of his writings (16.17.1). Cicero's use of the Greek word *kanōn* suggests that he is using the terms of their old intimacy.

The author composed for a lector (reader); therefore, first-person singular pronouns could refer to either the author or the reader in the capacity of narrator, and first-person plural pronouns, to the reader and audience (see 1:14; 21:24–25). John's narrator is not a character within the world of the narrative comparable to the narrator of *Moby Dick*, who invites his readers in the first line to "Call me Ishmael." John's first-person narrator belongs to the world of the audience.

Most modern theories of narration presuppose an individual silent reader, but any discussion of authorship and narration of John must take into account the performance art of ancient reading. John wrote for an oral reading. This commentary, therefore, refers to the narrator as the reader, the one who takes on the role of narrator by reading the words supplied by the author. A distinction is maintained between "the reader," who narrates, and "the audience" of the Gospel, which listens to the Gospel being read or recited. In the modern context, these two entities collapse into the solitary silent reader, who is free to linger over passages or flip pages back and forth to clarify meaning. In antiquity, reading moved forward through a text at a pace designed for an audience to follow.

Arguments to locate the place of composition for the Gospel tend to be tied to arguments regarding its intended audience and, hence, its purpose or the thought world to which it belongs. In his critique of heresies, Irenaeus claims that John resided and wrote the Gospel in Ephesus (*Haer.* 3.1.1) and asserts that John wrote to discredit a local gnostic heresy, against which Irenaeus now contends (3.11.1). Many scholars think that Irenaeus has inverted the relationship. Early Christian gnostics seem to have known John rather than John knowing or addressing Gnosticism (e.g., *Trimorphic Protennoia*).

Given that the earliest manuscripts and references to the Gospel come from Egypt, it is plausible that this is where it was written. However, manuscripts were better preserved in the dry Egyptian climate, so the argument for Egypt cannot rest on the manuscript evidence alone. Scholars who favor an Egyptian provenance do so because John seems to draw from a Hellenistic milieu similar to that of Philo of Alexandria (20 BC–AD 50). John's familiarity and references to Judea and the Galilee suggest to others that he wrote from and for an audience in that area. For many years, scholars argued back and forth, situating John within either a Jewish milieu or a Hellenistic milieu, but of late, scholars have recognized that their picture of Judaism has relied too heavily on imposing later forms, those of the sixth-century Babylonian rabbis, on first-century Judaism in order to draw distinctions. An observant Jew could obtain a Hellenistic education in Judea and even in the Galilee. The question of where John wrote has given way in recent years to inquiries about the education necessary to facilitate the composition of the Gospel.

References to reading in Jewish literature during the Roman period (1QS 6.6–8; 8.11–12; Josephus *Ag. Ap.* 2.204) suggest to some a high degree of literacy among Jews throughout the Mediterranean world, but recent studies argue that the documentary evidence represents only elite groups and that a literacy rate of about 10 percent, comparable to other populations, would have been normative (see Hezser 2001, 496–504). Consequently, it may not be logical to assume that the Jews had an education system alternate and parallel to the Greco-Roman rhetorical schools. Jews would have learned to recite Scripture from memory in the synagogues, but there is no evidence for formal rabbinical schools until the third century. Scribes were most likely educated in an apprentice system or within the context of family enterprises rather than in a scribal school. John's description of Jesus's education by the side of the Father suggests an apprenticeship (John 5:19–23). Similarity in exegesis in the writings of Philo of Alexandria and *Genesis Rabbah* suggests to Peder Borgen that John attended a synagogal school with a curriculum of exegetical questions and answers found in such schools (2003, 126–29), but this curriculum may have been more like catechesis than biblical studies. Like most NT authors, John demonstrates a familiarity with a narrow strip of Hebrew Scripture and not necessarily an expansive knowledge of the Torah, Prophets, and Writings. He does, nevertheless, represent Jesus as capable of the use of sophisticated exegetical techniques.

The Gospel's limited Greek vocabulary and grammar suggests someone working in a second language. Perhaps the most telltale sign of the author's

Greco-Roman Education

Formal education beyond instruction at home in religion, family, and civic traditions began at a preparatory school for sons of citizens that taught grammar, geometry, astronomy, literature, physical competition, and theoretical music, with rhetoric and dialectic as the crowning accomplishments. Imitation of pieces of classical writing was central to even the earliest stages of this education. Students learned to read and write by using exercises (*progymnasmata*) contained in handbooks that delineated the various styles and forms of rhetoric and contained well-known examples from classical literature for students to imitate (see Quintilian, *Inst.* 1.10–11). The most advanced students proceeded to a curriculum of *gymnasmata*, practice of oral declamations on a particular theme—a legal argument or a political or social concept—utilizing all the skills gained through imitation of the masters.

limited Greek is the nonuse of the optative mood with the exception of John 13:24. In contrast, Luke uses the optative twenty-eight times and Paul thirty-one times. By the Greco-Roman era, the optative mood had disappeared from letters and other forms of writing that did not deliberately seek to imitate Attic Greek. John's syntax does not demonstrate the linguistic refinement of the author of Hebrews (see J. Thompson 2008, 6) or the sophistication of the author of the Gospel of Luke, who was able to compose elegant periodic sentences (e.g., 1:1–4), but these limitations should not be confused with a diminished capacity to use language effectively and artfully. John either had some formal training or was a gifted student of public recitals of rhetorical, narrative, and dramatic works because he displays many of the rhetorical strategies and narrative conventions that were taught in the *progymnasmata* of Greco-Roman schools. Moreover, John demonstrates familiarity with many of the topics that are the focus of discussion by rhetoricians and philosophers: *parrhēsia* (frank speech), friendship, slavery and freedom, consolation, happiness, and *virtus* (manly virtue).

Relationship to the Synoptic Gospels

C. K. Barrett (1955, 43) notes ten incidents in the Gospel (including the work and witness of the Baptist, departure to Galilee, the feeding of the multitude, walking on the water, Peter's confession, departure to Jerusalem, entry into the city and anointing, betrayal and denial predictions, arrest, and passion and resurrection) that follow the same order as Mark and that, therefore, suggest some literary dependence. Nevertheless, large parts of John's narrative, his characters, and Jesus's proclamation are very different from what we find in the synoptic tradition. Clement of Alexandria († ca. AD 215) is the first on record to comment on these differences: he states that the first three Gospels recorded "bodily facts," whereas John wrote a "spiritual" Gospel (cited by Eusebius, *Hist. eccl.* 6.14.7).

Until the mid-twentieth century, the view that John knew one or more of the Synoptic Gospels prevailed, but during the latter half of the twentieth century, scholars began to account for differences by arguing that the Gospel of John represents a strain of the Christian tradition that broke away from the synoptic tradition early in the oral stage and then gave rise to different literary sources (e.g., a *sēmeia*, or signs, source and an *Offenbarungsreden*, or revelatory discourse source) on which the Gospel is based.

The language of the Gospel of John is often polemical, emphatic, and fraught with metaphor. Observations about the tone of this language combined with reconstructions of a multiple-stage composition history have given rise to a theory that the Gospel was written for a sectarian community that shared an "antilanguage," which set them apart from Jews in the synagogue as well as Christians who made use of the Synoptic Gospels (see Malina and Rohrbaugh 1998). "Antilanguage" is a term coined by linguist M. A. K. Halliday (1975) to refer to the imposition of specialized meaning on common words in order to exclude outsiders from understanding a group's discourse. The sect-versus-church typology is a sociological concept first developed by sociologist Max Weber (1864–1920). Church stands at one end of a continuum and signifies a religious organization that has influence on society or sees itself as making a claim on all members of its society. A church is allied with secular powers, hierarchical and bureaucratic, with a professional leadership. Sects are breakaway groups that stand in tension with society and define themselves over against the organization from which they have separated themselves and the society in which they reside. Given that the primitive church itself seems more like a sect of Judaism than what Weber calls church, and given that we have no empirical evidence for the existence of a Johannine community, this commentary takes note of where in the Gospel the sectarian hypothesis finds its support but does not argue for a sectarian reading.

The hypothesis that John knew one or more of the Synoptic Gospels remains viable. The significant distinction between the Gospel of John and those of Matthew, Mark, and Luke may lie in their use of rhetoric and narrative rather than different sources or sectarian tension. The authors of the Synoptic Gospels construct *chreia*, brief or pithy anecdotes that report either a saying or an edifying action. John constructs one sustained narrative, with episodes into which he embeds dialogues that are not chiefly the housing for Jesus's sayings. Dialogues and debates are the action of the Gospel. The form of the Synoptic Gospels is suited to paraenesis, practical ethical teachings informed by Jesus's proclamation of the reign of heaven. The form of the Gospel of John is suited to Jesus's proclamations about his identity as the Son of God.

The Rhetoric of the Gospel

The agonistic dialogues set John apart from the Synoptic Gospels. The purpose of these exchanges has preoccupied Johannine scholarship for several generations, beginning with the contribution of J. Louis Martyn (1968; 1979). Martyn posited that the Gospel was written in response to a major event in the life of the Johannine community. He identified that event as the addition of the "Benediction against Heretics" (*Birkat ha-Mînîm*) in the synagogue liturgy by the rabbis who met at the council of Yavneh (ca. AD 80), following the destruction of the temple. As a result of this addition, according to Martyn, Christians were effectively expelled from the synagogues. Martyn identified "a two-level" drama within the Gospel, in which the story of the church's conflict with the synagogue authorities becomes inscribed on Jesus's conflicts with the Jerusalem authorities. Because this theory explained both the anxiety of reprisals for making a confession regarding Jesus's divine status and the polemic against Judaism that seems to pervade the Gospel, it was quickly adopted as a near consensus by Johannine scholarship. That consensus soon began to unravel: scholars began to recognize that the decisions attributed to Yavneh occurred over many years, and that orthodox Judaism is a product of retrospection prompted in part by the rise of orthodox Christianity. Nevertheless, the puzzle put forward by Martyn (1979, 16) of why "the Johannine Jesus, himself a Jew, [would] engage in such an intensely hostile exchange with 'the Jews'" continues to invite proposals.

Largely under the influence of classical scholars such as George A. Kennedy (1984), more recent discussions have begun to situate the Gospel within the context of Greco-Roman rhetoric, the principal concern of which was to persuade. For example, Andrew Lincoln (2000) treats John's Gospel as a piece of forensic narrative that seeks to exonerate Jesus and condemn his accusers. Lincoln contends that the author structures the narrative by using a lawsuit motif, in which Jesus is put on trial by the Jews as a counterplot to the main plot, in which the world (with the Jews as its representative) stands accused. Lincoln's hypothesis does not give weight to the statement of purpose in John 20:31: "These are written so that you may come to believe that Jesus is the messiah, the Son of God, and that through believing you may have life in his name." The action of believing (*pisteuō*) can suggest a deliberative act of weighing out evidence; therefore, some readers treat the rhetorical focus of the Gospel as an invitation to listen to it as though it were a speech given in a legislature, and then hearers deliberate and come to the decision or reaffirm their decision that Jesus is the messiah (see Keener 2003, 214). This notion of belief fits with modern usage, which places emphasis on faith as volitional assent to doctrinal propositions; however, if one examines the language of belief in the Gospel, acts of belief or trust (another word with which we can translate *pisteuō*) are not about individual decisions or even certitude so much as a positive and

11

enthusiastic response to God's presence in the person of Jesus (see Kysar 2005, 214). The purpose of the Gospel is, therefore, not to bring its audience to faith but to stir up or express that faith. Consequently, this commentary treats the Gospel's overall rhetorical strategy as epideictic.

The action of the Gospel, Jesus's verbal duels, and the representation of his death all place the Gospel in the tradition of commemoration. The story of the loved one serves to comfort the community as it grieves the death. In the case of Jesus's death, the story not only consoles; it also subverts the humiliation of crucifixion suffered by Jesus and the shame imposed on his followers. Epideictic rhetoric, especially after a death, often takes the shape of narrative or lyric that reinforces the solidarity of its audience by encouraging them to identity with the person whose life is praised in the story and to celebrate by listening to that story. The emphasis on vivid representation of Jesus's actions and his poetic discourses mnemonically sustains the community's convictions. Within the context of epideictic rhetoric, the Gospel's language is not antilanguage; it is memorable language.

Johannine Narrative Art, Structure, and Interpretation

We tend to use the word "gospel" to refer to the genre of the first four books of the NT and forget that the authors of the NT used the word to refer to the proclamation or good news of Jesus Christ. A gospel is not a genre; it refers to the content or focus of a work, its message. The Gospel of John, as well as the three Synoptic Gospels and the apocryphal gospels, belongs to a literary milieu in which two new genres, the novel and biography, were emerging, both of which borrowed from the conventions of ancient histories, epics, and drama. Scholars, therefore, have found it helpful to treat the Gospel's composition as an example of either the early novel or the early biography.

The alignment with the novel, a category that modern readers associate with fiction, causes some consternation for readers who have thought of the Gospels as true histories, that is, faithful accounts of what Jesus actually said and the events as they happened. Whatever genre category we impose on our reading of the Gospel of John, it is helpful to recognize that ancient writers did not think of invention of events or details or speeches as a distortion of the truth but rather as conveying the truth. The writers of biographies and histories sought to reveal the true character of their subject or the nature of an action rather than lay down the bare facts for others to interpret. In order to achieve this, they made use of the literary and rhetorical conventions that they learned by imitating the masters of earlier genres in order to bring historic figures and past events before the mind's eye of their audience. Some dissembling of chronology and conflating of events and some invention of speeches and settings were not just tolerated but expected in order to tell the truth.

The style of the Gospel of John has been called dramatic in comparison to that of the synoptic authors. The conflict arises at the beginning of the narrative and develops steadily toward a climax so that the action is always fraught with tension. In fewer and longer episodes than are found in the Synoptic Gospels, the conflict arises out of the dialogues, and tension mounts within episodes. As in classical drama, the emphasis lies upon action that occurs through speech. Modern readers tend to focus on what language means and overlooks that language often does things. The Gospel's earliest audiences would have been much more sensitive to this distinction. This was a world in which oaths were central to the economy of the society, in which vows were made on a regular basis as part of piety, and in which social relationships were negotiated through verbal acts of supplication and blessing. John, like other pieces of Greco-Roman literature, constructs action around speech acts such as debate and supplication; therefore, this commentary introduces a number of these forms of speech in order to help modern readers follow the plot development.

John's author carefully demarcates episodes by using a number of recognizable conventions: entrances and exits or journeys and attention to time and place. As a result, it is readily apparent that he has a carefully developed structure, but this does not lead to a consensus about what that structure is. Some scholars have based their arguments about the meaning of the Gospel on a delineation of its structure. For example, the marking of time with reference to dates in the Jewish ritual calendar leads some to conclude that the Gospel reveals how Jesus replaces key elements of Jewish ritual. Rather than treating the conventions that he uses to demarcate episodes as the plot of the Gospel, the following outline looks for the dramatic structure that unfolds from beginning to end within the dialogues that are the main action of the Gospel. The plot is plaited with three major strands—prophetic narrative, tragedy, and heroic epic—each of which could be treated in isolation as the main plot, but to do so runs the risk of missing major plot elements in the narrative. Table 1 outlines the major elements in each form. Laying out the Gospel in a chart avoids reducing the plot to one story, but it can obscure elements of its structure that render the plot even more complicated. John introduces great variety and development into epicycles of recognition and fulfillment, as well as supplication, that run throughout the Gospel.

Table 1. Structure and Plot in John's Gospel

Structure	Prophetic	Tragic	Heroic
Prologue (1:1–18)			
From John's witness to the wedding at Cana (1:19–2:12)	Anticipation	The hero reveals his glory to his own	Arrival and acknowledgment of the champion, the Savior of the world
From the temple incident to the healing of the official's son (2:13–4:54)	Surprise		
From the first Sabbath violation to the raising of Lazarus (5:1–10:42)	Disappointment of Jewish expectations	His own do not recognize him	Challenges to the hero's honor
From the entry into Jerusalem to his entombment (12:12–19:42)	Fulfillment	*Pathos*: His own kill him	Triumph: Heroic death and consolation
From his entombment to his resurrection appearances (19:38–21:25)		*Anagnōrisis*: His own recognize him *Peripeteia*: Grief turns to joy, fear to peace, doubt to belief	

Hermeneutics and Method

When I began to study religious texts in an academic setting, I was impatient with professors who engaged their students in protracted discussions about the methods and objectives of the study itself. I complained that I wanted to study religions, not the study of religions. I hope that my reader is more patient than I was, because each act of reading, whether conscious or not, entails a hermeneutic, a notion of the goals and methods of interpretation that affects how one reads. Sometimes that hermeneutic might lead one to believe that the meaning one finds is what the author intended. If one suspects that various editors have constructed a text from various sources, then a hermeneutic may call for reconstruction of sources or close examination of editorial seams or evidence of earlier or later strata. This sort of reading requires a diachronic approach, which focuses on parts of the text and can disregard others as additions or insignificant residue from sources or earlier editions. Synchronic readings focus on the text itself rather than the process that gave rise to the text, but various hermeneutics are still possible. For example, one's hermeneutic may presuppose that the Holy Spirit directs one to an understanding

An Example of a Diachronic Reading

In his 1941 commentary on the Gospel of John, Rudolf Bultmann laid out a diachronic reading: first he located a stratum in which the Fourth Evangelist demythologizes Jesus's apocalyptic eschatology and replaces it with a realized eschatology, in which eternal life is a way of living fully here and now (see 3:16–21 and 5:19–24); then a later stratum added by an "ecclesiastical redactor" reconciled the Gospel with the synoptic accounts and reintroduced future salvation and sacramental interpretations of John's symbolic language (see 5:28–29; 6:51b–58; 19:34b–35). Bultmann then made sense of some of the aporias in the Gospel by arguing that at some stage in the manuscript history, pages were displaced and then edited together in a new order. Bultmann's commentary follows what he takes to be the original order of the Gospel (e.g., 4:43–54; 6:1–59; 5:1–47; 7:15–24; 8:13–20; 7:1–14; 7:25–29; 8:48–50; 8:54–55; 7:30; 7:37–44; 7:31–36; 7:45–52). Besides attributing large sections of the Gospel to a signs source, a sayings source, and a passion source, he also identified a Jewish gnostic source to which he attributed the prologue. Bultmann also treated many expressions and phrases as glosses (brief notes provided by a transcriber or commentator that are later treated as part of the original text), some because they are not found in all early manuscripts (e.g., "except the feet"; 13:10) and others because they seemed to him to disrupt the continuity of a thought (e.g., "You do not have a bucket for drawing water and the well is deep"; 4:11).

intended by God, or one's hermeneutic might call one to read with suspicion that the text encodes a deep-seated bias against women.

Western thought has become suspicious about efforts to recover the intent of the author, seeing it as a romantic but unattainable goal presupposing that we can find encoded in the text some fixed intent and meaning found originally in the private realm of an individual's consciousness (see Wimsatt and Beardsley 1946; Barthes 1977). To avoid the problem of reading for an ultimately inaccessible object, structuralists focus on the words and patterns in the text and seek some stable meaning that could be intentionally or unconsciously encoded in the text by the author. John's complicated narrative structures have provided rich material for this approach. At the farthest extreme lies the hermeneutics of poststructuralists such as Jacques Derrida, who argued that every attempt to find meaning excludes possibilities in the language of a text that permit other meanings—and forms different patterns, sometimes at direct odds with the meaning that a reader finds or even that the author intended. I began writing this commentary with a hermeneutic informed by the work of Hans-Georg Gadamer (1900–2002) and with the presupposition that writing is a substitute for speech: it intends an audience; therefore, reading is an act of communication, and interpretation is a dialogue between the reader or audience and the author.

15

In his major work *Wahrheit und Methode* (1960; ET: *Truth and Method* [1975]), Gadamer explains that each of us approaches a text with "fore-structures" or "anticipatory" structures that allow us to come to a preliminary understanding of what we read. This may mean that we impose ideas onto the text in order to find coherence because we are presupposed to find something understandable. This predilection to find meaning has a practical dimension insofar as our interpretations tend toward present concerns and interests. Gadamer asserts that understanding can occur only when one avoids reading a text to justify one's own preconceptions (prejudices), guarding against this by being self-conscious about what those prejudices are. Gadamer articulates a dialogic hermeneutic. Since our view is determined from our historical location, we have what Gadamer calls a horizon (*Horizont*) of understanding and interpretation, but we are not restricted by this horizon. We can bring our presuppositions into question precisely because we are aware that we read a text as a part of a tradition and because we acknowledge its authority, something written by another. In some cases, we read it as authoritative if we read as a member of a faith tradition. As a result, understanding is something that we negotiate with our dialogue partner, the author of the text, in order to come to a common framework that takes both our interests and the author's priorities into account, a process that Gadamer calls the "fusion of horizons" (*Horizontverschmelzung*). The process of interpretation is ongoing. The more that we can weigh out and integrate ideas that are native to the society in which the text arose that are strange or even anomalous to us, the more we can enter into dialogue with it. Consequently, we never arrive at a final or complete interpretation because we are not seeking direct access to the subjective meaning of the author's consciousness. Moreover, we cannot exhaust the process of learning the conceptual and linguistic horizon of the author, nor is our own situation static.

The format of this commentary is coherent with Gadamer's theory of interpretation. Each chapter begins with an introductory section that explains why what follows is treated as a literary unit. These introductions provide background material germane to the late Second Temple setting of the action, the rhetorical and literary conventions that a Jewish writer in the Greco-Roman world would have employed, and the topics of theological and philosophical concern to the ancient world that call for reexamination of our modern preconceptions about words and concepts. The center section of each chapter traces the logic or sense of the text as one proceeds in a synchronic reading. The final section engages in a discussion of some of the theological issues that arise from reading in our own context and as a result of the traditions that have sustained interest in the Gospel since its composition.

A number of features of Johannine narrative arrest the attention of a modern audience because of our historical situation. This Gospel is fraught with conflict. Conflict calls for a protagonist and at least one antagonist, and the Jews are Jesus's opponents in debates and the agents that move the action toward his arrest and execution. Seen from the vantage point of a post-Holocaust perspective, modern scholarship has become intensely concerned with the "anti-Judaism" of the Gospel and dualistic language that promotes a judgmental ecclesiology and soteriology. Consequently, this commentary focuses attention on the rhetorical and narrative conventions that John uses to construct not just conflict but also the characters who oppose or accept Jesus. The heated debates will be set within the conventions of classic literary dialogues. Then, in the theological issues section, the dialogue with the text will entertain the question of whether a modern reader ought to resist coming to an agreement with what one understands the text to mean. The dialogue will also entertain the possibility that some interpretations are informed more by creeds and doctrines that have developed *after* the Gospel was written than by what can be read *in* the Gospel. The purpose of the theological-issues sections is not to provide a conclusive argument for a particular interpretation but to facilitate the reader's own dialogue with the text.

This commentary is not intended to be an exhaustive compendium of all the textual variants, disagreements about translation, and meanings of words or significance of references. Students of the Gospel of John engaged in research for papers or other forms of communication with other readers and audiences would do well to procure Raymond E. Brown's Anchor Bible commentary on John (1966–70) and Craig S. Keener's more recent two-volume work *The Gospel of John: A Commentary* (2003).

John's Place in the Canon

Recent use of the term "maverick" within American discourse might cause one to hesitate to use the word to describe the Gospel of John, but when Robert Kysar wrote *John, the Maverick Gospel* (1993), he did not anticipate that a presidential contender would lay claim to the title in 2008. Kysar, like John McCain and running-mate Sarah Palin, uses the word "maverick" to signify breaking free of conventions and going one's own way. Throughout the history of Christian thought, John has been a maverick Gospel in another sense. It has defied being tamed and controlled. The history of its reception is a trail of repeated efforts to tie it down.

Until the last two decades of the second century AD, the Gospel of John seems to have been neglected in Christian thought. This silence ended when Irenaeus used it to defend his Christology and soteriology against Gnosticism. Paradoxically, at the same time that the Gospel of John earned a place within the orthodox canon, it seems to have been part of the canon of various movements deemed heretical. Students of the gnostic Valentinus (ca. AD 100–160) wrote commentaries on the Prologue and cited verses from the Gospel to support their views (see Culpepper 2000, 114–18). As new challenges to the core doctrines of the Roman Catholic Church arose toward the end of the Middle Ages, the Gospel of John once more became orthodoxy's champion. In the words of Thomas Aquinas, John "refutes all heresies" (*Joh.* 1.10). At the same time, early reformers such as Jan Hus found in the Gospel of John affirmation that they followed God's will.

Study of the Gospel of John seems to have brought to Christianity intellectual rigor and philosophical respectability. Origen of Alexandria (ca. 185–254) praised the Gospel of John as the firstfruits of the four Gospels but conceded that only the one who laid at the breast of Jesus had the mind of Christ necessary to understand his own book (*Comm. Jo.* 1.6). Origen seemed to relish the way that the Gospel allowed him to inform his Christian convictions with neoplatonic philosophy. Medieval theologians, unconcerned about historical context or authorial intent, looked for the spiritual sense of Scripture by using allegorical, moral, and anagogical meanings, and the Gospel of John provided material well suited to their methods. As a result, Augustine of Hippo (354–430) and then Thomas Aquinas (ca. 1225–74) produced longer commentaries on John's Gospel than on the Synoptic Gospels. John the Evangelist became "John the Divine" or "John the Theologian," a status not granted the other three evangelists.

While the Gospel of John was a favorite object of study for a small literate minority, it was mediated to the laity not simply through homilies and the lectionary, but also through its translation into paint and stone. The earliest iconographic depictions of Jesus are as the Good Shepherd and the Lamb of God. Many of the illustrations in this commentary are taken from Christian decorative relief work.

© Photo by Kleuske Museo Epigrafico, Rome

Figure 2. A fourth-century glyptograph of Christ as the Good Shepherd.

The Gospel helped define orthodoxy, but it also sat at the center of a conflict between East and West that rent the church in two. The debate over the question of whether the Holy Spirit proceeds from the Father or the Son led to a split in liturgical practice when the Roman church, at the Toledo Council of AD 589, added the *filioque* clause to the Nicene Creed, "We believe in the Holy Spirit, . . . who proceeds from the Father," so that it read "We believe in the Holy Spirit, . . . who proceeds from the Father *and the Son*." They found scriptural support for this insertion in John 14:26; 15:26; and 20:22–23. The Eastern Orthodox churches insist that the Holy Spirit comes from the Father through the Son. Contention over the *filioque* clause led, in large part, to the AD 1054 schism between the Roman Catholic and the Eastern Orthodox churches.

While scholastic theologians found confirmation of their sacramental theology in John, reformers such as Luther and Calvin shifted attention to John's pronounced use of the verb *pisteuō* (believe) and moved the practice of faith from participation in the mysteries of the church to confession of belief. In his *Preface to the New Testament* (1522), Martin Luther asserted that the Gospel of John, along with Paul's and Peter's Epistles, was "the true kernel and marrow" of the NT and the chief Gospel because it proclaimed Christ the most clearly. He directed the increasingly literate German-speaking people to begin with the Epistles and the Gospel of John and thereby set the Gospel of John at the center of the growing practice of private and silent devotional reading of Scripture.

With the rise of modern historical-critical methods, the distinction between the Gospel of John and the synoptic tradition led to neglect of its study as participants in the quest for the historical Jesus placed less confidence it its historical reliability than in material found in the Synoptic Gospels. Gotthold Ephraim Lessing (1729–81), the father of modern criticism, wrote that we have the Gospel of John to thank for the Christian religion (1784) but concluded that the Gospel was apocryphal, that is, not the product of an eyewitness (1777). The scholarly turn to literary, rhetorical, and social scientific criticism has brought John back into focus.

The Gospel of John has found an iconic place within the context of contemporary lay and popular culture. According to WikiAnswers™, perhaps not the most reliable source but certainly a reflection of popular perspectives, John 3:16 is the most-quoted passage in Scripture. The popularity of John 3:16 has led to a peculiar phenomenon. The phrase John 3:16, or simply the numbers 3:16, written on a sign, a lapel pin, a T-shirt, or a bumper sticker has come to signify a confession of faith.

Cultural critics describe postmodern culture as a kaleidoscope, with ever-changing fragmented images or a pastiche of imitations of images, phrases, and concepts borrowed from various cultural heritages. Glimpses of the Gospel of John appear in unexpected places. For example, in the climactic scene in the fantasy film *Inkheart* (Iain Softley, dir., New Line Cinema, 2008), a young girl with the power to read characters out of books and into reality furiously writes down a new ending to the book *Inkheart* and reads what she has written aloud. As a result, the monstrous shadow whom she has magically called from its pages turns upon the evil character rather than upon her mother, Toto from *The Wizard of Oz*, and the book's author. The word becomes flesh. If one watches the film after reading this introduction, what will now catch one's eye is the lectern from which the girl reads the book. Yes, it is an eagle.

Paradoxically, at the same time as Christian merchandizing reduces the message of the Gospel of John to one verse and Hollywood randomly borrows bits and pieces of Johannine themes and symbols, the methodologies used to study the Gospel facilitate reading from beginning to end. This commentary seeks to enhance the intelligibility of the Gospel for modern audiences and the gratification one finds in coming to know it as a unified work.

PART 1

John 1:1–2:12

In the Beginning

The Gospel of John drives a straight course to its end, Jesus's death upon a Roman cross. Jesus stands at the helm: fixed in his view is the route that God has charted. Appropriately, the narrative begins like the Gospel of Mark, within the public eye of John the Baptist's ministry, when Jesus is an adult in command of his life—rather than like Matthew and Luke, with the birth of a helpless infant. John 1:1–2:12 brings Jesus into the world of Second-Temple religious politics and establishes

> ### John 1:1–2:12 in Context
>
> ▶ **In the beginning (1:1–2:12)**
>
>   **The Prologue and More (1:1–18)**
>
>   **Come and see: Jesus reveals his glory to his disciples (1:19–2:12)**
>
> **Jesus's itinerant ministry (2:13–12:11)**
>
> **Jesus's triumphant hour (12:12–19:42)**
>
> **Jesus's resurrection: Endings and epilogues (20:1–21:25)**

him as the leader of a group of disciples who follow him because they seek a messiah but who find themselves witnesses to God's glory through signs they cannot anticipate. The opening chapters of the Gospel of John immediately establish its relationship with Hebrew Scripture, with which its first audience was surely familiar, but these chapters also make clear that this work is distinct from others with which that audience might be familiar. John's prologue reveals that Jesus's story neither begins with the Baptist nor ends with the cross. The origin of the story lies before the creation of the points of light by which we mark time.

John 1:1–18

The Prologue and More

Introductory Matters

For many years, a notion prevailed that John 1:1–18 was a hymn written for another occasion that was then tacked onto a preexisting gospel that had been cobbled together from several sources, but this idea has given way to a growing confidence that the prologue was crafted, either composed or reworked, as the original introduction to the Gospel. The external evidence points in this direction: there is no manuscript evidence for a gospel without the prologue, and second-century Christian scholars refer to it in their commentaries. Moreover, the way that it orients the reader to the entire body of the Gospel provides compelling internal evidence. The content and style of the prologue fulfill the prescription for an introduction provided by Cicero:

> One's opening remarks, though they should always be carefully framed and pointed and epigrammatic and suitably expressed, must at the same time be appropriate to the case in hand; for the opening passage contains the first impression and the introduction of the speech, and this ought to charm and attract the hearer straight away. (*De or.* 2.315, trans. Sutton 1942)

While the prologue serves to orient the reader to the rest of the Gospel, there are many aspects of the prologue that require some preliminary orientation for modern readers.

Genre

Placing a piece of prose or poetry into the conventions of an established literary form is often a necessary step in making good sense of its meaning or purpose. The abstract vocabulary of the prologue, the internal variations in prose style from grand or middle to plain, and its complicated structure all make determining its form or genre a challenge. Form critics have sought to fit the prologue into a Jewish convention, with some arguing that it is a hymn and others that it is a homily or midrash, a retelling of a biblical story grounded in the synagogue tradition of exposition on a passage from the Torah, in this case Gen. 1:1. The prominence of the word *logos* in the prologue invites some consideration of the Greco-Roman *logos* (*oratio* in Latin), an oration, which among its types includes encomium (a speech in praise of a person or thing), invective (a denunciation of the manners or morals or piety of a person), and apology (a speech of self-defense with regard to a particular challenge or accusation). The early church fathers integrated the Greco-Roman *logos* into the scripturally focused homiletic tradition inherited from the synagogue (Kinneavy 1996, 326). A homily is not simply instruction. The word means "social intercourse," and its rhetorical purpose is to have both the speaker and the audience affirm the truth of Scripture by the speaker proclaiming its meaning or significance and the audience listening in agreement.

Recent studies in rhetorical criticism have led to the discussion of lyric pieces in the NT, such as Paul's poem on love (1 Cor. 13:1–14:1) or the Christ hymn (Phil. 2:6–11) within the category of encomium. While the prologue does not line up point by point with the classical description of an encomium, discussing the prologue in light of some of the encomium's ingredients helps make sense of its twists and turns.

The Three Styles of Prose

Beginning in the Hellenistic period, teachers of rhetoric delineated three styles (see Cicero, *De. or.* 3.177). The grand, or dignified, style (*grave*) stirs the emotions by making liberal use of figures of speech, rhythmic organization, periodic construction, and devices such as impersonating the voice of the dead. It is most appropriate for ceremonial addresses, such as praise of a god or ancestors, and it allows the speaker to display the full range of his or her rhetorical skill. The middle style (*medium*), appropriate to deliberative speeches and narrative, aims to please and alternates use of plain language with more charming expressions such as metaphor or metonymy and figures of speech that play with word order. The plain style (*subtile*) seeks to teach with clarity, vividness, and persuasiveness. Its sentences tend to be staccato, and its vocabulary unadorned. (Cicero, *Or. Brut.* 21.69 uses *vehemens, modicum, subtile*; *Rhet. Her.* 4.8.11 uses *gravis, mediocris, extenuata*.)

The Logos

The study of no other word in John's vocabulary has preoccupied Johannine scholars as much as *logos*. To avoid reducing the range of possible meanings that the first audience could call to mind, *logos* will not be translated, but this requires a preliminary review of its range of possible meanings.

Early investigations into the meaning of *logos* emphasized its technical usage in Greek philosophy and Stoic thought. Heraclitus (sixth cent. BC) used the word *logos* to refer to the eternal principle of order in the cosmos. Gnostic Christians adopted the Stoic meaning for *logos* and the Stoic belief in God as an abstract principle immanent in the universe; they seem to have interpreted John's Gospel in this light. For example, *Trimorphic Protennoia*, a treatise discovered in the Nag Hammadi library (ca. AD 200), appears to be an amplification of John's prologue set on the lips of the Son of God. The *Corpus hermeticum*, a compendium of Near Eastern literature (ca. second and third cents. AD) purporting to contain secret wisdom revealed by the messenger god Hermes, and Mandean manuscripts (ca. second cent. AD), written by a gnostic group inspired by John the Baptist, provide glimpses into intellectual and spiritual milieus in which concepts similar to that of the *logos* figured prominently. Trying to work backward from these sources to reconstruct earlier movements that may have informed the prologue's form or concepts has produced a large body of scholarly works, yet without consensus regarding the necessity of such a venture.

Those who seek to ground John's meaning within Jewish midrash have treated *logos* as the Greek translation of either *dābār* (word) or *ḥokmâ* (wisdom). The Hebrew Bible contains many references to the word of God as not just the expression but also the agent of God's will (e.g., Isa. 55:11). In Proverbs, wisdom speaks and describes how she was created before the beginning of the earth (8:22–23) and how she was "beside him [God], like a master worker" and "was daily his delight" (8:30).

Encomium

An encomium is a composition in prose or poetry written to praise a human being, event, or idea. In the Greco-Roman traditions, encomia were often composed to celebrate the victory of an athlete or for recital at a funeral. The proper composition of the encomium is a common theme in the classical rhetorical handbooks. Aphthonius the Sophist includes the following subtopics:

Origins: *nation, homeland, ancestors, and parents' city*

Upbringing: *habits, skills, and principles of conduct*

Deeds: *of mind (e.g., prudence), body (e.g., beauty), and fortune (e.g., friends)*

Comparison: *superiority to someone or something worthy of praise*

Epilogue: *something fitting a prayer (Progymn. 35–36)*

Hermogenes asserts that the encomia of gods should be called hymns (*Progymn.* 15).

Many situate John's use of *logos* within Second Temple Jewish wisdom tradition as well as the speculative theology represented by the writings of Philo of Alexandria. John's description of the origin of the *logos* and its indwelling is comparable to descriptions of wisdom (*sophia*) found in Sir. 1:1–4; 24:8; and Wis. 9:1–2. Philo of Alexandria provides an example of a Jewish contemporary of Jesus who fuses neoplatonic or Stoic notions of the *logos* and the Jewish vision of a world called into being by God's words and informed by God's wisdom, in which heavenly agents play a role. There is a growing consensus that the prologue must be read within the context of a Jewish speculative theology and that the language of the prologue would have invited its audience to affirm the activity of God within history through agents of his wisdom. The word *logos* then prepares the audience to understand Jesus as an authoritative agent who reveals God's activity and glory through his speech and actions.

Structure and Purpose

While scholars who pursued diachronic readings of the Gospel found evidence for editing and insertions in changes of style within the prologue (e.g., Brown 1966, 23–39), those pursuing a synchronic reading have looked for an overarching design, and many have found a chiastic pattern. The sample chiasm is adapted from the model provided by Jeffrey Staley (1988, 57).

Chiasm of John 1:1–18a

A Relation of *logos* to God, creation, and humankind (1:1–5)
  B Witness of John (negative) (1:6–8)
    C Journey of the light/*logos* (negative) (1:9–11)
      D The gift of power to become divine children (1:12–13)
    C' Journey of the *logos* (positive) (1:14)
  B' Witness of John (positive) (1:15)
A' Relation of *logos* to humankind, re-creation, and God (1:16–18a)

Staley's pattern leads many to conclude that the fulcrum in 1:12–13 is the main point of the prologue. Although there may be a loose chiastic structure that helps one read the prologue, we need to be careful not to reconstruct the prologue to fit a rigid chiastic structure. As Peter M. Phillips (2006, 49) observes, "One wonders why, if the author of the prologue was so set on creating the kind of complex chiastic structure found by de la Potterie, Giblin and Culpepper and other eminent Johannine scholars, he did not do a better job."

It may come as a surprise to many students of the Gospel of John that exegetes and translations have treated John 1:1–18 as a discrete exegetical unit only since the late eighteenth century (Williams 2007). The Latin lectionary demarcated it as a unit only after Vatican II (AD 1962–65). Some ancient witnesses treat 1:14 as the prologue's conclusion (see Irenaeus, *Haer.* 1.8.5)

Chiasms

Students are introduced to this term in high school biology to refer to two chromosomes linking to form an X, the Greek letter *chi*. In NT studies, the term refers to an organizing principle in which literary elements form a mirror pattern, for example ABCB'A'. This pattern sometimes points to the ultimate importance of the central, unrepeated element. Because the pattern is used a great deal in ancient literature, readers may be tempted to force a pattern onto the text or to overread its significance and thereby obscure the importance of details that do not fit the pattern. The pattern may have more to do with the need to organize thoughts for oration and memorization than with pointing to the meaning of a passage.

and 1:15–18 as the words of John the Baptist (see Origen, *Comm. Jo.* 2.29; Aquinas, *Joh.* 191–222). This commentary follows this early tradition and treats 1:1–14 as the prologue proper and 1:15–18 as the beginning of John's witness, which continues in 1:19–34. The subsections of the prologue follow the prescribed topics of an encomium.

The prologue mirrors the incarnation by beginning with abstract language to signify the divine realm before the creation of the world and moves toward more-lucid language: the *logos* becomes light and then descends into the course of human history. Moreover, as the prologue moves through time from the primordial past to the present of the narrative action, its audience is transported from their own time back to the narrative present, in which they become witnesses to the action as it unfolds. The prologue (here) and the epilogue in 21:24–25 serve as a frame by beginning the Gospel and ending it with references to its audience in the first person. The final epilogue serves, in part, to transport the audience back to its own time.

Tracing the Narrative Flow

The Origin of the Logos (1:1–5)

The first part of the prologue uses poetic structure and figurative language not simply to explain from where Jesus comes but also to pay homage. Aelius Theon, in his teaching on encomia, observes that it is pleasant to use homonyms and nicknames as a topic of

---

John 1:1–18 in the Narrative Flow

In the beginning (1:1–2:12)

▶ The Prologue and more (1:1–18)

The origin of the Logos (1:1–5)

A comparison with John the Baptist (1:6–8)

The Logos's deeds (1:9–13)

The epilogue to the prologue (1:14)

John the Baptist's response (1:15–18)

Parallelism in John 1:1–5

Step parallelism:
  Beginning—Logos (1:1a)
  Logos—God (1:1b)
  God—Logos (1:1c)
  Beginning—God (1:2a)
Positive/negative parallelism:
  All came into being—
    Through him (1:3a)
  Nothing came into being—
    Without him (1:3b)
Step parallelism:
  Come into being—Life (1:4a)
  Life—Light (1:4b)
  Light—Darkness (1:5a)
  Darkness—Without compre-
    hension (1:5b)

praise (*Progymn.* 111). When the narrator calls Jesus the *logos*, that shows him honor.

The repetition and awkward word order of the first five verses is the product of its poetic structure. John 1:1–2 and 4–5 follow a pattern of step parallelism found in Hebrew poetics and Greek rhetoric called *anadiplōsis*, "doubling back," in which the word that ends one clause is repeated at the beginning of the next clause (see Ps. 92:9; Judg. 5:27). Verses 1 and 2 combine to form a chiasm. Then 1:3 is a form of parallelism in which the same idea is expressed in a positive and negative way.

In the beginning invokes a familiar passage, Gen. 1:1, and prompts the audience to begin to recite mentally "when God created the heavens. . . ." But John arrests the audience's attention by completing the thought with **was the *logos***, a clause that prompts the question, "What does he mean by *logos*?"

John will eventually answer the question in 1:17, not with a definition but with the name "Jesus." The departure from the text of Gen. 1:1 signals the reader that what follows will be a sort of commentary on Scripture informed by the broad semantic field for the word *logos* and the discourse of logos-theology. John will make a number of contributions to that logos-theology (see theological issues section below).

The tense of the verb "to be" (*ēn*) emphasizes that the *logos* is in place before creation. In later rabbinic discourse, one of the questions for discussion is What did God create before the things itemized in Genesis? The rabbis respond with various lists, which include such things as Torah and the throne of glory (e.g., *b. Pesaḥ.* 54a). If John is familiar with this question, his answer seems to be that the *logos* stands prior to all such things. In the terms of Greek philosophical discourse, the *logos* is an abiding reality. Any expectation that John will provide exposition on creation is cut short when he turns to step parallelism by using the noun that was in the predicate position of the first clause as the subject of the next clause. The focus will be on a poetic exploration of the relationship of the *logos* to the divine realm—**and the *logos* was with [*pros*] God**—rather than the story of creation.

Pros carries a great deal of weight. It can signify that the *logos* is oriented toward God (1 Thess. 1:9), that it has access to God (1 John 3:21), that it stands in a suppliant position to God (Jon. 1:5 LXX; Dan. 14:5 LXX [Bel and the Dragon 5]; Mark 6:25), or that it is in league with God (Josephus,

J.W. 7.221). In the Septuagint, Moses is described as one who is *ta pros ton theon* to signify his authority over Aaron (Exod. 4:16 LXX) and the people (Exod. 18:19 LXX). The clear implication seems to be that the *logos* is derived from God and has a close and authoritative connection with God. The step parallelism continues to accentuate this theological point. **And the *logos* was God** (1:1). The absence of an article before *theos* does not require that we translate *theos* as indefinite (a god) or as a quality (divine) as opposed to a predicate nominative, but the context suggests that the *logos* shares God's nature, and the syntax preserves a distinction between *logos* and God. John then reiterates what has been said. **This was in the beginning with God** (1:2). The repetition is poetic and reflects the oral reception of the piece rather than making a new point.

John now turns to the relation of the *logos* to creation. In the positive line of the parallelism, the *logos* is the agent or instrument of creation: **All things came into being through him.** This idea is not unique to John (see Col. 1:16; Heb. 1:2). All things (*ta panta*) is probably a broader concept than the world (*ho kosmos*), which in John generally signifies humanity. This thought is then repeated in a negative form for emphasis: **And apart from him not one thing came into being.** For those whose concept of *logos* is anchored in Greek philosophy, the introduction of the verb *egeneto* signals that, unlike the *logos* and God, all things are in a constant process of coming into being and passing out of being.

Versification presents a challenge at this point because the subject of the verb "was" in verse 4 has been left as part of verse 3. Shifting it to verse 4 preserves the step parallelism: **that which had come into being** (1:3) **in him was life** (1:4a). In the next step of the parallel structure, John narrows the focus from all of creation to humanity: **and the life was the light of humankind** (1:4b). Life (*zōē*) in 1:4a can refer to biological life, but in 1:4b John seems to use *zōē* to refer to eternal life, just as he uses it elsewhere in the Gospel. In Hebrew Scripture, God metes out life (e.g., Deut. 32:39; Job 12:10), and John now grants the *logos* this divine prerogative. Given that Dan. 12:2 contrasts the everlasting life of the resurrected with shame and everlasting contempt, *zōē* in 1:4 anticipates the *logos*'s sharing in God's glory in 1:14.

Eternal life in Judaism is typically seen as a future event, but in John it becomes an event that is begun in Jesus's presence and is a particular quality of life. In antiquity, life signified a social relation, the life of a people or nation (see Deut. 8:3; Prov. 19:23), rather than individual existence. Eternal life, therefore, is not about the continued existence of individual identity but continued existence of God's people. The concept of life becomes more explicitly social in 1:12, when "the light" makes it possible for those who believe to become "children of God."

The language of *logos* now slips out of John's vocabulary, and two other terms, "life" and "light," both of which are central to the remainder of the

Versification and Punctuation

The Greek of the earliest NT manuscripts has neither punctuation nor spaces between words, and line breaks often occur in the middle of words. Sentences, discrete thought units, had to be inferred by the placement of conjunctions and attention to cases and finite verbs. By the fourth century AD, scribes and translators had begun to divide the NT into paragraphs, but the division into the standard chapters was undertaken by Archbishop of Canterbury Stephen Langton in the first half of the thirteenth century. Versification and chapters were standardized only with the publication of the Geneva Bible in 1560. Textual critics continue to revise punctuation, based on how the earliest readers understood divisions. It is often helpful to ignore verse numbers while reading in order to follow the sense of a passage.

Gospel, become the main subjects. The end of 1:4 dictates the noun with which the next verse will begin: **And the light shines** [*phainei*] **in the darkness** (1:5). The verb *phainei* is without an object in its immediate context, but if we treat it in the context of the entire prologue, it illuminates or reveals glory (see 1:14).

The introduction of the opposition of light and darkness suggests to many scholars a heavy-handed dualism, such as that found in Gnosticism or the apocalyptic literature of Qumran. But the opposition between light and darkness is pervasive in human discourse about salvation, liberation, and wisdom; therefore, at this point it seems prudent to withhold filling in the identity or nature of darkness to the same degree by which the prologue invites identification of the *logos*. The attention to darkness in the next line of the parallelism—**and the darkness did not apprehend** [*katelaben*] **it** (1:5)—follows from the poetic structure and need not reflect some sort of cosmic battle. It seems more likely that the form of dualism found in the Wisdom literature is in play. In Wis. 7:29–30, wisdom is treated as superior to the light that gives way to the darkness of night because evil does not prevail against it. *Katelaben* is a double entendre: it requires translation with an English verb that captures the poetic image of darkness encroaching on light and its inability to both overwhelm and understand it.

A Comparison with John the Baptist (1:6–8)

By introducing the Baptist into the prologue, the evangelist provides someone whose reputation is widely recognized with whom to compare Jesus and a witness to Jesus who would have been deemed credible. The Jewish historian Josephus (AD 37–100) uses John the Baptist as an exemplar of Jewish piety (*Ant.* 18.116–19). To demonstrate Jesus's excellence, John begins with a standard of sufficient stature against which to proclaim Jesus's superiority; he provides the means to measure Jesus's greatness (see John of Sardis, *Progymn.* 139.5).

The poetic language structure of the prologue suddenly gives way from a grand to a simple style as the subject shifts from the realm of the divine to the realm of human activity. One can see why many scholars have treated 1:6–8 as an insertion, but the passage logically follows from 1:5 by identifying an agent of God who works against the darkness. **There once was a man** [the verb *egeneto* places John in the category of creation], **sent from God, by the name of John** (1:6). John the Baptist later refers to himself as one sent by God (1:33; 3:28). The absence of the title "the Baptist" suggests that the Gospel writer assumes that his audience will know to which John the narrator refers. Clearly John the Baptist is an important figure, but however the audience might understand the role of the Baptist, the prologue reduces his ministry to one purpose: **This one came for witness [*martyrian*] in order to witness [*martyrēsē*] concerning the light in order that all should believe through him** (1:7). Jesus later refers to himself as the light (3:19; 8:12; 9:5)

> ### Johannine Double Entendre
>
> John is fond of double entendre, ambiguous words that lend themselves to more than one interpretation. When two translations seem to work equally well, it is highly probable that John intends both meanings. The challenge for translators is to find a word in their own language that contains both senses of the Greek word, so that the reader, like John's intended Greek-speaking audience, entertains the two meanings. The following are prominent examples:
>
> > *Anabainō: Lift up as on a cross or to exalt (1:51; 7:8)*
> > *Egeirō: Build or resurrect (2:19)*
> > *Anōthen: From above or again (3:3–7)*
> > *Pneuma: Spirit or wind or breath (3:8; 19:30)*

and to John the Baptist as a lamp (5:35). John then repeats the same point by using a negative construction: **That one was not the light, but was to witness [*martyrēsē*] concerning the light** (1:8).

The verb *martyreō* occurs thirty-three times in John, but only once in Matthew, in polemic against the Pharisees (23:31), and once in Luke (4:22). The noun *martyria* (witness) occurs fourteen times, all in a positive sense, whereas in Mark and Luke it appears only with reference to witnesses against Jesus (Mark 14:55–59; Luke 22:71) or in a critique of the lawyers and Pharisees (Luke 11:48). Many of John's characters step into the role of witness (John the Baptist, the Samaritan woman, Scripture, the works of Jesus, Jesus, God, the Paraclete, the disciples, the Beloved Disciple, and even on occasion the crowd). Some translations translate *martyrein* as "to testify" to signify that the character gives testimony in defense of Jesus (Harvey 1976; Trites 1977). To witness preserves the emphasis on one who identifies Jesus for others by virtue of what the witness has seen and heard.

The Logos's Deeds (1:9–13)

The next section of the prologue serves as an apology. The general lack of acknowledgment of Jesus by the Jews and by the world presents a challenge.

John meets this by adopting an approach recommended by Aelius Theon, in which one makes clear that the subject of the encomium is not brought low by misfortune and that his actions are done for others rather than himself (*Progymn.* 110–11). Within the prologue, Jesus's rejection by some makes the gift that he grants to those who accept him all the more magnificent.

The reference to the "light" in 1:8 becomes a catchword for the resumption of focus on the main subject of the prologue and the beginning of a second telling of the story of the incarnation, now with light rather than the *logos* as subject. **The light was the true/real** [light]**, the** [one] **illuminating** [*phōtizei*] **everyone, the** [one] **coming into the world** (1:9). This translation makes the final clause refer to the light, thereby rendering the prologue a series of references to the incarnation, but it can be translated "illuminating everyone who comes into the world." In either case, the contrast between the Baptist and Jesus seems to be twofold. Jesus is the reality to which the Baptist points, and the Baptist's reach is limited compared to that of Jesus.

What is meant by illuminate? Certainly neither gnostic enlightenment through receipt of secret knowledge nor the altered consciousness of Asian thought is intended. In both the Jewish and early church tradition, language of enlightenment is used to describe the receipt of a pronouncement, either the gift of Torah or the proclamation of the good news of the Holy Spirit (see Heb. 6:4). John perhaps alludes to Isa. 49:6b, "I will give you as a light to the nations, that my salvation may reach to the end of the earth." In Rev. 18:1 and 21:23, *phōtizō* is used to describe the manifestation of God's glory; so once again John 1:14 may be anticipated.

In this second telling of the story of incarnation, the world or humanity stands in the place that darkness held in the first telling and shares its inability to recognize what is true or real. **He was in the world, and the world came into being through him, even so the world did not know** [*egnō*] **him** (1:10). As we shall see when we examine the trial and crucifixion, John makes it clear

---

Aristotle's Plot Elements

Aristotle identifies three kinds of action around which plots revolve: *anagnōrisis* (recognition), *peripeteia* (reversal), and *pathos* (suffering) (*Poet.* 1452a.13–1452b.14). *Anagnōrisis* is a point in the plot when the identity or the true situation of the protagonist is recognized by the protagonist or a character who holds the fate of the protagonist in his or her hands. In Greek tragedy, this moment often comes too late to change the course of events for the protagonist who in the course of the action experiences a reversal of fortune. When another character comes to *anagnōrisis*, they experience a *peripeteia* in their relationship to the protagonist. For Aristotle, *pathos* is an action, such as death, that causes distress or leads to destruction.

that the world and not just the Jews fail to recognize or acknowledge Jesus. John uses recognition (*anagnōrisis*) of Jesus's identity or the lack thereof as a major plot element in his Gospel.

The next two verses stand in parallel relationship to 1:10 by intensifying and then qualifying the action being narrated: **He came to his own** [people], **and his own** [people] **did not receive/accept him** (1:11). His own (*hoi idioi*) could signify either the Jews or all of humanity. Within the story told in the Gospel, Jews are the ones who reject Jesus, but John presents both the Romans and the Jewish authorities as handing Jesus over to death. The verb changes from *know* to *receive* and fits into the broader action of *anagnōrisis* as well as with the understanding of the light as a gift, something that one either accepts or rejects. Craig Keener (2003, 398) sees this as a play on the Jewish tradition in which God offers the Torah to the world, but only the Israelites accept it. Now the Israelites stand with the world and reject the gift that God offers humanity (3:16). The next line immediately qualifies the overstatement of the rejection of Jesus: **As many as did receive/accept him, he gave them authority to become children** [*tekna*] **of God, to those believing in his name** (1:12). The syntax of 1:12 is unusual. The sentence begins with *casus pendens* (a hanging case), when a word that normally appears later in a sentence moves into the first position. The subject of the first clause becomes the dative in a final clause in the same sentence. Given that "the name" is a circumlocution for God, this verse may suggest that those who receive him believe that he is God, but one should keep a number of possibilities in play. "His name" can also signify his authority or honor. The authority (*exousia*) that Jesus gives needs to be qualified with reference to the ancient Mediterranean world. It connotes a granting of privilege or a form of liberty. One who bears the name of his father exercises the authority of that father and bears the same social standing. One who accepts Jesus as God's agent has the right to call oneself a child of God.

The next verse adds a relative clause making clear that being a child of God does not depend on the same sort of factors required to be a human child. These are children **who were begotten** [*egennēthēsan*; this verb appears at the end of the sentence, but in English translation it needs to be brought forward] **not from blood** [*haimatōn*]. The plural for "blood" signifies the physiology of birth, in Aristotelian terms, the material cause. Adele Reinhartz (1999) makes a case for reading the entire prologue within the context of Aristotle's concept of reproduction. Ancient references to the reproductive process sometimes describe a child being formed by a father's seed and the mother's blood, but it seems unlikely that this reference is to the mother. Herodotus (*Hist*. 8.144) uses blood as an ethnic term, denoting a common genealogy. The Jews, like other ancient societies, thought of their common identity as an ethnos, a descent group bound together by common blood (see Cohen 1999, 133). In Hebrew Scriptures, blood is used to refer to the loss of life when it is shed (cf. Gen. 9:4;

> ### Aristotle's Four Causes
>
> Aristotle explains change in the material world or world of becoming as the result of four causes: material, formal, efficient, and final (*Phys.* 194b.17–195b.30). For example, a statue of Athena proceeds from a *material* cause, the marble; a *formal* Athena herself; an *efficient* cause, the skills and tools of the artisan; and a *final* cause, the purpose for which it was created, such as beauty, inspiration, or catharsis.

Lev. 17:11; Deut. 12:23), but this sense is not in view here. It is possible that John is making clear that being a child of God is not based on having a bloodline back to Abraham. John then turns to an efficient cause and a final cause for conception. God's children are conceived **neither from the will of flesh**, blind desire with no intent to procreate, **nor from human will**, the intent to produce descendents. In Jewish thought, sexual intercourse is wicked only if exercised outside the bounds of marriage. Within the Roman world, human intent can comprehend both biologically related children and a legally adopted son. Roman law allowed a man to choose someone unrelated to be his legal son and to deny paternity of his biological child and order that the child be exposed to death or slavery. God's children are not part of the order of creation, **but were begotten from God** (1:13). John seems to use language of procreation as a metaphor to express a concept of God's people similar to the one that Paul explains by using the concept or language of adoption (Rom. 8:15; Gal. 3:26; 4:5) or grafting (Rom. 11:17–18).

The Epilogue to the Prologue (1:14)

At the climax of the prologue, John introduces first-person plural pronouns. The audience now explicitly participates in proclaiming Jesus's virtue. The sentiment is celebratory and fulfills Nicolaus the Sophist's (*Progymn.* 58) recommendation that the expressions in encomia be polished (*glaphyros*) and theatrical (*theatrikos*), with some solemnity (*semnotēs*).

John begins by restoring the *logos* to the grammatical position of subject: **And the *logos* became flesh and dwelled among us.** The language of dwelling (*eskēnōsen*; in the NT this verb appears only here and in Rev. 7:15; 12:12; 13:6; and 21:3), literally residing in a tent, initiates a major theme in John's Christology: Jesus is the new temple. In Exodus, God's presence resides with Israel in a portable residence, the *miškan*, in Latin the *tabernaculum* (40:34, 35). In the Jewish concept of God's immanent presence, the *Shekinah* (*šĕkînâ*) dwells within a physical structure such as the ark, tabernacle, or temple—but not in human flesh.

The Greek word *skēnē* is the term adopted in Greek theater for the background building and platform upon which plays were enacted and from which we derive the English word "scene." The verb that John uses to describe how humans witness to the incarnation, *theaomai*, is semantically related to our word for theater: **and we were spectators to [*etheasametha*] his glory.** The narrative makes clear that seeing Jesus's glory is not a matter of seeing some sort of radiance. Glory is not like the blue skin of Krishna or a halo. Seeing is witnessing what Jesus does, how the story unfolds. We watch Jesus reveal his glory.

The next clause delineates to what sort of glory John refers: **glory as of an only offspring** (*monogenēs*; lit., one of a kind; Lat., *sui generis*). A strong distinction is drawn between children of God and the incarnate *logos*, who will be identified as God's Son. John uses the word "son" (*huios*) to refer only to Jesus. The language of "only begotten Son," with which many are familiar due to the KJV, is introduced by Jerome in his later translations when he uses *unigenitus* to translate *monogenēs*. Greek usage (e.g., Herodotus, *Hist.* 7.221; Hesiod, *Theog.* 426) does not warrant treating *monogenēs* as a reference to some sort of divine procreative process. Richmond Lattimore (1979, 196) uses the phrase "single son." The father's hopes, estate, and name—the things that in the ancient world constitute a father's honor—are handed on to this one child. The final two clauses of 1:14 make clear the nature of the glory that Jesus inherits. It is **from** [*para*] **a father**, and it is **full of grace** [*charis*] **and truth** [*alētheia*] (1:14). One can read grace and truth as modifiers of either God or Jesus without significant alteration to the import of the verse.

The equivalent signifiers for *charis* and *alētheia* in Hebrew Scripture seem to be *ḥesed* (loving kindness) and *ʾĕmet* (truth; e.g., Hosea 2:20, Ps. 85:10–11). In the Septuagint, *ḥesed* is usually translated with the word *eleos* (mercy; 28x in NT), but *charis* is so much a part of Christian vocabulary (e.g., Rom. 3:23–24) by the time of John's composition that its choice is logical. *Charis* denotes a favor or grant and captures the concept of God's abundant goodness being shared with humanity (see Pss. 23; 104; 150; or Isa. 25:6–8; 55:2). In the context of Hebrew Scripture, *ʾĕmet* signifies God's faithfulness to both his people and his promises—not the way we have come to refer to truth as empirical or forensic fact. If we treat this verse as the conclusion of the opening, its relationship to verse 1 becomes more pronounced. The *logos*—the word of God—signifies God's promise.

John the Baptist's Response (1:15–18)

John 1:15 marks a significant transition in the flow of thought. The narrator makes way for the voice of John the Baptist, who comments on the assertions made about the *logos* in 1:1–5 and 9–14 and affirms his role identified in 6–8. Scholars differ about where the Baptist's voice stops and that of the narrator resumes. In the following translation and commentary, the narrator's voice resumes only with 1:19. The purpose of the verses, to respond to 1:1–14, remains the same whether we put the words in the Baptist's mouth or the narrator's. In 1:1–14, the narrator proclaims that those who accept Jesus become children of God. In the response, John the Baptist, the paramount example of one who accepts Jesus, proclaims Jesus as the Son of God, who shares God's estate.

The narrator introduces the Baptist's speech with the present tense. If we read all four verses as coming from the Baptist, the speech takes on a dramatic immediacy as though the Baptist speaks from the grave to address the audience in the present time of a public reading. The impression that the Baptist speaks as though he were part of the audience is enhanced by the way that he quotes his own words. The verse has the complicated structure of a quotation within a quotation. **John testifies concerning him and has cried out saying, "This was the one about whom I said, 'The one coming after me came into being** [*gegonen*] **before me, because he was my prior** [*prōtos*, as in first in rank]'" (1:15; see 1:30). John the Baptist affirms two claims made in the prologue: Jesus exists before him (1:1–5), and he is subordinate to Jesus (1:6–8).

The language continues to address the audience by shifting to the plural first-person pronoun: **Because** [*hoti*] **from his fullness all of us we** [the subject is repeated, perhaps for emphasis] **received grace for grace** [*charin anti charitos*] (1:16). *Hoti* points back to 1:14 and substantiates the claim that Jesus shares in God's glory by affirming the receipt of grace. Fullness (*plērōma*) becomes a technical term in gnostic literature for the totality of divine power, but in this context, the more ordinary meaning makes sense. The measure that Jesus shares of God's glory is complete and not a fraction or a degree.

What *charin anti charitos* signifies is a matter of scholarly debate, but given what comes next, some contrast or complement to the covenant at Sinai seems to be intended. **Because the law was given through Moses,** [whereas] **grace and truth came into being through Jesus Christ** (1:17). Finally what, or rather who, is the *logos* becomes explicit. The unresolved issue for exegetes is whether this verse dismisses the gift of the law or uses the value of the law to point to the even greater value of the gift offered through Jesus. If John follows the guidelines for encomia, the comparison uses the law because the audience recognizes the law's excellence. If the comparison were intended to be between dissimilar things, one would expect language that blames the law for some ill.

In Exod. 33–34, a gracious God makes his covenant with the Israelites and allows Moses a glimpse of God's glory when he sees God's back. Earlier God says to Moses, "You cannot see my face; for no one shall see me and live" (Exod. 33:20). In John 1:18 the intertextual relationship between this story in Exodus and John 1:14 is made clear. The verse begins with the stark claim, **No one has seen God, not ever,** but then makes an exception for one who is the **only** [child of] **God** [*monogenēs theos*]. Later Greek manuscripts and the Latin fathers read *monogenēs huios*, but Irenaeus (*Haer.* 3.11.6), Clement of Alexandria (*Strom.* 5.12), and early Greek manuscripts attest to *monogenēs theos*. The language of *monogenēs theos* picks up the assertions made in the first verses of the prologue about the relationship of the *logos* to God and expresses it in terms of human relationship. The *monogenēs theos* is **the one who is to the breast** [*kolpon*] **of the Father** (see Luke 16:22; John 13:25). Modern translations tend to use idioms such as "close to the Father's heart" (NRSV) or "at the Father's side" (NIV) in order to make this image conform to our images of a father-son relationship, but John's ancient audience would have been comfortable with language associated with the mother-child relationship to express this relationship between father and son. Several of the *Odes of Solomon* contain images of believers drinking holy milk from God or Jesus's breast (8.14; 19.2–4). Isaiah uses the image of Israel sucking the breasts of kings (60:16) to signify the restoration of Jerusalem to the status of a royal city. It is quite possible that the image comprehends the idea that Jesus shares in God's nature the way that a child takes in a mother's nature while nursing.

The final clause expresses the role of the *logos* as light (1:9) in terms of human activity, **that one showed the way** (*exēgēsato*). The verb *exēgeomai* is the root for our concept of exegesis, walking someone through a text. *Exēgēsato* might signify that he explained about God, but the choice of language may also anticipate the image of the Good Shepherd, who will lead the way to life. Given the pronounced use of the demonstrative pronoun *that* (*ekeinos*), it makes sense to think of this line as pointing to Jesus, who in turn will point to the Father.

Theological Issues

The Prologue's Christology

John clearly draws on earlier Jewish literature, especially Wisdom literature's personification of God's speech that brings forth creation (e.g., Prov. 8:22–35) and the Hebrew prophets as the embodiment of God's word (e.g., Jer.

Odes of Solomon

These Syrian Christian psalms (ca. AD 100) are Jewish in "tone and perspective" and express joy and thanks for the coming of the promised messiah, the present experience of eternal life, and love from and for the beloved. The odes divide humanity "into those who walk in error (15.6; 18.14) and those who walk in the way of truth (11.3) or in the knowledge of the Lord (23.4)" (Charlesworth, *OTP* 2:726). Like John, the odes describe a realized eschatology in which the messiah has prevailed (31.1–2). The world has not yet recognized the messiah, but the narrative voice is not affected by this adversity because of the experience of the messiah's presence (7.3–4). The psalms anticipate a future in which the messiah is made known by those who sing his songs (7.19–26). James H. Charlesworth (*OTP* 2:729–30) contrasts the soteriology found in the odes with the narrow view of salvation found in works like *4 Ezra* (2 Esdras), "whose author, shattered by the collapse of the temple, Jerusalem, and the nation Israel, struggles with the eternal question of the meaning and purpose of evil in a world created by God and finally is distressed at the extremely few number of those who will be saved at the end of time."

1:9). Jesus, as the *logos*, is the means by which God communicates his intent. Through the incarnation of God's word in the person of Jesus, the believer now comes to know God as the Israelites once knew God through his words to the prophets. At the same time, the prologue redresses the propensity to categorize Jesus as a prophet (4:19; 6:14; 7:40; 9:17) by affirming the divine status that Jesus claims for himself (8:58).

What is actually being said about the relationship of Jesus to God in the prologue? Is the preexistent *logos* an hypostasis (a manifestation of the essence of God) or an emanation of God (something that issues from God)? The language of *monogenēs* does not necessarily imply that God generates Jesus; this is a term of relationship. The prologue presents Jesus as an autonomous eternal being who shares God's authority, power, glory, and righteousness, but who as a righteous son is obedient to God the Father. While the prologue places Jesus within the same station as God, it also corrects the accusation made on a number of occasions by Jesus's opponents that he is "making himself equal to God" (5:18; 10:31–33). Jesus is an agent, albeit a unique agent, who is subject to God's authority. Nevertheless, Jesus stands beyond the exalted agents of Jewish tradition: Abraham, Moses, and Elijah. He is and always has been God's Son. John places the accent on Jesus's creative life-giving work that he shares with God not because he has been delegated the task, but because, as God's Son, such tasks fall within his station. The world's failure to recognize that Jesus's actions are divine gifts to humanity and expressions of a true son's imitation of his father is the cause for its rejection of Jesus.

John is not introducing the terms for later debates about Jesus's ontological status. There is no apparent tension between the *logos*'s being God and living in the flesh. While John uses the dualistic terms of heaven and the world as above and below, as C. K. Barrett points out, John does not represent a strict cosmological dualism. The Son of Man is "a figure in motion" who bridges two realms (Barrett 1982, 108–9). The Christ hymn in Phil. 2:6–11 points to an early incarnational Christology in which Jesus empties himself of his equality with God. John seems to reject this exaltation Christology by making clear that Jesus loses none of his glory by becoming incarnate. The incarnation is a manifestation of divine glory (1:14). Moreover, Jesus is not humiliated by the crucifixion: his glory is not overwhelmed by the crucifixion (1:5).

The prologue makes clear that Jesus's divine status is not comparable to the elevation of Greco-Roman heroes and rulers to the rank of the gods. In the myths of Greco-Roman traditions, many heroes were deified or divinized. Greek heroes who were given divine honors were not thought to have ascended to Mount Olympus but were chthonic in nature: like Hecate and Persephone, they resided beneath the earth. The apotheosis of Roman emperors, by which they became divine, was a posthumous designation granted to them by the decree of the senate and the people (see fig. 3). While early emperors were

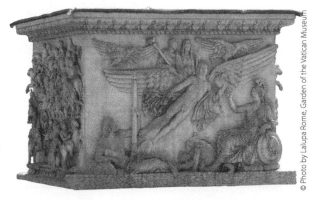

Figure 3. This relief from the base of a column (AD 161) depicts the ascent of Emperor Antoninus Pius (AD 138–61) and his wife, Faustina, during the ceremony performed by the Roman cavalry in which Pius is deified. Faustina had received the honors in AD 141 upon her death.

worshiped before their death, Hadrian was the first to make explicit claims to divinity during his reign (AD 117–138).

Rather than looking for precedents for John's high Christology in other traditions, Larry Hurtado (2005, 29) recognizes the power of religious experience to account for significant religious innovation. By accenting the proclamation that "we have seen his glory," one situates the prologue within epideictic rhetoric, which affirms the convictions of the audience. It is possible that in the prologue, John finds a way of articulating a Christology that reflects the liturgical and worship practices of his community, which were already in place. Most Jews expected some sort of messiah who would restore Israel to its proper status and relationship with God. Jesus comes and dies and is resurrected. The early church must then pay homage to a transcendent rather than an earthly messiah, so they quickly adopt practices that Hurtado has labeled binitarian. Once these practices become normative, something that occurs very quickly, thought or articulation of theology and Christology follow. John's Gospel with its prologue is an important step in this process; it tells the story in such a way as to make clear that binitarian worship is sound.

The Prologue's Story of Salvation

Does the rejection of the *logos* by his own in 1:11 and the contrast between Moses and Jesus in 1:17 signal an abrupt end to God's covenant relation with the Israelites and the rejection of the Jews? The dualistic language of the prologue pairs the world with darkness and divides humanity into those who do not know the light and reject it versus those who accept him and believe and, as a consequence, become children of God. Such categories lead many exegetes to conclude that the prologue treats the Jews as disinherited. This reading of the prologue is often paired with a sectarian version of the story of salvation in which those who are not children of light belong to a realm of darkness and are, therefore, condemned (see Petersen 1993, 20–36). If this is the case, the dualism points in the direction of a sectarian audience comparable to that of the Qumran community, which had fled the world for the desert and was awaiting vindication. Militating against this conclusion is the absence in John of the sort of dualism found in passages like the following from 1QS 1.9–11 (trans. Qimron and Charlesworth 1994, 7):

> . . . in order to love all the Sons of Light
>   each according to his lot in the Council of God,
> and to hate all the Sons of Darkness
>   each according to his guilt at the vengeance of God.

Nor does one find injunctions such as this one from CD 13.14–15 (trans. Baumgarten and Schwartz 1995, 55):

> None of those who have entered the Covenant of God shall buy from or sel[l] to the Sons of Dawn; rather (let them give) hand to hand.

If John's Gospel were the product of a sectarian community bound by a sharp dualism, one would expect to see evidence of community rules more restrictive than washing each other's feet and loving one another.

Binary thought, or dualism, seems to be a propensity of human thinking in general, which becomes more pronounced in certain situations and modes of discourse. If we set the prologue within the same milieu that gave rise to the *Odes of Solomon*, the dualistic language does not necessarily require that we anticipate a soteriology that restricts salvation to a small, circumscribed group. In the *Odes of Solomon*, the dualistic language is used to express the worshipers' joy in the knowledge that the messiah brings salvation rather than to delineate the distinction between salvation and damnation. When the messiah of the *Odes* describes the condemnation he receives from those who are in error, he affirms that he bore their bitterness so that he might save his nation and fulfill the promises to the patriarchs to save their descendants (31.12–13).

The solution to this question may be to ask, What is the rhetorical thrust? Rather than seeking to delineate who is in and who is out, the prologue's purpose may be to evoke an unequivocal response from its reader about what it means to acknowledge Jesus and receive his instruction or follow his commands. The claim that Jesus is the light that illuminates everyone (1:9; see also 3:16) suggests that readers should not dismiss the possibility that the prologue presupposes the story told in Isaiah in which the word of God becomes the light by which all the nations will come to know God, who up until now has been known, albeit mediated through the Torah, by only the Jews (see 4:22).

In order not to allow John's dualistic language to draw one into the issues of false and true religion in the context of our own pluralistic society, readers may find it helpful to think of belief as the act of putting complete trust in God and in Jesus as his Son rather than thinking of belief as an act of putting complete trust in one's own ability to articulate the truth and recognize what is wrong with other peoples' traditions.

Logos versus Sophia

If the Hebrew and apocryphal Wisdom literature is the correct context in which to read the prologue, why does John translate wisdom (*hokmâ*) with *logos* rather than *sophia* as it appears in the Septuagint? The simplest answer is based on grammar: *sophia* is female gender; *logos* is male gender. In order for the pronominal references to Jesus to line up with the symbolic or metaphoric signifiers for Jesus, a male noun works best (Scott 1992, 105). In several places in Jewish Wisdom literature, *sophia* and *logos* are often paired, for example, "by *logos* shall *sophia* be known" (Sir. 4:24 AT). Burton Mack notes that *sophia* and *logos* are interchangeable in Hellenistic Judaism (1973, 96–107, 141–54). Colleen Conway provides evidence that Second Temple literature is fluid in its gender representation of wisdom as either female or male (e.g., Wis. 7:23–27; 2008, 152–55). It is unlikely that the shift happened as a reaction against using the feminine gendered noun. Paul and Q refer to Jesus as *sophia* personified (1 Cor. 1:21–25; Matt. 11:19b; Luke 7:35). John probably follows in a tradition reflected by Philo of Alexandria, in which the use of *logos* allows the integration of Stoic and neoplatonic thought into Hebrew wisdom theology to produce a *logos* theology.

John the Baptist versus Jesus

The content and style of the verses about John the Baptist raise the question of whether polemic against him is one of the prologue's major rhetorical aims. During Jesus's life, John the Baptist had a much larger following and was more widely known, and his followers remained active for a number of decades after the Baptist's death. Acts contains an account of Paul's encounter with Apollos, who had received John's baptism but had no knowledge of baptism in the name of Christ Jesus (18:24–19:10). Strong opposition to the Baptist in second-century Christian literature suggests that followers of John and Jesus viewed each other as rivals (see Tertullian, *Marc.* 4.18). The majority of scholars seem to agree that these verses have a negative function. They make clear that John is subordinate to Jesus, they withhold a title, and they limit the purpose of his ministry to witnessing to Jesus. Subsequent episodes in which John the Baptist rejects the title of messiah or prophet (1:19–21) and his disciples are threatened by Jesus's own baptizing ministry (3:26) lend weight to this conclusion.

Ernst Käsemann and C. K. Barrett provide more-positive accounts for the emphasis upon the Baptist. Käsemann (1969, 165) notes that the Gospel would not exist without a confessing community of which John is the first representative; therefore, the prologue pays homage to the role that the Baptist played in the life of the disciples. Barrett (1971, 44) argues that the Baptist fulfills the same role in the Gospel of John as in the Synoptic Gospels: he is the voice of the Hebrew Scriptures (4:22; 5:46), who makes the coming of the Lord intelligible (1:17). Moreover, in the narrative that follows, the audience first sees Jesus through John's eyes, a technique of explicit embedded focalization suggesting that John the Baptist's witness is more rather than less important to John the Evangelist (see sidebar on *focalization* in 1:19–2:12). Reading the rhetoric of the Gospel as epideictic reduces the tendency to find polemic by looking at comparisons as favorable and placing the accent on celebration of Jesus's virtues and the benefits of being his followers.

John 1:19–2:12

Come and See:
Jesus Reveals His Glory to His Disciples

Introductory Matters

The stories of the Baptist's identification of Jesus (1:19–34), how Jesus comes to have disciples (1:35–51), and the wedding at Cana (2:1–11) are three episodes within one narrative, the unity of which is demarcated by the progression of seven days. The timing of the sign at Cana seems to take advantage of the number seven's capacity to symbolize fulfillment or completion as well as the power of the number three (2:1) to evoke anticipation of the resurrection. In later units, the narrator shifts from the passage of days to the succession in feasts in order to mark the lapse of three Passover festivals. The unit also has geographic coherence: it begins with the arrival of a delegation from Jerusalem and is set in the region of the Galilee. In contrast to Mark's breathless action, the Johannine Jesus strikes a leisurely and seemingly more intentional pace as though he were following an itinerary. John takes care to identify the setting in which the action takes place. Although the precise locations of Bethany (1:28) and Cana (2:1) are unknown and Bethsaida (1:44) is in Gaulanitis, not the Galilee, the names establish the unity of action and create the impression that the narrator is relating accurate recollections. Jesus's identity is first acknowledged and his glory is first revealed in the hinterland. References to crossing the boundary into Judea by the narrator or characters within the Gospel consistently signify danger. At the end of this unit, Jesus travels to Jerusalem, where his identity and authority are challenged.

Unity of Space and Time

A common misunderstanding of Aristotle's concept of unity requires that a story take place within one day and in one place because this degree of unity is achieved in Sophocles's *Oedipus Tyrannus*, which Aristotle deemed the best tragedy. Aristotle's actual standard of unity is met by the following conditions: a plot is about one action, the removal or transposition of any part of the narrative changes the plot, all characters are caught up in the same action, one episode follows logically from the last, and any change of location is necessary to the plot (*Poet.* 1451a.16–36).

John 1:19–2:12 in the Narrative Flow

In the beginning (1:1–2:12)

The Prologue and more (1:1–18)

▶ **Come and see: Jesus reveals his glory to his disciples (1:19–2:12)**

Day 1: The inquisitors' eyes are on the Baptist (1:19–28)

Day 2: The Baptist turns the inquisitors' attention to Jesus (1:29–34)

Day 3: The Baptist directs the disciples' attention to Jesus (1:35–42)

Day 4: Jesus observes the disciples and announces that they will see his glory (1:43–51)

Day 7: The disciples observe Jesus's glory (2:1–11)

Transition (2:12)

Although the action within each episode is distinct, together the three form a prelude and contain the actions that initiate Jesus's public career. No event, like the baptism of Jesus in the synoptic tradition, inaugurates that ministry by signifying a change in Jesus's status. Jesus's glory is revealed; he is not glorified. The narrator accomplishes this through first bringing Jesus into view, building anticipation of what Jesus will make visible, and then carefully managing who sees the water become wine. Jesus's glory becomes visible for both the Gospel's audience and Jesus's disciples. The action dramatizes claims made in the prologue: the Baptist bears witness about Jesus (1:6–9), and the disciples who accept this witness see Jesus's glory (1:14).

Although John reveals the plot of his story in the prologue and refers to the certainty of Jesus's death, he also generates anomalous suspense (see Gerrig 1996, 93–106). In a study of suspense in the book of Tobit, Ryan S. Schellenberg (2009, 3–7) explains how such anomalous suspense heightens the audience's confidence in God's providence. John also uses this tension to demonstrate Jesus's trust in God. While Jesus remains calm, those around him do not. John juxtaposes the urgent search for the messiah by two conflicting groups: one that seeks to suppress him, and one that seeks to proclaim him. John brings the antagonists of the Gospel into view from the onset. He sets his plot within a political atmosphere of suspicion and vigilance comparable to that of the Spanish Inquisition (AD 1480–1530) or the McCarthy era of the late 1940s and early 1950s in the United States.

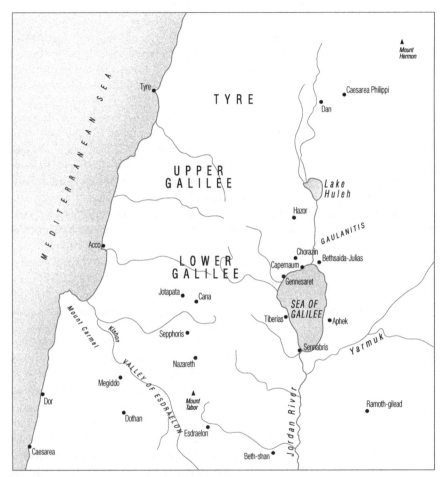

Figure 4. Map of the region around the Galilee during the early Roman period.

Tracing the Narrative Flow

Day 1: The Inquisitors' Eyes Are on the Baptist (1:19–28)

The opening line—**and this is the witness of John**—immediately directs the audience's attention to the statements that the Baptist will make about himself and about Jesus and sets his witness within a context **when the Jews [*hoi Ioudaioi*] sent priests and Levites from Jerusalem in order to question him.** (Note that John the Evangelist does not give John the Baptist a title. This commentary refers to the latter as the Baptist to avoid confusion about to which John it refers.) There is no scholarly consensus about to whom John refers when he uses the term *Ioudaioi*. Some contend that it refers to Judeans, and others say to various Jewish authorities (see "Anti-Judaism in John" in the theological issues section of 7:1–8:59). On some occasions, John uses *Ioudaioi* to refer to Pharisees (8:22; 9:18) and, on other occasions, to the general population (18:20). *Hoi Ioudaioi* seems to signify different Jewish constituencies rather than simply adherents of Judaism. The picture of a concerted and undifferentiated effort to suppress John, and later Jesus, contributes to the suspense.

The delegates' abrupt question, **"Who are *you*?"** (*Sy tis ei*; 1:19), with an emphatic use of you (*sy*) as the first word, suggests an adversarial relationship between the two parties. The Baptist does not treat this as an open question but rather as an indirect accusation that he represents himself as a messiah through his actions. John uses verbs to describe the Baptist's response that are appropriate to an interrogation: **And he admitted [*hōmologēsen*] and did not refuse to answer [*ērnēsato*], but he admitted [*hōmologēsen*] that "I am not [*egō ouk eimi*] the anointed one [*ho christos*]"** (1:20). The three verbs used by John to introduce the short answer draw attention to either the contrast between the Baptist's "I am not" with Jesus's "I am" assertions, thereby pointing to Jesus's superiority or the contrast between the Baptist and Peter, who three times denies that he is a disciple (John 18:17, 25–27). Translations often pair confession and denial, but *ērnēsato* can also mean refuse, and in the context of the action, refuse may be the more logical verb. The *hōmologēsen-ērnēsato-hōmologēsen* sequence also serves to emphasize that while the interrogators are indirect in their questions, the Baptist is not evasive in his answer. He answers the real question, "Are you the Messiah?" which leads them to press for identification with other eschatological candidates by asking **"Who then? Are *you* [*sy*] Elijah?"** John, like Mark and Matthew (Mark 9:11; Matt. 17:10), seems to treat Elijah as a messianic forerunner or a harbinger of the eschaton (Mal. 4:5–6; Sir. 48:9–10). John's inclusion of deictic pronouns helps to accentuate the confrontational tone of the exchange. The word *you* points like a finger at a suspect. The continued use of deictic pronouns is indicated with the use of italics in the translation.

Rather than explaining the significance of the Baptist's ministry, John dramatizes the tension it generates with the Jerusalem

Deictic Pronouns

Although the inflection of Greek verbs often makes the use of personal pronouns unnecessary, the author of the Fourth Gospel frequently includes grammatically superfluous pronouns in sentence constructions for rhetorical emphasis. The effect is lost in English translation; to capture it requires emphasis to be thrust upon the pronouns as if the speaker were either touching one's breast when using the first-person pronoun or pointing to the person or group being addressed when using the second- or third-person pronouns. When used in dialogue, these deictic pronouns make clear that speech is filled with challenges and self-defense in a manner similar to the way that hand gestures in the illustration make clear that the figures are engaged in an argument.

authorities. Given that the appearance of one claiming to be a messiah or his agent would lead to political unrest and social instability, those who held power and were invested in maintaining the status quo would be motivated to quash any eschatological or messianic movement. The Baptist's ministry may have been politically provocative because its location and symbolic action fulfilled the call of other millennial prophets such as Theudas (ca. AD 44–46; Josephus, *Ant.* 20.97–99; Acts 5:36–38) to retreat to the wilderness of Perea in order to cross the Jordan westward and undertake a new conquest of the land (Crossan 1991, 231–32).

Those familiar with the synoptic tradition might expect an affirmative answer from the Baptist, but he responds with a clipped answer **"I am not,"** which accentuates his antipathy to their investigation. The interrogators, and the audience, are forced to move down their list to another eschatological figure and ask, **"Are *you* the prophet?"** The single word answer **"No"** measures the Baptist's increased belligerence. The prophet to whom they refer is probably the prophet like Moses, whom God promises to raise up at some unspecified future date (Deut. 18:18), whom the Samaritan and Qumran communities treated as a messianic figure (e.g., 1QS 9.11; 4QTest [4Q175] 5–8), and to whose status Theudas seems to have laid claim (see Josephus, *Ant.* 20.97–98). In refusing these roles, the Baptist seems to be distancing himself both from titles of honor, in keeping with what he will say about his relationship to Jesus in 1:27, and from traditional messianic categories, in a manner similar to Jesus, but he does not deny that he serves an eschatological role. When the Baptist's negative replies force the interrogators to ask an open question, he declares, **"*I* am a voice shouting in the wilderness, make straight the way of the Lord, just as the prophet Isaiah said"** (1:23). All four Gospels associate this passage from Isa. 40:3 with the Baptist, but only John puts it directly on the Baptist's lips. Like Jesus, who declares himself the bread of life and living water rather than the Davidic king or the prince of peace, the Baptist calls himself a voice rather than Elijah.

The next line creates some confusion because it states that **those having been sent were out of the Pharisees** (1:24). Many see this as a second group because it makes no historical sense that Pharisees would send priests and Levites as their agents. Raymond E. Brown (1966, 51) observes that this second question "is more theoretical and worthy of the theologically minded Pharisees." Although John does not stress distinctions between Jerusalem groups and seems to treat them as a collective antagonist, he does seem sensitive to Pharisaic distinctions (see John 3:3–8, 11; 7:52; 9:13–14), but in this context the Pharisees' question is not a new agenda. It builds upon the Baptist's refusal of an eschatological title; therefore, there is no need to see this as indicating an interruption in the action.

The inquisitors ignore the Baptist's declaration and, thereby, point to their lack of interest in seeking new understanding. Two verbs mark the persistence of their allegiance to a predetermined conclusion: **And they questioned him and they said to him, "Why then are you baptizing if you are neither the anointed one nor Elijah nor the prophet?"** John presupposes that his audience is familiar with a baptizing ministry. The Pharisees presuppose that baptism has eschatological significance. Although documentary evidence for such a conviction outside the NT is thin, ritual bathing does seem to have eschatological significance in the Qumran material (e.g., 1QS 3.6–9; 4.20–22). When **John answered them saying, "I baptize in water,"** he begins to draw a contrast between himself and Jesus, although the distinction between their baptisms does not become clear until 1:33. The Baptist begins his suspenseful introduction of Jesus with the sudden claim that **in your midst stands one whom *you* do not know** (1:26). It is not clear whether he means in the immediate presence of those standing around him, in which case Jesus has been listening to the dialogue, or poetically, as in living in the present time. Nor is it clear that he himself knows to whom he refers. He may also be in suspense. The Baptist builds anticipation by describing the status of this unknown person, the **one coming after me,** by devaluing his own status, **of whom *I* am not worthy even to loosen** [*hina lysō*] **the strap of his sandal** (1:27). John's use of the *hina* subjunctive clause is epexegetical: it explains what the Baptist means by unworthy. A more elegant translation would be "I am so unworthy that I would not even try to loosen the strap of his sandal." Honor and shame is scripted on the body: the head is the point of honor; the feet are a sign of shame or humility. His words do not signify his humility so much as they point to the height of Jesus's status.

John brings this episode to a close by giving its geographic location: **This happened in *Bethany*, across the Jordan, where John was baptizing** (1:28). The delay in providing this information may serve to accentuate a mood of foreboding because the Baptist is working in territory that falls under the jurisdiction of Herod Antipas, who will eventually order his execution.

Day 2: The Baptist Turns the Inquisitors' Attention to Jesus (1:29–34)

John marks a progression in time but does not introduce a new party to the dialogue; therefore, it is reasonable to assume that the Jerusalem delegation is still the Baptist's audience. He focalizes the introduction of Jesus through the eyes of the Baptist, who continues to subvert the Jerusalem authorities' preoccupation with traditional eschatological roles by directing their attention to the unexpected: **"Look! The Lamb [*amnos*] of God who takes up [*airōn*] the sin [*hamartian*] of the world!"** (1:29). Note the rhythm created by the diction. The action of taking up suggests an understanding of sin more ontological than psychological. Jesus does not remove guilt. The sin of the world is failure, corruption, degradation; it is a dying, decaying thing. Jesus takes away death and brings life. The Baptist's words are not simply an assertion; they are also a gesture by which he points to Jesus and directs the attention of the Jerusalem delegation, as well as that of the reading audience and his disciples, to Jesus. This gesture is repeated in 1:38 and is comparable to Jesus's and Philip's invitations to "come and see" (1:39, 46).

To tell the story, John now demonstrates his propensity to use the direct speech of his characters rather than a narrator. The Baptist's next assertion is an analeptic reference to something said in the past. The line appears in 1:15 and perhaps warrants treating 1:15–18 as the beginning of this unit rather than leaving it attached to the prologue. "**This is concerning whom I said, 'After me comes a man who has become before me, because he was** [existed] **before me** [has priority over me]'" (1:30). C. H. Dodd (1953, 274) sacrifices the emphasis provided by the pronouns and tidies up the awkward grammar by translating, "There is a man in my following who has taken precedence of me, because he is and always has been essentially my superior." If

---

Focalization

Development of the concept of focalization, introduced to literary criticism by Gerard Genette, is credited to Meike Bal (1997, 263–96). Reports of events, characters, settings, and so forth as seen through the eyes of a narrator, often in hindsight, are external focalization, and those seen through the eyes of a character within the story are internal focalization. John uses variable focalization, shifting from what is seen through the eyes of one or another character as well the narrator.

Dodd's translation is correct, the Baptist's confession points to his failure to recognize Jesus's status until now rather than to lack of a prior acquaintance. While the ambiguity of the Greek allows for the possibility that Jesus was a disciple of the Baptist, the disciples' question in 1:38 suggests that he now is not one of their company. Moreover, the Baptist continues by admitting that, until recently, "*I did not know him.*"

The Baptist delays finishing the recognition story that he has begun to tell and returns to the question asked the previous day about the basis of his baptizing. He links his baptizing ministry to the revelation of Jesus's identity. He does not present baptism as initiation into a penitent community, "**but in order that he** [the Lamb of God] **might be made manifest to Israel; therefore, I came baptizing in water**" (1:31). Is his ministry his own preparation to serve as witness to Jesus, or is Jesus's appearance dependent on contrition? Or can only one who is looking with the open eschatological perspective of the Baptist's ministry recognize Jesus? Adoption of one reading does not exclude the other two.

The Baptist now resumes his story: **And John witnessed** [*emartyrēsen*], **saying that "I have watched the Spirit descend like a dove out of heaven and remain** [*emeinen*] **on him**" (1:32). Translators often favor "testified" rather than "witnessed," but testify does not capture the emphasis on what the Baptist has seen. In this Gospel, *menō* becomes an important verb to describe the relationship of disciples to Jesus (see esp. 14:4–16). The comparison to a dove may simply point to a slow circling descent or to the role that Noah's dove plays as a sign of new life (Gen. 8:8–12). No baptism of Jesus is narrated. Unlike the synoptic tradition in which the receipt of the Holy Spirit marks a rite of passage, like an anointing or commissioning or coronation, in John the descent of the Holy Spirit is a sign by which the Baptist can recognize who Jesus is. The Baptist makes this clear by reiterating, **"And *I* did not know him,"** and then adding, **"but the one sending me to baptize in water, that one said to me, 'On whomever you shall see the Spirit descending and remaining on him, this is the one who baptizes in [the] Holy Spirit'"** (1:33). John finally arrives at the distinction between the Baptist and Jesus. Jesus is the eschatological agent who brings the anticipated eschatological gift (Joel 2:28–32; Isa. 44:3–5; Ezek. 36:26–27; Zech. 12:10). Note how the Baptist uses circumlocutions rather than naming God as the agent who sent him and makes his recognition of Jesus possible. His speech reflects typical Jewish piety. The Baptist ends his story by completing the speech act introduced in 1:19: **"*I* have seen and have witnessed that this is the Son of God"** (1:34). Rather than providing a narrative that allows his audience to witness this divine revelation, the evangelist makes clear that the story is mediated through a trusted eyewitness.

Rather than the voice from heaven quoting Ps. 2:7, "You are my Son, the beloved, in you I take pleasure" (Mark 1:11; par. Matt. 3:17; Luke 3:22), the Baptist becomes the voice declaring that Jesus is the Son of God. The Baptist's confession need not signify that he has perfect understanding of who and what Jesus is. In its original context in Ps. 2, "son of God" simply means a person appointed by God to sit as his agent on an earthly throne (see Ps. 89:26–27; 2 Sam. 7:14). In John's Gospel, witnesses as well as opponents speak words truer than understood by the one who utters them (see 11:50). The narrator says nothing about how the Baptist's audience receives his words, but given what happens later in the Gospel, it seems reasonable to imagine them treating his testimony as though he were a witness at a McCarthy inquest who has identified someone as a member of the Communist party. The inquisition can now treat Jesus as "a person of interest."

Day 3: The Baptist Directs the Disciples' Attention to Jesus (1:35–42)

The next day, John had again been standing [inactive] **and two of his disciples** (1:35). **And** [after] **intently observing Jesus walking about, he says, "Look! the Lamb of God"** (1:36). The succession of tenses from pluperfect to aorist to present indicates a clear and leisurely progression of events and focalization. Whatever the Baptist intends by directing his disciples' attention to Jesus, they seem to understand the messianic implications. **And his two disciples listened to him speaking and followed Jesus** (1:37).

John's strategy of focalization now switches to Jesus as the principal observer: **Turning, Jesus** [after] **watching them following says to them, "What are you seeking?"** Although "seeking" (*zēteō*) is a verb often used for obedience to God (see, e.g., Isa. 9:12 and 34:16 LXX), John tends to use it to refer to engagement in the wrong activity. The crowd seeks to make Jesus king (6:24, 26; 7:11); the authorities seek to arrest and execute him (7:1, 11, 25, 30, 34, 36; 8:37; 10:39); Mary seeks the body of Jesus (20:15); Jesus's opponents do not seek the glory of God (5:44). Jesus alone seeks to please God rather than himself (5:30). John signals the disciples' discomfort with answering the direct question by having them reply with the question **"Rabbi" (which translated** [into Greek] **is teacher), "where are you staying** [*meneis*]**?"** (1:38). The banality of their question helps capture the awkwardness that comes to characterize most of their interaction with Jesus. Its simplicity, coupled with the polite address, encodes a sense of social reserve and a high degree of anticipation. To the disciples' ears, Jesus's response **"Come and see"** might seem to contain nothing noteworthy, but the Gospel's audience ought to anticipate that this is an invitation to come and be a witness to the signs of Jesus's glory. The immediate consequence is a literal fulfillment of their question: **Therefore they went and saw where he stays and they remained beside him that day; it was about the tenth hour** (1:39). If one begins counting at dawn, the tenth hour means that it is late in the afternoon, and so, perhaps, the disciples remain with Jesus overnight. If it signifies the Egyptian method of counting from midnight, it signifies that the disciples spent the whole day with him, but a teaching ministry in which Jesus directs long sermons to his disciples (e.g., Matt. 5:1–7:27) is neither narrated nor a plot element in John's Gospel. This is not the story of Jesus's equipping his disciples to spread the gospel.

The revelation that **Andrew, the brother of Simon Peter, was one of the two disciples who, hearing from John, also followed him** (1:40) comes late. Once again, the narrator presupposes an audience familiar with key characters. The second disciple remains anonymous. John does not always name all the disciples, but given that the Beloved Disciple is always represented as being in the company of Simon Peter (13:24; 20:2; 21:20), one is compelled to ask if this is his first shadowy appearance.

The narrator follows Andrew's movement. No longer in Jesus's presence, Andrew now provides a candid answer to Jesus's unanswered question from 1:38 when he **first finds his own brother Simon and says to him, "I have found the Messiah (which translated** [into Greek] **is *Christos*** [the anointed one])" (1:41). In the wake of the Baptist's rejection of the title Messiah, these disciples seem to be on the quest for a new candidate to follow. This is the first of only two occurrences of the word *messiah* in the NT. Both are in John (see John 4:25). Other authors use the Greek *Christos*. John points to the singularity of his usage by providing the translation. John does not narrate how or when Andrew makes the leap from rabbi to messiah. The disciples will continue to address Jesus as Rabbi (1:49; 4:31; 9:2; 11:8; cf. 13:13), as others do (3:2; 6:25; 8:4; 11:28), and on occasion Lord (*kyrie*), a title more appropriate to the messiah but probably intended only as a polite address (e.g., 6:68; 11:12).

The pattern of those encountering Jesus going to others to report, for good or ill, dominates the Gospel from the onset. Jesus does not call Peter. Instead Andrew leads **him to Jesus.**

Jesus now displays one of the key attributes of his role as the Good Shepherd: he names his followers (see 10:3). Curiously, after this episode, Jesus will not refer to them by name again until after the resurrection. **Then looking at him intently Jesus said, "You are Simon the son of John; you shall be called Cephas, which translated** [into Greek] **is Peter"** (1:42). The nickname Cephas (Aramaic for *rock*) seems to signify intransigence or thickheadedness more than a firm foundation; this Gospel never identifies Peter as the central leader of the church. In Matthew, Jesus seems to play on a name by which Simon is already known and makes it signify his election to, or a prophecy about, the role he will play in the growth of the church (Matt. 16:18). John does not make Jesus's purpose clear, but the silence at this point may be a narrative strategy to generate suspense rather than polemic against Simon Peter's role as a leader (see "Two Models of Discipleship" in the theological issues section of 21:1–25).

Day 4: Jesus Observes the Disciples and Announces That They Will See His Glory (1:43–51)

John marks the passage of time by counting days and noting a geographical transition. **The next day, he wished to go out to the Galilee, and he finds Philip.** The use of pronouns creates some confusion. Because Jesus is in the subject position in the last sentence, it is syntactically logical to conclude that Jesus is the subject, but given that Andrew is said to go *first* to Simon Peter, one ought to anticipate a second initiative from Andrew, and given that Andrew is twice paired with Philip (6:5–8 and 12:22), the intended sense may be that Andrew is still rounding up his associates. Jesus's invitation to Philip, **"Follow me"** (1:43), is more like the synoptic tradition's call narrative, but the pattern of disciples coming to Jesus rather than Jesus seeking them persists. The next line—**Now Philip was from Bethsaida,** a city in the province of Gaulanitis, **from the city of Andrew and Peter**—explains the relationship of three of the first disciples; this might cause some consternation for those who try to reconcile John with the synoptic tradition that identifies Capernaum as Peter and Andrew's home (Mark 1:21, 29). John's accent on Philip's association with a city in a region with a prevalently Syrian and Greek population figures more prominently later in the narrative (12:21) and demonstrates the coherence of his narrative.

The actions and conclusion of Andrew set into motion a chain of cause and effect. Right away **Philip finds Nathanael and says to him, "The one of whom Moses wrote in the Law and the Prophets, we have found . . ."** The asyndeton and word order seems to encode his excitement. The timing of the precise identification of the messiah as **"Jesus son of Joseph from Nazareth"** (1:45) becomes a setup for Nathanael's sarcastic response. **Nathanael** delivers a jab, "**From Nazareth, is it possible anything good is** [from Nazareth]?" The word order encodes Nathanael's disdain. His reaction may be startling given the pattern established so far, but it is not illogical. There is nothing in the tradition of messianic expectations to point to Nazareth as the home of a messiah. Nazareth is not mentioned in the Hebrew Scriptures, Josephus, or the Talmud. Moreover, there is no archaeological record for the town dating to the biblical period. The NT is the only witness to its ancient existence. Here, as in John 7:52, Jesus's home is a reason for rejecting rather than accepting him.

The final joke on Nathanael is delayed, but **Philip** facilitates the setup when he repeats Jesus's invitation "**Come and see**" (1:46). The reader is left to fill in Nathanael's acceptance of this invitation while the narrator jumps ahead in the action and once more begins with what Jesus sees and his power to name. **When Jesus saw Nathanael coming toward him, he** [immediately] **says concerning him, "Look, a true Is-**

The Jab-and-Punch-Line Joke

John uses a comic convention in which an apparent fool builds expectations about the content of an announcement. When the facts do not line up with the buildup, the receiver says something to underscore the foolishness of the sender with a jab. But the banter is a setup, and the receiver steps into the role of the fool when the sender delivers a punch line. For example:

Sender: *How is a mountain like an elephant? (the* Setup)

Receiver: *I don't know. How is a mountain like an elephant?*

Sender: *They both have ears?*

Receiver: *What! Mountains don't have ears. (the* Jab *line)*

Sender: *Sure they do. Haven't you heard of mountaineers? (the* Punch *line)*

---

raelite in whom there is no guile [*dolos*]" (1:47). Homer uses the word *dolos* to denote traps like the Trojan horse (*Il.* 6.187–89; *Od.* 8.494) and Penelope's robe (*Od.* 19.137). The identification of Nathanael as a true Israelite raises the question With whom is he being compared? Isaac accuses Jacob, later renamed Israel, of stealing Esau's birthright with such a deception (*dolou*; Gen. 27:35 LXX). In the context of the narrative, Jesus may implicitly chastise the disciples. The Baptist has said that his mission is to make Jesus manifest to Israel (1:31); therefore Nathanael seems to represent the fulfillment of this objective by virtue of the fact that, unlike the Jerusalem delegation or the first disciples, he has not sought a pretext to determine the Baptist's or Jesus's true identity.

Nathanael's response to Jesus's pronouncement "**How can it be that** [*pothen*, signifying impossibility; see Euripides, *Bacch.* 465; *Alc.* 781; *Phoen.* 1619–20] **you know me?**" is a piece with his response to Philip. Jesus meets his incredulity with a direct answer to the literal meaning of his question "**From where** [*pothen*] **do you know me?**" and affirms the narrator's characterization of him as the one who sees by saying, "**Before Philip spoke to you when you** were under the fig tree, I saw you" (1:48). In the Prophets, the fig tree often signifies Israel under judgment for its lack of fidelity to the law (Jer. 8:13; Mic. 7:1) or Israel in its early fidelity to God (Hosea 9:10). Sitting under a fig tree can also signify well-being (Mic. 4:4). In the messianic age, those whose sins are forgiven will sit under the prophet's vine and fig tree (Zech. 3:10). Perhaps the fig tree's significance is not symbolic but an index to Nathanael's own contentment. He, in contrast to all the others thus far introduced in the Gospel, seeks nothing but relaxes under the shade of a tree. Jesus's prescience provokes Nathanael to a pronouncement that rivals, if not surpasses, that of Philip: **"Rabbi, you are the Son of God."** Modern readers must take care not to take Nathanael's meaning too literally too quickly because he follows it with a synonymous parallelism, **"You are king of Israel"** (1:49). He expresses traditional expectations that the messiah will be a son of David who is called the son of God insofar as he is God's anointed regent (1 Chron. 17:12–13; Ps. 2:7–12).

How Nathanael would find confirmation of Jesus's messianic identity in Jesus's one piece of unaccountable knowledge is not obvious. Calling him a prophet, as the Samaritan woman does (4:19), seems a more logical response. **Jesus** seems to concur when he asks, **"Because I said that I saw you sitting under a fig tree, *you* believe?"** Nathanael's response calls for a corrective, a revelation. **"You will see greater [things] than this (1:50). . . . Truly, truly, I say to you [pl. *hymin*], you shall see [pl. *opsesthe*] the sky opening and God's angels ascending and descending upon the Son of Man"** (1:51). In the synoptic tradition, Jesus habitually begins pronouncements with a single "Amen," whereas John doubles it, seemingly for emphasis (see Num. 5:22; Neh. 8:6; Pss. 41:13; 72:19). David Daube (1944, 27–31) thinks that John preserves the authentic habit of Jesus. This is the first appearance of the title "Son of Man" in this Gospel; it will appear twelve more times (3:13, 14; 5:27; 6:27, 53, 62; 8:28; 9:35; 12:23, 34 (2x); 13:31), all but twice on the lips of Jesus. The two exceptions, found in the crowd's question in 12:34, are prompted by Jesus's use of the term (see "The Johannine Son of Man" in the theological issues section of 9:1–10:42). Once again, traditional eschatological figures are replaced with a less conventional term.

Jesus combines two scriptural images—Jacob's ladder (Gen. 28:12–15) and the ascent of "one like a son of man" (Dan. 7:13 NIV)—to signify what the disciples will see. Scholar of religion Mircea Eliade (1957, 52–53) uses the term *axis mundi* to describe objects or symbols that connect the realms of the sacred and profane. Jesus becomes the means by which divine revelation is possible. The ladder alludes to but is not limited to the cross. Jacob names the place where he saw the ladder meet the earth as Bethel, the house of God (Gen. 28:19). The temple, also known as God's house, is also an *axis mundi*, and Jesus may be anticipating the claim that he will make in 2:19 that he is the temple.

Day 7: The Disciples Observe Jesus's Glory (2:1–11)

Besides the symbolic use of time and geographic locations, the story of the wedding at Cana is linked to the preceding episodes because it completes John's version of the call of the disciples. The final accent falls on how they receive what they witness. The episode also provides the catalyst for the beginning of Jesus's public career.

Because the story draws on the symbolic significance of a wedding setting (precisely how will be explored in the theological issues section below), it is important not to impose modern concepts of marriage on a close reading. Modern readers like to imagine a wedding similar to that depicted in films such as *Fiddler on the Roof* (Norman Jewison, dir., United Artists, 1971), complete with a canopy, a tradition from the weddings of the Babylonian Jewish community that dates no earlier than the fifth century AD. There is no evidence for a Palestinian wedding ceremony other than the procession in which the woman is led from her father's house to her new home with the family of the bridegroom. The marriage was constituted by a contract and cohabitation. The banquet celebrated the union and provided witnesses to the event. The banqueting could last as long as two weeks—wedding gifts probably took the form of contributions of meat and drink—and could require the oversight of a servant or guest honored with the role of *symposiarchos* (Tob. 8:20; 10:7; Sir. 32:1–2; Plautus, *Pers.* 770) or in John's vocabulary an *architriklinos*. While evidence is scant for what the rituals or formalities of a Second Temple Jewish wedding entailed, Michael L. Satlow (2001, 20) finds sufficient grounds for concluding that they signified the establishment of both the man as a member of the civic body and a household in which children (future members of society) were produced and raised. Jesus's departure from the Galilee at the end of this unit constitutes a significant break with what its society would consider to be the responsibilities of a son. His ascent to heaven fulfills these responsibilities (see 14:2–3).

By beginning **On the third day a wedding took place in Cana of Galilee,** John employs a rhetorical strategy comparable to an enthymeme by leaving the task of adding up the days and drawing conclusions to his audience. John arranges the order in which he brings the participants of the scene into view with an eye toward the action that will follow. The disciples are bystanders, who play no direct role in the action but fulfill an important role in the

Figure 5. The western front of the Abbey Church of Saint Peter and Saint Paul (Bath, ca. sixteenth century), depicting Jacob's Ladder.

© Photo by Mattes

narrative by witnessing what happens. He begins by noting **And the mother of Jesus was there** (2:1). The omission of the name Mary is puzzling but not necessarily troubling. Her status comes from her son, and to refer to her as the "mother of" is respectful. Moreover, anonymity in this Gospel seems to be a sign of intimacy rather than obscurity. By adding **What is more, Jesus was invited,** John sets the stage for tension. Jesus still has one foot in the world of his earthly family; he stands in the context of a celebration of family obligations. In a manner comparable to the beginning of the last unit (1:35), John uses a singular form of the verb to invite and then adds **his disciples** to the wedding party without providing a plural verb (2:1). One must be careful not to impose the picture suggested by the synoptic tradition of a master constantly followed by his entourage of disciples. When John notes the disciples' presence, it has a purpose. John does not explain Jesus's relationship to either family in the wedding party, prompting earlier generations of scholars to speculate about kinship ties (for examples, see Brown 1966, 98), but more-recent sociological studies focus more on the role of those present: Jesus and other guests are there as witnesses to the union. The disciples are there to witness Jesus's glory.

The word **then** indicates that some time passes, and **when the wine was running short** (*hysterēsantos*), the main action begins. The Greek word *hysterēsantos* suggests two different possibilities for what is amiss: there is either insufficient wine or only wine of very poor quality. While the first reading tends to dominate in translations (e.g., NRSV, NIV) and makes sense given what Mary says, the second possibility fits with what the president of the banquet says (see 2:10). **The mother of Jesus says to him, "They do not have wine"** (2:3). While Mary's intent is far from explicit, almost every culture uses assertions as veiled criticisms or requests. Within a society of honor and shame, it would be inappropriate for the mother of a grown man to make a direct rebuke for failing to bring wine as a gift or to request that he redress the shortfall. If Jesus were to ignore her request, she would run the risk of either being put in her place, a woman is defined by shame, or opening Jesus to the shameful accusation of failing to honor his mother (see Exod. 20:12). Early exegetes are very sensitive to this dynamic (see John Chrysostom, *Hom. Jo.* 22).

Jesus's response, **"What's that to me and to you, woman?"** renders his mother's words a request. His words are a Semitism and are indicative of the degree of verisimilitude to which John tends to strive in his dialogues. The phrase *Ti emoi kai soi*

Enthymeme

Aristotle called the enthymeme the very body or substance of proofs (*Rhet.* 1.1.3 [1354a.11]). In formal logic, an enthymeme occurs when one or more premises and/or a conclusion is missing. Enough of the argument is provided so that the audience can easily complete the thought. Enthymemes either avoid stating the obvious, obscure a weak argument, or encourage the audience to think on the same line as the speaker.

appears several times in the Septuagint and marks the speakers' antipathy for the actions of the party to whom the question is directed (Judg. 11:12; 1 Kings 17:18; 2 Kings 3:13). Many scholars seek to soften what appears to be a rebuff of his mother by arguing that *gynai* is a polite address, but the examples cited mark social distance or the guise of a stranger (John 4:21; 20:15; Homer, *Od.* 19.221). Adriana Destro and Mauro Pesce (1995, 280) suggest that Jesus's address marks his social independence from his mother's kinship status. The reason that Jesus gives for resisting his mother's request is **"My hour has not yet come"** (2:4). Later, Jesus will use the phrase "my hour" to refer to his death and resurrection (7:30; 8:20; 12:23–27), but "hour" can also refer to the eschatological reality that Jesus's actions inaugurate (4:21–23; 5:25–28). By virtue of performing the sign at Cana, his "hour" begins; Jesus embarks on his journey to the cross. This leads Craig Keener (2003, 506) to conclude, "The primary reason for the rebuff must be that his mother does not understand what this sign will cost Jesus."

What happens next strikes modern readers as humorous and just what a mother would do: Mary ignores what Jesus has just said. But Mary is not a modern woman, and we need to be sensitive to the honor-and-shame dynamics with which John plays. Jesus's honor stands at risk if he does not comply when **His mother says to the servers, "Whatever he says to you, do"** (2:5). Though in the Gospel of Mark the family tries to remove Jesus from his public ministry (Mark 3:21), in John they seem to be pushing him into it (see 7:3). Mary clearly expects that Jesus is capable of doing something extraordinary.

John then provides a piece of scenic detail with enough precision to provoke speculation about intent. **There were six stone** [or stoneware, hard-baked clay] **water jars unattended there in accord with the purification** [rites] **of the Jews with the capacity to hold up to two or three measures** (2:6). The number six may signify incompletion or labor. Six is the number of days God works before resting on the Sabbath. References to stone vessels (Exod. 7:19; *m. Beṣah* 2.3) indicate that stone was used because it was less susceptible to impurity, but simple stoneware satisfies the requirements for keeping drawn water pure (see *m. Kelim* 10.1). It is not clear if the total volume is two to three measures or if each jar holds that amount, making the total twelve to eighteen measures. A measure is about nine English gallons, so whatever the volume, it is copious. Why jars for purification are present is not clear. They may have been used for cleansing of utensils in preparation for the wedding or filling basins for hand washing, in which case the number and size of the empty jars could be an index to the number of guests. John's underscoring that these are according to Jewish practice may point to conformity to Judean practice in the Galilee and may signify a response to Southern polemic. Judeans thought that Galileans did not keep their high standards for purity.

Through Jesus's direct speech, John makes clear that the jars are empty: **"Start filling the water jars full of water!" And they filled them to overflowing**

(2:7). John's emphasis on the sequential relation of command and action produces a cinematic effect and heightens the anticipation as the audience watches the miracle unfold in their mind's eye. The use of the historic present adds to the effect. **And he says to them, "Now start drawing out [some] and bring [it] to the president of the banquet." And they brought [it]** (2:8). The servants' silent but obedient response underscores the authority with which Jesus speaks (see 5:8–9; 9:6–7; 18:8; 21:10–11). **But when the president of the banquet tasted the water, it had become wine, and he had no idea from where [*pothen*] it had come.** John uses *pothen* twelve other times (1:48; 3:8; 4:11; 6:5; 7:27 (2x), 28; 8:14 (2x); 9:29, 30; 19:9), primarily when underscoring the failure of others to look to heaven for the source of intervention. **But** the narrator points out that **the servers who had drawn the water knew.** There is ironic pleasure when someone who is ostensibly in charge is in the dark and when the servants who are not wedding guests become the insiders. From time to time, John seems to offer glimpses of the reversal of the social order so prominent in the synoptic tradition.

John returns to the consequences of the miracle. Rather than serving the wine, something is still amiss, for the president of the banquet calls the bridegroom (2:9) and says to him, **"Every man first sets out the good wine and as soon as they have been made intoxicated, [he sets out] the worse. You have reserved the good wine until now"** (2:10). This is either a challenge to the integrity of the groom, a suggestion that he has been holding out on his guests, or simply an expression of pleasant surprise. In any case, Jesus has spared both president and groom the social embarrassment of having no wine to serve. The way the story is told places the accent on the ignorance of the hosts and that though one may have the empirical evidence of a miracle in front of one, another, more rational account of what has happened is always available. The silence of the bridegroom is humorous. Although he does not know where the wine came from, he does not betray his ignorance or correct the president's mistake. As long as no one knows the truth, no honor is lost.

The narrator then turns his attention to the epistemological gain of the story. **Jesus did this—the first [or beginning] of his signs—in Cana of Galilee, and it made manifest his glory, and his disciples believed in him** (2:11; see "The Role of Signs" in the theological issues section of 2:13–4:54). Throughout this story, honor has been at stake, a commodity given through public recognition or lost through public humiliation. Jesus's act goes publicly unacknowledged and so lies outside the economy of honor and shame. Rather than honor (*timē*) as a currency of status, Jesus possesses glory (*doxa*). Jesus's works do not bring him honor, that is, public recognition; they reveal or make manifest a quality that is intrinsic to his being (1:31; 3:21; 7:4; 9:3; 17:6; 21:1, 14).

The act of believing is important in this Gospel and should not be confused with knowing. At this point the disciples do not fully understand who Jesus is (cf. John 12:23; 17:24), but they trust him or put faith in him or feel confident about him. The sign at Cana thus confirms their initial inclination to follow him because they believe him to be the messiah.

Transition (2:12)

The line **After this, he went down to Capernaum—he and his mother and his brothers and the disciples** serves as a transition from one episode to another by marking the change in setting as a consequence of what has happened. The sudden introduction of his brothers makes it possible that they are silent witnesses to the event, a possibility that provides logical background to their demeanor toward Jesus in John 7:1–9. Now that Jesus has begun to make manifest his glory, returning to a permanent residence is no longer a viable option **and** [so he] **did not remain there many days** (2:12). John Chrysostom's (*Hom. Jo.* 23) comment that Jesus tarries only to honor his mother is, perhaps, apologetic for the dishonor that his departure from home signifies in the context of the ancient world. Home signifies responsibility, well-being, and life, whereas travel signifies danger and even death.

Theological Issues

The narrative brings Jesus into focus and introduces the main action: the manifestation of Jesus's glory and its acceptance or rejection. There is no hint that Jesus is building a new Israel or a new sort of society. Jesus is represented as God's agent through the sign given to John the Baptist, Jesus's unearthly knowledge of others, and his capacity to change water into wine. Beyond this, exegetes have drawn other conclusions about the theology of the Fourth Gospel.

The Symbolism of the Wedding Banquet

Scholars have reconstructed a tradition of the "Messianic Wedding Banquet" by conflating prophecies about an eschatological banquet (Isa. 25:6–7, a coronation banquet), the abundance brought by the messiah (9:6–7), and the metaphor of a marriage to signify the restoration of the covenant (54:4–8; 62:4–5). The intertestamental literature elaborates on the theme of abundance, including abundant wine, but is not explicit about a banquet (*1 En.* 62.12–16; *2 Bar.* 29.1–8). Michael Satlow notes that "it is very difficult to ascertain if the marital metaphor was 'live' during the postexilic period" (2001, 43) and that "among Jews writing in Greek, the description of the relationship between God and Israel as a marriage was stunningly uninfluential" (44). 1QSa 2.11–21 provides the clearest reference to a banquet attended by the messiah and the congregation of Israel. It appears that NT writers revive the covenant as marriage metaphor found in Hosea and Jeremiah and create the concept of a messianic wedding banquet. John may not be drawing from tradition so much as creating tradition by making Jesus's inaugural sign take place at a wedding.

If we take our cues from literature contemporary to the Gospel, the setting of the eve of Jesus's journeys at a wedding may have significance for the plot of the Gospel. Many ancient Greek novels begin at a wedding, from which the couple sets off intentionally or unintentionally on a perilous journey (e.g., Chariton, *Chaer.* 1.1, 11; 3.3; Xenophon of Ephesus, *Ephes.* 1.8–10). In ancient literature, marriage and death are homologous: elements of one may signify the other. Both begin with purification of the body and libations, the bride and the corpse are both veiled, and both end with a body in a chamber. For the bride, marriage is a death to her former state as a virgin daughter in the household of her father and birth to a new life in the household of her husband, where the death of her virginity makes possible new fruitfulness. Euripides makes extensive use of this homology in *Iphigenia at Aulis*: Agamemnon uses the ruse of a wedding to lure Iphigenia and her mother to Aulis, where she will be sacrificed. A wedding as a point of departure may then signal the beginning of Jesus's journey toward his death.

The wedding setting shines a light on Jesus's subversion of concepts of what eternal life requires. An apocryphal work dating to the first centuries, by Pseudo-Phocylides (175–76), captures the prevailing Jewish attitude in giving this piece of advice: "Do not remain unmarried, lest you die nameless. Give nature her due, you also, beget in your turn as you were begotten" (P. W. van der Horst, *OTP* 2:580). While marriage is not commanded in the law, in Jesus's day it was treated as a halakic obligation (Satlow 2001, 17), the celebration of which overwrites fulfillment of other commandments and even purity laws. For example, one early rabbi states that if signs of leprosy appear on the bridegroom during the seven days of festivity, inspection is to be deferred until after they are over (*m. Neg.* 3.2). Jesus's participation in the wedding and his provision of wine have him participating as a guest within the civic order, within the mundane understanding of life and abundance. The story of the gift of abundant life should perhaps be read against the backdrop of a society that would question Jesus for failing to take a wife and then to father children in order to secure his name.

Mariology

Beginning with the early church fathers, Christian theologians saw the Johannine mother of Jesus as a symbol of the church or a new Eve, mother of a new creation. Raymond E. Brown (1966, 108–9) continues in this tradition when he points to the depiction of the woman giving birth in Isa. 26:17–18 and Rev. 12:1–2 as a symbol of the people of God in order to explain why Jesus calls his mother "woman." Recent symbolic readings focus on her place among the other women of the Gospel as exemplary witnesses (e.g., Culpepper 1983, 154).

Increasingly attention has turned to social and literary questions and the significance of the role of Jesus's mother, as his mother, in the Gospel and in the particular episodes in which she appears (see, e.g., Gaventa 1999, 79–99). Within the literary structure of the Gospel, Jesus's mother fits into a complex of elements that include wine, blood, and water and references to Jesus's hour and glory that demarcate an enveloping structure, with the wedding at Cana at one end and Jesus's crucifixion at the other. John perhaps balances Jesus's emphasis on his descent from the Father with recognition of his human parentage (see also 1:45; 6:42; 7:3–4). At the wedding at Cana, Jesus's mother expresses her intimate knowledge of her son's ability and anticipates satisfaction of her veiled request, and Jesus responds as an obedient son. At the foot of the cross, Jesus makes provision for his mother. The presence of Jesus's mother allows for the representation of Jesus as the good son, thereby enhancing the representation of Jesus as the good Son.

Replacement Theories

Scholars often situate the interpretation of the wedding at Cana within the context of a "replacement motif," in which Jesus supplants Jewish institutions and replaces them with Christian ones. The earliest discussion of the motif seems to appear in a 1930 work by Adolf Schlatter and is then developed by Aileen Guilding (1960, 58–68) and Raymond E. Brown (1966, 953–56). Many proponents of this theory contend that the Gospel presents Judaism as a failure to fulfill God's intent as encoded in the Law and the Prophets. According to this theory, the purification rites alluded to in the Cana wedding story are then the first Jewish institution to be replaced. Other replacements include:

Passover lamb (1:29, 36; 19:14, 31, 36)
temple (2:19–21)
temple worship (4:21–24)
manna (6:51–58)
Sukkoth rituals of light and water (7:37–39; 8:12)
Torah (e.g., 1:14, 18; 8:51; 13:34; 14:15, 21–24; 15:10–15)

As Brown (1966, 104) puts it, "All previous religious institutions, customs and feasts lose meaning in his [Jesus's] presence." Brown argues that in the light of the messianic banquet, "Mary's statement, 'They have no wine,' becomes a poignant reflection on the barrenness of Jewish purifications, much in the vein of Mark 7:1–24" (1966, 105). Gail Yee (1989, 25–26) contends that "the Johannine Jesus now nullified and replaced all the Jewish liturgical institutions that the community lost in its divorce from the synagogue: Sabbath, Passover, Sukkoth, and Dedication." If one treats the wedding at Cana as the messianic banquet, Jesus replaces Jewish purification rites with eschatological abundance.

This interpretation depends largely on an early date for the conscious split between the Jewish and Christian traditions. It is often easier to see in hindsight the moment at which an act or decision (or a set of these in close proximity) sends either or both traditions on a trajectory that means inevitable separation. A number of observations about the Cana wedding story throw its contribution to the replacement motif theory into question. The argument that Jesus replaces purification rites rests on the premise that under Jewish law he misappropriates the water pots to create wine and renders them impure, but what evidence we have on the matter states that rain water can be drained from broken wine pots to fill a *miqweh* (*m. Miqw.* 2.7); therefore, filling the jars with wine does not render them impure. Moreover, the celebration of a wedding can take priority over some *halakot* (see *m. Neg.* 3.2). Judith Lieu (1999, 67) observes that "although commentators will find numerous links between Jesus's teaching and the details of the festival rituals, John makes no attempt to draw attention to these, or to suggest that Jesus in some way replaces them."

Another way to articulate the relationship of past practices to Jesus's life and ministry is to see John as appropriating and building upon their significations. If purification prepares one for the joy of God's abundance, Jesus provides that abundance. Given the treatment of Jesus as the one sent by God to bring life and to reveal God's glory, the choice of festivals and rites associated with that glory seems to be the framework in which to emphasize that Jesus is who he says he is. Rather than Jesus's doing away with these festivals and practices, Jesus's presence, not the temple or some other agency, gives festivals and practices their sanctity. Jesus is the new temple, but given that the temple is not standing when the Gospel is written, rather than Jesus's replacing the temple, Jesus fulfills the place left after its destruction. Jesus negates the necessity of rebuilding the temple.

From time to time the possibility resurfaces that a Greco-Roman background informs Johannine Christology and that it is a Greco-Roman cult that Jesus replaces: the cult of Dionysus or Bacchus. The cult of Dionysus was widespread in the Hellenistic and Roman periods and was sanctioned by the state. In 2 and 3 Maccabees, Seleucid and Ptolemaic rulers seek to suppress Judaism and impose Dionysian practices on them (2 Macc. 6:7; 14:33; 3 Macc. 2:29–30). Numerous Hellenistic and Roman rulers represented themselves as Dionysus incarnate (e.g., Plutarch, *Ant.* 24). Skeptics, such as Craig Koester (1995, 80–81), tend to argue that Dionysus does not turn water into wine. Nevertheless, questions about the relationship of the Gospel to Dionysian traditions persist because of the influence that Dionysus's iconography has on Greco-Roman representations of heroes and divinized men in literature and art and, consequently, on Christian representations of Jesus (see Jensen 2000, 126–27; Salier 2004, 67–70)

Lamb of God

Looking at the Baptist's invitation to see Jesus as the Lamb of God who takes up the sins of the world, looking through the lens of two thousand years of Christian doctrinal development, one can easily impose a substitutionary atonement theory on the Gospel. A sacrifice must be offered to expiate for humanity's sins; Jesus presents himself as the perfect sacrifice, a creature without blemish. This view of atonement has come under close scrutiny and stern critique in the last few decades. Current reflections on the meaning of the title Lamb of God within the Gospel of John focus on the ambiguity of the image and the lack of antecedent in earlier Jewish Scripture and literature for the association of a lamb with the act of lifting up sin. The Passover lamb is not an expiatory sacrifice but rather a meal that commemorates God's deliverance of Israel from bondage. It is possible that John refers to Isaiah's comparison of God's servant who "has borne [LXX: *pherei*] our infirmities and carried our diseases" (53:4) to a "lamb led to the slaughter" (53:7). If John refers to the

> ### Dionysus
>
> Dionysus is the son of Zeus by a human mother, Semele, who dies while giving him birth and whom he subsequently rescues from Hades. In stories, his identity is hidden by his human guise until he manifests his divinity. He provides wine and fertility and is associated with the abundance of the afterlife. Euripides's play, *The Bacchae*, follows a plot often compared to that of the Gospel of John (e.g., Stibbe 1992, 126–46). Dionysus has been traveling through the world, making himself manifest and introducing his worship practices, when he arrives at Thebes, where the new king, Pentheus, is hostile to the new cult. Pentheus exemplifies the limits of human reason to recognize Dionysus and to understand the life that he brings.

tamid, a twice-daily offering of a lamb (Exod. 29:38–42) that signifies the communion between God and Israel, sin signifies the alienation of humanity from God rather than guilt. Readers should also bear in mind that sin has two meanings in John's Gospel. Jesus's opponents, and at times Jesus, treat sin as a transgression of the law (5:10, 14; 8:34; 9:2–3, 31), but it also means ignorance of Jesus (8:21, 24, 46; 9:41; 15:24; 16:9). The Baptist may be saying that the revelation of Jesus as God's agent eliminates the sin of ignorance.

It seems likely that John's habit of playing with language serves to subvert conventional meaning and to open up a cognitive space receptive to fresh meaning (see Nielsen 2006, 227). The role that the verb *airō* (to lift up) plays in the Gospel points to the ironic dimension of the designation of Jesus as the Lamb of God who takes up the sin of the world. In John, the act of lifting Jesus up onto the cross becomes an act of exaltation (3:14–15; 8:28; 12:32–33; 19:15). Jesus, God's glorified lamb (Isa. 52:13), exalts the sin of the world; the act of crucifixion, which could be seen as Jesus's humiliation and a dishonor to God, is now seen as an act that honors God. What can be said with certainty is that the Baptist's pronouncement marks Jesus for death, that Jesus is God's agent, and that his death signifies glorification and not humiliation.

John 2:13–12:11

Jesus's Itinerant Ministry

While Jesus has his eye fixed upon his death upon a cross in Jerusalem, his prescience about the desires of the crowd and the Jerusalem authorities to either crown him or stone him keeps him on the move. In the synoptic tradition, Jesus wanders about in a peripatetic ministry, proclaiming an atopic kingdom (i.e., not of this world; John 18:36), but in John, he moves about to evade capture. The unit begins with his departure from the Galilee and then proceeds through three cycles of Passover until his last appearance in Jerusalem. Because the sacred calendar both commemorates past events and the agrarian calendar and includes pilgrimage to the temple in Jerusalem, time and space are

John 2:13–12:11 in Context

In the beginning (1:1–2:12)

▶ Jesus's itinerant ministry (2:13–12:11)

    Transforming sacred space (2:13–4:54)

    God works on the Sabbath (5:1–47)

    Bread and circuses (6:1–71)

    Verbal sparring at the festival of Sukkoth (7:1–8:59)

    A second Sabbath violation at a second pool (9:1–10:42)

    The sweet scent of death (11:1–12:11)

Jesus's triumphant hour (12:12–19:42)

Jesus's resurrection: Endings and epilogues (20:1–21:25)

unified principles in this Gospel. Accusations against him arise when Jesus's assertions about his identity as God's Son and his signs take place at the geographic center of God's holiness and on his holy days. Resolve to stop him happens when his signs are seen as a threat to the nation's holy place (11:48).

Figure 6. Map of the Galilean, Samarian, and Judean settings in the Gospel of John.

John 2:13–4:54

Transforming Sacred Space

Introductory Matters

The emphasis that John places on the passage of time and the approach of Jesus's hour ought not obscure the importance of space in the Gospel. Mikhail M. Bakhtin introduced the language of chronotope into literary studies in order to describe the spatiotemporal matrix of narrative and to thwart the predilection of the human intellect to treat what is one reality as though it were two different things (Bakhtin 1981, 84). The following reading focuses on the care that John takes in bringing the spatial dimension of events before the mind's eye and how the narrative follows the transformation of space through the encounter with Jesus.

John 2:13–4:54 contains at least five discrete stories: the incident in the temple, the dialogue with Nicodemus, John the Baptist's resignation, the encounter with the Samaritan woman at the well, and the healing of the royal official's son. The episodes in the previous unit (1:19–2:12) are bound by temporal markers. These episodes now are points on Jesus's first journey to Judea (2:13–3:22), with the Baptist's contemporaneous action in Samaria (3:23–36), and then back through Samaria (4:1–42) to the Galilee (4:43–54). The end of the unit is marked by a refrain, "Jesus did this second sign when he came from Judea to the Galilee" (4:54), that takes special note of this itinerary. The subtitle "Transforming Sacred Space" points to this topographic design as more than the setting in which Jesus's work takes place. Jesus becomes the new sacred geography, and thus participating in Christ, a theme developed more fully in the Farewell Address (13:31–17:26), is the means of entering

67

God's kingdom. The temples on Mount Moriah and Mount Gerizim, which were once major centers of worship (neither of which stood at the time the Gospel was written), do not need to be rebuilt in stone for they have been rebuilt through Jesus's resurrection. Jesus's movement through space entails border crossings, and with each crossing the border is transformed. Those who were previously at the center of the sacred landscape, such as Nicodemus, lose their place and must find it again. Those formerly excluded from the sacred order of the Jerusalem elite, such as the Samaritan woman, stand in God's presence. The mighty, those who collaborate with imperial power, become the needy.

Two major closely entwined value systems exert a force upon social interactions during the first century AD and factor into John's rhetorical construction of space. The first is the concept of purity, and the second is the twin concepts of honor and shame.

Purity is not a concept limited to Judaism, but Second Temple Judaism had its particular list of things that caused impurity and various methods for restoring it, although there does not seem to have been consensus about which method to use. An analogy to dirt informs language and practices regarding impurity, but the modern analogy of radioactive contamination explains better how impurity could spread. Evidence from later rabbinic literature indicates that what caused impurity and which methods and what sources of water could purify were the subject of debates that divided groups such as the Pharisees, Sadducees, and Essenes (e.g., *m. Yad.* 4.7). *Miqwā'ôt*, ritual baths, that date to before AD 70 have been discovered that follow the prescription found in the Mishnah (*m. Miqw.* 6.8). One's degree of purity determined how deep into the temple courts one could enter and with whom one could have physical contact.

The concept of purity intersects with broader cultural anthropological concepts of honor and shame. Within the minds of the Second Temple elite, purity could be a source of honor, and impurity a source of shame. Anthropologists describe honor as public recognition of social standing that is ascribed by one's inherited status or acquired through competition. Shame comes when one's actions cross the boundaries of one's social status or when challenges to one's honor are met with resignation or defeat. Paradoxically showing a proper sense of shame, especially in the case of women, by keeping one's place through modesty or humility maintains one's family honor.

John uses the deictic language of his narrator and characters, as well as their entrances and exits, to rhetorically construct the sacred and social dimensions of space. His poetics articulate space, material properties, and actions in order to generate what modern theorists call *mise en scène* (a term borrowed from cinematic arts) and what classical rhetoricians called *ekphrasis*. The order—the linear imposition of time on space inherent in writing—with which he brings these elements to the mind's eye imposes a point of view.

Social exchanges in ancient Mediterranean societies could easily become caught up in a zero-sum game in which honor is gained or lost as though honor were a limited commodity (see Moxnes 1996). The literary dialogues embedded in Greco-Roman narratives often take the form of verbal duels or flyting (insult-and-boasting competitions), analogous to fencing matches, in which challenges to honor are parried (deflected) and then met with riposte (a counterinsult and/or boast). John's dialogues are fraught with comparable agonistic repartee that can disturb modern readers expecting a gentle Jesus, who issues invitations and offers forgiveness. An ancient audience would receive these dialogues as a representation of the broader action of the Gospel, in which Jesus's identity or status is challenged and confirmed, and would have treated Jesus's aggressive rhetoric as points scored in a contest that demonstrates his authority.

As the main action of the Gospel begins to unfold, the centrality of dialogue to John's narrative becomes evident.

> ### Ekphrasis
>
> Modern usage of the term *ekphrasis* narrows its application to literary descriptions of a work of art. In ancient rhetorical exercises, students imitated Homer's description of Achilles's shield (*Il.* 18.578–608), and we find many examples of detailed descriptions of works of art embedded in narratives (e.g., Achilles Tatius, *Leuc. Clit.* 1.1). Ancient rhetoric manuals also applied the term broadly to the art of lingering on details in lengthy digressions or in brief sketches so that persons and actions and times and places and seasons and many other things could be brought before the eyes with clarity (*saphēneia*) and vividness (*enargeia*; Hermogenes, *Progymn.* 22–23). Nicolaus the Sophist adds festivals, meadows, harbors, and pools to Hermogenes's list (*Progymn.* 68) and explains how the use of *ekphrasis* in narrative both turns the audience of a written work into spectators (70) and works on the emotions (71).

Much of the action of the Gospel is constituted by a series of encounters between one person and Jesus. Before one makes symbolic sense of this or begins talking of a personal relationship with Christ, it is important to recognize that John is working within ancient literary conventions of having two, and occasionally three, characters engage in a dialogue at one time. He also seems to draw from the stock of character types found in Greco-Roman literature that are described in detail in *The Characters* by Theophratus (371–287 BC). This typicality leads some scholars to treat John's cast as representatives of types of believers or members of different groups within the actual world of John's audience. But ancient writers take care to situate characters within the realities of social and physical settings: they work within the logic of the action to transform types into individuals. Meir Sternberg (1985, 247–48) observes that Hebrew narrative presumes upon the readers' propensity to type characters and then deliberately destroys the readers' comfort in their conclusions. John appears to follow the same method. For example, Nicodemus seems to be pulled by his Pharisaic status to conform to the group's judgment, but then he shows up at Jesus's entombment with more than enough myrrh for a royal burial. Readers need to begin by treating each character as an individual but to be sensitive to the sorts of presuppositions about their shared identity with a social or ethnic group in order to see how John forces his audience to adopt a new point of view. Moreover, his use of character types forces his audience to recognize the nature of human folly.

Tracing the Narrative Flow

Jesus in the Temple (2:13–25)

Scholars continually seek answers to the question of why John places the temple incident at the beginning of Jesus's public ministry rather than at its end. John's account is at odds with that of the synoptic tradition in many ways. The following reading will focus on three prominent differences: the careful sequencing of action, the concentration on setting, and the focus on zeal rather than the eschatological act of preparing the temple. The thrust of the episode is not a critique of the economy of the temple or purification in preparation for reception of the nations or judgment on the temple cult. The focus of the passage is on Jesus's assertion that his body is the temple and how his words foreshadow his death and resurrection.

The narrative begins with the customary specification of time or occasion and place: **And the Passover of the Jews was approaching, and Jesus went up to Jerusalem** (2:13), ascending from 686 feet below sea level (at Capernaum) to 2,500 feet above sea level. The clarification that this is the Passover of the Jews (see also references to festival of the Jews in 5:1; 7:2–3; 11:55) can be understood as a topographical reference to a feast that calls for a pilgrimage to Jerusalem. The inclusion of the phrase "of the Jews" suggests some social distance between the audience and the Jews or evokes more clearly the memory of the Passover as the liberation of the Jews.

The action begins with what Jesus sees, an *ekphrasis* describing the space and its activity into which Jesus will step in medias res. **And he found in the temple precincts** [*hieros* versus *naos*] **those exchanging oxen and sheep and doves and the seated money changers** (2:14). The presence of money changers should be expected. Given that Judeans could not mint their own coins, it was necessary to change money into Tyrian coinage, its high percentage of silver providing a reliable standard, in order to pay the temple half-shekel tax

(Exod. 30:11–16). Jesus's elaborate and varied actions are shown in sequence by using diction dominated by repeated hard or repeated consonant sounds that give the narrative a rhythm appropriate to the action: **And having made** [*poiēsas*] **a whip out of cords** [*ek schoiniōn*], **all** [*pantas*] **he drove out** [*exebalen ek*] **of the temple precincts, both the sheep** [*ta te probata*] **and the oxen** [*tous boas*], **and of the small money changers** [*kollybistōn*] **he poured** [*execheen*] **out the small coins** [*kerma*] **and the tables** [*tas trapezas*] **he upset** [*anatrepsen*] (2:15). As is his habit, Jesus commands others to complete the action (2:7–8; 9:11; 11:44; 18:8, 11): **And to those selling the doves, he said, "Take those things out of here!"** This is followed by a prohibition to all the merchants not to undo Jesus's work: **"Do not make the house of my Father a house of merchandise** [*emporiou*]**!"** (2:16).

> ### Diction
>
> Aristotle treats diction (*lexis*) together with delivery (*taxis*) because in an oral society the written word became the spoken word (*Rhet.* 3.1.2–7.12 [1403b–14a]). Silent and solitary reading was not an ancient pastime. Classical rhetoricians chose words not just with a view to meaning but also rhythm, cadence, and sound, because they were conscious of how diction could convey emotion and aid the memory of both the one who recites the words and those who hear them (see Quintilian, *Inst.* 11.3.1–9).

The Latin word *emporium* (from Gk. *emporion*) was used in the nineteenth century to describe a store that sold all sorts of goods; in antiquity, it referred to a market center or trading center. Jesus seems to be fulfilling the prophecy in Zech. 14:21 that "there shall no longer be traders in the house of the LORD of hosts on that day."

John uses the recollections of Jesus's disciples **that it was written** (a circumlocution for Scripture), **"The zeal of your house will devour me"** (2:17), to turn attention away from critique of how the temple is run to what the action says about Jesus. The allusion to Ps. 69:9, a psalm of lament, looks forward to the crucifixion: the psalmist's zeal for God's house is both the reason for his persecution and metaphorically an agent of self-destruction. John tends to use the word "remember" to refer to Jesus's death and resurrection (2:22; 12:16; 15:20; 16:4, 21; see Coloe 2001, 75). The verse suggests that the disciples see Jesus's actions as a sign of his passion about the temple and not its condemnation. They are looking for confirmation of their conclusions and not signs that point to either the destruction of the temple or the death of their chosen messiah.

John signals the resumption of the action in the temple precinct with his characteristic use of the word *oun*: **The Jews then** [*oun*] **responded to him and said to him, "What sign** [*sēmeion*] **do you offer us that you do this?"** (2:18; see Matt. 12:39–40). Their response seems rather mild. When Jeremiah smashes a pottery jug to prophesy the destruction of Judea, the chief officer of the temple strikes him and places him in the stocks (Jer. 20:1–2). In Mark,

Figure 7. Drawing of the second temple with Antonia in the background.

the officials ask no questions and jump directly to strategies for killing Jesus (11:18), but the actions of the Johannine Jesus lead to dialogue.

Jesus meets their demand for a proof with a counterchallenge that uses deictic language to anchor the argument in its physical setting: "**Destroy** [*lysate*; aorist imperative is used for commands for specific acts rather than general conduct] **this temple** [*ton naon touton*; recall that Jesus is standing in the temple precinct and that he is pointing to the temple proper], **and in three days I will raise it** [*egerō*]" (2:19). John has turned the taunt of those who mock Jesus at his crucifixion (Mark 15:29) into Jesus's boast. D. B. Wallace (1996, 490–91) offers this paraphrase: "Go ahead! Destroy this temple, if you dare! I will still raise it up!" The Greek contains a play on words: buildings are erected (*egeirō*) and the dead are raised (*egeirō*). The boast that Jesus will raise the building is not simply a claim to miraculous powers but to a social status shared by few. In Roman society, triumphant generals (see "The Triumph" sidebar at 12:12–50) were allowed to restore temples in Rome with their plunder; this was one of the good works (*euergesiai*) that normally would be permitted only to the emperor (Suetonius, *Aug.* 29). No doubt Herod regarded his own act of temple renovations as this sort of *euergesia*. Jesus's words anticipate the language of victory used later in the Gospel (12:31–32; 16:33).

Without the power of hindsight, the Jews logically take Jesus's words to point to the structure in front of them and find his boast to be preposterous. Once more, the setting becomes part of their argument: "*This* **temple was under construction** [*oikodomēthē*] **forty-six years, and** *you* **in three days will raise it?**" (2:20). Their dismissive comment ends the battle of words and

Herod's Temple

In his attempt to make his kingdom important in the Roman world and his rule popular among the Jewish people, Herod the Great undertook a major renovation and expansion that doubled the size of the temple precinct and gave the temple a beautiful facade of radiant marble gilded with gold. Work was begun in 20 BC and seems to have been completed (in AD 63) only a few years before its destruction in AD 70 (Josephus, *J.W.* 5.184–226; *Ant.* 15.380–425; cf. John 2:20). Adjacent to the temple, Herod also built a fortress, Antonia, which became the position from which Rome exercised control over its precincts and operations. The presence of Roman soldiers so close to the temple adds to the potential for violent protests within the temple precinct (see Josephus, *Ant.* 17.254–64; 18.261–309; 20.105–12).

seems to point to their conclusion, at this point, that Jesus is harmless. The Jerusalem authority's hostility will begin to mount when Jesus returns to Jerusalem for the Feast of Sukkoth (7:14). Just in case his audience did not catch the wordplay, the narrator explains, **He said this about the temple of his body** (*sōmatos*; 2:21). John uses the noun *sōma* only in reference to Jesus's crucified body (19:31, 38, 40; 20:12) and links this reference with the end of the story by adding a prolepsis (a reference to a future act) that disrupts the chronology of his account: **Therefore when he had arisen from the dead, his disciples remembered that he said this, and they believed in the Scripture and the word that Jesus said** (2:22). "Scripture" should be taken as a reference to the Torah and Prophets in toto rather than a particular verse.

The narrator then provides his assessment of the immediate consequences of the Jerusalem visit. **While he was in Jerusalem at the Passover** [participating] **in the festival, many trusted in his name** [after] **seeing** [*theōrountes*] **his signs that he did** (2:23). The choice of the verb *theōreō* underscores that they are watching Jesus's actions the way that one watches a spectacle. Who these many are is not specified, but given what we learn in 4:45, they are possibly Galileans. The phrase "trusted in his name" (*episteusan eis to onoma autou*) seems to signify that they grant him the authority to disrupt temple activity rather than the idea that they have the sort of faith to which the disciples come at the end of the Gospel. **However, Jesus himself has no trust** [*episteuen*] **in them on account of his knowing everything** (2:24). Rather than treating this as a statement about a general sort of omniscience, it is perhaps best taken as a reference to his godlike knowledge of the intents, desires, and stories of all people he encounters. The narrator's final qualifying remark—**And that he had no need for someone to testify about humanity** [*tou anthrōpou*], **for he knew what was in humanity** (2:25)—seems to support this understanding of Jesus's insight.

73

Nicodemus Visits Jesus (3:1–21)

In the next scene, the narrator brings forward one person with whom Jesus can engage in a dialogue. The Fourth Gospel contains two dialogues and one narrative without direct speech in which Nicodemus takes part. Analyses of the first discourse have tended to focus on how Nicodemus misunderstands Jesus. This analysis will focus on the give-and-take of the rhetorical moves, the way that they seek to create either solidarity or division or to establish honor and rank. Nicodemus arrives while thinking of himself as Jesus's dialogue partner, but when Jesus speaks about himself as the source of salvation in language that is veiled by double entendre, Nicodemus struggles to keep up his end of the banter. When Jesus moves into pure monologue, Nicodemus falls behind, but the last lines of the monologue keep Nicodemus in sight.

The narrator begins with an introduction that includes an identifying marker just used with reference to Jesus's distrust (2:25) and that often signals anonymity: **There was a person** (*anthrōpos*), then a marker that typically signifies Jesus's opponents, **from among the Pharisees**, then another that signifies a unique identity, **by the name Nicodemus**, and finally one that points to his honored status as **an official [***archōn***] of the Jews** (3:1). *Archōn* covers everything from club leader to someone in political office with real power. The narrator then uses the setting for rhetorical effect by adding **This [man] came to him at night** to invoke the prologue (1:5). Nicodemus is drawn to Jesus's light, which shines in the darkness, but darkness is also a cover. He seems not to want others to see whose company he seeks.

John's introduction to Nicodemus as well as the way Nicodemus frames his words provokes questions about his character or intent. Set within Theophrastus's delineation of characters, Nicodemus resembles the dissembling man who "comes to his enemies and willingly converses with them." Jesus's characterization of Nicodemus's words and silence capture the sort of phrases that Theophrastus (*Char.* 1) describes as habitual to the dissembler, phrases such as "I do not believe it," "I cannot accept that," and "I am shocked."

Nicodemus uses a polite address that places Jesus on his own social level, and he uses the plural to represent himself as one who speaks for others: **"Rabbi, we know that you have come from God, a teacher, for no one is able to do these signs that you do unless God is with him"** (3:2). He makes claim to certainty and the authority to delineate the criteria by which one recognizes whether someone is from God or not.

Within the context of many cultures, including Mediterranean cultures of the Greco-Roman era, such praise of Jesus's virtues calls for some sort of reciprocal compliment, but Jesus immediately turns the engagement into a verbal duel by rejecting Nicodemus's claim to knowledge and later by returning Nicodemus's politic address with a challenge to Nicodemus's right to call himself a teacher (3:10). Jesus asserts his own claim to delineate criteria to recognize the divine: **"Truly, truly, I say to you, unless one is born again/from** above [*anōthen*], he or she shall not be able to see the kingdom of God" (3:3). In the Gospel of John, Jesus refers to the kingdom only here and once in his trial (18:36), a theme that was certainly central to the preaching of the historical Jesus. John has Jesus boldly use "kingdom of God" and not the circumlocution "kingdom of heaven."

Nicodemus seems to be as practiced in nuanced speech as Jesus. By responding, **"How is a person able to be born who is old? Surely he is not able a second [time] to enter into the womb of his mother and be born?"** (3:4), he takes advantage of the double entendre that Jesus's word choice has made possible. Rebirth is a metaphor used in rabbinic Judaism to signify conversion (for a detailed discussion, see Keener 2003, 542–43) and may have had currency in Second Temple Judaism, particularly among Pharisees who seem, according to the Gospel of Matthew, to be engaged in proselytism (Matt. 23:15; 28:16–20). Nicodemus would not see himself as one in need of such a "rebirth." By rendering Jesus's assertion absurd, Nicodemus tries to take control of the discourse by forcing Jesus to answer his question and clarify his meaning. Jesus, however, maintains control by responding with yet another double entendre: **"Truly, truly, I say to you, unless one be born from water and wind/ spirit [*pneumatos*], one is not about to enter into the kingdom of God"** (3:5). *Pneumatos* must be translated with two words in order to capture Jesus's sustained wordplay. He completes his counterattack with an argument based on the premise that the effect shares the same properties as its cause: **"The one who is born of the flesh** [metonymy for the physical body; we would say flesh and bones] **is flesh, and the one who is born from the spirit/wind is spirit/wind"** (3:6).

Jesus's command, **"Do not be astonished because I said to you, it is necessary for you [pl.] to be born again/from above!"** (3:7), points to how Nicodemus is receiving what Jesus says. Now Jesus turns to terms of common discourse by citing a maxim: **"The spirit/wind breathes/blows where it wishes, and you hear its sound, but you do not know from where it comes and where it withdraws. Thus is [the experience of] everyone who is born from the spirit/wind"** (3:8). According to ancient understanding, wind did not die down but rather it retreated to an unseen

Flesh and Spirit

Socrates speaks of the body as something that is mortal, transient, and corruptible—and of the soul as eternal and belonging to the transcendent realm along with the forms, all of which belong to the Good. Gnostics tended to denigrate this body as something that holds the soul captive. Judaism tended not to treat flesh as evil or corrupt. Evil is about inclinations, what one chooses to do with physical desires that are natural. John appears to follow the Jewish notion that spirit animates flesh that is not yet living and can reanimate that which is dead (see Gen. 6:9; Ezek. 36:25–26; Eccles. 11:5; *L.A.E.* [*Apoc.*] 13.3–6; 32.4; *4 Ezra* [*2 Esd.*] 7.26–38; 2 Macc. 6:18–31; 7:22; Philo, *Opif.* 135).

location for a time. Jesus's figure undercuts Nicodemus's pretension of knowing, but his words may also answer Nicodemus's question by invoking language associated with God's power to resurrect that became part of the second benediction (of 18) in the Shemoneh Esreh, as it is recited from Sukkoth to Passover: "Your miraculous powers are eternal, Lord, and are exercised in many ways. You make the wind blow and the rain fall. You generously sustain the living and most mercifully restore the dead to life" (trans. Reif 2006, 151). Jesus repeats the command "Do not be astonished" in 5:28 with reference to the eschatological event of the general resurrection. Through the course of the Gospel, piece by piece, Jesus will describe how a person achieves eternal life through abiding in Jesus, who is the resurrection and the life.

Nicodemus's response, **"How are these things able to happen?"** (3:9), is comparable to a technical question raised frequently in Second Temple literature: "How will the dead be raised?" Paul answers the question with the expression "in the twinkling of an eye" (1 Cor. 15:52). Nicodemus's second question is not a refutation of the terms of the discussion, nor is it necessarily an indication of misunderstanding. His question calls for an account of how the resurrection can be accomplished without observation. Jesus's sarcastic question, **"You are the teacher of Israel, and you do not know these things?"** (3:10), provides the riposte to Nicodemus's polite address of "Rabbi" (3:2) and suggests that Jesus is indeed talking about something for which Nicodemus claims expertise. What follows are Jesus's proofs, substantiating that his own resurrection is a future fact and drawing on conventions of classical rhetoric.

First proof: On Jesus's origin. Jesus makes an argument based on *ethos*, his own character or person, in particular his origins (see "Logos, Ethos, and Pathos in John" sidebar at 5:1–47). Because he has descended from heaven, he can speak of what he knows, and he can ascend to heaven. The first assertion contains Jesus's counter to Nicodemus's initial claim to speak knowingly on behalf of a group regarding Jesus's origins: **"Truly, truly, I say to you that what we know we speak, and about what we have seen we testify, and our testimony you have not received"** (3:11). The use of the first-person and second-person plural verb forms in this verse suggests that Jesus is quoting conventional wisdom. He then employs a form of argument common in early rabbinic discourse, *qal wahomer*, "light and heavy," that was probably normative for the Pharisees. **"If I spoke to you [about] the terrestrial phenomena**

Maxims

Maxims are a form of enthymeme that require their audience to provide the premise and conclusions of an argument (Aristotle, *Rhet.* 2.21.1–16 [1394a–95b]). The implicit argument in John 3:8 is as follows:

Premise: Rebirth is caused by a heavenly power.
Premise: Heavenly powers cannot be comprehended.
Conclusion: Therefore, you cannot comprehend rebirth.

[*epigeia*] **and you did not believe [*pisteuete*, pl.], how then shall I speak to you [about] the heavenly phenomena [*epourania*] so you will believe?"** (3:12). Jesus then classifies himself as belonging to heavenly phenomena with a proleptic nod to his future ascension—**"And no one ascends to the heaven except one descending from heaven, the Son of Man"** (3:13)—in which he obliquely refers to himself as the Son of Man (see "The Johannine Son of Man" in the theological issues section of 9:1–10:42). The claim to be unique is a standard feature of the ancient rhetoric of boast or praise (see Aristotle, *Rhet*.1.9.38 [1368a.10–15]; Quintilian, *Inst*. 3.7.16; Aelius Theon, *Progymn*. 114; see also John 1:18; 6:44, 65; 14:6). As Jerome Neyrey (2007a, 82) observes, to be unique "is a rhetorical marker for the deity" (see 2 Macc. 1:24–25).

Second proof: An analogy. Jesus moves from possible allusions to the resurrection onward to an unmistakable reference by offering an analogy to Num. 21:7–8: **"And just as Moses raised up the serpent in the wilderness, so it is necessary for the Son of Man to be raised up"** (3:14). No analogy is perfect, and each requires one to ask what precisely is being compared. The comparison may be as simple as something being lifted up as a sign: Moses holds up a serpent, and Jesus is held up on the cross (see Keener 2003, 565). It could be as complicated as Augustine's (*Tract. Ev. Jo.* 12.11) interpretation that sees an allusion to both death brought by the serpent in Gen. 3 and the story in Num. 21: just as gazing on the bronze serpent prevented death by the bite of a snake, so gazing at the cross brings death to death. If the latter is the case, John is anticipating Caiaphas's logic that through one man's death the nation will be saved (11:50). Whatever the analogy, Jesus now completes his answer to Nicodemus's question in 3:4. Jesus is lifted up in his death and resurrection **"in order that all who believe in him shall have eternal life"** (3:15). One is born again by trusting in Jesus's death and resurrection.

Third proof: On motive. The next argument explains why the Son of Man descends to earth. Quintilian (*Inst.* 5.10.33) describes two types of motive: the enjoyment of a great good and deliverance from some evil. Jesus's answer satisfies both types. **How [*houtōs*] God loved the world that [*hōste*] he gave the Son, the one and only!** (3:16). The Greek in the first line invites archaic English wording used now only occasionally in pop song lyrics such as "How I wish, how I wish you were here" (Pink Floyd, "Wish You Were Here," London: Harvest/EMI, 1975). The emphasis is not on the quantity but on the character of God's love. *Hōste* expresses result with emphasis. Jesus's death is an

---

Proofs

Aristotle calls the means of persuasion proofs (*pisteis*) and divides them into two categories. Inartificial proofs include laws, witnesses, contracts, torture, and oaths. These are the proof appropriate to the courtroom (*Rhet.* 1.15.2 [1375a]). Artificial proofs are rooted in discourse and argument and, depending on the form, are suited to forensic, deliberative, and epideictic rhetoric (for a concise description of these proofs, see Quintilian, *Inst.* 5.9).

expression of God's willingness to give a life so that others may live. Jesus will later describe this as the greatest demonstration of love (15:13). He closes this argument by rejecting popular expectations that God's eschatological agent comes to separate the righteous from the wicked and to condemn the world for its treatment of Israel or its idolatry: **For God did not send the Son into the world in order to judge the world, but in order that the world might be saved by him** (3:17).

As Quintilian (*Inst.* 5.10.35) points out, arguments from motive are usually raised as a defense in order to repel an accusation. The logic of the argument makes most sense if one reconstructs an objection to Jesus's assertion that his death is a sign of God's love and is the means to eternal life. The assertion in Deut. 21:23 that "anyone who is hung on a tree is under God's curse" provides a possible basis for the accusation that Jesus's execution is a sign of God's wrath and the result of condemnation.

Final proof: On the ethos of disbelievers. The final verses are not a proof in support of Jesus's assertion but rather an argument that explains why some continue to doubt in the face of Jesus's signs. The underlying point is that to believe in Jesus's name is virtuous. In order to makes sense of Jesus's argument, modern readers should set aside concepts of innocence or guilt, or pardon and condemnation, and recognize that the concepts of honor and shame are operative in this passage. **The one who believes in him is not judged** [not subjected to humiliation] **whereas the one who does not believe has already been judged** [has become subject to shame] **for he** [or she] **has not believed in the name of the only begotten Son of God** (3:18)—the person has not shown honor where it is due. The next verse explains why they choose not to honor Jesus by believing: **This then is the judgment that the light has come into the world, and the human beings loved the darkness greater than the light, for their deeds have been base** (*ponēra ta erga*; 3:19). Jesus then clarifies how the nature of their deeds causes them to love the darkness, using antithetical parallelism to contrast those who have been judged with those who are not. **For everyone who practices pettiness** [*phaula*] **hates the light and does not come to the light, lest one's deeds be censured** (3:20). The change in noun from *ponēra ta erga* to *phaula* may reflect John's habit of varying his vocabulary, or it may be an example of an early rabbinic form of argument from the general case to a particular example. Pettiness is a kind of baseness. Most translations treat *phaula* as synonymous with *ponēra*, but by doing so they miss a possible reference to the historical Jesus's assessment of Pharisaic practice. In Matt. 23, Jesus delivers a long diatribe against the Pharisees' obsession with minutiae and their neglect of what matters to God. At the end of Jesus's ministry, the Johannine narrator will level a similar accusation against those who do not acknowledge their belief in Jesus, charging that they wish to preserve the honor they receive from others (John 12:42). Jesus now moves to the second line of the antithesis. **While the one who exercises the truth comes to the light, in** order that their deeds might be made known that they are things done in God (3:21). The gist of the argument is that Jesus shares in God's deeds, which are necessarily glorious; therefore, whoever sides with him shares in his glory.

Nicodemus does not speak after 3:9, and Jesus ceases to use first-person and second-person pronouns after 3:12. It is reasonable to conclude that the narrator's voice has replaced that of Jesus and speaks to the Gospel's audience rather than to Nicodemus. Nevertheless, the final passage (3:16–21) ends with language that points back to where the episode begins, with a Pharisee coming covertly in the night to speak with Jesus. The use of the metaphor of darkness recalls Nicodemus's choice to come to Jesus under the cover of night lest he be seen coming to someone whom the temple authorities have dismissed as not worthy of their consideration. When the reader next encounters Nicodemus (7:45–52), he will be challenged to take sides. In the last encounter (19:38–42), he does a deed that honors Jesus. Nicodemus's movement toward the light is gradual.

The Baptist Resigns (3:22–36)

The next episode is marked by a change of location and seems to be a return to earlier action. Historical critics have treated this as an aporia, but the return to the Baptist's territory allows John to use characters within the story to comment on the rise of Jesus's following. As we shall see, John uses the corporate voice in the same way that the tragedians use their chorus to accentuate the ambiguity and conflict that arise from the actions of the main characters (Brant 2004, 178–87).

After this Jesus came (and his disciples) into Judean territory and spent his time [*dietriben*] with them and baptized (3:22). Homer uses the verb *diatribō* to signify wasted time or an unwanted delay (*Il.* 19.150). Jesus does not move through John's landscape with the same sort of urgency or frenetic pace of activity that characterizes the synoptic Jesus's ministry. The idea that Jesus's ministry was initially modeled after that of John the Baptist seems to be suggested here. John, however, expresses little interest in the ideology of baptism but instead in Jesus's precedence over the Baptist and the shift of "the Jews'" attention from the Baptist to Jesus.

The narrator then proceeds to give a precise geographic orientation and brings the Baptist into the scene: **And there was John baptizing in Aenon near Salim because water was plentiful there, and they were continuing to arrive and were being baptized (3:23).** The picture is of a very successful ministry and of people not simply coming but also joining his movement as followers (see John 4:1, where baptism is treated as the initiation of a disciple). The Baptist seems to be in Samaria. Jesus's move into Judea suggests some sort of geopolitical distinctions in the two baptismal ministries. The narrator then points to an unseen, malevolent force that casts a shadow over the Baptist's ministry: **For John had not yet been put under guard (3:24).** The Gospel writer assumes that his audience knows the story found in Josephus (*Ant.* 18.109–19) and the synoptic tradition (Mark 6:14–29; par. Matt. 14:1–12; Luke 9:7–9) that the Baptist openly criticized Herod Antipas and, as a result, was imprisoned and later executed. John's narrator employs a technique used with some frequency by Herodotus's narrator. At the moment that he narrates a person's success, he will add a proleptic reference to the person's end in order to point to the instability of fortune or to comment on the significance of an event (e.g., Herodotus, *Hist.* 7.213; de Jong 2004, 106).

A more proximate opponent than Herod now comes into view: **An inquiry then occurred [between] some of John's disciples with a Jew concerning purification** (3:25). Once again, John shows no interest in distinguishing to which Judean interest group this lone "Jew" belongs, but his questioning seems to cause the Baptist's disciples to look at Jesus's activity as unwanted competition and to try to draw the Baptist's attention to it as such: **"Rabbi, the one who was with you on the other side of the Jordan, of whom you have testified—look, this one is baptizing, and all are going to him"** (3:26). The contrast between how the narrator characterizes the health of the Baptist's ministry and his disciple's use of "all" points to the disciples' unreasonable rivalry. The Baptist presents the voice of Johannine reason and provides several arguments to correct their attitude. He begins with an enthymeme in the form of a maxim, piling up negatives (in the Greek) for emphasis: **"A person is not able to undertake anything at all unless it be given to him from heaven"** (3:27). The Baptist then turns from a theological principle to his own past statements to persuade them that he does not view Jesus as a rival: **"You yourselves [can] attest for me that I said, 'I am not the Christ but one who has been sent before that one'"** (3:28). He places himself in a subordinate position and, therefore, not as one who can or should contend with Jesus. He then turns to an analogy underscoring that he is a supporter of Jesus rather than a rival: **"The one having the bride is the bridegroom, while the friend of the bridegroom, who stands and hears him, rejoices in joy** [*chara chairei*] **because of the voice of the bridegroom; therefore, my joy has been fulfilled"** (3:29). The Baptist describes his joy as exceeding what is culturally prescribed for wedding guests. Mention of the bridegroom's voice introduces an element that either compares Jesus's voice to his own voice crying in the wilderness (1:23) or looks forward to the voice of the Good Shepherd, who calls his sheep by name (10:3). Or it may be a synecdoche, in which a general class, the voice, is used to refer to a more-specific class, the sound of joy expected from the bridegroom (see Jer. 7:34). He then returns to an argument based on their chronological relationship: **"It is necessary for that one to increase** [*auxanein*] **[in power or honor] and for me to suffer loss** [*elattousthai*] **[in power or status]"** (3:30). Jerome Neyrey and Richard Rohrbaugh (2001, 464–83) set the Baptist's view of his relationship to Jesus (and that of his disciples) within the zero-sum game of ancient society, in which power and honor are treated as a "limited good." A similar view of the waxing and waning of divine champions is expressed by Aeneas: "Zeus builds up and Zeus diminishes the strength in men, the way he pleases, since his power is beyond all others" (Homer, *Il.* 20.242–44, trans. Lattimore 1951). Rather than rivals, the Baptist characterizes their relationship as one champion passing on the role to a newcomer who is his superior.

The end of the passage is comparable to the end of the Nicodemus discourse. First-person and second-person pronouns and verb forms disappear. The voice of the Baptist, like that of Jesus, seems to be subsumed within that of the narrator. Attention returns to the Johannine distinction between knowledge based on divine and human experience, but now from the perspective of one looking back on Jesus's earthly career. **The one coming from above is above all. One who is from the earth is from the earth and speaks of the earth. The one coming from heaven** [is above all] (3:31). He now echoes a dichotomy found in 1:11–12: **What he has seen and heard, to this he testifies, and no one accepts his testimony** (3:32). This absolute language is then tempered with an exception: **The one who accepts his testimony certifies** [*esphragisen*] **that God is true** (3:33). The metaphor depicts a person's putting a seal of authentication on a document (see John 6:27). If this is still the Baptist's voice, he is responding directly to his disciples, "You may not accept Jesus's authority, but I do, and my testimony carries sufficient weight that you ought to accept it."

The remainder of the passage then elaborates upon confirmation of Jesus's authority and repeats what has been said at the end of the Nicodemus discourse. **For he whom God sent speaks the words of God, for he does not give the Spirit by measure** (3:34): there are no half-truths or incomplete acts, for Jesus has been given complete power and authority by virtue of his relationship to God, as the Baptist has spelled out in 1:18. Once more divine love is named as the efficient cause of Jesus's power: **The Father loves the Son and has given everything in his hand** (3:35). The passage then ends by drawing a clear line between two fates: **The one who believes in the Son has eternal life, while the one who refuses to comply with the Son will not see life, but God's wrath remains on him** (3:36). If this is the Baptist speaking, the language of wrath (*orgē*) may belong to the vocabulary of his call for repentance (Matt. 3:7; Luke 3:7) rather than the soteriology of John's Gospel.

The Samaritan Woman at the Well (4:1–42)

The next episode contains a series of scenes marked by entrances and exits, a standard convention of classical drama adopted by John here and in a number of episodes (see 9:13–34; 18:28–19:16). A number of scholars have treated the narrative as a parody of a type-scene from Hebrew Scripture in which a man or his agent meets his bride at a well (Isaac and Rebekah; Jacob and Rachel; Moses and Zipporah; see Brant 1996, 211–16). The following reading underscores the complexity of the narrative. Besides elements of the betrothal type-scene, the scenario of water disputes, the speech act of supplication, and the plot elements of recognition and reversal—all combine to constitute the action.

Some readers may be struck by the absence of the language of penitence in the above list. While some commentators persist in characterizing the Samaritan as a fallen woman, to do so is to make assumptions about the woman's capacity to act as an agent and what it means to live with a man who is not one's husband. The woman's morality is nowhere at issue in the dialogue, and it therefore seems inappropriate to make it an issue in the interpretation of the story. This does not mean that the woman does not live with shame. Without a husband or children, she is a woman without family honor (see Day 2002, 170–71).

While the Baptist treats Jesus's rise in status as a divinely sanctioned progression, antagonistic forces see his rise as problematic and drive Jesus to move on. Once again, no specific threat is named, but John sustains a sense of foreboding by referring to Jesus's prescience: **Since Jesus knew that the Pharisees heard that Jesus makes and baptizes more disciples than John** (4:1)—**although Jesus himself did not baptize but his disciples** [did] (4:2)—**he gave up on Judea and departed and arrived** [*aperchomai*; one verb, two actions] **again in the Galilee** (4:3). The editorial qualification about Jesus's delegating the task of baptism seems designed to distinguish Jesus's ministry from that of the Baptist.

The narrative moves through a topography of potential conflict by having him leave Judea, then stating: **But it was necessary for him to pass through Samaria** (4:4). It was possible to take a longer route to avoid Samaria. The necessity seems to lie in leaving Judea in a hurry. He does not, however, seem to be driven by the goal of reaching his next destination quickly. He is not so much God striding upon the earth (Käsemann 1968, 73) as God strolling through the countryside.

Having provided the rationale for the sojourn in Samaria, John fixes the precise location of the story. Use of the historic present becomes prevalent in the telling of the tale, giving the impression that one is watching the action unfold in present time: **He comes to a city of Samaria called Sychar, near the piece of land that Jacob gave his son Joseph** (4:5). The narrator then zooms in on a precise spot, making it clear that the setting is significant. **In that place was a spring** [-fed well] **of Jacob.** With the well in view, the action plays against the backdrop of the general significance of a well as a source of refreshment. The way the narrator brings Jesus into view—**Jesus then, having grown weary from the journey, was sitting down at the spring** [-fed well]; **it was about the sixth hour** (4:6)—throws the accent on Jesus's humanity, his vulnerability to the body's needs for sleep, food, and water, and perhaps more important, the need for a body to occupy space. The choice of *pēgē* to denote *well* signifies that it is fed by living water, running water. Water signifies life, but a well signifies water rights, over which men compete (see Gen. 21:22–34;

The Samaritans

This people emerged in the historical record during the second century BC and share a religious heritage with the Jews. They followed the same laws from the Torah governing Sabbath observance, diet, purity, and circumcision, but they worshiped in different temples. During the Hasmonean expansion of Judean territory, Samaria was annexed, and in about 107 BC, John Hyrcanus ravaged the capital at Shechem and destroyed the temple on Mount Gerizim. The Jews barred the Samaritans from worshiping in Jerusalem (Josephus, *J.W.* 2.232–44; *Ant.* 18.29–30; 20.118–36). The Samaritans hoped for the reconstruction of their temple at the coming of a prophet messiah (the *Taheb*, the "Restorer"), whom many scholars identify as Moses or the fulfillment of Deut. 18:18. The Mishnah's references to the Samaritans probably reflect the views of Jesus's contemporaries: "Rabbi Eliezer used to say, 'He that eats of the bread of Samaritans is as one who eats the flesh of swine'" (*m. Šeb.* 8.10); "the daughters of Cutheans [Samaritans] are menstruants from their cradle" (*m. Nid.* 4.1).

26:17–22). This well is named for Jacob, claimed as ancestor by both Jews and Samaritans, but the Jews denied their kinship with Samaritans (Josephus, *Ant.* 9.288–91). The scenario of a stranger at a well requires an act of hospitality, something denied if the stranger is an enemy. The Jew must recognize the kinship claimed by the Samaritans.

The introduction of another player adds complexity to the narrative: **A woman of Samaria comes to draw water.** In the betrothal type-scene, the woman passes the test of hospitality by offering water and is then recognized as the appropriate wife for the patriarch. John phrases Jesus's words without conjunctions and particles, giving the impression that Jesus's request, **"Give me [some] to drink"** (4:7), is immediate and abrupt. The narrator then provides an important analepsis (flashback) that provides the rationale for Jesus's asking the woman and not one of his disciples: **For his disciples had left and gone into the city in order to buy groceries** (4:8). This raises a more-significant social tension in antiquity: two strangers, one a man and the other a woman, are alone at a well. Jesus's request would also have been even more shocking to a Jewish narrative audience: Jesus invites impurity. Jesus, cast in the role of a suppliant, provides yet another twist.

John has included the elements typical to a suppliant act, as outlined by F. S. Naiden in his work *Ancient Supplication* (2006, 4):

1. The suppliant approaches an individual or place (in this case, the well).
2. The suppliant makes a gesture of supplication (Jesus sits; therefore, his head is below the woman's).

3. The suppliant requests a boon.
4. The benefactor responds.

The synoptic tradition often plays with this pattern by moving the gesture of supplication to the end, where it takes the form of thanks or worship. In his suppliant stories, John finds a variety of ways to play with the convention.

Rather than entering into the betrothal type-scene, the woman acts out the conflict narrative by implicitly denying his request. **"How is it that you, being a Jew, beg [*aiteis*] [something] to drink from me, a Samaritan woman?"** (4:9). Her question delivers an insult by marking the two boundaries of gender and ethnicity that Jesus has breached. Jesus is a Jew, but not a good one by the Jews' standards. Logic dictates that she refuse his supplication, given their peoples' mutual antipathy. Jesus then returns her insult first by denying her identification of him and then with a boast: **"If you knew the gift of God and who it is who says to you, 'Give me [something] to drink,' you would have begged him, and he would have given you living water"** (4:10). She has water: he has living water. Jesus engages in double entendre. The well water was considered to be living water because it drew from an underground spring. The living water in the area of Gerizim sprang from the rich aquifer that lay below Samaria. As such it fulfilled the definition of living water required for Jewish (and probably Samaritan) purification rites and temple worship (Lev. 15:13). Living water is also a metaphor in Jewish tradition, signifying God's life-giving power (e.g., Jer. 17:13) or wisdom (e.g., *1 En.* 48.1; 49.1). Rather than allowing Jesus's riposte to put her on the defensive, she makes a quick countermove to gain the upper hand by pointing to Jesus's lack of means by which to act: **"Lord, you do not have a bucket for drawing water, and the well [*phrear*] is deep. From how then do you [plan to] hold the living water?"** (4:11). By taking living water at its literal meaning, the woman engages in the play on words rather than misunderstanding Jesus. Before he can respond to this question, she makes a direct attack on his person by asking a question in a form that anticipates a negative response: **"Surely you are not greater than our father Jacob, who gave us this well, and he drank from it and his sons and his sheep and goats"** (4:12). At the same time as she calls Jesus's status into question, she makes a counterclaim to Jewish aspersions against Samaritans by claiming Jacob as "our father." Her use of polysyndeton (a series of words linked by conjunctions) is comparable to the expression "here and there and everywhere." In John's Gospel, this is the first of a series of such challenges that Jesus will face, each of which raises the bar higher since Jesus must demonstrate his superiority to Moses (6:30–31) and Abraham (8:53) and his equality with God (9:29; 10:33).

Rather than countering her attack, Jesus makes a boast about the water that he offers: **"All who drink from this water will be thirsty again (4:13), but whoever drinks from the water that I will give to them, will definitely not [*ou*** *mē*] be thirsty for the age [*aiōna*]." The word *aiōna* can signify a lifetime or an epoch, so the next line makes the duration of satisfaction clearer: "**Instead, the water that I will give one will become in them a well of water leaping into eternal life [*zōēn aiōnion*]**" (4:14). The animated action of the water fits into the characterization of the water as living.

The woman challenges the truthfulness of Jesus's claim by requesting that he fulfill it: "**Lord, give me this water, in order that I might neither thirst nor pass through here to draw water**" (4:15). The lack of a particle or conjunction signals the rapidity with which a role reversal takes place. The woman now plays the role of suppliant. Jesus's next move is calculated to demonstrate his power; he presents her with a task that he knows she cannot fulfill: "**Go away, call your husband [*andra*] and come here!**" (4:16). Again the Greek grammar and syntax emphasizes the rapid pace of the dialogue. The command makes sense within the cultural context, in which it would be inappropriate for Jesus to make a gift directly to a woman, but it functions as a test that the woman passes by answering Jesus's question truthfully: "**I do not have a husband [*andra*].**" Jesus says to her, "**You speak rightly that you have no husband** (4:17). **For you had five husbands, and now the one you have is not your husband [*anēr*]; this you have spoken truthfully**" (4:18). The relationship of a man (*anēr*) to a woman is determined by pronouns and context, so stress must be laid on the pronoun "your." That the man with whom she lives is not her husband does not necessarily mean that he is someone else's husband or that they have physical relations. She may be living with a close kin. The humiliating fact of having been married five times and five times widowed or rejected and not to be married at present would be sufficient cause to conceal her status. Jesus's word of praise for a painful admission indicates that he has moved from playful banter to sincere speech.

With the woman's response, "**Lord, I observe that you are a prophet**" (4:19), perhaps a reference to the *Taheb*, the subject of the dialogue moves from the water that either the woman can draw or Jesus can give and shifts to Jesus's identity, and the action shifts from supplication to recognition. She implicitly adopts the metaphoric meaning of living water by turning to the status of the temple. Among the traditions that inform Jesus's promise of living water stands Ezekiel's and Zechariah's identification of the temple as a source of living water (Ezek. 47:1–12; Zech. 14:16–19). "**Our fathers worshiped on this mountain** [Mount Gerizim] **and you** [pl.; the Jews] **say that in Jerusalem is the place where it is necessary to worship**" (4:20). Craig Keener (2003, 612) suggests that Jesus and the woman might have been able to see the ruins of the Samaritan temple from where they stood.

The woman expects Jesus to speak as a Jew. Jesus's language—"**Believe me, woman, that the hour is coming when neither on this mountain nor in Jerusalem you will worship** [pl.] **the Father**" (4:21)—begins to break down the distinctions based on where their different forebears worshiped by speaking to her as a representative of both Jews and Samaritans who will worship "the Father." Jesus avoids possessive pronouns at this point but adds a qualification with marked pronouns that seems to assert Jewish precedence: **"You** [*hymeis*] **worship what you do not know; we** [*hēmeis*] **worship what we know, because salvation is from the Jews"** (4:22). Given that the Gospel of John calls into serious question how well the Jews know God, this seems to be in tension with much of the Gospel. The comment may refer to Jewish Scriptures. The Gospel of John draws heavily on the Prophets for proof of Jesus's identity, texts that the Samaritans would not have held to be canonical. Jesus's next assertion suggests that both Jewish and Samaritan worship have been inadequate: **"But the hour is coming and is now, when the real worshipers will worship the Father in spirit and truth. For indeed the Father seeks after those who worship him"** (4:23). Although "the hour" is an allusion to Jesus's execution, Jesus provides no hint of an ordeal. The representation of God as a seeker provides a theological complement to the radical concept of atopic worship: humans do not have to travel to a particular place to worship because God meets them wherever they worship in spirit. Jesus continues to develop this theology by pointing out that **"God** [is] **spirit,"** that is, God is not a physical being and so has no need for a physical building or temple worship, **"and it is necessary for those worshiping him** [as spirit] **to worship in spirit and truth"** (4:24). "Spirit and truth" seem like psychological terms describing inner dispositions, but it may be that the phrase refers to the worship practices of the early church and Jesus as the object of worship. Paul describes speaking in tongues and their interpretation, prayer, and blessings as acts facilitated by the Spirit (1 Cor. 12:7–11; 14:14–16), along with the singing of "spiritual songs" (Eph. 5:19–20; Col. 3:16). Truth, later in the Gospel, refers to Jesus (14:16, 26; 15:26).

To make sense of what Jesus is saying, the woman makes logical recourse to traditional expectations: **"I know that the Messiah is coming, the one called Christ** [see 1:41]; **when that one shall come, he will proclaim to us everything"** (4:25). Samaritan messianic expectations were in an excited state shortly after the time of Jesus's ministry. In AD 36, a man who seems to have been followed as the *Taheb* led a group of Samaritans up Mount Gerizim, where they were met by a detachment of Roman soldiers sent by Pilate to violently put down the movement (Josephus, *Ant.* 18.85–97). If Josephus's story is any indication, the "everything" that the Samaritans hope to learn concerns the location of the sacred vessels needed to restore temple worship on Gerizim. **Jesus** then makes a rare explicit admission to a messianic identity and **says to her, "I am the one speaking to you"** (4:26). Jesus's words bear some resemblance to the wording of Isa. 52:6 LXX, a passage about the restoration of knowledge of God's name that compares the redemption of Jerusalem and Zion to the deliverance from Egypt.

The return of the disciples interrupts the dialogue. John registers their amazement at the impropriety of the conversation by recording what is unsaid:

No one, of course, said, "What do you seek [*zēteis*; what are you about]?" or "Why are you talking to her?" (4:27). What they have witnessed is unspeakably shameful. To draw attention to Jesus's inappropriate act would bring even more shame to their master. The woman's reaction to the disciples' presence also may be an index of her response to being caught in the act: **Then the woman let go of her water jug and departed to the city.** It is also possible to read into the action symbolic import about not needing a jug because of the gift of living water, but this seems excessive. It might be a gesture of hospitality. Though at the beginning of the dialogue, she hesitates to give Jesus water, now she leaves the means by which the disciples can help themselves. The narrator then follows her to the city, where she **says to the people** (4:28), **"Here!** [*deute* is an adverb but functions as an imperative] **See a man who said to me everything whatsoever** [that] **I did."** This exaggerated statement is anticipated by her claim that the messiah will explain everything and therefore prepares for her speculation: **"Could he not be** [*mēti houtos estin*] **the Christ?"** (4:29). Her choice of words expresses her desire that Jesus be the messiah. The uncertainty of the expression fits into a Johannine pattern in which Jesus's demonstrations of his powers lead to dialogues in which people discuss his identity. The woman's question about Jesus's identity opens up dialogic space in which the townspeople will come to their own conclusions.

The next two verses demonstrate the sophistication of Johannine narrative as he interlaces the interaction of Jesus with the disciples and the woman with the townspeople (see "Simultaneous Action in Ancient Narrative" sidebar at John 18:1–19:42). **They** [the townspeople] **came out of the city and went to him** (4:30). **In the meantime the disciples had been questioning him, saying, "Rabbi, eat up!"** (4:31). John uses their direct speech to point to the food that they have procured. Jesus continues to speak in metaphor: **"I have food to eat that you do not know"** (4:32), leaving the disciples puzzled: **"Surely no one brought him** [something] **to eat?"** (4:33). The introduction of a metaphor into a context in which Jesus's words can easily be taken for their literal sense seems like a verbal trap designed to frustrate the disciples; however, it should be placed within a cultural context in which wordplay is appreciated more than it is in many modern cultures and in the context of a narrative constructed of dialogue. The disciples' logical failure to grasp Jesus's metaphor opens up discursive space in which Jesus explains himself: **"Food for me is to do the will of the one who sent me and to complete his work"** (4:34). Jesus then extends the metaphor by moving into a figurative landscape with which the disciples are more familiar, citing what seems to be a familiar proverb (as opposed to a reference to the actual season): **"Do you not say that there are still four months and the harvest comes?"** The point seems to be that labor is rewarded in the future rather than immediately. Conventional wisdom is replaced by the realities of the eschaton to which Jesus directs their mind's eye: **"Look, I say to you, lift up your eyes and gaze at the estates** [*chōras*] **because they are white** for the harvest" (4:35). The use of harvest to refer to eschatological judgment is found in Jewish Scripture and literature (Jer. 51:33; Joel 3:13; 4 *Ezra* [2 Esd.] 4.29–39; 2 *Bar.* 70.1–2) as well as in the Q account of the Baptist's preaching (Matt. 3:12; Luke 3:17). In John, as well as in the synoptic tradition (see Matt. 9:37–38; 13:39; Mark 4:29; Luke 10:2), Jesus uses the metaphor for mission and perhaps draws from the tradition of harvest as a metaphor for God's abundant future blessing (Amos 9:13–15) and the early church's treatment of Jesus and his followers as the "firstfruits" (Rom. 8:23; 1 Cor. 15:20). **"Already (4:35) the one who harvests receives a reward, and he gathers together fruit [as in profit] for eternal life, so that the one who sows might rejoice together with the one who harvests"** (4:36). Herod awarded large land grants in the area west of Gerizim to six thousand gentile colonists (Josephus, *J.W.* 1.403; *Ant.* 15.296). This metaphor may not simply signify realized eschatology but also realized economic justice or a reversal of the economic order. Jesus cites yet another proverb: **"For in this [regard] the saying is true that one person is the sower and another the one who harvests"** (4:37): others often benefit from one's hard labor. But now Jesus tells his disciples, who belong to the social class who would see themselves as the victims of this truism, **"I sent you to harvest that [for which] you have not labored. Others have labored, and you have entered into their labor"** (4:38).

John then returns to the Samaritan story line as a dramatization of Jesus's metaphor and his earlier boast that the woman will beg for living water. **Many of the Samaritans from that city believed in him on account of the word of the woman who testified that "He said to me all that I did"** (4:39). Given what follows, "belief in him" does not necessarily signify a particular conviction about Jesus's identity or his divine status so much as an openness to receive him and accept whatever identity he reveals. **Then when the Samaritans came to him, they begged him to remain with them, and therefore he remained there two days** (4:40). In a major role reversal, the Samaritans become friends, and they paradoxically become the suppliants who beg Jesus to accept their hospitality.

Rather than narrating how Jesus passes his time or what he says, John obliquely alludes to Jesus's preaching, leaving it to his readers' imagination or familiarity with Jesus's teachings to fill in the blank. John is more concerned with the conclusions that the Samaritans draw from what Jesus said: **And many more believed through his word** (4:41), **and they said to the woman that "We no longer believe on the basis of your speech, for we ourselves have heard and we know that this is truly the savior of the world"** (4:42). The episode then ends with words that signify an act of recognition. They are represented as moving from an understanding of who Jesus is that seems to be defined by Samaritan interests, onward to using a title that is not rooted in Jewish or Samaritan eschatological traditions and has universal implications. They now adopt royal messianic expectations, but rather than embracing a title from the Jewish or Davidic tradition, they choose a title associated with Roman imperial power.

The Royal Official's Son (4:43–54)

The reference to Jesus's imperial status at the end of the Samaritan episode prepares for the introduction of a character who labors in a royal household. Because John does not represent Jesus's preaching ministry, but instead the debates about his identity generated by his healings (particularly his Sabbath healings), it is easy to overlook the social issues that might inform the Gospel. The distance that the royal official travels physically and the social boundaries he must cross to seek healing for his child—both point to his desperation. Death and disease are the great levelers.

This is the second of three signs that follows a pattern in which someone (Jesus's mother, 2:3; the official, 4:47; Lazarus's sisters, 11:3) makes a request of Jesus, Jesus makes an oblique reference to his crucifixion, the person persists, and then Jesus performs the sign. The remaining signs are initiated by Jesus, and in several cases resistance comes from those who benefit from the sign.

The narrator picks up the action with Jesus's travel itinerary—**After the two days he departed from that place to the Galilee** (4:43)—and then provides the reason for moving on that seems to refer to Judea rather than Samaria or the Galilee: **For Jesus himself had testified that a prophet has no honor in** [his] **own fatherland** (*patridi*; 4:44; see Matt. 13:57; Mark 6:1; Luke 4:24). Jesus may be quoting a well-known proverb (see Epictetus, *Diatr.* 3.16.11; Dio Chrysostom, *Cont.* 6; Philostratus, *Ep.* 44) or simply be drawing an obvious conclusion from the stories of the prophets, particularly Jeremiah. The choice of the term *patridi* either requires knowledge of Jesus's Davidic heritage or reflects the reference in 1:11 to "his own people," who "did not accept him." If the latter is the case, the story of the Samaritans becomes a narrative illustration of John 1:12: "To all who received him, who believed in his name, he gave power to become children of God."

In contrast to the Judeans, **the Galileans did welcome him, all having seen how much he did in Jerusalem at the festival, for they also came to the festival** (4:45). More events than the incident in the temple, as well as satisfaction in seeing him prevail over the Judean authorities, seem to lie behind their positive reception of Jesus. In the language of the Russian formalists, the way the story is narrated, the *sjuzet*, reshapes an underlying sequence of events, *fabula*, that is represented but not necessarily narrated in its entirety.

John treats the Galilee as a place more hospitable to Jesus, and so it is important to understand the historical north-south tension that seems to inform the Gospel. Josephus treats Judeans and Galileans as distinct ethnic identities with respect to habits. In the Palestinian Talmud, a saying attributed to Rabbi Yochanan ben Zakkai, one of the reputed architects of the Judaism that emerges after the destruction of the temple, reflects Judean contempt:

"Galilee, Galilee, because you hate the torah, your end shall be destruction" (*y. Šabb.* 16.8, trans. Freyne 2004, 10). As much as Judeans may have looked down on Galileans as inferior in their piety, the Galileans may have resented the Judeans for treating the Galilee as its hinterland and may have seen their region as a blessed land (see Josephus, *J.W.* 3.41–43) and Judea as a wasteland. The Galilee was an independent region until the Hasmonean program of territorial expansion (ca. 104 BC), at which point a pattern began that lasted throughout the Herodian era: large estates were absorbing small independent farms (see Horsley 1995, 34–61). Seán Freyne (2004, 44), in his study of the ecology of the Galilee, notes that the abundance of the land had fallen into the hands of a few in defiance of the shared blessing envisioned in Deuteronomy and Leviticus. Moreover, under the strain to pay taxes and tributes, the land was intensively cultivated. Freyne situates many of the synoptic parables and sayings about sowing and reaping in this socioeconomic context. John may also have this reality in view when Jesus speaks of eschatological abundance. When Jesus says that some harvest what others sow (4:37), he describes a reality that the Galileans would resent, but in his realized eschatology, this inequity is addressed.

Jesus's career takes place at the beginning of a period of Romanization of the province by Herod Antipas, who establishes major urban centers at Sepphoris and Tiberius, draining off even more of the resources of the countryside. Josephus (*Life* 71–73, 119) provides several stories that illustrate how the agents of imperial power, such as he, profited from access to the imperial storehouses filled by Galilean peasants. Josephus (*Ant.* 14.451) describes how in 38 BC the Galileans rebelled against the nobility and drowned Herod's supporters in the Gennesaret. The Galilee continued to nurture insurgents against imperial power until the First and Second Jewish Revolts (AD 66–70 and 132–135). The royal official ought to be treated not as a neutral character but rather as a representative of "Herodian opulence" (Freyne 2004, 16), who from a Galilean perspective ought to suffer at the eschaton.

Once more the travel narrative arrives at a precise destination: **Then he came again to Cana of Galilee,** and through an analeptic epithet—**where he made water wine**—the narrator prepares the reader to anticipate a similar sign. He immediately adds a twist: **and there was a certain royal official,** someone who ought to take issue with the Samaritans' recognition of Jesus as "savior of the world," and then yet another twist—**whose son fell ill in Capernaum** (4:46). Whether the official is a Jew or a gentile or a Herodian or Roman employee is not specified. All that seems to be significant is that he is a member of the elite, a factor that might have reduced the anticipation of pleasure in seeing his son's health restored for John's intended audience. The story subverts any *Schadenfreude* that John's audience might feel.

The story then proceeds along the framework of supplication. In the first step in which the suppliant approaches an individual or place, the official comes to Jesus in a series of actions that denote a movement down the social ladder. (1) **This [man] heard that Jesus has come from Judea to the Galilee.** As an official, he hears reports, but instead of summoning Jesus in accord with his superior status, (2) **he went out to him.** The royal official then makes a gesture of supplication; (3) **he begged him,** an action appropriate to someone subordinate to Jesus, **in order that he would come down and cure his son** [*ton huion*]**, for he was about to die** (4:47). The request makes the basis for the man's startling behavior clear: he is desperate, and he believes Jesus to be a wonder-worker and healer. At this point, the narrator adds suspense to the story by delaying confirmation that the request will be fulfilled. Jesus makes a general comment about the ultimate *telos* of all signs, **"Unless you see** [pl.] **signs and portents** [*sēmeia kai terata*]**, you will not believe** [pl.]**"** (4:48). When set beside Jesus's remark to Thomas about those who have not seen and yet believe (20:29), Jesus's statement is often taken as a critique of a sign-based faith. Willis Hedley Salier (2004, 57) challenges this conclusion by arguing that the conditional clause followed by an emphatic negative signifies a statement of fact (cf. John 20:25). Within the narrative context, Jesus's words suggest that Jesus performs signs not as a healer but to make his identity as the Son of God evident. The phrase *sēmeia kai terata* also appears in Exod. 7:3 and Deut. 4:34–35 LXX, where it signifies proof of God's sovereignty. The official acknowledges that he has been lowered to the position of a suppliant by calling Jesus **"Lord/Sir** [*kyrios*]**"** and makes his appeal to **"come down before my little child** [*to paidion mou*] **dies"** (4:49), a plaintive request to travel the fifteen to twenty miles from Cana to Capernaum rather than a command. The use of the diminutive underscores his pitiful state. Jesus's first words, **"Get along,"** continue to play with the audience's expectation that the request should be denied, but they are followed quickly by a performative utterance that enacts the healing: **"your son lives."** As is normative to the Gospel, the man obeys Jesus's command: **The man** [immediately] **trusted the word that Jesus said to him and went along** (4:50).

The travel narrative now moves in the opposite geographic and social direction: **But by the time the man was going down, his slaves met him, saying that his child lives** (4:51). Both his status as one to whom others report and his child's life are restored. John then focuses on the substantiation that the child's improvement is no coincidence. **Then he learned the hour from them in which he had improvement** (4:52)**, as soon as they said to him that yesterday at** [the] **seventh hour the fever let go** [of] **him.** The language used here reflects ancient understandings of a fever not as a symptom but as a force that is either the disease itself or that evacuates the excess of blood, phlegm, or bile that is the disease. **Then the father realized that** [it was] **that hour in which Jesus said to him, "Your son lives" and he, and his entire household, believed him** (4:53). What he believed is not made explicit. It may be as simple as the fact that Jesus was the agent of his son's restored health. The inclusion of the entire household here seems to establish parity with the Samaritan story. Rejection or acceptance is a social reality, but at this point it is limited to a domestic circle that has had a private glimpse of a sign. Within the Mediterranean world, religious activity was divided between public worship of civic gods in temples and private worship in homes. The full implications of the exclusive claims that Jesus will make about salvation are slowly working themselves out.

John then ends with a line that refers back to 4:46: **Again, Jesus did this second sign** of the two performed at Cana **when he came from Judea to the Galilee** (4:54). The enumeration does not limit the total number of signs that Jesus has performed to two; the narrator narrates only those witnessed by a select few and those that do not provoke controversy. This will change when Jesus travels back to Jerusalem, where he becomes the instigator of his signs and chooses the occasions for performing them.

Theological Issues

Many of the issues that arise from these chapters revolve around the characters introduced in the narrative: their function, their faith, and their fate. In some cases, the debates prompted by John's depiction of his characters contain forceful arguments on either side. This had led recent scholarship to seek shades of gray and positions that admit truth on either side.

The Role of Signs

John uses the word *sēmeia* (sign) to refer to Jesus's miracles rather than the word *dynameis* (mighty works) used in the synoptic tradition. The narration of a limited number of signs, how characters respond to them, and what Jesus says about them raise the following three issues: (1) Is there symbolic significance to the number of signs and, if so, what counts as a sign? (2) How does a sign function differently from a miracle? (3) What role do signs play in faith?

Signs seem to provide structure to John's narrative by serving as the actions around which dialogues are formed. In the Synoptic Gospels, teaching and mighty acts are seldom as tightly interwoven as in John's narratives. Many exegetes count seven signs, a number that signifies completion. Those who subscribe to the theory that John used the so-called *sēmeia* source in composing the chaps. 1–12 generally offer the following list:

1. Water to wine (2:1–11)
2. Healing official's son (4:46–54)
3. Healing infirm man (5:1–18)
4. Feeding of the thousands (6:1–15)
5. Walking on water (6:16–21)
6. Healing blind man (9:1–41)
7. Raising Lazarus (11:1–44)

Many substitute the crucifixion for walking on water in order to construct a chiasmus that highlights the comparable elements at the wedding at Cana and the crucifixion and place the feeding at the center, to support a sacramental reading of the Gospel (e.g., Grassi 1986). Though it does seem that John selects a reduced number of signs with care as though he were providing a representative and symbolic number, he refers to many more signs that take place outside the narrative (2:23; 6:2), and a number of other events function as signs: the temple demonstration (2:14–15), the revelation of the Samaritan woman's past (4:18), the miraculous landing of the boat (6:21), and the catch of many fish (21:6), as well as the resurrection itself (see 2:18–20). The limited number recounted may be the result of his narrative strategy rather than determined by symbolism. (For a discussion of the absence of exorcism in John, see "The Ruler of This World" in the theological issues section of 12:12–50.)

The word *sēmeia* suggests a broader category of phenomena than miracle. In the recognition scenes of Greco-Roman literature, scars and possessions function as signs pointing to the identity of the protagonist. The word also suggests a purpose beyond the act itself. In ancient studies of rhetoric, signs serve as a form of argument, a proof. Aristotle provides the following example: the fact that a woman gives milk is a sign that she has recently given birth (*Rhet.* 1.2.18 [1357b.16]). This use of the word *sign* requires that modern readers become conscious of modern usage. We tend to use the word in three ways: as icons (signs that bear resemblance to what they signify), as symbols (signs that can be arbitrary or conventional and denote an association of ideas), and as indices (signs that refer to the object they denote because they are causally related). The familiar road signs in figure 8 illustrate these distinctions. The iconic walking figure looks like the permitted action; the symbolic nuclear zone sign relies on convention to be understood; the leaping deer warns drivers to exercise caution by indicating the potential hazard of a deer on the road. Jesus uses a great deal of symbolic language, but his signs function as indices pointing to his identity and glory.

Jesus's signs do not function as conclusively as Aristotle's example of mother's milk. Many people witness the signs and do not believe. John presents

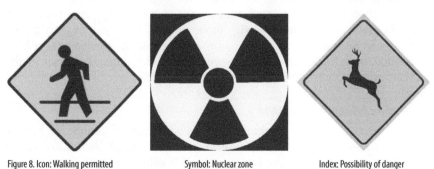

Figure 8. Icon: Walking permitted   Symbol: Nuclear zone   Index: Possibility of danger

two pictures. One shows different people working out the sense of what they have seen or heard in terms of traditions that they know; the other reveals the consequences of those deliberations. Some characters come to believe in Jesus. John uses the verb *pisteuō* with great frequency, approximately one hundred times, but the noun form *pistis* never appears. Faith is not an object that one possesses. David J. Hawkin (1996, 25) proposes working with B. F. Meyer's notion of prophetic understanding: faith is seeing signs or events through the lens of symbolic imagery and thus recognizing divine intervention.

In the Synoptic Gospels, the word *sign* has negative connotations. Whenever a group asks for a sign, Jesus reprimands them and denies their request (Matt. 16:1–4; Mark 8:11–13; Luke 11:16–17). The healing miracles are done in response to faith. In John, the order is reversed. Jesus performs a sign, and believing in Jesus follows.

Jesus's response to the royal official, "Unless you see signs and portents, you will not believe," triggers a scholarly debate about whether John treats faith based on signs as incomplete, as merely a step toward belief based on what Jesus says. Rudolf Bultmann (1955, 45) contends that a signs-based faith is altogether dispensable, as though one can come to faith based on Jesus's word, without any demonstration of his divine power. Jesus's words to Thomas, "Because you have seen me, do you believe? Blessed are those not seeing and yet believing" (20:29), seem to support Bultmann's dichotomy. Ernst Käsemann (1968, 21–23, 52–53) rejects Bultmann's conclusion and argues that one must place John's concept of faith within a first-century context in which manifestation of God was inconceivable without being accompanied by the miraculous and marvelous. In his study of the rhetorical function of signs, Willis Hedley Salier finds that in ancient Jewish Greek literature, signs perform a positive function on which John draws. They point to the authority of God's messengers and demand that witnesses respond with obedience and trust. Signs also become the events that God's people remember and celebrate (Salier 2004, 18–25, 27–34). The Gospel writer himself presents a positive role for signs when he claims that the signs he has presented "have been written in order that you believe that Jesus is the Christ, the Son of God, and in order that believing you may have life in his name" (20:31). The distinction between hearing and seeing is a false dichotomy. In the Gospel, they belong to a single process: those who see tell others, who learn of the sign by hearing. The Gospel, by providing a narrative to be read aloud, is an audible representation of what others have witnessed, both Jesus's actions and words. The reader and audience see events in their mind's eye (see Larsen 2008, 189–90).

Reading Johannine Characters

In John, the emphasis on the individuals who have encounters with Jesus gives rise to discussion about their possible symbolic import. Some have argued that the characters represent kinds of faith (Collins 1976, 26–46, 118–32);

others, that they fit into a strategy of polemic against constituencies or groups with which the Johannine community related or contended (Brown 1979, 71–88). Since the publication of R. Alan Culpepper's *Anatomy of the Fourth Gospel* (1983), increased attention has been given to the nuances, details, and literary strategies giving the impression that Johannine characters are real people with private thoughts and individuality. Under the influence of Paul Ricoeur, reading for character has become an ethical issue. Ricoeur (1992) calls readers to task for treating the other as though one can fathom them, a tendency that lies at the roots of judgment, prejudice, hatred, and ultimately violence.

Johannine characterization seems to reflect conventions that can be traced to principles found in Aristotle's *Poetics* and *Rhetoric*. Aristotle subordinates characterization to action. Character confers coherence on an action (*Poet.* 1450b.7–9). Modern literature often works in the opposite direction as psychological dramas have come to the fore. Aristotle explores the nature of an act or an emotion or cognitive state with a view to whether it is noble or ignoble, worthy of imitation or not. In Aristotle's analysis, the choices that a person makes do not reveal their character, they shape them, whether "they will live well or the reverse" (*Poet.* 1450a.15–20). This distinction has significance for how one reads the Gospel. Those who look at characterization as an index of a person's character try to reconstruct thoughts and motive. Those who look at characterization as part of the coherence of action watch as choices lead to tragic consequences, not only for Jesus, but also for those who make the choices.

John's use of character types comparable to those found in Theophrastus should not be confused with the idea that his characters function as types rather than as individuals. Shakespeare uses classical types in his plays so that one recognizes that Jacques in *As You Like It* is a killjoy, but he is nonetheless lifelike. It is easy to forget that he is just words on a page and to feel a sense of grief that he cannot overcome his melancholy, perhaps because readers recognize that they know people of that type. John takes care to use his characters' words and deeds as indexes to the sorts of consciousness or intentionality and biographies that make it possible for readers to imagine them as real people.

Historical and socioanthropological research adds another dimension to the discussion of character by reminding readers that identity in antiquity came from being a member of a group. Modern identity focuses much more on individual inclinations and personality; in antiquity, however, family, ethnicity, citizenship, social status, and occupation defined identity. Whatever honor or standing a person had belonged to the group and not the individual unless the individual was some sort of hero whose victories brought honor to the group that associated with him. John's characters belong to social and ethnic groups, and their actions determine whether their membership within these groups remains stable or whether they become members of a new community to which Jesus brings honor through his noble death. Believing in Jesus had social implications and was not simply a matter of individual salvation.

Nicodemus and the Samaritan woman stand at the center of much of the discussion of Johannine characterization and its purpose; many see them as foils within John's narrative, paired for the purpose of contrast. Nicodemus, a member of the Jerusalem elite, approaches Jesus in the night; the Samaritan woman, a member of a rejected group, approaches Jesus when the sun stands at its apex (see, e.g., Trumbower 1992, 73, 79; or Koester 1989, 333–36). Winsome Munro captures the two different ways of reading these characters in her article "The Pharisee and the Samaritan in John: Polar or Parallel?" (1995). She rejects reading Nicodemus as an example of a person who has a weak character or understanding and the Samaritan as a fallen woman whose presence at the well is a sign of her shame; instead, she reads their actions as movements across social borders toward relationship with Jesus.

Johannine Ecclesiology

In this unit, John presents several glimpses of what constitutes the people of God, but the terms he uses are too ambiguous for us to be certain that he is referring to the church as we know it. Do Jesus's words to Nicodemus that "unless one be born from water and . . . spirit, one is not about to enter into the kingdom of God" (3:5) signify baptism (cf. 1:33)? Is the kingdom of God the church? These questions lead to a soteriological question: does one need to be baptized to be saved? The Gospel of John refers to Jesus's baptizing ministry (3:26) but does not mention baptism of the Samaritans or the household of the royal official. Their inclusion among the children of God must be inferred from the prologue (1:12–13).

Two disagreements have taken shape with regard to such questions. One is the long-standing debate between those who, within John, find confirmation of a sacramental theology, and those who argue that salvation comes through faith alone. Given the epideictic nature of the Gospel's rhetoric, it is not surprising that it produces a greater sense of confidence in doctrines and practices that develop from two different reading trajectories. The other is a more-recent debate about whether the language of the Gospel is an antilanguage, produced by a sectarian community, which is designed to make insiders feel that they are "in the know" (see Malina and Rohrbaugh 1998, 65–107)—or metaphoric language, intended to be unfamiliar so that the fresh metaphors provoke new insights or observations (see Kysar 2005, 183–98). With regard to this latter debate, this commentary consistently treats the language as metaphoric.

John 5:1–47

God Works on the Sabbath

Introductory Matters

This unit begins a lengthy section of the Gospel—framed by Jesus's healing the man at the pool of Bethzatha, and Jesus's restoring a man's sight at the pool of Siloam—that provides an account of the mounting opposition to Jesus. In the middle stands the miraculous feeding and the Bread of Life and Light of the World discourses. (For the many aspects of the framing episodes indicating that the two healings should be considered side by side, see table 2.) The key contrast in the two healings is the disposition manifest in the first man's willingness to name Jesus to the authorities, and the second man's willingness to be tossed from the assembly rather than denounce Jesus. John uses the rhetorical construction of illness and his representation of each character in order to turn what would be simply healing miracles in the Synoptic Gospels into short dramas in which recognition and reversal play a significant role. Kasper Bro Larsen (2008, 145–47) calls the story of the man at Bethzatha a recognition parody: the recipient of the healing ought to come to the realization of who Jesus is and acknowledge him, but in this story he fails to do so.

Rather than serving to place the benefactor in a good light, as miracles tend to do in ancient biographies, Jesus's signs now serve to set the stage for argument. If one looks at the rhetorical purpose of the healing in chapter 5 within the context of the broader unit, the story is the first element in the standard outline of a persuasive speech found in the ancient rhetorical handbooks (Cicero, *Inv.* 1.19.27–1.21.30; cf. Quintilian, *Inst.* 4.2.1–132). The healing functions as the *narratio*, the statement of the case on which to base the charges that Jesus breaks the Sabbath and makes himself equal to God.

Table 2. Parallels: The Healings of the Infirm Man and the Blind Man

	Chapter 5	Chapter 9
Physical setting	Jerusalem pool of Bethzatha	Jerusalem pool of Siloam
Temporal setting	Sabbath	Sabbath
Duration of affliction	thirty-eight years	since birth
Severity of affliction	immobile	blind
Jesus's statement on sin	"Do not sin any more, so that nothing worse happens to you" (5:14)	"Neither this man nor his parents sinned; he was born blind that God's works might be revealed in him" (9:3)
Initial interrogation	The man is unable to reveal Jesus's identity or location	The man is unable to reveal Jesus's location
Final disposition	informant	defender
Accusation	Breaks the Sabbath and makes self equal to God (5:18)	Breaks the Sabbath (9:16) and makes self a God (10:33)
Jesus's self-defense	"The Son can do nothing on his own, but only what he sees the Father doing; for whatever the Father does, the Son does likewise" (5:19)	"I have shown you many good works from the Father. For which of these are you going to stone me?" (10:32)
Jesus's counter-accusation	"You have not heard his voice at any time nor have you seen his form" (5:37)	"If you were blind, you would not have sin, but now you say that 'we see,' your sin remains" (9:41); "the sheep hear his voice" (10:3)

When one recognizes that John's structure resembles this convention, the logic and progression of Jesus's subsequent arguments become much clearer. The dramatic setting calls for omitting the second element of a standard speech, the *partitio*, a quick summary of the arguments. Jesus leaps immediately into his first argument. From 5:19–30, he proceeds through the *confirmatio*, a series of arguments refuting the charge. John 5:31–47 contains the *reprehensio*, in which Jesus anticipates his opponents' arguments and launches a counterattack. The *conclusio* awaits Jesus's summation in 12:44–50.

Narratio (5:1–18)
    Setting (5:1–4)
    Healing story (5:5–9a)
    Discovery of Sabbath violation (5:9b–14)
    Accusation against Jesus (5:15–18)

Confirmatio (5:19–30)
    First argument: A son imitates his father (5:19–20)
    Second argument: A son practices his father's trade (5:21–23)
    Third argument: A father delegates tasks to his son (5:24–29)
    Fourth argument: A son does what his father desires (5:30)
Reprehensio (5:31–47)
    Regarding the charge that he testifies to himself (5:31)
    John [the Baptist] testifies (5:32–35)
    Jesus's deeds testify (5:36)
    The Father testifies (5:37–38)
    Scripture testifies (5:39–40)
    Reproach (*obiurgatio*): Accusers fail to receive testimony (5:41–47)

Before beginning to trace the progression of the unit line by line, two other aspects of the rhetoric warrant preliminary attention: the roles played by figures of speech and boasting. The progression or logic of Jesus's speech is difficult for modern readers to follow because it conforms to many ancient conventions, both Jewish and Greco-Roman (if such a distinction makes sense with respect to the first century AD). Andrew Lincoln (2000, 73–81) draws attention to the forensic setting of the speech. Jesus is on trial and defends himself. But just as in Plato's *Apology*, where Socrates is on trial, his argument is designed not to persuade his narrative audience but rather to impress the Gospel's audience. Throughout, Jesus uses figures of speech—such as epistrophe (a series of clauses or lines ending with the same wording), alliteration, and anaphora (repetition of the same wording at the beginning of clauses or lines)—that serve as much to delight the audience of the Gospel and to present Jesus as an orator as to present his case. When trying to make sense of an argument or draw conclusions about subtleties in theology, it may be important to remember that word order and choice can be dictated by concern for style rather than logic.

Chapter 5 marks the narrative's turn from an emphasis on reception of Jesus to rejection. Now Jesus's claims about his identity are received as hubris, insolence, or a lack of restraint appropriate to one's position. Set within a Jewish forensic context, the question of who can serve as a witness and the need for two independent witnesses is central to the discussion; John also draws from Greco-Roman conventions in which sound argumentation included not just logic (*logos*) but also appeals to the emotions of one's audience (*pathos*) and the character (*ethos*) of the speaker, including the status of one's family (Aristotle, *Rhet.* 1.2.3 [1356a.1–4]; 2.11.12–2.17.17 [1389b–91b]). In the heated debates of Greco-Roman narratives, the appropriate response to an accusation of hubris is to boast about one's entitlement to the position into which one has placed oneself (Cicero, *De or.* 2.342; e.g., Homer, *Il.* 21.157–60).

Logos, Ethos, and Pathos in John

Logos entails deductive forms of argument, such as syllogisms, in which conclusions follow necessarily from the premises presented, or inductive arguments, such as analogies, in which conclusions are supported by facts or comparison. Jesus tends to favor deductive logic in John (see 8:34–47). Jesus's logic does not always meet the standards of philosophical reasoning, but it generates the impression that Jesus's arguments are reasonable and promotes certitude for the believer.

Ethos refers to appeals to character, either to the character of the speaker, to the defendant on trial, or to a witness. Aristotle focuses on the virtues of the individual based on station in life. High birth is not enough; one must also not depart from one's inherited nature (*Rhet.* 2.14.3 [1390b]). John's Jesus defends his own character by repeatedly emphasizing his conformity to God's will and ways (e.g., 5:19–23).

Pathos entails persuading an audience by appealing to its emotions and inviting it either to pity those who suffer or are on trial so that it will not think them totally without goodness and deserving of punishment (*Rhet.* 2.8.2 [1385b]), or to be angry so as to redress wrongs (*Rhet.* 2.1.4 [1378a]), or to fear so that it will choose a course of action to avoid or face that which it fears (*Rhet.* 2.5.1–15 [1382a–b]). John tends to focus on the assurance that the act of belief already taken is sufficient to prevent disaster, or he makes those who are fearful of the consequences of believing in Jesus appear pitiable.

Tracing the Narrative Flow

Narratio: *The Sabbath Healing Recounted (5:1–18)*

The narrator begins with a conventional transition often used in classical Greek literature—**After these things** [*meta tauta*]—and then provides a quick orientation to time and place: **there was a festival of the Jews, and**

John 5:1–47 in the Narrative Flow

In the beginning (1:1–2:12)

Jesus's itinerant ministry (2:13–12:11)

  Transforming sacred space (2:13–4:54)

▶God works on the Sabbath (5:1–47)

    Narratio: The Sabbath healing recounted (5:1–18)

    Confirmatio: The arguments refuting the charge (5:19–30)

    Reprehensio: Jesus refutes objections to his arguments (5:31–47)

Jesus went up to Jerusalem (5:1). The lack of specificity about which festival had scholars speculating during the heyday of historical criticism, but John may be purposeful in his vagueness. The critical element is that the healing

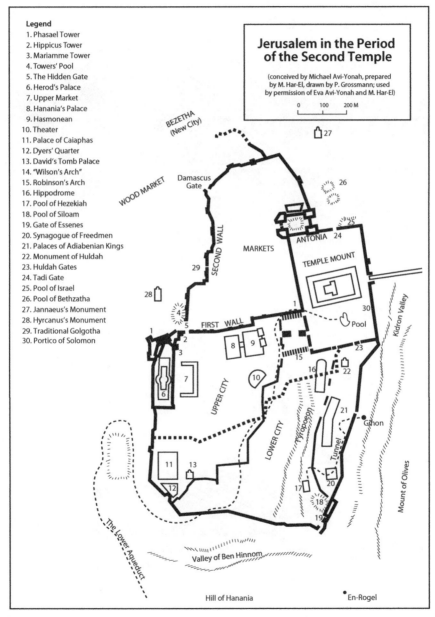

Figure 9. Map of Jerusalem in the Second Temple Period.

Legend
1. Phasael Tower
2. Hippicus Tower
3. Mariamme Tower
4. Towers' Pool
5. The Hidden Gate
6. Herod's Palace
7. Upper Market
8. Hanania's Palace
9. Hasmonean
10. Theater
11. Palace of Caiaphas
12. Dyers' Quarter
13. David's Tomb Palace
14. "Wilson's Arch"
15. Robinson's Arch
16. Hippodrome
17. Pool of Hezekiah
18. Pool of Siloam
19. Gate of Essenes
20. Synagogue of Freedmen
21. Palaces of Adiabenian Kings
22. Monument of Huldah
23. Huldah Gates
24. Tadi Gate
25. Pool of Israel
26. Pool of Bethzatha
27. Jannaeus's Monument
28. Hyrcanus's Monument
29. Traditional Golgotha
30. Portico of Solomon

Jerusalem in the Period of the Second Temple

(conceived by Michael Avi-Yonah, prepared by M. Har-El, drawn by P. Grossmann; used by permission of Eva Avi-Yonah and M. Har-El)

0   100   200 M

Figure 10. Archaeological excavations of the pools of Bethzatha (Bethesda).

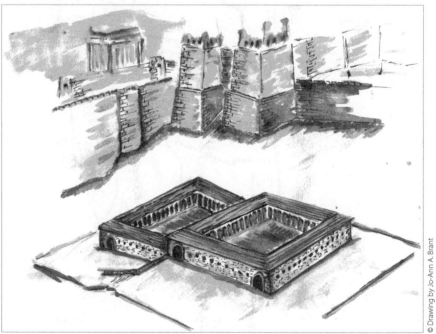

Figure 11. Reconstruction drawing of the pools of Bethzatha.

takes place on a Sabbath, but John delays revelation of this fact so that his audience experiences a reversal. From an event that should bring Jesus praise, the healing becomes controversial and potentially shameful.

John provides great specificity about the location of the action. **There is in Jerusalem by the sheep** [gate] **a bathing pool that is called in Hebrew Bethzatha, which has five porticoes** (5:2; see figs. 10 and 11). For the location of the pools, see figure 9: the map of Jerusalem. The sentence construction is awkward and requires the addition of a noun in one of two places. Rather than sketching out the festival preparations and activities as he does in chapter 2, John provides a description of those who would be excluded from the celebration (Thomas 1995, 96). **In these** [galleries] **a great number of infirm were lying—those who were blind** [*typhlōn*], **lame** [*chōlōn*], **wasting away** [*xērōn*]—**waiting for the movement of the water** (5:3). The next verse provides an explanation of why they wait: **For an angel of the Lord on occasion descended in the pool and disturbed the water. The one then first stepping in after the disturbing of the water became restored in whatever way he** [or she] **was constrained by disease** (5:4; see Ps. 77:16 [76:17 LXX]).

The narrator then focuses attention on the principals of the action. **There was a particular man there who had been infirm for thirty-eight years** (5:5). The duration of his infirmity may draw symbolic import from the story of the exodus, which according to Deut. 2:14 lasted thirty-eight years, but thirty-eight years also signifies a generation, and that is probably the point here (Thomas 1995, 7). The duration of his illness is sufficient cause to arouse pity (see Aristotle, *Rhet.* 2.8.8–11 [1386a]), and so **Jesus, seeing this man lying and knowing that he has already** [had his ailment] **a long time, says to him, "Do you wish to become restored?"** (5:6). After underscoring Jesus's omniscience, John leaves it to the reader to deduce from this verse and the subsequent dialogue that the affliction from which the man suffers impedes his ability to stand and walk. The man does not take Jesus's question as an indirect offer but instead rationalizes his inaction as though Jesus's words criticize him for his continued state of impairment: **"Lord, I do not have a man to put me in the pool whenever the waters do get disturbed. And when I am on the way, another steps down ahead of me"** (5:7). John provides no reason at this point to question whether the man has done something to deserve his suffering and thereby warrant our withholding pity (see Aristotle, *Rhet.* 2.8.2 [1385b.14]). The account explains why he would not expect to be healed at this time. The man's friendless state is yet another sufficient condition to pity him (Aristotle, *Rhet.* 2.8.10 [1386a.10]). The man's speech here and in 5:11 performs the act of blaming. Although he acknowledges Jesus with the polite address *Kyrie*, he does not employ the sort of deictic language found in earlier dialogues that would signify his orientation toward Jesus as one who might be important to his flourishing. For example, in response to Jesus's question, the man does not ask, for example, "Would you be willing to carry me to the water?"

Jesus provides an alternate and more-direct remedy to the problem that is not limited by assistance or speed: **"Get up [aron], pick up your mat and walk about"** (5:8). The verb *airō* and the language of healing, *hygiēs*, used in John only with reference to this man (5:6, 9, 11, 14, 15; 7:23), may render this healing a sort of resurrection. In ancient conception, a limb that was not usable was dead, and so its restoration would be a restoration of life itself (see Salier 2004, 100). The narrator reports first the healing, **And immediately the man became restored, and** then the man's compliance with Jesus's commands, **he picked up his mat and walked about.**

The emphasis on signs of the man's frustration or anger lays the ground for an emotional reversal, but rather than describing a response of joy or gratitude, the narrator immediately sounds the bell that signals danger: **And it was a Sabbath on that day** (5:9). The timing of the event now stands at the center of the reversal.

The Mishnah permits carrying a man on a bed (*m. Šabb.* 10.5) but names carrying an object from one domain to another as the last in its list of thirty-nine prohibited actions (*m. Šabb.* 7.2). Regardless of whether the irony that Jesus would be permitted to carry the man on the mat to the water would have been known in the late Second Temple period, it is clear from Scripture that carrying the bed constitutes a Sabbath violation (see Exod. 31:14–15; Num. 15:32–36; Jer. 17:21–22).

The action that follows reestablishes the climate of inquisition apparent in the opening dialogue with the Baptist. The Jews who see the man indict him: **"It is a Sabbath, and you are not permitted to pick up your mat"** (5:10). In contrast to the Baptist's denials and witness to Jesus, this man deflects the investigation: **"The one who restored me, that one said to me, 'Pick up your mat and walk about'"** (5:11). **So they interrogated him, "Who is the man who said to you, 'Pick up and walk about?'"** (5:12). **But the one who was healed did not know who he is, for Jesus slipped away [into] the crowd that was in the place** (5:13). Whereas the man's first act of blame was an index to his own frustration or suffering, this act of blame points to the anger of the Jews and suggests either his own shame or his fear of suffering their wrath for violating the Sabbath. The man's ignorance of Jesus's identity or whereabouts sharpens the glaring contrast between the recognition owed Jesus and what has been given. The question of whether the man's suffering is a just desert now comes into view when **Jesus finds him in the temple, and he said to him, "See, you are restored; stop sinning, lest something worse happen to you"** (5:14). Whether Jesus is referring to some sin that led to the man's paralysis or to what he has done subsequent to his restoration is not clear, but John has laid the ground for the reader to think of the man as a sinner. His following actions confirm this supposition as fact: **The man went away and announced to the Jews that it is Jesus who made him whole** (5:15). **And on account of this** [either the act of betrayal or the Sabbath healing], **the Jews were persecuting Jesus, because he did this on a Sabbath** (5:16).

In the synoptic tradition, Jesus's healings are controversial because they take place on the Sabbath, but John uses the dialogue that follows to shift quickly to a more-controversial charge related to Jesus's claim to a status equal to that of God. The action picks up in medias res, with Jesus responding to the allegation that he has violated the Sabbath: **"My Father until this moment is working, and I am working"** (5:17). In contrast to the synoptic Jesus's disclaimer that he keeps the Sabbath as it was intended to be kept (Mark 2:27; Matt. 12:1–13), John's Jesus implies that he is not required to keep the Sabbath because he is a creator and not part of the creation. John seems to be aware of a tradition found in the contemporary and later Jewish literature that recognized God's continued labor on the Sabbath. Philo (*Cher.* 86–90; *Leg.* 1.5–6) argues that God rested but continued to work because his labor does not cause him to be weary (see also *Let. Aris.* 210; *Jub.* 2.21, 30). The rabbis understood birth, death, and rainfall to be divine activity and evidence that God works on the Sabbath (see *b. Ta'an.* 2a; *Gen. Rab.* 11.10). While these discussions find apologetic grounds to excuse divine activity, they do not justify human labor on the Sabbath. Jesus's self-justification on these grounds is provocative. **On account of this, then, the Jews sought all the more to kill him, because he not only broke the Sabbath, but he also said God was his own father,** [thereby] **making himself equal with God** (5:18; see 10:33; 19:7). The narrator gets ahead of the action—there have been no references to death threats at this point—but in doing so underscores that Jesus knows where his speech is leading.

Confirmatio: *The Arguments Refuting the Charge (5:19–30)*

Jesus constructs a complicated argument to refute the allegation that he makes himself equal to God by arguing that by virtue of his relationship to God, whose work and will he does and whose glory he receives, he shares God's status (see Meeks 1990, 310–11).

First argument. First, Jesus places his work within a divine economy, using a figure that draws from ancient practices: **"Truly, truly, I say to you, the Son is not able to do anything himself unless he sees the Father doing it, for whatever that one does, this also the Son likewise does** (5:19). **For the Father loves** [*philei*] **the Son and shows all to him that he does, and he will show him works greater in order to amaze you"** (5:20). Note: the Synoptic Gospels do not describe God's love for his Son. This is a unique Johannine theme (see M. Thompson 2001, 98). In an ancient economy, one is entitled to do a job by virtue of heredity and apprenticeship. Imitation is the key pedagogical method of instruction. The appeal to pedigree and rearing to substantiate his fitness to be engaged in the task at hand is common to ancient agonistic discourse of boasting and insult (e.g., Achilles's speech in Homer, *Il.* 21.187–93; Paul's boasts about his education in Acts 22:3; Gal. 1:11–12).

Second argument. From a figure based on education through imitation, Jesus moves to a figure based on a son's practicing his father's craft, trade, or profession. **"For just as the Father wakes the dead and makes alive, likewise also the Son whom he wishes to make alive** [he wakes from the dead]" (5:21). Note the epistrophe, the repetition of the same word at the end of successive clauses. This reference to resurrection supports the notion that the restoration of the man's limbs to health would be understood as a partial resurrection. Jesus then moves to the figure of a father's delegating tasks to the son. The first clause contains a double negative that should be rendered as an emphatic negative. **"For** [indeed] **the Father judges no one, but he has given all judgment to the Son"** (5:22). As the agent, the son ought to be given the honor due to the father whom he represents. Jesus appropriates this cultural norm into his defense in lines heavy with alliteration and antithesis: **"in order that all honor the Son** [*pantes timōsi ton huion*] **to the degree that they honor the Father** [*timōsi ton patera*]. **The one who does not honor the Son** [*timōn ton huion*] **does not honor the Father** [*tima ton patera*], **the one who sent him** [*ton pempsanta auton*]"** (5:23). Jesus states directly what is implicit in the parable of the tenants of the vineyard in Luke 20:9–19.

Third argument. Jesus then defines the task that his father has assigned to him. The picture seems to be comparable to that found in Dan. 12:2, in which "those who sleep in the dust of the earth shall awake, some to everlasting life, and some to shame and everlasting contempt," or *1 En.* 61–62, in which God places the Son of Man on his throne of glory, from which he judges humankind. Unlike *1 Enoch*, Jesus does not paint a picture of a terrifying cosmic event in which death is a place of eternal punishment. Jesus depicts himself in the role of eschatological agent of resurrection: **"Truly, truly, I say to you that the one who hears my word and trusts the one who sent me has everlasting life and does not come to judgment, but has moved over from death into life"** (5:24).

At first glance, this verse might suggest that faith in Jesus has become the critical factor in salvation, but John's emphasis lies on Jesus's agency. John seems to draw on a tradition that the dead will be called to life by the sound of God's shofar, or trumpet, at which time they will be judged (see 1 Cor. 15:52; 1 Thess. 4:16; *Tg. Ps.-J.* to Exod. 20:18). Jesus's voice replaces the shofar. Lazarus provides an example of one who hears Jesus voice and is called back to life (John 11:43–44). Jesus adds two items to traditional Jewish eschatology: he is speaking not about those who are dead but about the living; the experience of being called from death to life is not limited to those in the grave. Moreover, those who are called by Jesus's voice are assured of eternal life.

Jesus then reiterates what he has said with reference to the actual dead: **"Truly, truly, I say to you that the hour is coming and is now when the dead will hear the voice of the Son of God, and those who have heard will live"** (5:25). The point seems to be that the eschatological event of resurrection and judgment has begun with Jesus's ministry, and those who follow him are part of the resurrected community. Jesus then reasserts that his ability to act as the agent of resurrection is a task assigned by God: **"For just as the Father has life in himself, so also he has given life to the Son to have in himself** (5:26). **And he has given to him authority to make judgment, because** [he is the] **Son of Man"** (5:27). With the suggestion that he is the Son of Man, Jesus now makes his identification with the divine agent in Dan. 7:13 clear.

In the next verse, Jesus briefly interrupts the flow of his speech with the rhetorical flourish of an apostrophe (a direct address) followed by a rhetorical question: **"You are not amazed at this, are you?"** Such questions add a tone of indignation (*iracundia*) to heighten the emotional effect of a speech (*Rhet. Her.* 4.15.22; see Quintilian, *Inst.* 4.1.63–70; 9.2.38–40). The direct address to his audience also serves to create the impression that Jesus is in dialogue with his narrative audience even though Jesus is the only one who speaks.

When he resumes, Jesus continues with the delineation of his work, using more-conventional language to reiterate what he has said in 5:26. **"For the hour is coming in which all who** [are] **in the grave will hear his voice** (5:28), **and they will come forth, those having done good things to resurrection of life, those practicing things that are contemptible** [*phaula*] **to resurrection of judgment"** (5:29). Most translators use the word "wickedness" or "evil" to translate *phaula*, but its usage in Greek literature suggests that its meaning is informed by a culture of honor and shame and that it refers to a wide range of acts, including those that are base or thoughtless or acts that are the easy way out, such as lying. Daniel 12:2 contrasts waking to eternal life with waking to the shame of everlasting contempt. Earlier exegetes thought John 5:29 was a product of later redaction, but it is a logical rhetorical move. Jesus anchors his claim in what strikes his opponents as an unprecedented authority within established tradition.

Fourth argument. Jesus then concludes his arguments by returning to the main premise with which he began in 5:19, that he does not make himself God's equal, by asserting that he follows God's will. He begins with an emphatic denial, using a double negative: **"I am** [utterly] **unable to do anything for myself."** He then makes the positive case with a line that repeats the hard sound of *k* in almost every word: **"Just as I hear I judge** [*kathōs akouō krinō*], **and my judgment is just** [*kai hē krisis hē emē dikaia estin*]**."** He then provides the concluding argument: **"because I do not seek my own desire but the desire of the one who has sent me"** (5:30). Implicit within this statement is the understanding within the Jewish context that doing God's will or following God's judgment is an act of righteousness (see Amos 5:24; Mic. 6:8).

Reprehensio: *Jesus Refutes Objections to His Arguments (5:31–47)*

In the next section, Jesus begins by anticipating the logical objection to his argument: any claim that Jesus makes for himself can be accepted as true, according to biblical law, only if it is corroborated by two witnesses (Num.

35:30; Deut. 17:6; 19:15). The demand for two witnesses appears to have been part of standard Jewish judiciary practice (Josephus, *Life* 256; *Ant.* 4.219; *b. Sanh.* 37b; 2 Cor. 13:1; 1 Tim. 5:19; Matt. 18:16; Rev. 11:3–4). Jesus concedes the point: **"If I testify concerning myself, my testimony is not true** [as in not valid]**"** (5:31). He then produces a witness who is acceptable to his opponents and ties this inquisition to the earlier interrogation of John: **"Another is the witness concerning me, and I know that true is the testimony that he testifies concerning me** (5:32). **You have sent to John** [an analeptic reference to John 1:19], **and he has testified to the truth"** (5:33).

Jesus, like a true orator, interrupts his thought with a parenthesis that conforms to Cicero's (*Inv.* 1.42) recommendation that one raise and refute one's opponent's position and take care to select something that will be treated as probable or sound, but then treat it as insignificant or disparage it by holding up one part that is sound and invalidating another part: **"But I do not receive testimony from man; rather, I say this in order that you may be saved** (5:34). **That one was the lamp who burned and shone, and you have wished to rejoice for a time in his light"** (5:35). Jesus both praises and dismisses the Baptist's witness. Jesus's allusion to the Baptist seems to be based on a description of Elijah found in Sir. 48:1 and the historical probability that the crowd received the Baptist joyfully (see Josephus, *Ant.* 18.118). Jesus then provides a superior witness: **"But I have a witness greater than John for the deeds that the Father has given me in order that I might complete these things: these deeds that I do testify concerning me that the Father has sent me"** (5:36). Jesus speaks of works, not signs, as his first witness in accord with the argument he lays out in 5:19–30. For his second witness, he offers God: **"And the one who has sent me, that Father, has testified concerning me."**

Jesus now moves from self-defense to the offense by attacking the capacity of his opponents to serve as witnesses against him. The problem is not that Jesus is without witnesses, but that his opponents are deaf and blind to them. **"Neither have you heard his voice at any time nor have you seen his form"** (5:37). In Jewish tradition, witnesses must be male adults with no impairment of their critical faculties. At the end of the story of the blind man, Jesus will follow up the charge of blindness (9:39–10:39). Jesus then adds a further but unconventional disqualification by using a tautological argument: **"And his word you do not have abiding in you, because the one whom that one sent, this one you do not trust"** (5:38). Jesus's opponents can hear the testimony of God only if they have a priori accepted the truth of that to which Jesus claims God testifies. Given the trickiness of this argument, Jesus moves quickly to an appeal to yet another witness: Scripture. He uses the rhetorical strategy of inviting the audience to provide the desired answer. **"Search the Scriptures, because you suppose in them to have everlasting life, and those are the witnesses concerning me"** (5:39; see also 7:52). The problem is not a matter of the lack of witnesses but the willingness to accept that to which they witness: **"And you are not willing to come to me in order that you might have life"** (5:40).

In the next step, Jesus employs reproach (*obiurgatio*) by reprimanding his audience for not fulfilling the social requirement identified in 5:23 of honoring the Father by honoring the Son. **"Glory from men I do not receive (5:41), but I know you, that the love of God you do not have in you (5:42). I have come in the name of the Father, and you do not receive me. If another were to come in the name of his own, you will receive that one"** (5:43). To modern ears, reproach suggests violent anger, but in the context of ancient rhetoric, it is an effective strategy for persuading a crowd that objects to something one says that they ought not disapprove (Cicero, *De or.* 2.339). Jesus continues to strike a tone of indignation by employing the rhetorical question, **"How are you able to trust glory that you receive from each other, and the glory that [is] from the only God you do not seek?"** (5:44). He then makes explicit that his opponents now stand accused, and he adds further clarification to the picture of eschatological resurrection that he has begun to paint earlier. While he stands in the role of the one who raises people to eternal life, he does not stand in the role of prosecutor. **"Do not suppose that I will accuse you before the Father. Your accuser is Moses, in whom you hope"** (5:45). Moses, in this context, is a synonym for the Torah or metonymy for all Jewish Scripture. Jesus turns his defense witness into a witness for the prosecution of his opponents.

In a final flourish, Jesus refutes the integrity of their charges by challenging their commitment to the authority on which the charges are grounded: **"For if you were trusting Moses, then you would be trusting me, for he wrote concerning me (5:46). But if you do not trust those writings, how will you trust my words?"** (5:47). John leaves open the rhetorical trap that Jesus has laid. Any objection to what Jesus has said would substantiate, within the confines for true witness that Jesus has established, that they place their trust in human glory rather than Moses or God. Set within the context of a verbal contest, Jesus ends this round the victor.

Theological Issues

The issues that arise from a reading of John 5 center on Jesus's relationship to God and matters related to the timing of salvation and the execution of judgment.

Jesus's Equality to God

By denying that he does wrong in restoring life to limb on the Sabbath because he is working just as God works, Jesus provokes the accusation that he makes himself equal with God. Bianca Lataire (2000) clarifies that Jesus is not claiming divinity (a substantial or essential likeness) for himself so much as granting honor to himself; he is accused of hubris or impiety (see 2 Macc. 9:8–12; Philo, *Leg.* 1.49). Craig Keener (1999, 42) suggests that in the context of the argument, the accusation "makes himself equal with his Father" signifies that Jesus acts as though he were independent of God, just as a rebellious son declares himself emancipated from his father. Jesus denies the charge and makes the case that he acts on God's behalf. His arguments put into question the degree to which Jesus shares God's status. As Keener (1999, 40) notes, John states that Jesus is fully divine (1:1, 18; 20:28), but that God, to whom Jesus submits, has the greater rank. The realization that John does not offer a full-blown trinitarian doctrine, coupled with the admission in 10:31–39 that men can be called gods, raises the question for some of whether the Christology of the Gospel should be situated within Jewish notions of righteous individuals.

Perhaps no other scholar has contributed more to this discussion than Wayne Meeks (1990). As Meeks shows, in both Greco-Roman and Jewish thought, it was possible for humans to share God's attributes, to be like God. Heroic and powerful individuals were often called the son of God. As Jesus suggests in 10:31–39 and as Meeks (1990, 314) puts it, "the title *theos* is innocuous because there are accepted occasions when it is appropriately used of humans." Working within the framework articulated by J. Louis Martyn, Meeks situates the defense—that Jesus does not make himself God's equal—in the level of the conflict between a church that has parted ways with the synagogue. The Gospel makes clear that Jesus's sonship is not just honorific but also derives from a unique relationship with God.

The language of persons, being, and essence found in the fourth-century creeds used to define the relationship of Jesus and God is not in sight. While questions of ontology logically follow from claims that Jesus is the Son of God, John's interest in the father-son relationship does not lie with generative principles but with social status or authority. Within the context of ancient Mediterranean cultures, the status and occupation of a father are handed down to a son intact unless the son does something to diminish that honor or to be disinherited through disobedience, but while the father is living, this is a hierarchical relationship. The issue in the context of the Gospel is whether Jesus is to be treated with the same respect and deference that is shown God. Marianne Meye Thompson (2001, 118–20) notes that in John 5, Jesus does the work of giving life that is reserved for God, and he shares two prerogatives with God: he grants eternal life and he judges. It is these things for which God deserves worship and honor; therefore, Jesus also deserves honor. Moreover, if one does not honor the Son, one does not honor the Father. The unity rather than the sameness of Jesus and God is the point.

Realized and Future Eschatology

In his defense, Jesus blends language of future eschatology, in which general resurrection of the dead is followed by judgment and then the granting of eternal life (5:28; see 21:21–23 for a reference to Jesus's return), and realized eschatology, in which the gift of eternal life happens in this life (5:25). On numerous occasions in the Fourth Gospel, Jesus refers to final judgment as a time when one's actions are scrutinized and reward or punishment is meted out (3:19–21; 5:29; see also 6:39–40, 54; 10:9, 28; 12:48; 14:3). Influenced by the work of Rudolf Bultmann (1971, 261), who sought a philosophic notion of judgment in John free of what he considered to be mythic elements, many twentieth-century scholars treated the statements in 5:25 and 28 as irreconcilable and attributed them to later redaction of the Gospel. Statements of realized eschatology were then favored as more authentically Johannine, and views that seemed most compatible with traditional Jewish thought were treated as editorial additions.

Rather than seeing this as an irreconcilable tension and consigning these verses to different stages in the development of the Gospel, scholars working within conservative traditions adopted the language of *schon jetzt* (already now) and *noch nicht* (not yet) to describe the tension in early Christian eschatology that seems most pronounced in the Gospel of John. More recently scholars have moved to language of inauguration (Keener 2003, 323) or complement (O'Donnell 2008, 751). Jörg Frey (2005, 47–65) points to evidence found in 1 John to argue that the Johannine community understood the parousia, judgment, and resurrection to be part of their future but did not allow expectations to dominate how they expressed their faith. Jesus does not simply call people from the grave; he also calls them into new life on this side of the grave. John's rhetorical focus is on freeing those who acknowledge Jesus from the anxieties of death and judgment through the assurance of eternal life. Jesus's followers do not face two possible verdicts at the judgment. John emphasizes Jesus's authority and power to act as an agent in the process and the confidence that believers ought to feel about their own status as those who belong to Jesus (see 6:39–40).

If one limits one's understanding of Johannine judgment to realized eschatology, one might be left to suppose that those who have not believed are condemned with no appeal to their righteousness or God's mercy. Within traditional Jewish eschatology, those who stand outside the covenant are judged by their merits. While the emphasis on realized eschatology provides certainty about the future for Jesus's followers, the presence of future eschatology confutes one's ability to state with certainty the ultimate fate of those who do not believe at present.

Sin and Affliction

In chapter 5, John continues to play with the literary form of supplication by flouting the pattern (see 2:13–4:54): the beneficiary does not seek out the healer, makes no gesture of supplication (either before the healing or afterward in the form of gratitude), and makes no request. Jesus initiates all the action.

111

In glaring contrast to a synoptic healing, faith plays no role at all in the granting of the gift. The presence of Jesus's warning, "See, you are restored; stop sinning lest something worse happen to you" (5:14)—coupled with absence of acts of repentance, forgiveness, or gratitude—raises the question of the relationship of sin and illness. Jesus's words suggest to some that the man's affliction is a divine punishment (Thomas 1995, 14–19), but John does not make clear to which sin Jesus refers. It could be that Jesus refers to the man's act of shifting blame for Sabbath transgression from himself to Jesus. It is even possible, as Jeffrey Staley (1991, 62) suggests, that Jesus refers to the act of carrying around the mat, which constitutes the Sabbath violation. The present imperative form of the verb to sin (*hamartane*; 5:14) does suggest that Jesus is prohibiting a continuing action rather than a potential future act (Thomas 1995, 15; "stop sinning"). While Jesus, as the Son of God, works without violating the Sabbath, the Gospel does not challenge the notion that people are to keep the Sabbath by refraining from labor (contra Borgen 1987, 97). Mark W. G. Stibbe offers a solution that fits within the narrative structure of the story. In this Gospel, sin is the failure to recognize Jesus by believing that he is the Son of God and acknowledging him publicly (Stibbe 1993, 116).

The notion that sin necessarily causes affliction is prevalent in later Jewish thought. In her study of disabilities in ancient Jewish thought, Judith Abrams (1998, 90–91) describes the principle of *middâ kěneged middâ* (measure for measure). For example, if one feigns a physical disability such as lameness or blindness to receive charity, one will be afflicted with that disability (*m. Pe'ah* 8.9). Jesus's warning that sin may lead to affliction should not be read backward to signify that all affliction is caused by sin. The idea that suffering and death were the result of sin does lie within the purview of ancient Judaism, but Larry P. Hogan, in *Healing in the Second Temple Period* (1992), finds four additional causes for illness frequently identified within Second Temple discourse: God for his own purposes, intermediaries of God, evil spirits, and the movement of the heavenly spheres. John seems to anticipate his readers' fixing on sin as the cause of affliction and confutes their conclusion when he puts the question, "Who sinned, this man or his parents, that he be born blind?" (9:2) on the lips of the disciples and records Jesus's response, "Neither" (9:3). (For a continuation of this discussion, see "Sin, Blindness, and Begging" in the theological issues section of 9:1–10:42.)

John 6:1–71

Bread and Circuses

Introductory Matters

Jesus's miracles of healing and even resurrection often find parallels in ancient biographies about healers and divine men (see Cotter 1999). The two miracles in this story—Jesus feeding the five thousand and Jesus walking on water—however, figure in the lives of kings and emperors. The Roman emperor demonstrated the beneficence of his reign by distributing grain to the people of Rome (*Res gest. divi Aug.* 5.2; 15.1–3; 18.1; Suetonius, *Claud.* 18; Cicero, *Sest.* 103). One of Emperor Caligula's greatest spectacles entailed spanning three and a half Roman miles (roughly equivalent to 3.25 of today's statute miles) across the Bay of Naples with a flotilla of ships and then riding across it on a chariot (Suetonius, *Cal.* 19). Juvenal (*Sat.* 10.81) satirizes the emperor's means of exercising influence over Roman crowds by writing that he offered them *panem et circenses*, bread and entertainment.

The sign with which this major episode in the Gospel begins (Jesus multiplying the loaves and fish) is the miracle that John clearly shares with the synoptic tradition. Raymond E. Brown (1966, 240–43) dedicates four pages of his commentary to a chart that delineates all the parallels and minor differences. The key difference lies not in the narration of the event so much as with what happens as a consequence of the miracle. The synoptic event leads to an increase in the number of people seeking healing from Jesus; John's account provides the catalyst for discourse and dialogue about Jesus's identity that push disciples away.

The Bread of Life discourse has been the focus of much debate since the Reformation, with Catholic readers finding confirmation of their understanding of the sacraments and Protestant readers finding confirmation of the

The Purpose of Repetition

Modern readers may find repetition tedious, but in antiquity it was considered charming or pleasing to the ear because it makes prose more rhythmic. Repetition points to the importance of the idea to the speaker and gives to its expression energy and vehemence (Quintilian, *Inst.* 9.3). As the bellman says in Lewis Carroll's "The Hunting of the Snark" (1876), "I have said it thrice. What I tell you three times is true." Perhaps most important, repetition makes an idea memorable (Quintilian, *Inst.* 11.2.34).

requirement of faith for salvation. Much of this controversy is generated by the repetition that dominates the discourse as scholars have sought patterns to determine a central point or a development in Jesus's argument or Johannine thought. In the following reading, the purpose or function of the repetition will be situated within the norms of Greco-Roman rhetoric that emphasize the audible reception of a speech.

Greco-Roman narratives often employed a speech act—such as lament, the *agōn* (debate) of a trial, prophecy, or supplication (see "Introductory Matters" at 2:13–4:54)—as the frame or content of the action in an episode. In John's Gospel, the act of supplication is frequently central to the action; this is especially true in the narrative that precedes the Bread of Life discourse and the discourse itself. Jesus makes it clear that he can provide eternal life; the crowd makes a supplication and asks what gesture, what work, is necessary to receive the boon that Jesus offers. Jesus rejects their request and clarifies that the crowd has not made the necessary gesture of believing in him.

Scene 1: Supplication for physical bread (6:1–15)
    Step 1: The crowd approaches Jesus (6:1–2)
    Step 2: Jesus makes the request on behalf of the crowd (6:3–7)
    Step 3: Jesus fulfills the request (6:8–13)
    Step 4: The crowd attempts a gesture of supplication (6:14)
    Step 5: Jesus rejects the gesture of supplication (6:15)
Scene 2: Jesus crosses the sea (6:16–21)
Scene 3: Supplication for bread from heaven (6:22–59)
    Step 1: The approach (6:22–26)
    Step 2: The request (6:27–34)
    Step 3: The presentation of Jesus's terms (6:35–59)
        Part 1: Stipulation of the gesture (6:35–40)
        Part 2: The crowd considers the terms (6:41–42)
        Part 3: Jesus repeats his conditions in stronger terms (6:43–59)
Scene 4: Some disciples refuse the suppliant gesture (6:60–71)

John adds a complication to the action by placing the disciples in the position of one who overhears. Overhearing or eavesdropping is an important device in classical drama. Plautus and Terence employ it multiple times in every one of their plays. Rather than the dialogue moving the plot along, it is frequently the reaction or limited understanding of the character listening in on the conversation that sets the action rolling. This is the case in John 6. The climax of the scene is the recognition on the part of some of Jesus's disciples that they are not prepared to make the gesture necessary to receive the life that Jesus offers. The unit ends by naming one of these, Judas Iscariot, who will hand Jesus over to the authorities.

Tracing the Narrative Flow

Scene 1: Supplication for Physical Bread (6:1–15)

Step 1: The crowd approaches Jesus. The transition to this next episode is signaled by the passage of time, **After these things,** and movement in space, **Jesus departed and went to the other side of sea of the Galilee, the Tiberias** (6:1; see map of Galilee, fig. 4 at John 1:19–2:12). Historical critics working with the hypotheses that John was dependent on a signs source and that the extant Gospel is a restructured and heavily edited version of the autograph see the setting of this episode as an aporia suggesting that the order of chapters 5 and 6 should be flipped. More recently, scholars working with ancient rhetoric and dramatic conventions have noted that the present order of the scenes makes sense given the way that tension mounts in the Gospel.

Like the Synoptic Gospels, John identifies the lake with the region on its western shore rather than by its ancient name Gennesaret. He also refers to it by using the name of a city on its southwest shore, Tiberius, a city named for the Roman emperor and in AD 24 established on a graveyard by Herod Antipas as the region's capital. In our own postcolonial era, people are discarding names imposed on places by colonial powers and restoring ancient names (e.g., Bombay is again Mumbai). John's invocation of an imperial name reminds his ancient audience that Jesus's actions ought to be set within the context of empire.

The narrator then sets Jesus within the action that is in progress: **A large crowd was following him because they had observed the signs that he was doing on behalf of those who were sick** (6:2). Here is another instance where the formalists' distinction between *sjuzet* (the representation of events through

---

John 6:1–71 in the Narrative Flow

In the beginning (1:1–2:12)

Jesus's itinerant ministry (2:13–12:11)

　　Transforming sacred space (2:13–4:54)

　　God works on the Sabbath (5:1–47)

▶**Bread and circuses (6:1–71)**

　　　　Scene 1: Supplication for physical bread (6:1–15)

　　　　Scene 2: Jesus crosses the sea (6:16–21)

　　　　Scene 3: Supplication for bread from heaven (6:22–59)

　　　　Scene 4: Some disciples refuse the suppliant gesture (6:60–71)

what is given, what is told) and the *fabula* (the events implied in a narrative, what has happened) is helpful. The reader must reconstruct a story from what is given, in which a number of public healings have been witnessed by the crowd.

Step 2: Jesus makes the request on behalf of the crowd. The action begins when **Jesus went up the mountain, and he took a seat there with his disciples** (6:3). The ascent up a mountain places Jesus in the role of Moses, and John's insertion of a more precise designation of time—**the Passover, the festival of the Jews, was approaching** (6:4)—confirms the association. When Jesus ascends a mountain in Matt. 5:1, he instructs his disciples. In the action that follows, John's disciples function as servants rather than students.

John focalizes the scene through Jesus's vantage point. **Jesus, upon lifting up his eyes and observing that a large crowd was coming toward him, said to Philip, "How can I shop for bread in order that they might eat?"** (6:5). John then makes clear that the question does not point to any inadequacy on Jesus's part: **He said this, drawing him in, for he knew what he himself was going to do** (6:6). Many scholars treat Jesus's question as something akin to the test of the mettle of Abraham's faith in Gen. 22:1 or that of the Israelites in Exod. 15:24, but a number of oddities in this question and John's use of the verb "drawing in" (*peirazōn*) suggest that Jesus is being wry. The disciples have been Jesus's personal shoppers (4:8), and the verb "shop" (*agorasōmen*) paints a picture of Jesus struggling through a market, trying to pick up more bread than he could possibly carry. By making Jesus's question a riddle to which Jesus knows the answer, John points to Jesus's superiority to Moses, who asks in sincerity, "Where am I to get meat to give to all this people?" (Num. 11:13; Thatcher 2000, 210–11). Jesus's superiority to Moses, who is depicted as a divine king in contemporary Jewish literature, is a major theme in this episode (see Meeks 1967). Philip plays the part of the straight man and answers from the practical perspective of finances: **"Two hundred denarii** [one denarii is a day's wage for a laborer; see Matt. 20:2] [is] **not sufficient** [to buy enough] **loaves of bread for them so that each might receive so much as a morsel"** (6:7).

Step 3: Jesus fulfills the request. **One of his disciples, Andrew the brother of Simon Peter, says to him** (6:8), **"There is a lad here who has five loaves made from barley and two small preserved fish, but what are these to so many?"** (6:9). John artfully brings the boy into view through Andrew's speech. In the synoptic version, the food belongs to the disciples (Matt. 14:17; Mark 6:38; Luke 9:13). Taking the food from a child adds to the distress of the situation or the disciples' folly. The fish (*opsaria*) serve as a sort of relish; bread is the substance of the meal. The need for a relish signifies that the bread may satisfy hunger, but not one's appetite. Alone, barley bread is not easily swallowed (Dalby 1996, 91).

The similarity of what follows with the ritual of the Eucharist is covered in the theological issues section. Jesus's instructions—**"Make the people recline!"**—anticipates the miracle. In antiquity a free person reclined at a banquet.

Figure 12. Fish plate, ca. 350–325 BC, Louvre. Imported and locally produced fish plates were popular in Palestine during the Hellenistic period.

The narrator begins with a wide angle and then narrows focus upon Jesus's actions. There was a large pasture in the place. Then the people reclined, the number about five thousand (6:10). Jesus then took the bread and returning thanks [*eucharistēsas*] he handed [it] around to those reclining; in the same manner [he distributed the fish, and they took] from the fish as much as they wanted (6:11). The setting perhaps anticipates Jesus's command to Peter to feed his sheep (21:15–17). Ancient tendencies to count only men could mean that we can picture an even larger crowd. The language of *eucharistein* is a Greek rendering of the Hebrew verb *bārak*, to bless. It would be odd for Jesus to distribute the food without a blessing.

The action at the end of the meal recalls the exodus and anticipates the implicit comparison of Jesus to Moses in the next day's dialogue. When they had eaten their fill, Jesus says to his disciples, "Gather the surplus fragments lest any be wasted" (6:12), in contrast to the manna that could not be saved (Exod. 16:19–20). Then they gathered and stuffed twelve baskets of fragments from the five loaves of bread made of barley that were left over from the feeding (6:13). The number twelve suggests that either twelve disciples did the gathering, hence twelve baskets were used, or the remainder of the bread feeds a restored Israel.

Step 4: The crowd attempts a gesture of supplication. Then the people seeing the sign he did were saying that "This is in fact the prophet, the one coming into the world" (6:14). Given that this acknowledgment of Jesus's authority is prompted by the receipt of bread and the centrality of Moses to the Bread of Life discourse, it seems likely that this is in reference to the promise in Deut. 18:18 that God will raise up a prophet like Moses. Their association of Moses with a royal messiah is borne out by Jesus's prescience of their intent in 6:15.

Step 5: Jesus rejects the gesture of supplication. Then Jesus, knowing that they were about to come and seize him in order that they might make him king, withdrew again to the mountain [to be by] himself alone (6:15). In Mark 6:53–56, the crowd's reaction to the feeding is to recognize that Jesus is a miracle worker and to bring him more infirm people to heal. In John, the crowd advances the plot by providing tension between their notion of messianic fulfillment and Jesus's purpose, thus necessitating Jesus's hasty retreat.

The narrative of the miraculous feeding then sets the stage for the tension between the crowd's supplication and Jesus's insistence that the gift of life entails an act tantamount to death. Unless the crowd trusts in Jesus's death, it can have no part of his life.

Scene 2: Jesus Crosses the Sea (6:16–21)

Walking on water in Jewish and Greco-Roman tradition is unambiguously a divine act. In Job 9:8, the image of God treading on the waves of the sea depicts his power over nature. In Ps. 77:19, a similar image signifies God's deliverance of his people from Egypt. Persian King Xerxes builds a bridge of boats across the Bosphorus so that he can imitate Poseidon (ca. 480 BC; see Dio Chrysostom, *3 Regn.* 3.30–31). Caligula imitates Xerxes by crossing the Bay of Naples. Trajan's conquest of the Dacians is represented on his victory column by depicting his troops crossing the Danube on a flotilla of boats (see fig. 13). It is possible that the story of Jesus's walk on the water is set into the episode simply because it follows the feeding miracle in the oral tradition (see Mark 6:30–56), but given the accent on kingship at the end of the last scene, it is also possible that John is making clear that Jesus deserves the title of king even though he has just rejected the crowd's bid to enthrone him. John also seems to take advantage of the juxtaposition of the signs to dramatize the disciples' lack of comprehension in preparation for the final act in the episode. The disciples fail to draw any conclusions from Jesus's miraculous ability and try to rescue him.

Again the transition to a new episode is marked by a reference to time and movement. **When it became late, his disciples went down by the sea (6:16). And boarding a small boat** [as in a fishing boat]**, they were trying to cross the**

Figure 13. This imprint from a relief on Trajan's Column (AD 113), Rome, depicts Roman troops crossing the Danube.

© Conrad Cichorius, 1896

sea to Capernaum. John gradually adds the elements that signal the danger of their situation. First, **it had already become dark,** and second, **Jesus had not yet come to them** (6:17), and third, **the sea was churned by a mighty wind** (6:18). The position of the sea in the Jordan Rift Valley and the hills that surround it make sudden violent storms a frequent event. Those who have been caught in a small craft such as a canoe or rowboat in such conditions are familiar with the need to keep the boat going forward in order to stay in control and to prevent being swamped with water from side waves. **Then having rowed about twenty-five or thirty stadia** [3.125–3.75 land miles, or 2.75–3.25 nautical miles, placing them at about a third of the distance across the sea], **they spotted Jesus walking upon the sea and drawing near the boat, and they were afraid** (6:19). The order of information suggests that the sight of Jesus is what frightens them. Anxiety about drowning is dwarfed by fear of an apparition. Jesus's response, *Egō eimi,* can be translated as "It is I," but given the place of this phrase in the Gospel, it should perhaps be associated with God's name and power to deliver (Exod. 3:14) and translated as **"I am; do not be afraid"** (6:20). John's Gospel ends the episode with a piece of irony by describing the contrast between the disciples' intention to rescue Jesus—**They wanted then to take him into the boat**—and Jesus's miraculous rescue of the disciples—**at once the boat happened upon the land to which they were heading** (6:21).

Scene 3: Supplication for Bread from Heaven (6:22–59)

Step 1: The approach. John picks up the narrative **on the next day** with the focalization of **the crowd that was standing on the other side of the sea, who saw that no other small vessel was over there other than the one and that Jesus did not go with his disciples into the vessel but only his disciples departed** (6:22). This is an awkwardly worded sentence, the import of which is that the crowd saw that only one boat was gone. The Greek seems to suggest that they are stranded on one shore but that they can see the shore upon which the boat had landed. Their problem is solved: **but small boats arrived from Tiberias near the place where they ate the bread after the Lord had given thanks** (6:23). Perhaps John plays with the irony: the boats that deliver them from their plight come from the emperor's namesake. **When the crowd saw that neither Jesus nor his disciples were there, they climbed into the boats and came to Capernaum, seeking Jesus** (6:24). John lingers over the realization that Jesus has left and lets us see the crowd looking at the evidence of the disciples' stormy crossing. The crowd is left to puzzle over how Jesus got from point A to point B while the Gospel's audience has had the privilege of witnessing the miracle.

The crowd then approaches Jesus, **and finding him on the other side of the sea, they said to him, "Rabbi, however did you come to be here?"** (6:25). John underscores the crowd's suppliant position by having them arrive into Jesus's space and ask a question that points to their ignorance of the time and means of Jesus's arrival. Their polite address of "Rabbi" suggests that their enthusiasm for making Jesus king has cooled. The puzzle of Jesus's arrival diverts them from their original intent to make Jesus king and puts the miraculous feeding out of mind. A dialogue then ensues in which Jesus sets the stage for the act of supplication for bread from heaven. **Jesus responded to them and said, "Truly, truly [amēn amēn], I say to you, you seek me not because you saw signs, but because you ate the bread and were sated"** (6:26). This is an insult. Jesus accuses them of being ruled by their stomachs. Set within Greco-Roman literature, concern for food places the crowd in the category of the fool. The comic fool in Roman comedy talks incessantly about his hunger and thirst (e.g., Aristophanes, *Vesp.* 56–60; Plautus, *Capt.* 492–97; Juvenal, *Sat.* 5.156–74; Lucian, *Sat.* 4, 9). Much of what Jesus says in this dialogue is a characterization of the crowd as an entity that does not belong to him rather than a clarification of his identity.

At this point, the terms to be repeated come into use. Jesus has used the distinctive Johannine doubling of the word *amēn* (*epizeuxis*, repetition of words with no words in between) with the phrase "I say to you" already in his first dialogue with the disciples (1:51), in conversation with Nicodemus (3:5, 11), and in his self-defense (5:19, 24–25); he will use it four times in this dialogue to punctuate his speech. The repetition of this and many other words lends rhythm and energy to Jesus's speech.

Repeated Vocabulary in the Bread of Life Discourse

Word	Form	Occurrences
bread	declensions of *artos*	14
from heaven	*apo/ek tou* (*ex*) *ouranou*	10
descend	conjugations of *katabainō*	6
eat	conjugations of *phagein*	9
eat	conjugations of *trōgō*	4
work	forms of *ergazomai* or *ergon*	5
life	declensions of *zōē*	12
everlasting life	*zōēn aiōnion*	5
give	conjugations of *didōmi*	10
believe	conjugations of *pisteuō*	9
the last day	*eschatē hēmera*	4
flesh	declensions of *sarx*	7
drink	conjugations of *pinō*	4
blood	declensions of *haima*	4

Step 2: The request. **Jesus then admonishes them, "Don't work for perishable food but for food that lasts for everlasting life, which the Son of Man will**

give to you, for this the Father, God, approved" (6:27). The word "approved" (*esphragisen*) means, literally, to put a seal upon something to certify or appoint it. For people from the British Commonwealth, it conjures up images of products that bear the label "by appointment to her Majesty the Queen," signifying that the product is served in the royal household. Herodotus (*Hist.* 2.38) uses the verb in a similar way to describe the seal that Egyptian priests affix to sacrificial animals upon inspection. Jesus has established what the boon is and makes the implicit offer that will end this part of the discourse with the crowd making a supplication (John 6:34).

The contrast between perishable and imperishable food does not provoke a question. Within Jewish eschatological conventions, such a distinction is understood. The issue delineated is what one must do, what the appropriate gesture is that will ensure a supplication being fulfilled: **"What might we do in order that we may work the works of God?"** (6:28). One ought not to be quick to impose a Pauline or Lutheran faith/works distinction on this exchange. "What must I do to do God's will?" is a familiar question in Jewish discourse, here reworded to fit the Johannine dialogue. There is no need to treat the question as inadequate, but John takes the answer in a christological direction. By putting things into his own distinct terms, **"This is the work of God, to trust in whom that one sent"** (6:29), Jesus destabilizes the dialogue and throws the crowd off balance. Belief in this context is not necessarily reducible to believing that God has sent Jesus but could connote that they should follow Jesus. The defection or commitment of the disciples is then the culmination of the story.

The crowd's response—**"What sign then are you doing, so that we may see and we may trust you? What do you work?"** (6:30)—seems puzzling in light of how they had taken the feeding on the prior day as sufficient basis to make Jesus their king. Now the stakes are higher. If Jesus is the new prophet-king of Deut. 18:18 who will deliver them from their oppressors, he should be able to provide something better than bread, specifically manna, the food that Moses provided in the wilderness: **"Our fathers ate manna in the wilderness, as it has been written, 'Bread from heaven he gave for them to eat'"** (6:31). This seems to be a paraphrase of a combination of Exod. 16:4, 15 and Ps. 78:24 that serves as the second in a series of challenges in which Jesus's dialogue partners suggest that Jesus is overstepping his bounds: they ask if he is greater than a Hebrew forefather, each one more eminent than the last. The Samaritan woman asks if he is greater than Jacob (4:12). This crowd asks indirectly if he is greater than Moses, and a later crowd asks him if he is greater than Abraham (8:53). In Jesus's response—**"Truly, truly, I say to you, Moses did not give you the bread from heaven, but my Father gives you the bread from heaven, the real [bread] (6:32). For the bread of God is that which descends from heaven and gives life to the world"** (6:33)—he persuades the crowd to make their supplication by offering something better than manna, something from God that is not a temporary solution or salvation through a national movement; it is the redemption of the world. The Gospel's audience knows that Jesus is referring to himself, but on a narrative level, the crowd has no reason to suspect that Jesus does not offer a better form of manna, so they word their request as **"Lord, always give us this bread!"** (6:34).

Step 3: The presentation of Jesus's terms. The request prompts Jesus to make his intention clear that he is the bread of life, but he also changes his use of pronouns in anticipation of the crowd's rejection of the terms.

Step 3, part 1: Stipulation of the gesture. Jesus's use of first-person declarations and the third-person statements to describe the beneficiary of this gift generates a social distance between him and the crowd. **"I am the bread of life; the one who comes to me shall not be hungry, and the one who believes in me shall definitely never be thirsty"** (6:35; see Isa. 55:1–3). "I am the bread of life" is the first of a series of seven "I am" statements, in which Jesus asserts that, rather than bringing eschatological blessings, he is himself the blessing (8:12; 10:7, 9, 11, 14; 11:25; 14:6; 15:1). Jesus seems to imply that what he offers is superior even to wisdom. Wisdom does not quench thirst but rather provokes greater thirst (see Sir. 24:19–21). Jesus repeats this claim again in 6:48.

Next Jesus makes it clear that the crowd does not perform the gesture that completes their supplication by returning to direct second-person address: **"But I told you that you have neither seen nor do you believe"** (6:36). The remainder of this part of his speech (vv. 36–40) reiterates Jesus's defense arguments in 5:27–38. The accent falls on Jesus's assigned task as God's agent and his obedience in accepting all who come to him. **"All that the Father gives to me will have come to me, and I will certainly not cast out the one coming to me** (6:37). **Because I have descended from heaven not in order to do my will but the will of the one having sent me** (6:38). **This is the will of the one having sent me, that of all that has been given to me, I should lose nothing, but I shall raise him** [or her] **on the final day"** (6:39). The next verse repeats the point, thereby enhancing the speech's poetic rhythm and emphasizing the gestures of witnessing and believing: **"For this is the will of my Father in order that everyone observing the Son and believing in him shall have life everlasting, and I will raise him** [or her] **on the final day"** (6:40).

Step 3, part 2: The crowd considers the terms. Jesus's words push the crowd away, and the crowd's actions reflect their disengagement. They drop Jesus as a dialogue partner and begin to speak among one another, referring to Jesus in the third person. The introduction of the Jews (*hoi Ioudaioi*) at this point raises the question of whether this is a different crowd, but the continuity with the preceding dialogue suggests that this has been a Judean crowd all along or that the Galilean crowd is referred to as Jews as a way of emphasizing their antipathy toward Jesus's words. The narrator characterizes their speech with the onomatopoeic verb *gongyzō*, bringing back into play the story in Numbers in which the people were grumbling (*gongyzōn*) in the wilderness (Num. 11:1 LXX; see also LXX: Exod. 16:2, 8; Num. 14:27; 17:25 [10]; Ps. 77 [78]:17–22).

Then the Jews were grumbling about him because he said, "I am the bread that descends from heaven" (6:41). And they said, "Isn't this Jesus the son of Joseph? Don't we know his father and mother? How then can he say that 'I have descended from heaven'?" (6:42). The claim that Jesus is the bread is not at issue for them but rather the implication that he has descended from heaven. Thus far Jesus has used his claim about his pedigree in his defense, but now the crowd challenges that claim.

Step 3, part 3: Jesus repeats his conditions in stronger terms. Scholarship has typically treated 6:43–51 and 53–58 as revelatory speeches that correct the crowd's misunderstanding, but the crowd has correctly treated Jesus's claim that he is the bread of life as a metaphor for being God's heavenly agent. Jesus's so-called clarification compounds rather than reduces ambiguity by playing with words rather than explaining them. Jesus stands in solidarity with the narrator by dismissing their concerns as complaining: **"Do not grumble among yourselves! (6:43). No one is able to come to me unless the Father who has sent me impels [*helkysē*] him, and I will raise him on the final day"** (6:44). The next verse is a digression that explains what it means to be impelled by God, using the same picture of education that Jesus uses in 5:19–20. **"It has been written in the Prophets, 'And they will all be divinely instructed'** [see Isa. 54:13; Jer. 31:33]. **Everyone having listened at the side of the Father and having learned comes to me** (6:45). **Not that anyone has seen the Father other than the one being beside God; this one sees the Father** (6:46). **Truly, truly, I say to you, the one believing has life everlasting"** (6:47). The correction in 6:46 is a device that, on the narrative level, lends the speech verisimilitude as though Jesus is thinking on his feet and, on the rhetorical level, emphasizes Jesus's knowledge of what he speaks.

Suddenly Jesus begins to escalate the rhetoric by repeating **"I am the bread of life"** (6:48) and then drawing a stark distinction between manna and the true bread by using the verb "to die" (*apothnēskō*) as punctuation. **"Your fathers fed in the wilderness on manna and died (6:49). This is the bread that descends from heaven, in order that anyone may eat from it and shall not die"** (6:50). The next line expresses the same thought in antithetical form, repeating many of the same words yet shifting the emphasis from his heavenly descent to his identity with the bread: **"I am the living bread that descends from heaven; whoever feeds upon this bread shall live into eternity, and the bread is my flesh that I will give on behalf of the life of the world"** (6:51). Jesus becomes the willing agent of the act of love described in 3:16.

The Jews' response, **"How can he possibly give us his flesh to eat?"** (6:52), in which they continue their internal debate, stands at the center of a chiasmus (see below; Talbert 2005, 142). Jesus escalates the rhetoric by using more-controversial terms in 6:53–58 to repeat elements from the first half of the chiasmus (6:49–52). The first line adds the element of blood to the mix, calling to mind the wine of the Eucharist, but in the narrative context, flesh and blood is a Hebraic way of speaking of the whole person (see Brodie 1997, 285): "**Truly, truly, I say to you, unless you eat the flesh of the Son of Man and drink his blood, you do not have life in yourselves**" (6:53). Jesus repeats his statements once more with language that employs cacophony (harsh-sounding words) and places emphasis on the first-person and third-person pronouns, thereby underscoring the crowd's difficulty with accepting Jesus's words. "**The one consuming [*trōgōn*] my flesh and drinking my blood has life everlasting, and I will raise him [or her] on the final day (6:54). For my flesh actually is food and my blood actually is drink (6:55). The one consuming my flesh and drinking my blood abides in me and I in him (6:56). Just as the living Father sent me, I also live through the Father, and the one consuming me, he also will live through me (6:57). This is the bread descending from heaven, not just as the fathers ate and died; the one consuming this bread will live forever**" (6:58). With the introduction of the word *trōgōn*, a verb that connotes the actual chewing of the food, and language of hematophagy, the drinking of blood, Jesus moves away from persuasive to offensive speech even if he speaks metaphorically. Jesus makes clear that his victory comes at the cost of his life and that participation in the life he offers requires that one either render oneself unclean to the Jewish community or celebrate that death by treating it as a feast.

Chiastic Outline of John 6:49–58

    A Ate . . . died/eat . . . not die (6:49–50)
       B My flesh/eat . . . live (6:51)
          C How . . . eat (6:52)
          C′ Unless . . . eat (6:53–54)
       B′ My flesh/eat . . . live (6:55–57)
    A′ Ate . . . died/eat . . . live (6:58)

John marks the end of the dialogue with the crowd with a reference to its setting **in the synagogue in Capernaum, where Jesus has been teaching**

Figure 14. Ruins of the Synagogue at Capernaum.

(6:59). As is evident in 5:10, John can purposely withhold details. Juxtaposed against the action that follows, it seems possible that the location marks the choice that the disciples must make between fellowship with the synagogue or communion with the community that eats the bread and drinks the wine of Christian fellowship and shares Jesus's teachings. Whether or not expulsion from the synagogue was a major crisis in the early church or the Johannine community, John makes the synagogue a signifier of impending conflict.

Scene 4: Some Disciples Refuse the Suppliant Gesture (6:60–71)

Rather than focusing on the end of the crowd's deliberation, John shifts attention to the disciples, who have been silently observing the debate. **Then many of his disciples listening said, "His speech is unbearable. Who can listen to him?"** (6:60). Their characterization of Jesus's speech as more than they can handle, in the ancient context, says more about the disciples than Jesus. Philodemus of Gadara (110–40 BC) distinguishes between two types of students using language associated with digestion: those who are tender (*hapaloi*) accept what they are taught, and those who are tough (*ischyroi*) cannot accept the criticism of their teacher and violently resist frank speech (*Lib.*, P.Herc. 1471, col. 7.1–5).

Once more the scene is focalized through Jesus, who sees the disciples react like the crowd. **Jesus, perceiving that his disciples were grumbling about this, said to them, "Does this offend you?"** (6:61). Rather than returning to the images of his death found in the discourse, he focuses on the consequence of that death. The implication is that to treat the death as an offense is to ignore its necessity for his ascension. His use of a rhetorical question presses his point and also captures his indignation: **"What if you should watch the Son of Man ascend where he was in the first place?"** (6:62). He points to the relative unimportance of physical life compared to the spiritual life he offers: **"The Spirit is that which makes alive; the flesh is of no use, none at all; the**

125

saying that I have spoken to you is spirit and is life" (6:63). Both Jesus and the narrator's words emphasize Jesus's intimate knowledge of his disciples and make clear that the intended audience of his argument has been his disciples and not the crowd. Jesus reveals, "But some of you are those who do not believe." For Jesus knew from the beginning who those were who did not believe and who was the one who will hand him over (6:64). And he said, "On account of this, I have said to you that no one is able to come to me unless it [the ability] is given to him by the Father" (6:65). From this [time] many of his disciples went back to things [they had left] behind and no longer walked about with him (6:66). The narration of the defection is a piece of apologetic. The disciples do not reject Jesus: God rejects the disciples.

Jesus's words sort out those who do not trust him and reduce his following to the size of a group familiar to readers of the Synoptic Gospels. Once more Jesus engages them with a question, but it serves as an invitation to remain. Then Jesus said to the Twelve, "Don't you also want to go away?" (6:67). Simon Peter puts himself forward as the spokesperson for the group in the first of a series of acts in which he represents himself as Jesus's committed follower (13:9, 37; 18:10). The ancient audience would perhaps have treated his action and words within the role of what Theophrastus calls the *periergos*, the overzealous servant who promises more than he can deliver (*Char.* 13). Simon Peter responded to him, "Lord, who will we go after [follow]? You have words of everlasting life (6:68). And we have believed and have known that you are the holy one of God" (6:69). Peter uses the same title for Jesus that Dan. 4:23 uses to refer to a divine messenger and that Satan uses in Mark 1:24 when he addresses Jesus. The latter association may come to the modern audience's mind when Jesus responded to them, "Did I not choose the Twelve? And from you one is a devil" (6:70). The rebuke is aimed at Peter's arrogant assumption that he can speak for all those disciples who remain. The narrator then makes explicit to whom Jesus refers: He was speaking about Judas Simon of Iscariot, for this one out of the Twelve was about to hand him over (6:71). With this ominous note, the unit comes to a close.

Theological Issues

The Bread of Life discourse fuels three discussions. The first concerns the necessity of eating Jesus's flesh and drinking his blood. Does Jesus simply refer to how one receives his death, or is he referring to the Eucharist? If the latter is the case, what sort of understanding of the role of the sacrament is implied? Is it a commemorative meal of thanks and remembrance, or does John presuppose that Jesus is present or acts through the elements of the meal? The second issue, the more recent to emerge in scholarly discussion, is the relationship of Jesus to Moses and of the bread of life to manna. Does this unit support a replacement theory, or does it signify a christological interpretation of traditional Jewish eschatology? The distinction may be subtle but significant in light of the history of Christian persecution of the Jews. The final issue revolves around the freedom to believe in Jesus and the notion that God determines who will belong to Jesus.

John 6 and the Eucharist

The Gospel of John contains no narration of the institution of the Lord's Supper. The disciples gather for a final meal with Jesus, but Jesus does not comment on the food that they consume. The presence of eucharistic words in this narrative and discourse—such as a prayer of thanks (*eucharistēsas*), fragments (*klasmata*, the word used for eucharistic bread in *Did.* 9:3), give (*didomai*), on behalf of (*hyper*), bread (*artos*), blood (*haima*), eat (*phagein*), and drink (*pinein*)—has led to a debate about whether the Bread of Life discourse is a commentary on the Lord's Supper and the conclusion that, while John does not include that supper in his narrative, he presupposes that it is a ritual of the community for which he writes. Catholic sacramental theology finds support for the doctrine of transubstantiation, which asserts that Jesus's real presence is found in the consecrated bread and wine.

Evidence of early disagreement about whether the Bread of Life discourse is about the importance of participating in the Lord's Supper can be found in the writings of the church fathers. Justin Martyr (AD 100–165), the earliest known interpreter of John, read this text through the lens of his understanding that the Eucharist was a ritual marker of the true believer (*1 Apol.* 66; ca. AD 151). Clement of Alexandria (AD 150–215; *Paed.* 1.6.46–47) and Origen (AD 185–254; *Hom. Job* 6.43; 10.17; 20.41–43) treated the language of eating flesh and drinking blood as a metaphor for gaining nourishment from Christ's teachings.

The omission of the Lord's Supper led Rudolf Bultmann to conclude that the Gospel writer rejected rituals as markers of commitment in favor of a metaphoric treatment of eating and drinking as an existential commitment. Bultmann (1971, 218–19) treated 6:44–48, the verses in which Jesus becomes more adamant about eating and drinking, as the additions of an ecclesiastical editor. Bultmann's concern was that belief in the necessity of sacraments turned faith into superstition rather than leading to authenticity. Those who persist in denying that John 6 alludes to a ritual meal (e.g., Gary Burge 1987, 106, who contends that 6:51–58 signifies a "redirection away from material religion") tend to presuppose that the language of spirit is highly individual, and they discount the idea that people need tangible ritual markers in order to claim a group identity.

In opposition to Bultmann's case for disunity, Donald A. Carson (1991) argues that the language in the second half of the discourse is not necessarily sacramental, as if the bread and wine themselves effect salvation. He points

127

to the prevalence of metaphors of eating and drinking in modern English to signify one's full engagement or commitment: "We devour books, drink in lectures, swallow stories, ruminate on ideas, chew over a notion, and eat our own words. Doting grandparents declare they could eat up their grandchildren" (Carson 1991, 279). John himself uses the metaphor when he cites Ps. 69:9, "Zeal of your house will devour me" (2:17).

Oscar Cullmann is a modern scholar often cited in support of a sacramental reading. Cullmann (1953) contends that in the second half of the discourse (6:48–65), eating is to be taken literally, but "my body" is a metaphor for bread, informed by the metaphoric reference to Jesus as the bread of life in 6:27–47. He situates the Gospel within the debates against docetism (the belief that Jesus's physical body was an illusion) and Gnosticism, which informed the early church fathers' use of John 6 (Cullmann 1953, 93–102). The main point of the Bread of Life discourse is then the assertion of the presence of Jesus in history. Jesus really was flesh and blood, and belief in the incarnation is a prerequisite for participating in the rituals of the church.

More-recent scholarship has focused on the importance of ritual and the conventions of ritual meals in antiquity. This trend will be treated under "Significance of the Last Supper" in the theological issues section of 13:1–38.

Manna and the Bread of Life

Reference to a future banquet in which Israel shall eat a meal of manna is a repeated motif in early Jewish eschatological and rabbinic literature: "And it will happen at that time that the treasury of manna will come down again from on high, and they will eat of it in those years because these are they who will have arrived at the consummation of time" (2 Bar. 29.8, trans. A. F. J. Klijn, in OTP 1:631; see also Sib. Or. 7.149). Mekilta on Exod. 16:25 reports that "you will not find it [manna] in this world, but you will find it in the world to come" (trans. Hammer 1995, 125; see also Pesiq. Rab Kah. 5.8; Num. Rab. 11.2; Ruth Rab. 5.6; Eccles. Rab. 1.9). The identification of manna as one of the rewards for members of the church in Pergamum who remain steadfast (Rev. 2:17) corroborates that this Jewish tradition has its roots in the Second Temple period.

Second Temple literature associates manna with wisdom and Torah (e.g., Philo, Mut. 259–60; Leg. 3.162, 169–76; Neh. 9:20; Mek. 13.17; Exod. Rab. 25.7; Jos. Asen. 16; see Hylen 2005, 101). The basis of this association lies perhaps in Deuteronomy's claim that God feeds his people with manna to teach them that one "does not live on bread alone, but by every word that comes from the mouth of the LORD" (Deut. 8:3). Peder Borgen (1981, 20) argues that John worked fragments from the haggadah (the traditions informing the order of Passover meal) into the composition of 6:31–58.

The current scholarly discussion centers on whether the Gospel of John presents Jesus as a replacement for these Jewish traditions (e.g., Lindars 1972;

Yee 1989), in which case Christianity supersedes Judaism, or whether the Gospel develops these Jewish traditions (e.g., Rensberger 1999, 146; Hylen 2005, 181–88). At stake is whether one sees the Gospel of John as a document of a religion that defines itself apart from Judaism, or whether one sees the Gospel as a document of a group that sees itself in continuity with Jewish tradition. If John 6 is seen in continuity with John 5, Jesus's work stands in continuity with God's life-giving gift of the manna in the wilderness. The dualism of the language of death versus life that marks the contrast between the manna eaten in the wilderness (6:49, 58) and the consumption of Jesus's flesh (6:33, 51, 54, 56–58) builds upon eschatological expectations. Nothing that Jesus says about the manna offends his audience; otherwise their request for the bread from heaven in verse 34 would make no sense. It therefore makes sense to treat the comparison as an example of an encomium comparing its subject favorably with an established standard. The paradox that Jesus will bring life through his death becomes the polemical edge of the discourse.

Predestination, Providence, and Free Will

On the one hand, John 6:43–45 and possibly 6:37, 39 (see also 12:32) depict God selecting who will accept Jesus in advance of their encounter with Jesus. On the other hand, John 6:35 and 40 as well as 6:51–66 seem to depict the believer as exercising choice. The tension in these verses becomes acute in theological discussions of God's control of the future, and human ability to affect the course of events through the exercise of their free will. Augustine of Hippo (AD 354–430) first raises the problem with reference to John 6:44 when he notes that one might ask how a person can believe if they are drawn by force against one's will (*Tract. Ev. Jo.* 26.2–3, NPNF[1] 7:168–69). He resolves the problem by quoting Virgil and calling the divine force "love" so that the believer is drawn not by necessity but by "pleasure; not obligation, but delight" (*Tract. Ev. Jo.* 26.4, NPNF[1] 7:169). John Calvin was not satisfied with this answer and resolved the tension in favor of predestination. The notion that someone could reject the gospel raised the possibility in his mind that the gospel was somehow flawed. In *Concerning the Eternal Predestination of God* (written in 1552), Calvin cites John 6:37, 44–45 to make the case that faith is a gift that God bestows upon a select group whom he deems worthy (1997, 5.2). Calvin deemed human will to be too weak an instrument to overcome pride or to persevere and do the will of God (5.3).

Given that making a case for either determinism or free will is not the point of Jesus's argument and given that Jesus makes assertions that support both sides of the debate, an understanding of his position may need to proceed from a middle ground. While individuals may exercise choice, the range of choices possible is determined by preceding events and existing conditions. Paul Anderson contends that the Bread of Life discourse makes visible the "dialogical character of revelation." God initiates a dialogue with humans but how they respond is voluntary. As Anderson (1997, 260) puts it, "On one hand, *no one can come* to God without divine facilitation; on the other, *all who come and believe* are enabled to become children of God." Paula Fredriksen (2000, 22) contends that John does not offer a theology of predestination but rather makes clear that those who believe are then chosen insofar as God and Jesus then confer a status on them. Juxtaposed with the narrative of the feeding that features Jesus's absolute control of the situation, the rhetorical purpose of the assertion that God draws believers is to reassure those who trust in Jesus that they are God's people and that Jesus's incarnation, death, and resurrection are divine providence.

John 7:1–8:59

Verbal Sparring at the Festival of Sukkoth

Introductory Matters

Direct speech dominates in the next two chapters. This can prove daunting for modern readers who must negotiate a complicated narrative structure containing dialogue in which Jesus uses shocking insults and makes long complicated arguments, with little narrative reprieve. The narrator refers to Jesus's teaching in the temple (7:14, 28; 8:2). That speech appears in fragments interrupted by debate or verbal contest (*agōn*) with his audience, in which Jesus puts forward a series of arguments in defense of his teaching. John periodically inserts a series of debates within the crowd that show the Gospel's audience how Jesus's words are being received. John also interlaces the story of the growing conspiracy by presenting the simultaneous deliberations of the Pharisees who first eavesdrop on Jesus and the crowd, next send agents to stop Jesus's speaking by apprehending him, then disagree with Nicodemus about the legality of their actions, and finally enter into direct dialogue with Jesus (see sidebar "Simultaneous Action in Ancient Narrative" at 18:1–19:42). Added to this are periodic asides from the narrator. To complicate matters, the story of the adulterous woman has been interpolated into the narrative. Table 3 provides a picture of the complexity of the action. Through these debates, John dramatizes both the world's inability to recognize Jesus and makes visible the doggedness of the Jewish authorities to resist Jesus's rhetoric and to cling to their decision to repress him.

131

Table 3. Narrative Complexity in John 7–8

Jesus's Speech	The *Agōn*	Crowd Debates	Simultaneous Action	Narrator's Aside	Interpolated Action
		Where is he? (7:11–12)			
				No one spoke openly because . . . (7:13)	
	You teach without authority (7:15–24)				
		Is he the Christ? (7:25–27)			
	continues (7:28–29)				
			Authorities send agents (7:30–32)		
I am with you still for a short time (7:33–34)					
		Is he traveling to the Diaspora? (7:35–36)			
Come to me and drink (7:37–38)					
				He said this regarding . . . (7:39)	
		Is he the Prophet? (7:40–44)			
			Agents report (7:45–52)		
				They were putting him to the test (8:5–6)	Adulterous woman (7:53–8:11)

Jesus's Speech	The *Agōn*	Crowd Debates	Simultaneous Action	Narrator's Aside	Interpolated Action
I am the light of the world (8:12)					
Father testifies on my behalf (8:13–19)					
				He spoke these words because ... (8:20)	
I am going away (8:21)					
		Who are you? (8:22–27)		They did not know ... (8:27)	
Then you will know that I am (8:28–32)					
	Our Father is Abraham (8:33–47)				
I honor my Father (8:48–58)					

Agōn

Greco-Roman epics, tragedies, and histories frequently include an *agōn*, a debate that imitates the standard oratorical and rhetorical features of the debates heard in courtrooms and political assemblies (e.g., Euripides, *Med.* 1323–60; Thucydides, *Hist.* 3.52–68). In Homer's *Iliad*, the warriors fight with words more than with swords. The *agōn* includes long speeches that move through a series of legal, logical, or moral arguments. In some cases the opponent responds with shorter speeches or ones of equal length. The setting can be a formal trial or an interlude in the action, in which the losing side or victim is provided an opportunity to speak. According to Elton T. E. Barker (2009, 1–30), the purpose of a literary *agōn* is to allow the audience to listen to the dissenting voice, which is often silenced in actual public life.

Parrhēsia

The Greco-Roman world valued *parrhēsia*, frank or candid speech, as a hallmark of a freeborn status. Slaves were not free to speak their minds (Euripides, *Ion* 668–75; *Phoen.* 391); citizens were (Dionysius of Halicarnassus, *Ant. rom.* 7.31.2). Tyranny deprived one of the freedom to speak (Demosthenes, *Halon.* 7.1; Plutarch, *Dion* 34.3). One's wisdom and virtue were measured in part by one's use of *parrhēsia*. One did not withhold the truth from friends, especially truthful criticism (Plutarch, *Adul. amic.* 50b; Seneca, *Ep.* 52.12; 75.5). But in public, it was more judicious to be circumspect about what one said. *Parrhēsia* is a gift of the Spirit at Pentecost (Acts 4:23–31) and appears on the list of Christian virtues (2 Cor. 3:12; 7:4; Phil. 1:12–20; 1 Thess. 2:2; Philem. 8–9).

John 7:1–8:59 in the Narrative Flow

In the beginning (1:1–2:12)

Jesus's itinerant ministry (2:13–12:11)

 Transforming sacred space (2:13–4:54)

 God works on the Sabbath (5:1–47)

 Bread and circuses (6:1–71)

▶ Verbal sparring at the Festival of Sukkoth (7:1–8:59)

  The narrative setup (7:1–13)

  Day 1: The source of Jesus's teaching (7:14–36)

  Day 2: The deliverance Jesus offers (7:37–8:59)

While Jesus's violation of the Sabbath remains in focus, the conflicts do not revolve around what he does, as in the Synoptic Gospels, so much as around what he says in his self-defense and the frankness (*parrhēsia*) with which he speaks. When reading these dialogues, it is crucial for the audience to recall that John employs dramatic irony. We know what the narrative audience does not know. Alicia Myers points out that the failure of Jesus's words "to persuade characters *within* the Gospel" is "a key component to the believability of his character for those listening *to* the Gospel as a whole." The reaction of the Jews is an index of how candidly Jesus speaks. The incredulity of Jesus's audience is paradoxically an indicator of the truth with which Jesus speaks. Those who find Jesus's words to be inappropriate respond appropriately, given their limited knowledge. Jesus's words are shocking unless one is given a special revelation of Jesus's identity, such as that found in the prologue or witnessed by individuals such as John the Baptist or the Beloved Disciple. The purpose of these dialogues is to persuade the Gospel's audience, not the narrative audience, of the truth of his words (Myers 2009).

Tracing the Narrative Flow

The Narrative Setup (7:1–13)

The episode begins with a reference to the plot to kill Jesus, of which he is cognizant, that prevents him from returning to Judea and keeps him **wandering about in the Galilee** (7:1). Once again, John represents Jesus's itinerant status as evasion of authorities rather than the nature of his teaching ministry. To those unaware of the plot—his brothers and the crowd—Jesus's words or actions provoke criticism. When **Sukkoth**, or Tabernacles, one of three Second Temple Jewish pilgrimages to Jerusalem, **draws near** (7:2), Jesus's brothers taunt him: "**Get going and go up to Judea in order that your disciples** [there] **will also take in** [*theōrēsousin*] **the deeds that you do**" (7:3). Their use of the term "disciple" to refer to the ambivalent crowd in Jerusalem mocks Jesus's following. They continue to goad him: "**For no one does such things in secret; he seeks to be candid** [*parrhēsia*]. **If you do these things, make yourself known to the world**" (7:4). The narrator adds an aside—**For not even his brothers were believing in him** (7:5)—so that one cannot mistake their encouragement for sincerity even if one does not know the cultural norms that render such a speech sarcastic. Within the ancient social context, seeking fame is a dangerous act. Philodemus of Gadara (ca. 110–35 BC, a teacher of Virgil) notes that becoming renowned does not lead to security and that the safer route is to withdraw from the crowd and keep company with friends (*Vit.* 9, P.Herc. 1424, col. 23.11–18). Frankness of speech is something that one tends to limit to the private realm in antiquity unless one's power and authority is supreme.

Whereas the synoptic kin try to stop Jesus from teaching because he is shaming the family (Mark 3:21), the Johannine brothers goad him into public humiliation. Jesus seems to be acknowledging that they are trying to score points at his expense: "**My time is not yet come, but your time is always at hand**" (7:6). He then demonstrates frankness of speech by naming the reality of his situation. "**It is not possible for the world to hate you, but me it hates, because I am testifying concerning it that its deeds are evil**" (7:7), but he withholds the truth when he says, "**You go up to the festival; I am not going up to this festival, because my** [measure of] **time has not yet been completed**" (7:8). Given the forthrightness with which Jesus speaks elsewhere in the Gospel, its absence here is startling, but within the context of the Greco-Roman world, his deception would be considered prudent rather than wrong. Jesus's speech reveals the quality of the brothers' relationship and not his own character. His lack of frankness is prompted by their disingenuous flattery. Given their lack of belief in Jesus, thus their lack of friendship, frankness is denied them.

After saying these things, he remained in the Galilee (7:9). **But when his brothers went up to the festival, then he also went up, not openly but in secret** (7:10). Once again, Jesus's stealth offends some modern sensibilities, but within the ancient Mediterranean context, deception can be seen as necessary and admirable. A short-term strategy to mislead in order to achieve a noble end, such as Odysseus's disguise when he returns home (Homer, *Od.* 13.429–38), could be worthy of praise.

John sets the scene for Jesus's arrival, showing his audience that his presence is anticipated but that his reception will be mixed. **Then the Jews were seeking him at the festival and were saying, "Where is that** [man]**?**" (7:11).

And there was much grumbling about him in the crowd. Some were saying that he is a good [man], but others were saying, "No, on the contrary, he leads the crowd astray" (7:12). The wording of the accusation suggests that he is considered a false prophet (see Deut. 13:1–15). John handles the collective voice of the crowd in a manner comparable to the chorus in a Greek tragedy. The tragic chorus is a spectator on the stage that deliberates about the possible significance of what it sees and, in doing so, dramatizes the ambiguity of the human predicament. Both the chorus and John's crowd make visible that they either do not know their own minds or that they are of two minds.

The narrator provides a foil for Jesus's frank speech by describing the crowd's reticence: **Nevertheless, no one spoke about him openly on account of fear of the Jews** (7:13). John uses a classic technique for creating suspense by describing fear and its effects but not the object of their fear (e.g., Amos 2:14–16). He depicts a climate of repression in which frank speech is most dangerous. At the back of the audience's mind ought to be the contrast with Jesus's final entry into the city (12:12–19). The sorts of things that Jesus has been doing do not prompt a spontaneous and enthusiastic chorus of hallelujah. It will be the raising of Lazarus that leads the Jerusalem crowd to hail Jesus as king (12:13).

Day 1: The Source of Jesus's Teaching (7:14–36)

Only in the middle of the feast did Jesus go up to the temple, and he was teaching (7:14). What he teaches is not the issue; John chooses not to cloud the controversy with too much detail. That he teaches is the problem.

The accusation. Jesus's teaching provokes amazement and an accusation presented as a question: **"How does this [fellow] know [so much] without having studied letters?"** (7:15). The wording suggests that Jesus can do more than read; it implies Jesus possesses some level of erudition. This is not necessarily a compliment. The degree to which Jesus's knowledge deserves respect depends on at whose feet he sat to gain it. Knowledge in antiquity was the repository of sage tradition, not the invention of genius or the result of a process of discovery. Being an autodidact is not something to which one aspired in antiquity (see Gerhardsson 1998, 204–5).

Jesus's self-defense. Jesus must demonstrate the authority of his teaching by establishing the line of transmission: **"My teaching is not mine but of the one who sent me"** (7:16). Jesus throws the onus for refuting this claim back on his dialogue partners. **"If anyone wants to do his will, he will know regarding the teaching whether it is from God or if I am speaking from myself"** (7:17). This is an indirect way of saying, "I have received it from God; it is not my own invention." Jesus proceeds by making a point with which his audience is meant to agree. **"The one who speaks from himself [invents ideas] seeks his own glory, whereas the one seeking the glory of the one who sent him, this one is honest, and unrighteousness is not in him"** (7:18). In antiquity, art was discovered; it followed rules. Poetry was inspired. The invention of an individual was not knowledge or insight. According to educational philosopher Kieran Egan (1992, 13), "The imagination in both ancient Greek and Hebrew traditions represents a rebellion against divine order, it disturbs the proper harmony between the human and the divine worlds, and it empowers people with a capacity that is properly divine."

Jesus then proceeds to an example of a teaching with an accepted provenance from God by using the rhetorical strategy of asking a question that forces the audience to answer in the affirmative and therefore to agree with him. "**Has not Moses given you the law?**" But he quickly turns to an accusation: "**And** [yet] **not one of you keeps the law.**" Rather than stating what commandments they violate, he implies that they act unjustly by asking them, "**Why do you seek to kill me?**" (7:19). John later places on Nicodemus's lips the explanation of how this violates the law (7:51).

An interruption. The crowd dismisses the question as unfounded and returns once more to the issue of the source of Jesus's words. Since they do not come from a recognized authority, they attribute them to a malevolent force: "**You have a demon. Who is seeking to kill you?**" (7:20). Paranoia is a modern diagnosis for unwarranted fear. This is not what they accuse Jesus of experiencing. The notion that a demon controls Jesus points to the slanderous nature of his words. Jesus also associates lies with the devil (8:44). Their question supports their assertion, because indeed, at this point, no one has said or done anything life threatening. The Gospel's audience, however, knows that Jesus demonstrates his prescience.

Jesus resumes. Jesus does not address the charge but rather continues to impugn the judgment of the crowd: "**I did** [one] **deed, and you are all amazed** (7:21) **on this account.**" The one deed seems to be the healing of the lame man and the amazement that he would heal a man on the Sabbath. Jesus proceeds to an argument in the form of a comparison. He begins with a premise about which there is a consensus: "**Moses has given you circumcision—not that it is from Moses but from the fathers—and on a Sabbath you circumcise a man**" (7:22). He includes a self-correction that underscores both that the practice of circumcision is older than Moses and that Jesus is knowledgeable. He then asks a rhetorical question, comparing his violation of the Sabbath with a permitted violation in order to challenge the warrant of their anger. "**If a man receives circumcision on a Sabbath in order not to violate the law of Moses, are you filled with black** [bile] **because I made a man entirely healthy on a Sabbath?**" (7:23). Jesus's wording reflects the ancient understanding that emotion is the product of an imbalance of bodily humors. Anger is the result of an excess of black bile (*cholē*). This is a very clever argument that deserves close attention. Jesus puts forward a case where one works on the Sabbath in order to keep the patriarchal law central to fidelity to the covenant. The implication is that Jesus works on the Sabbath in order to be obedient to God, one of the essential aspects of righteousness. In doing so, he does not accuse the crowd of breaking the law. He accuses them of making an issue of something that is not an issue. Jesus ends the argument with an imperative that makes his point explicit: "Do not judge based on sight, but [with] righteous judgment judge" (7:24). If they persist in treating his actions as a violation of God's will, they exercise poor judgment.

The crowd debates internally. John takes a break from the main action to allow the crowd to reveal its confusion and to comment on the action. This interlude functions like the *stasimon*, a choral ode in Greek tragedy in which the chorus comments on or reacts to the preceding action in order to measure the mood of the scene. The crowd's anxiety about Jesus is not assuaged but heightened. Some members of the crowd of Jerusalemites seem to have privileged knowledge: "Is this not the one whom they are seeking to kill?" (7:25). They know what Jesus knows: some unnamed agents do have lethal intent. Jesus's frankness provokes a line of reasoning opposite to that pursued in 7:20: "And look, he is speaking openly and no one is speaking to him." The fact that no one in authority is telling Jesus to stop talking or taking issue with what he says leads to a suspicion: "Do the authorities perhaps in fact know that this man is the Christ?" (7:26). Here, as elsewhere, John underscores the uncertainty that tempers their conclusions by putting them in the form of a question. This sort of speculation provides warrant for the authorities' later observation that if Jesus is not stopped, everyone will follow him (11:48).

The crowd's thoughts are kept in a state of unrest because they have mitigating evidence with which to contend: "But we know from where this man comes, while at such time as the Christ comes, no one is to know from where he comes" (7:27). John presents the corporate voice's deliberating in a manner that shows that looking at Jesus through the lens of traditional expectations leads to confusion. This verse also prevents one from lining up John's representation of the crowd's knowledge with some sort of normative Judaism. If people are expecting a Davidic messiah, they should anticipate that he comes from Bethlehem (Mic. 5:2).

Jesus's concluding assertion begins. While the crowd describes its own confusion, Jesus denies the validity of this mental state by asserting the contrast between what they ought to know and what he does know: "But me you know, and you know from where I am [i.e., from where I come], and on my own accord I have not come, but he is trustworthy, the one who sent me, whom you do not know (7:28). I know him because I am from him, and that one sent me" (7:29). John then interrupts Jesus's speech to show how it is being received.

The Pharisees' simultaneous action. Rather than seeing the following account as a series of failed arrest attempts, it is possible that John captures simultaneous action by quickly describing the efforts of the authorities to arrest Jesus; then he gives an expanded account in which we see the behind-the-scenes activity of the authorities, which leads to the arrest attempt (7:32–36). The narrator responds to the crowd's bewilderment in 7:20 by describing in summary the thwarted actions of the authorities: **They were seeking in fact to grab him, and yet no one laid hands upon him, because his hour had not yet come** (7:30). In Greek, the imperfect tense "were seeking" (*ezētoun*) can denote a parallel event. John makes clear that it is the crowd's reaction and not Jesus's words that is the provocation for the arrest: **Many from the crowd believed in him and were saying, "At such time as the Christ comes, will he not do many signs such as this man has done?"** (7:31). John shows their thoughts moving in the right direction, but their

> ### Allo-Repetition
>
> Allo-repetition is repetition of another's words, which can serve various rhetorical purposes. Children often use this form of rhetoric to ridicule the other. It can also signal incredulity, lack of comprehension, or disagreement in preparation for a counterclaim.

habit of projecting the coming of the messiah into the future prevents them from recognizing that he has come. He then provides an expanded account of the efforts noted in 7:30. **The Pharisees heard the crowd grumbling these things about him, and the high priests and Pharisees sent attendants so that they might nab him** (7:32).

Jesus resumes his speech. **"I am with you still for a short time, and [then] I go away to the one who has sent me** (7:33). **You will seek me, and you will not find me, and where I am, you are not able to come"** (7:34).

The crowd debates internally. John's readers and audience enjoy the privilege of knowing what Jesus means and watching the crowd's comic confusion: **Then the Jews said to one another, "To where is this one going to travel that we will not find him; surely he is not going to travel to the Greek Diaspora to teach the Greeks [is he]?"** (7:35). John provides a glimpse into one way in which Jesus's audience is able to make sense of what he is saying by using the knowledge they have of the world. Stories of heavenly ascent do not inform their imagination at this point. The Jews' questions point to frustration by taking the form of allo-repetition: **"What is [the meaning of] this word that he said, 'You will seek me and you will not find me, and where I am, you are not able to come?'"** (7:36). At this point the Jews can be either the temple attendants or the crowd or both. Given what happens when the attendants report back to the authorities, it seems as though John refers to the attendants who have entered into the crowd's deliberations.

Day 2: The Deliverance Jesus Offers (7:37–8:59)

Jesus resumes his speech. John marks the passage of time and the resumption of Jesus's speech. It seems that the attendants have lost sight of their orders and have joined the crowd. **On the next day, the major day of the festival, Jesus stood and shouted out, saying, "If anyone thirsts, come to me and drink** (7:37); **the one who believes in me [come and drink], just as the**

Writing [one of the *Ketubim*] said, 'Out of his belly will gush rivers of living water'" (7:38). The awkward construction allows the belly to belong to either the believer or Jesus. This translation throws the accent on Jesus by repeating the invitation in 7:37 and treating the fulfillment text as yet another example of Scripture's witness to Jesus (see 5:39–40). Maarten J. J. Menken (1996) suggests that Jesus refers to Ps. 77:16, 20 LXX (= 78:16, 20 Eng.), with the addition of the epithet "living" from Zech. 14:8, and appropriates imagery associated with the water ritual that took place on the first day of Sukkoth. Joel Marcus (1998) concurs that Jesus quotes both the psalm and Zechariah but suggests that the backdrop is the joyful ritual of drawing waters from Siloam that, according to the Talmud, took place on the second night of the festival.

However much modern readers might want to speculate about the associations invoked by Jesus's words, the narrator focuses attention on Jesus's reference to a future event: **He said this concerning the Spirit that those who believed in him were going to receive; for [the] Spirit was not yet [received] because Jesus was not yet glorified** (7:39). For those familiar with the book of Acts, John seems to refer to the gift of the Spirit at Pentecost, but John will confute Luke's timeline by narrating the receipt of the Spirit in a resurrection appearance scene (20:22).

The crowd debates internally. Jesus's words provoke a dispute about whether Jesus fulfills messianic expectations. **Some of the crowd, upon hearing these words, were saying, "This is surely the prophet"** (7:40); **but others were saying, "This is the Christ," while some were saying, "No, for does the Christ come from the Galilee?** (7:41). **Does Scripture not say that Christ comes from the seed of David and from Bethlehem, the village where David was [born]?"** (7:42). The crowd now appears to know what the crowd speaking in 7:27 did not. John does not develop a consistent identity for the crowd or distinguish between groups that he calls the crowd or the Jews. Emphasis is on the action. The crowd is paralyzed by indecision, leaving the timing of Jesus's arrest to God's providential schedule: **So a rift then developed in the crowd on account of him** (7:43). **Some of them wanted to nab him** [presumably including the attendants], **but none laid hands upon him** (7:44).

The simultaneous action. John turns his audience's attention to the attendants' uncompleted mission. **Then the attendants came to the chief priests and the Pharisees, and those** [authorities] **said to them, "Why have you not brought him?"** (7:45). **The attendants replied, "Never [before] has a man spoken in this way"** (7:46). The audience now sees retrospectively that the attendants have indeed joined the crowd. The Pharisees then invoke Deut. 13:6–11 that warns the Israelites against being led into worship of other gods by a prophet-enticer: **"You haven't also been led astray?** (7:47). **Surely none of the authorities has believed in him, nor [have] the Pharisees?** (7:48). **But this crowd, which does not know the law, is accursed"** (7:49).

At this point, John brings Nicodemus in sight. Nicodemus will try to lead the authorities into a deliberative mode and away from the false sense of certainty that their words reflect. John underscores Nicodemus's Pharisaic status: **Nicodemus, who had come to him** [Jesus] **earlier** [see 3:1–2], **being one of them, says to them** (7:50), **"Our law does not judge a man unless it first hears from him and knows what he does, does it?"** (7:51). Nicodemus voices conventional legal opinion (see Josephus, *Ant.* 14.167; *J.W.* 1.209; *Exod. Rab.* 21.3). The authorities dismiss his point by making an ad hominem argument (an attack upon his person that betrays their fallacious reasoning) by suggesting that he is acting as if he is one of Jesus's accursed followers: **"Surely you are not from the Galilee** [are you]?**"** They then impugn his judgment directly: **"Search and see that a prophet does not arise from the Galilee"** (7:52). Their invitation to search Scripture (something that Pharisees do) is a piece of irony, for they circumvent the task of inquiry by providing Nicodemus with the conclusion he must reach in order to be one of them. At first, Nicodemus speaks with frankness as one who corrects, but when he does not reply, he is shown to lack the steadfastness (*asphaleia*) requisite to a virtue such as *parrhēsia*. Philodemus points to how this scene would be received by a Greco-Roman audience: "If, then, the wise know each other, they will gladly be reminded by one another . . . and will feel a biting sting and will be gracious" (*Lib.*, P.Herc. 1471, col. 8b.6–13). In this quick exchange, John captures the Pharisees' sacrifice of their own reputation as accurate interpreters of the law as well as Nicodemus's struggle to be both constant and loyal to his associates. Greek and Roman philosophers identify *asphaleia* and *pistis* (loyalty), in Latin as *constantia* and *fides*, as two of the principal qualities that are hallmarks of a friend (e.g., Epictetus, *Diatr.* 2.22.29–30; Cicero, *Amic.* 19, 65). To fulfill these virtues, Nicodemus needs to switch his allegiance to Jesus.

An interpolated story. Any study of John 7:53–8:11 should begin with Gail O'Day (1992). Manuscript evidence indicates that John 7:53–8:11 was not an episode in the Gospel before the fifth century. The number of textual variants in the manuscripts that do contain it and the way it disrupts the flow of the broader unit also point to its status as an interpolation. Some scholars believe that it was inserted to illustrate that Jesus could write, but it seems significant that it follows an episode in which due process is discarded. Jesus demands a stricter process.

The action in 7:53 seems to pick up after 7:44, when some want to seize Jesus but do not. **And they each one walked away to his house** (7:53), **but Jesus walked away to the Mount of Olives** (8:1). John assumes that his audience knows this is where Jesus and the disciples camped while in Jerusalem. **At dawn he was again in attendance in the temple, and all the people came to him, and taking a seat, he taught them** (8:2). John now switches to the historic present as though his audience watches the action unfold: **The scribes and the Pharisees** bring a woman caught in adultery and placing her in the middle (8:3), they say to him, "Teacher, this woman has been caught blatantly committing adultery (8:4). In our law Moses commanded such [women] to be stoned. What do you then say?" (8:5). The narrator then interrupts to provide their motives. **They were saying this, putting him to the test, so that they might have [grounds] to accuse him.** Such a test would serve to support the allegation that Jesus's teachings are his own invention rather than based on the authority of the law and tradition. Though John provides little content to Jesus's teaching upon which to reconstruct the answer they anticipate, it seems logical to assume that Jesus is supposed to disagree with the penalty.

John emphasizes that Jesus at first ignores their question: **Jesus, stooping over, was etching in the dirt with a finger** (8:6). Some manuscripts include **affecting not to listen.** Etching (*katagraphō*) can signify a wide range of actions from scratching to writing to drawing, but given that the Pharisees do not comment on the action, precision in translation is not necessary. **As they continued interrogating him, he lifted up his head and said to them, "The one of you without sin throw a stone [at] her first"** (8:7). **And stooping down again, he etched in the dirt** (8:8). John does not indicate that the men look at what takes shape in the dirt; he describes their dramatic and deliberate response to Jesus's words. The gesture of etching seems to signal that Jesus has nothing more to add and is not interested in debate. **Those listening exited one by one, beginning with the elders** [some manuscripts include *heōs tōn eschatōn*, **until the last**], **and the woman was left alone being in the middle** (8:9). The verb and the parade are evocative of the *exodos* (recessional) of a Greek chorus from a stage. **Jesus then lifting his head said to her, "Woman, where are they? Is there no one to condemn you?"** (8:10). **But the [woman] said, "No one, Lord."** **Then Jesus said, "Neither do I condemn you. Walk away, and from now on sin no more!"** (8:11).

Rather than using the language of forgiveness to describe what has happened, it is more appropriate to note the agreement with what Jesus says to the lame man in 5:14 or will say in 12:47 in his climactic public speech. Jesus, in keeping with what he says in 3:16; 8:17; and 12:47, chooses not to judge her.

Jesus resumes his speech. The chronology of events is quite complicated and again gives the impression of concurrent rather than sequential action. Jesus resumes the speech interrupted after he invites those who are thirsty to drink (7:37–38): **"I am the light of the world. The one listening to me shall definitely not walk about in the dark but will have the light of life"** (8:12). Isaiah uses the phrase "light of the world" as a metaphor to describe the role of God's servant in the deliverance of the nations (42:6; 49:6). Jesus makes a bolder claim. In the context of the Feast of Sukkoth, the emphatic language of "I am" echoes the divine name *YHWH*. Jesus claims to be a theophany of God's glory that led the Israelites from bondage in Egypt and that now dwells in the temple (see Coloe 2001, 135–36, 142–43).

The days of Jesus's words going uncontested by the authorities have come to an end. Pharisees now enter the main action and take issue with him. What follows is some of the most difficult argumentation to understand and to accept. Jesus attacks his opponents with language that, especially in a post-Holocaust setting, many regret. The series of speeches that stretch from 8:12–59 resemble the patterns of the legal and moral arguments found in the classical *agōn*. The unit contains three discrete arguments. In the first (8:13–19), the Pharisees appear as the plaintiff, and Jesus responds as the defendant by arguing that the witnesses on his behalf are valid. In the second (8:33–47), Jesus takes the opposite approach by questioning the validity of his opponents' judgment. In the third (8:48–58), Jesus defends his honor.

First argument: "My testimony is valid." The Pharisees articulate the objection that Jesus has anticipated in 5:31: **"*You* are testifying on your own behalf; testimony of yours is not valid"** (8:13; italics indicate deictic pronouns). Jesus repeats their allegation because he cannot refute the fact that he is testifying on his own behalf; therefore he argues that his testimony is valid because he knows the facts of the case: **"Even if *I* testify on my own behalf, valid is testimony of mine, because I know from where I came and where I am going. But *you* do not know from where I come or where I am going"** (8:14). Unlike his opponents, he does not have to determine whether a witness is true or false. **"*You* judge according to the flesh; *I* do not judge anyone at all"** (8:15). He backtracks from this point by arguing that as God's agent, he is an authoritative judge. **"And even if *I* did judge, my judgment is truthful, because I am not alone, but *I* and also the Father who sent me** [are truthful]" (8:16). He then appeals to the law and argues that he has two witnesses: himself and God. **"And in the law of your own it is written that the testimony of two men is valid** (8:17). *I* am the one testifying on my own behalf, and the Father who sent me testifies on my behalf"** (8:18). This argument provokes the Pharisees to demand that Jesus bring forth the witness to whom he appeals: **"Where is** [this] **father of yours?"** Jesus can now end his argument with a condemnation of his opponents for failing to know God: **"You know neither me nor my Father; if you knew me, then you would also know my Father"** (8:19). As far as logic goes, this argument is too tautological (circular) to qualify for great deliberative or forensic rhetoric. It simply demonstrates that Jesus knows more than his opponents.

Jesus resumes his speech. The narrator begins with some scenic detail and repetition of the observation that efforts to arrest Jesus have failed. **He spoke these words in the treasury while teaching in the temple, and no one nabbed him, because his hour had not yet come** (8:20). Jesus picks up an assertion that he makes both in 7:33–34 and in his argument to the Pharisees in 8:14. **Again he said to them, "*I* am going away, and you will seek me,"** and adds the assertion **"and in your sin you will die; where *I* go away, *you* are not able to come"** (8:21).

Dialogue with the crowd. In the final interruption by the crowd, Jesus enters into dialogue with it. The crowd's questions lag one step behind Jesus's answers with comic result. The crowd does not respond to his words of condemnation but continues its deliberations begun in 7:35–36: "**Surely he isn't going to kill himself** [is he], **given that he says, 'Where** *I* **am going away** *you* **are not able to come'?**" (8:22). Jesus responds to their speculation: "*You* **are from below,** *I* **am from above.** *You* **are from this world,** *I* **am not from this world**" (8:23). He then draws attention to the fact that he is reiterating his initial words of condemnation. The implication is that they have not attended to the significance of what he has said. "**As I was saying to you, you will die in your sins; for unless you believe that** *I* **am, you will die in your sins**" (8:24). The repetition indicates that Jesus is emphatic, but it also points to Jesus's perception of his narrative audience as slow to understand. John measures the foolishness of their question "[And] *You* **are who?**" by capturing Jesus's exasperation: "**What have I been saying** [durative present] **to you from the beginning?**" (8:25). He then repeats what he has said: "**Many things** *I* **have about you to say and to judge, but the one who has sent me is trustworthy, and what** *I* **heard from him, these things I am saying to the world**" (8:26). The suggestion that one could say much more than one says is a common rhetorical device. The narrator ends with an aside just in case his audience has not caught on to the humor that **they did not know that he spoke to them** [about] **the Father** (8:27). Jesus continues to speak in language that is comprehensible to the Gospel's audience but enigmatic to his narrative audience.

Jesus resumes his speech. "**When you lift up the Son of Man, then you will know that** *I* **am, and that I do nothing on my own behalf, but even as the Father taught me, I speak these things**" (8:28). Jesus comes around to the point with which he began in 5:19–20: what he says and does he has learned from his Father. He reasserts that what he does he does in obedience to his Father: "**And the one who sent me is with me, and he has not left me alone, for** *I* **always do that which is acceptable to him**" (8:29). Something surprising now happens—**Upon his saying these things, many believed in him** (8:30)—but Jesus turns to them and challenges the depth of their conviction. **Then Jesus said to the Jews who believed in him, "Whoever of you abides in my word, truly are my disciples** (8:31), **and you will know the truth, and the truth shall free** [*eleutherōsei*] **you**" (8:32). The placement of the second-person pronoun at the end of the sentence is tantamount to a surprising turn in a trial in which a witness points past the defendant to the prosecutor as the guilty party. To free can mean acquittal from the indictment of sin. It can also play on the theme of frank speech and signify that Jesus's disciples speak boldly about what they know to be true (see Acts 4:13).

Debate over the identity of Jesus's opponents. John tends to switch from one group of speakers to another within a crowd in his dialogues; therefore, numerous scholars posit that the group who believed and those who now speak are different entities (see Hunn 2004), but the explicit identification of Jesus's addressees and his emphasis on true discipleship suggest that those who speak in 8:33 are the same group identified in 8:30.

The crowd now pulls away from Jesus by taking his words at a literal level and offense at their implication: **"We are the seed of Abraham and have been enslaved to no one, never. How can *you* say, 'You will become free'?"** (8:33). Calling someone a slave in antiquity was an insult. They overlook that Sukkoth celebrates God's care for the Israelites after he has delivered them from slavery in Egypt. Jesus begins his response with an argument that answers their question, but then he breaks into an accusation. He starts with a premise to which all should agree: **"Truly, truly, I say to you that everyone who does sin is a slave of sin"** (8:34). He then uses an enthymeme beginning with a premise that is sound in his cultural context: **"The slave does not abide in the house forever; the son abides forever"** (8:35). A slave can be sold to another household or be manumitted. Jesus leaves the next premise unstated: the son has authority to execute the father's commands. He then states the conclusion that follows from the two premises: **"If then the son should set you free, you will really be free"** (8:36). He begins the next statement by conceding to their first assertion, **"I know that you are [the] seed of Abraham."** Yet then he levels an accusation, **"but you seek to kill me, because my word [*ho logos ho emos*] does not find room in you"** (8:37). He then follows with an admonition that they should imitate God, building on the unstated premise that a son follows a father's orders: **"What *I* have seen by the Father's side I speak, and therefore, what *you* have heard from the side of the Father, you should do"** (8:38).

The Jews respond by reasserting Abraham's paternity: **"Our father is Abraham."** Jesus discredits their claim by using a form of deductive argument called *modus tollens.* Jesus begins with a conditional statement: **"If you were children of Abraham, you would do the deeds of Abraham"** (8:39). He then demonstrates that the consequence of the condition is not the case. **"But now you are seeking to kill me, a man who has been speaking the truth to you that I heard from the side of the father. Abraham did not do this"** (8:40). Once more Jesus uses an enthymeme and leaves it to his audience to supply the obvious conclusion that they are not Abraham's children. Jesus quickly follows with an accusation—**"*You* do the deeds of your father"**—based once more on the unstated premise that a son does what a father commands. This prompts them to name a different father: **"*We* were not begotten of fornication; we have one father, God"** (8:41). They seem to have trumped Jesus by claiming

---

Modus Tollens

Modus tollens (the way of denying) takes the following form:

If P, then Q
Not Q; therefore, not P

For example:

If it rains, then the ground will be wet.
The ground is not wet; therefore, it did not rain.

God as their father before Jesus has made explicit his claim to be the Son of God. They also imply that Jesus was fathered through an illegitimate act.

Jesus must now refute their claim that God is their father. He begins with an enthymeme in the form of modus tollens: "If you were from God the Father, you would love me, for *I* issue forth from God and I have arrived; for I have not come on my own accord, but rather that one sent me" (8:42). He leaves it to his audience to complete the thought: "You do not love me; therefore you are not from God." Jesus then inserts a rhetorical flourish, asking and then answering his own question (*sibi ipsi responsio*): "Why do you not comprehend my speech? Because *you* are not able to hear my word" (8:43). Jesus steps up the rhetoric by making a counterassertion to their claim that Abraham and then God is their father: "You are from your father the devil and want to do the wishes of your father." He supports his allegation with two assertions that his opponents will agree are valid:

1. "That one was a manslayer [*anthrōpoktonos*; see 1 John 3:15] from the beginning and has not stood in truth, because there isn't truth in him."
2. "Whenever he speaks as he is wont, he speaks the lie, for he is a liar and the father of it" (i.e., lies; 8:44).

Within these assertions lies an implicit argument that can be reduced to a syllogism:

> A son imitates his father.
> You are doing what the devil does by seeking to kill me.
> Therefore, the devil is your father.

The theological issues section of this chapter will take up the consequences of this statement for anti-Judaism. At this point we recognize that the context for this statement is the *agōn* in which Jesus defends himself by dismissing the honor of his accusers rather than part of his proclamation of deliverance with which he began.

Jesus then comes around to his main point. Their inability to discern the truth prevents them from accepting his witness: "Precisely because *I* say the truth, you do not believe me" (8:45). Jesus then uses the rhetorical touch of direct address in which he asks questions that he does not allow his accusers to answer: "Who among you reproaches me concerning sin? If I speak truthfully, why do *you* not believe me?" (8:46). He immediately launches into one more *modus tollens* argument: "The one who is from God hears the words of God; by reason of this—that you are not from God—you do not hear" (8:47).

Jesus defends his honor. The focus of the dialogue shifts back to Jesus's authority when the Jews resort to an ad hominem comeback indicating that they have taken Jesus's attack as an insult rather than a serious allegation about their status. The Jews responded and said to him, "Are we not right in saying that you are a Samaritan and have a demon?" (8:48). Jesus returns to the task of defending himself by denying their second allegation. Jesus replied, "*I do not have a demon*," and then makes a counterassertion, "but I honor my Father, and you hold me in no honor" (8:49). Once more this is implicit criticism based on the social norm that one dishonors a father by failing to give honor to a son. He then provides an amplification of his assertion in the form of an antithetical parallelism: "*I, on the other hand, do not seek my* [own] glory; [while] the one who seeks [glory] is also the one who judges" (8:50). The act of judging Jesus is dishonorable. The more-conventional reading is that the one seeking and judging is God, but in the immediate context, Jesus seems to be implying that those who reject him are seeking their own glory.

The next line seems to begin another thought, but it follows logically from the discussion of glory, for in the Greco-Roman literature and in this Gospel, glory or humiliation is dependent on the nature of one's death or the death that one inflicts on one's opponent: "**Truly, truly, *I* say to you, Whoever keeps my word shall not look on** [*theōrēsē*] **death forever**" (8:51). This line has been construed as a poetic way of saying, "You will have eternal life," but it could equally mean, "You shall not be a spectator of death," or "You will not perceive death." When Jesus's followers look at his crucifixion or their own demise, they ought not to see death at work.

The Jews now take the offensive by ridiculing his assertions with allo-repetition and then either challenge him to make bolder statements at which they can scoff or try to make him back down from his claims: "**Now we know that you have a demon. Abraham died and the prophets, and *you* say, 'Whoever keeps my word, shall not taste death forever'**" (8:52). The Samaritan woman has asked whether Jesus is greater than Jacob. Now the Jews chose an even more prestigious patriarch to demonstrate that Jesus reaches too high: "**Surely *you* are not greater than our father Abraham, one who died? Even the prophets died. Who do you make yourself** [out to be]?" (8:53).

Jesus now defends himself by returning to his main contention in this debate that he does not seek his own glory: "**If ever I suppose myself** [to be greater than Abraham], **my glory is nothing; it is my Father who is glorifying me, the one you are saying is your God**" (8:54). The Greek word for glory, *doxa*, is etymologically related to the verb *doxazō*, "to have an opinion." In the system of honor and shame, honor can exist only in the eye of the beholder. While one can inherit a position of honor, it is nothing if others do not acknowledge it. In what he says next, Jesus implies that his opponents are incapable of honoring him because they do not acknowledge the source of his honor, his Father: "**And you do not know him, whereas *I* [do] know him. If I were to say that I do not know him, I shall come to be like you, a liar.**" The word order delays the insulting punch. Jesus then sets the record straight: "**But I do know him and I keep his word**" (8:55). In other words, Jesus acknowledges and honors his Father's status through his obedience. The verb "keep" (*tēreō*) takes on the nuance of keeping a promise. Jesus fulfills God's promise made to Abraham, "In you all the families of the earth shall be blessed" (Gen.12:3). He therefore adds, **"Our father Abraham rejoiced exceedingly in order that he might see my day, and he saw and rejoiced"** (8:56). Jesus either means "saw" in the metaphoric sense of foresaw, as in "He anticipated it," or he refers to something like the tradition found in the *Apoc. Ab.* 21.3–29.21, in which the archangel Michael gives Abraham the privilege of seeing the whole world through the eyes of an immortal prior to his death.

The Jews seize upon the apparent absurdity of Jesus's claim. **Then the Jews said to him, "Fifty years you have not yet had** [you are younger than fifty years old], **and Abraham have you seen?"** (8:57). Jesus ends with a claim that agrees with 1:1–5. **Jesus said to them, "Truly, truly, I say to you, before Abraham came to be, I am"** (8:58). This seems to be an implicit but clear claim to the divine name *YHWH*, which solicits an expected response within the religious milieu in which Jesus lives. **Then they lifted up stones to throw at him. But Jesus hid and exited the temple** (8:59).

John brings this scene to a clear ending by using Jesus's exit. Until this point, he has neglected actions that demarcate the end of a scene and has used the narrator's comments to close the action and entrances to mark the beginning of a new scene. Exits as well as entrances begin to play a more significant role in the action through the remainder of the Gospel.

Theological Issues

Anti-Judaism in John

This unit adds very little to Johannine Christology and serves more to represent the growing hostility of the authorities. John makes polemical use of the term Jews (*hoi Ioudaioi*) throughout his Gospel, but it becomes most pronounced in these chapters. While the insults that Jesus hurls at his opponents occur in the context of a social milieu in which verbal dueling allowed for creative ad hominem attacks, the statement "You are from your father the devil and want to do the wishes of your father" (8:44) becomes enshrined in later Christian art and literature when Jews were made to look like Satan. The insult becomes justification for blaming Jews for catastrophes such as the bubonic plague. In the last few decades, the question of whether John's Gospel contains or promotes anti-Judaism has come to stand at the center of much of Johannine scholarship. (See Bieringer, Pollefeyt, and Vandecasteele-Vanneuville 2001 for an in-depth discussion.)

John often seems to use *hoi Ioudaioi* as a metonymy for the world. While it is the world that does not know the *logos*, it is people who were Jews with whom Jesus contended; therefore it makes sense that the Jews are named as

Jesus's opponents. Because of the way that John constructs his action and the sense that there is a looming force of opposition, John ignores the realities of subgroup identities. A few scholars entertain the possibility that the author of the Gospel thought of the Jews as others because he was not a Jew or no longer thought of himself as a Jew and was careless of distinctions. As Richard Bauckham (2006, 59) observes, Jews referred to themselves as Israelites, whereas gentiles referred to them as Jews. The Johannine Jesus does not enter into the sectarian debates over such things as purity, divorce, tithing, or fasting that define Second Temple discourse. Jesus speaks only of those who believe or do not believe.

For a number of decades, scholars tried to identify a particular subgroup with which John or his community had particular problems. For example, Marinus De Jonge (1972) argued that it was Jewish Christians and their prophet-messiah Christology with which John took issue (see John 6:60–66; 7:3–5; 8:31). If the Jews are treated as a fictional construction, the question changes from "With whom does the Gospel stand in a polemical relationship?" to "What is the polemic about?" In 7:1–8:59 the central allegation is that it is the nature of the world to seek its own glory by judging manifestations of God's work as sin.

Whatever argument one uses to qualify John's usage, the repeated references to "the Jews," rather than to a particular subgroup, and Jesus's accusation, "You are from your father the devil," cannot be brushed over. Géza Vermès's (2001, 34) contention that "John's hatred of the Jews was fierce" remains a possibility. Modern interpreters ought to be cautious where John is not. Demonizing one's opponent when one is powerless, as early Christians were, is a protest against one's status, but demonizing them when one stands in a position of power or when one knows that such words can incite violence is considered a hate crime in many modern nations.

The Truth Will Free You

The language of freedom (*eleutheria*) belongs to Paul's habitual vocabulary, not John's. John favors the language of everlasting or eternal life when writing of the gift of salvation that Jesus brings. It is only in John 8:33–36 that he employs this language.

The translation "You shall know the truth, and the truth shall make you free" (8:32 KJV) has taken on a life of its own in American culture. It is engraved on the foyer floor of the CIA headquarters and is cited by conspiracy theorists on their webpages as though the truth is something to be uncovered. In contrast, the truth that Jesus proclaims stands right before his audience's eyes. Yet the freedom that he offers may require some uncovering.

In modern discourse, freedom generally refers to personal freedom and the ability to choose a way of life without the interference of an authority. In antiquity, the concept of freedom was tied more closely to the social order.

When Paul uses language of freedom, he frequently refers to the ability of Jews and Greeks, men and women, slaves and masters to enter into fellowship in a time when these distinctions prevented people from sitting at table with one another or speaking frankly with each other (Gal. 3:28). Slaves and women could not enter into contractual relations in Greco-Roman society without approval, but they could freely bind themselves to Christ without permission of masters and husbands.

Some take Jesus's words metaphorically to refer to release from sin's consequences, such as illness (5:14) or guilt (9:41), so that freedom becomes John's language for forgiveness (Talbert 2005, 160). The terms and setting of the discourse, however, point to usage comparable to Paul's meaning. The crowd's claim that they have never been slaves becomes all the more ironic given its timing during the Feast of Sukkoth, in which the Jews are celebrating release from obedience to Pharaoh as his slaves and the joy of obedience to God as their sovereign and protector. Jesus's proclamation that he is the bread of life, the source of living water, and light of the world draws from the rituals associated with Sukkoth and associates him with the gift of divine protection (see Coloe 2001, 115–43). If one knows that Jesus is God's true Son, then one can acknowledge Jesus, openly secure in the knowledge that God will call the believer his own. As the prologue states, those who accept Jesus are granted the privilege to become children of God (1:12). Freedom is then a social status in which one dwells within God's glory.

John 9:1–10:42

A Second Sabbath Violation at a Second Pool

Introductory Matters

The story of the restoration of a man's sight and its aftermath contains three rhetorical features unique to this Gospel. The unit begins with the narration of a Sabbath healing, then moves to a series of scenes comprised of shorter dialogues, in which the blind man's capacity to serve as a witness stands on trial before the Pharisees. This section shares the same dramatic structure as Jesus's trial before Pilate, as well as a number of other elements, that render it what literary critics call *mise en abyme*, or the "Droste effect," a miniature

---

Mise en Abyme

Novelist André Gide first used the term *mise en abyme*, borrowed from a practice in heraldry of putting a smaller shield within one of the quadrants or at the center of a shield, to describe a portion of a work that displays the proportions and subject of the larger work (1954, entry dated 1893; see fig. 15). Literary and art critics also use the term "Droste effect," derived from an early twentieth-century advertisement for Droste cocoa that features a nurse carrying a tray on which is placed a package bearing a miniature version of the advertisement. Examples of this literary technique include "The Murder of Gonzago," the play within a play in Shakespeare's *Hamlet*; the Nisus and Euryalus episode in Virgil's *Aeneid* (9.176–503); and the battle of the Centaurs in Ovid's *Metamorphoses* (12.210–535).

151

Figure 15. Coat of arms of John the Fearless, Duke of Burgundy (AD 1404–19), featuring *mise en abyme*.

version of the story inserted within the story. In the final two sections of the unit, Jesus returns to center stage, and the action pivots to a challenge to the Pharisees' status. Jesus accuses them of being blind, then employs an extended *paroimia* (a proverb), and then a rhetorical, exegetical trap to confute and convict them before escaping their grasp. Within the context of the broader narrative, the healing of the man stands in parallel and tension with the healing in chapter 5. Both are Sabbath healings with pools as part of their setting; both lead to controversy, but when the man who was blind stands as a positive witness to Jesus's identity, Jesus's opponents stand on the defensive. (For parallels, see table 2, at 5:1–47.)

Tracing the Narrative Flow

Jesus Restores a Man's Sight (9:1–7a)

John does not provide a particular place or time for the first scene. The narrator picks up the action immediately after Jesus leaves the temple at the end of chapter 8. That he does not name Jesus suggests that this is a continuation of the narrative in chapters 7–8. John begins the scene through Jesus's focalization: **And as he was walking along, he saw a man blind from birth** (9:1). The duration of the man's blindness makes his suffering pitiable and makes restoration of his sight all the more miraculous. The narrator then brings the disciples into view. Jesus seems to go to Jerusalem by himself in 7:10. This is the first mention of their presence since the defection of a number of their members in 6:66–71. The disciples find cause not to pity the man, asking, **"Rabbi, who sinned, this man or his parents that he be born blind?"** (9:2). John situates the disciples in the company of the authorities as

© Photo by Zev Radovan

Figure 16. Byzantine pool
until recently identified
as the Pool of Siloam.

those who stand in judgment. One should not infer from the disciples' question
that blindness was automatically equated with sin in Second Temple Jewish
societies. This story stands between evidence to the contrary. Tobit (ca. third
cent. BC) is the tale of a man whose blindness is an accidental result of his
righteous actions (2:7–10). A review of later rabbinic literature reveals that the
blind were categorized with the destitute and those incapable of being valid
witnesses and not with sinners. (This discussion continues in the theological
issues section below.)

Jesus turns the disciples' attention away from judgment toward God's creative work: **"Neither did this one nor his parents sin."** The editors of NA[27]
follow the decision of the scribes or interpreters who put a full stop at the
end of the next *hina* clause, thereby suggesting that God made the man blind
so that Jesus would have someone to restore to sight. This translation follows
John C. Poirier's (1996) suggestion by putting a full stop in the middle of 9:3
and making the *hina* clause modify Jesus's actions in the next line: **"But in
order that [*all' hina*] the works of God might be made manifest to you (9:3),
it is necessary for us to work the works of the one who has sent me while
it is day; night is coming, when no one is able to work"** (9:4). The focus of
Jesus's speech is on his role: **"Given that I am in the world, I am [the] light of
the world"** (9:5). The task assigned to Israel in Isa. 61:1–3 and the disciples in
Matt. 5:13 becomes christological in John. Jesus then takes his own metaphor
literally. Not only does he make truth clear; he also makes the blind see.

John continues to reconfigure the typical supplication scene (see my comments on 4:8). The royal official comes to Jesus, and Jesus asks the infirm man

153

Figure 17. Steps to pool discovered in 2004 that dates to the late Second Temple period.

© Photo by Todd Bolen

if he seeks healing, but the blind man, whose suppliant act is begging for money or food, receives healing without dialogue. Without addressing the man, Jesus **spat on the ground and made mud from the spittle and smeared the mud on his eyes** (9:6). The use of what seems to be a therapeutic technique is startling, given that the power of his words are sufficient elsewhere to achieve restoration. As a plot element, the action of making mud eliminates any ambiguity about whether Jesus's actions constitute violation of the Sabbath if the standards enumerated in the Mishnah are applicable in the first century AD (cf. *m. Šabb.* 7.2). As a narrative technique, Jesus's methodical steps slow down the action. He then puts the moment of healing at a distance by directing the man, **"Go along, wash up at the pool of Siloam"** (**which means "having been sent"**) (9:7a), and thereby removes himself from the conflict that follows. By providing a translation of the Hebrew name for the pool, the narrator may simply draw attention to a happy coincidence rather than suggest that the pool's name has symbolic import for the story. If the pool served as a *miqweh*, Jesus's choice indicates that he intends the healing to be a public event (see Shank 2005; for the location of the pool, see fig. 9, map of Jerusalem, at 5:1–47).

The Mise en Abyme *(9:7b–34)*

John hands over a surprising amount of narrative space to the blind man, whose story duplicates, in part, Jesus's narrative (see table 4). The only other Gospel narratives of comparable length in which Jesus is not present appear in the infancy accounts of Mathew and Luke prior to Jesus's birth. For twenty-seven verses, the man who was blind is the principal character in an inquisition narrative marked by a series of dialogues and delineated by exits and entrances. The purpose of *mise en abyme* varies from context to context. John appears to use it as a way of showing his audience that imitation of Jesus is honorable.

Table 4. Parallels between Jesus and the Blind Man

Jesus	Blind Man
Crowd repeatedly deliberates about his identity (e.g., 7:12, 25–27, 40–42)	Crowd deliberates about his identity (9:8–9)
Series of scenes marked by exits and entrances in the trial before Pilate (18:28–19:16)	Series of scenes marked by exits and entrances in the interrogation by the Pharisees (9:13–34)
"I am," *egō eimi*, assertions (e.g., 9:5)	"I am," *egō eimi*, assertion (9:9)
Speaks frankly (e.g., 10:25–30)	Speaks frankly (9:25, 27, 30–33)
Argues with logic (e.g., 8:39–40)	Argues with logic (9:31–34)
Expresses sarcastic astonishment that Nicodemus, a Pharisee, does not understand (3:10)	Expresses sarcastic astonishment that the Pharisees do not understand (9:30)
Accused of being an invalid witness (8:13)	Treated as an invalid witness (9:18)
Accused of being a sinner (e.g., 9:24)	Accused of being a sinner (9:34)
Authority of his teaching questioned (e.g., 7:15)	Accused of trying to teach without authority (9:34)
Jesus throws out (*ekballō*) traders from the temple (2:15) and the "ruler of this world" (12:31) but not his own (6:37). The good shepherd leads out (*ekbalē*) his own (10:4)	Pharisees throw him out (*exebalon*) of the assembly (9:34)

Scene 1: The crowd's inquiry. The formerly blind man becomes the protagonist: **Then he went off and washed and he started seeing** (9:7b). **Then the neighbors and those observing him earlier that he was a beggar were saying, "Is this not the one who was seated** [*kathēmai* suggests that he was placed in a suppliant's position] **and begging?"** (9:8). That the man begs raises a question about his relationship to his family (see the theological issues section below). Once more the crowd begins to deliberate, but now the once-blind man is their object: **Some were saying that, "This is [he]," but others were saying, "Not so, but he is like him."** The man now steps into the role of Jesus by asserting his identity frankly and with the phrase **"I am [*egō eimi*] [he]"** (9:9), a phrase otherwise associated with Jesus. When they ask him **how he comes to be able to see** (9:10), he recounts each detail: **"The man, the one called Jesus, made mud and smeared it on my eyes and said to me that [I should] go along to Siloam and cleanse. Then after going and cleansing, I recovered my sight"** (9:11). The degree of repetition from 9:6 allows the Gospel's audience to check his story against the facts: his words render him an accurate witness. When he is asked, **"Where is that [man]?"** he replies truthfully, **"I do not know"** (9:12). Though the infirm man did not know who had healed him, this man knows who Jesus is but not where to find him.

Scene 2: The Pharisees interrogate the man. This miracle does not immediately generate controversy about Jesus's authority or identity. The first two of three Pharisaic interrogations (both of which are instances of true *stichomythia*—alternating lines given to alternating characters—something not achieved in the Synoptic Gospels) focus on establishing the blind man's identity. **They brought him to the Pharisees, the formerly blind** [man] (9:13). In keeping with the McCarthyesque climate, the man is handed over for interrogation. John withholds why this matter would concern the Pharisees until the next verse. **It was the Sabbath on the day Jesus made the mud and opened his eyes** (9:14). Pharisees seem to have been particularly concerned about what constituted violation of the Sabbath and, therefore, the man would be of interest to them, but first they must establish if a healing has indeed taken place. Besides the fact that the man's blindness disqualifies him as a witness, there are reasons to suspect the man's testimony. If a person who seems to be blind is seen begging one day and then walking about able to see the next, accusation of fraud might also be possible. When the Pharisees inquire about how his vision came to be restored, the man gives an abbreviated recounting of his story: **"He put mud on my eyes and I wash and I see"** (9:15). In classical Greek literature, repeated stories are tailored for the recipient (see the retellings of the Oresteia in Homer, *Od.* 1.298–302; 3.193–200; 11.409–56). He omits Jesus's name and the command to go and wash, raising the possibility that he is protecting Jesus by taking full responsibility for the act of cleansing. He stands in contrast with the infirm man, who continued to point back to Jesus and say, "He told me to do it," as if to absolve himself from any Sabbath violation. Moreover, the more the Gospel's audience hears the story, the more redundant it becomes and the more absurd the narrative audience appears (cf. repeated elements in Dan. 3:1–18).

The Pharisees step into the role of the crowd by engaging in an internal debate. **Then one of the Pharisees said, "This is not a godly man, for he does not keep the Sabbath." Others were saying, "How is a sinful man able to do these signs?" And there was rift among them** (9:16). **Resuming their interrogation, they ask the man, "What do *you* say about him, since he opened your eyes?"** The deictic use of "you" is a challenge to the man to reevaluate what has happened and resolve the problem by denouncing the healer. The man's answer, **"He is a prophet"** (9:17), stands in tension with their question.

Many exegetes focus on the inadequacy of the man's answer. Raymond E. Brown suggests that he makes the following faulty inductive argument: Jesus miraculously cured blindness. Elijah and Elisha also perform miraculous cures. The source of their power is their divine office. Jesus's source of power must be the same divine office; therefore, Jesus is a prophet (Brown 1966, 373). According to Craig Keener (2003, 1:787), "The healed man still can reason only from his experience and lacks an adequate grid for interpretation" until his final encounter with Jesus. Set within the action of the narrative, however, the response makes good sense. "He is a prophet" is a defiant counterassertion to the accusation that Jesus is not a godly man.

Scene 3: The Pharisees interrogate the man's parents. Rather than taking issue with the man's assertion, the authorities doubt that a healing has taken place. **The Jews therefore did not believe these things about him, that he was blind and his sight was restored, not until they summoned the parents of the man whose sight was restored** (9:18). The interrogation resumes with the introduction of new dialogue partners: **"Is this your son, who you say was born blind? How does he now see?"** (9:19). His parents begin by confirming that a healing has taken place: **"We know that this is our son and that he was born blind (9:20), but how he now sees, we do not know; or who opened his eyes, we do not know. Ask him, he has come of age, he will speak for himself"** (9:21). The parents assert that he is a valid witness, and at the same time, they distance themselves from him. They also respond to a question—"Who opened his eyes?"—that they were not asked. Once again, John seems to be constructing the *Zeitgeist* of a repressive regime in which people are dragged in for interrogation in order to denounce others. The response "I don't know" does not necessarily indicate a lack of sufficient data to answer a question. It can point to either (a) a lack of sufficient desire to go through the reflexive thought process needed to produce an answer, or (b) a lack of conviction that producing an answer will be to one's own benefit. The narrator implies that they do know the identity of the one who restored his sight by providing reason *b*: **His parents said these things because they were afraid of the Jews, for already the Jews had contrived [*synetetheinto*] that if anyone should admit that he [Jesus] is Christ, he [or she] would find himself [or herself] out of the synagogue [*aposynagōgos*]** (9:22). The word *aposynagōgos* is unique to this ancient Greek text (see also 12:42; 16:2). The alliteration with the word *synetetheinto* makes it possible that the unusual word choice is motivated by the poetic rhetoric of the narrative. Although it probably was not a technical term, the seriousness of its possible import makes John's use of it a major issue with which scholarship contends (see the theological issues section below). John makes it clear that the parents seek to escape their interrogation by renouncing their responsibility for their son: **On account of this, his parents said that, "He has [come of] age, put your questions to him"** (9:23).

Scene 4: Pharisees reinterrogate the man. Now that the Pharisees can no longer dispute that a healing has taken place, they must return to their former line of questioning, and the interrogation with the formerly blind man resumes. They now seek a condemnation of whoever has healed him. John gives the impression that they know it is Jesus, but the narrator never makes this explicit. **They then summoned the man for a second time, [the one] who was blind, and said to him, "Give glory to God; *we know* that this man is sinful"** (9:24). John uses a technique common in pieces written for the stage in which characters refer to their own thought processes. In a theater piece, this heightens the impression that the actors delivering the lines indeed experience the emotions, intentions, or cognitive states to which they refer. When this occurs in stichomythia, it intensifies the expression of conflict (e.g., Sophocles, *Oed. tyr.* 553–84). The man's resistance to the authorities' efforts to have him denounce Jesus is punctuated with the repetition of the verb "I know" (*oida*) and asyndeton (a missing conjunction between the independent clauses) that suggests that he fires back with rapidity: **"Whether he is sinful, *I do not know*; one thing *I do know*, that I was blind; now I see"** (9:25). His words point to his positive assessment of what has happened to him rather than to the question of Jesus's identity.

The Pharisees then return to their efforts to find something wrong with the act itself by repeating their opening question. John now puts it in direct speech: **"What did he do to you? How did he open your eyes?"** (9:26). That the questions follow the claim that Jesus is a sinner adds to the impression that they do not seek the truth but are pressing the man for a denunciation. John has the man underscore the pretense of the questions and the tense mood of the scene by adopting sarcasm: **"I already told you and you did not listen. What do you want to hear again? You do not want to become his disciples** [do you]?" (9:27). His sarcasm stands in contrast with his parents' evasiveness. The harder the Pharisees push, the more passionate he becomes in his insistence that Jesus is a man of God. As a result, the Pharisees use the fallacious argument of guilt by association: **"*You* are that man's disciple, whereas *we* are disciples of Moses (9:28). *We know* that God spoke to Moses; as for *this*** [man], **we do not know from where he is** [i.e., his origins]" (9:29). The addition of deictic pronouns and the antithetical repetition in 9:25 and 28 are two additional techniques for representing the ferocity of the debate.

The man's response employs the rhetorical device of *exclamatio* to express strong emotion, in this case indignation: **"This is bizarre, because *you* do not know where, even though he opened my eyes"** (9:30). The Gospel's audience is surely meant to applaud the daring of his frank speech, but in the ancient context, one would also have anticipated the outcome. He has stepped out of his station and continues to do so when he provides a theological syllogistic argument. Premise 1: **"We know that God does not listen to** [the] **sinful but to whoever is God-fearing** [*theosebēs*] **and does the will of God; to this one he listens"** (9:31). Note the use of the plural first-person pronoun to underscore the validity of the premise. Premise 2: **"From of old** [*ek tou aiōnos*] **it has not been heard that someone opened the eyes of a person born blind"** (9:32). The appeal to an oral tradition may signify that John places the words of a Pharisee upon the lips of a Pharisaic opponent as well as emphasizing that the second premise is valid. Irrefutable inductive conclusion: **"If this man were not godly, he would not be able to do anything at all"** (9:33). In the face of such tight logic, the authorities can respond only with an ad hominem attack, considered a fallacious argument in modern logic and as something that only resembles a proof by Aristotle (*Soph. elench.* 178b.16–23): **"You were born wholly in sin, and are you teaching us?"** Left with no more arguments, they turn to brute force: **And they ousted him out** [*exebalon auton exō*] (9:34). The final alliteration and repetition points to the energy with which they expel him.

Resumption of Jesus's Narrative (9:35–38)

In the next scene, the action reverses the man's situation. When the Pharisees throw him out, Jesus seeks him out. **Jesus heard that they expelled him and, finding him, said, "Do *you* believe in the Son of Man?"** (9:35). In the final encounter between Jesus and the man, the terms of identification take a major leap from "prophet," which provides many options and is a logical possibility (see John 1:21; 4:19; 6:14)—even Jesus identifies himself with the prophets (4:44)—to "the Son of Man," a singular designation that no one uses other than Jesus. The man's clarifying question suggests that he is receptive to taking Jesus's lead but not that he has a clear idea of what sort of figure Jesus intends: **"And who is he, Lord, in order that I may believe in him?"** (9:36). His response makes sense only if he receives Jesus's question as encouragement. His words are an index to his eagerness. **Jesus said to him, "You have seen him, and the one speaking with you is that one"** (9:37). **Whereupon the [man] exclaimed, "I believe, Lord," and he worshiped him** (9:38). This gesture of prostration completes the act of supplication.

The Paroimia *of the Good Shepherd (9:39–10:21)*

The blind man's part in the narrative is now over, and John returns the reins of the story to Jesus. Jesus resumes the speech he left off in 9:4–5: **"For judgment I came to this world, in order that those who do not see shall see, and those who see shall become blind"** (9:39). The principal action—Jesus's response to allegations and his counteraccusations—begins once more when the narrator brings into view some Pharisees who overhear the conversation. The interrogation with the blind man did not provide them with Jesus's name, so apparently they have followed the blind man to see to whom he would lead them. Once again, the action follows the consequences of the eavesdropping (see 6:60–71). They catch that there is an implicit insult in Jesus's speech that has been hurled at them: **"Surely we are not blind, are we?"** (9:40). Jesus comes back with a loose form of *modus tollens* (see 8:39) that serves to confirm the insult rather than justify it: **"If you were blind, you would not have sin, but now you say that 'we see,' your sin remains"** (9:41).

The chapter break makes it look like this is the end of the episode, but 9:40–41 is the beginning of a debate in which the *paroimia* of the sheepfold serves as an analogy, a deductive form of argument in which Jesus implies that the Pharisees are false leaders and demonstrate their blindness through their incomprehension. The dialogue ends where the controversy over the healing of the blind man began with the question of whether it is possible for a sinner to do a godly work (10:21). The next line does not introduce the speaker;

therefore, the action from 9:41 is not interrupted. **"Truly, truly, I say to you, The one who does not enter through the gate into the sheepfold, but climbs over another way, that one is a thief and a plunderer"** (10:1). The doubling of attributes may simply be a rhetorical flourish, but given that the Gospel's first audience would have fresh memories of the First Jewish Revolt, the term plunderer (*lēstēs*) may conjure the image of insurgents who lead the people to a bloodbath. In contrast, **"The one entering through the gate is the shepherd of the sheep** (10:2). **To this one, the doorkeeper opens, and the sheep hear his voice, and he calls his own sheep by name and leads them out"** (10:3). The presence of a doorkeeper signifies that this is a common pen that contains several flocks. **"Whenever all of his own exit, before them he proceeds, and the sheep should follow him, because they know his voice** (10:4). **That** [voice] **of another one they will** [definitely] **not follow, but they will flee from him, because they do not know the voice belonging to another"** (10:5). The designation "another" (*allotriō*) can be synonymous with "a stranger." This proverb presents a space, the sheepfold, normally associated with safety and a space beyond a gate, where hungry wolves prowl, an area normally associated with danger. In the synoptic parables of the lost sheep, the shepherd seeks to return the sheep to the fold. In the Johannine story, the action inverts the values of the space as thieves and robbers enter the fold and kill and destroy the sheep, and as the shepherd leads the sheep out to safety and to life.

The narrator pauses to make a comment in which he characterizes the story as a *paroimia*. Given the prominence of parables in the Synoptic Gospels and their absence in John's Gospel, much attention has been given to the question of whether John 10:1–18 counts as a parable (see, e.g., Lindars 1970, 318–29). The complexity of the figure suggests that it is not one *paroimia* but a series of proverbs, images, and explications (for a detailed discussion of the structure, see Kysar 2005, 161–82). Set in the context of a debate, the allegorical nature of the *paroimia* renders it an insult; therefore, it will be treated as a single speech act.

The narrator gives his audience a glimpse into the cognitive state of Jesus's opponents, thereby providing the

Paroimia

According to Quintilian, a *paroimia* is a proverb or short fable (*Inst.* 5.11.21) that functions as an allegory in contrast to a *parabolē*, which provides a comparison (*Inst.* 5.11. 21–22; 8.6.57). In Greco-Roman rhetoric, such embedded pieces of folk wisdom serve to delight the audience by speaking of "melancholy things in more cheerful words" (*Inst.* 5.11.19; 8.6.57). Quintilian states that when such figures are used as periphrasis (a circuitous way of speaking), they veil offensive or hurtful speech (*Inst.* 8.6.59–61). For example, Emperor Tiberius answered a group of governors who petitioned to increase provincial taxation with a proverb comparable to those cited by Jesus: "A good shepherd shears his flock; he does not flay them" (Suetonius, *Tib.* 32, trans. Graves 1957, 131).

rationale for Jesus's second version of the story but also presenting them as inexorably blind to its meaning. **Jesus told this proverb [*paroimian*], but those [men] did not know what it was he was talking about to them** (10:6). The *paroimia* becomes a trap: Jesus's opponents are baffled by Jesus's obliqueness and prove themselves blind to his meaning. As a result, Jesus presses his point by repeating the insult in a modified version of the *paroimia*: **"Truly, truly, I say to you that I am the entrance of the sheepfold"** (10:7). Rather than identifying himself as the shepherd, Jesus first aligns himself with the boundary between the two spaces, the gate: **"All, as many as came before me, are thieves and plunderers, but the sheep did not listen to them** (10:8). **I am the entrance; through me whoever shall enter will be saved and will come in and go out and will find pasturage** (10:9). **The thief does not come unless in order that he might steal [*klepsē*] and slaughter [*thysē*] and lay waste [*apolesē*]; I came in order that they might have life and they might have abundance"** (10:10). In 10:10, Jesus uses a series of nearly synonymous verbs, adding poetic weight and emotional force to the contrast. The Greek verb endings also give a cadence to the first half of 10:10, which is weakened by translation. The choice of verbs may simply be for emphasis, but again, for many in John's first audiences, they might also recall the devastation of the First Jewish Revolt. The asyndeton marks the strong contrast between the actions of the thief and those of Jesus. Thieves (and by extension Jesus's opponents) take life, whereas Jesus gives life. The truth of this statement is demonstrated by the action that follows in chapters 11 and 19.

Jesus takes advantage of the indeterminacy of the *paroimia* and identifies himself with the shepherd: **"I am the Good Shepherd. The Good Shepherd lays his life down on behalf of the sheepfold"** (10:11). Jesus lays out a second pastoral scenario in order to hurl another insult at his opponents. Most flocks were attended not by their owner but by paid laborers, who were at the bottom of the Mediterranean social order and not always trusted (cf. Aristotle, *Pol.* 1.3.4 [1256a.30]; Longus, *Daphn.* 4.35; Xenophon of Ephesus, *Ephes.* 3.12; and Heliodorus, *Aeth.* 6.7 uses "herdsman" as a euphemism for "bandit"). Jesus continues, **"The hireling is not even a shepherd—his sheep are not his own—he watches the wolf coming and leaves the sheep alone and flees, and the wolf snatches them away and scatters [them]** (10:12). **Because he is a hireling and he does not take the sheepfold to be his concern** (10:13). **I am the Good Shepherd and I know my own and my own know me** (10:14). **Just as the Father knows me and I know the Father, and I lay down my life on behalf of the sheepfold** (10:15). **And I have other sheep that are not from this tenancy [*aulēs*]."** Jesus's vocabulary points to a complexity in the agrarian economy that requires the use of antiquated English. The word *aulēs* implies that in the background stand a landowner and a large estate broken up into small tenant farms. **"It is necessary for me to lead these as well, and they will hear my voice and become one flock for one shepherd** (10:16). **For this reason, the**

161

Father loves me, because I lay down my life in order that I receive it again" (10:17). Translators favor the active sense of the verb receive (*lambanō*), "I take" (e.g., NRSV, NIV). The passive sense makes God the agent. The next verse does suggest that Jesus, in effect, raises himself from the dead, although only at the Father's command: **"No one lifts it up [*airei*, an allusion to the particular form of Jesus's death] from me, but I lay it down by myself. I have authority to lay it down, and I have authority to receive it again. I receive this command from my Father"** (10:18). To modern sensibilities, this can sound like suicide, but in the Greco-Roman world a self-inflicted death is more virtuous than execution, and aristocrats were often given that option. Jerome Neyrey (2007a, 180–81) provides a list of forms of death deemed "noble" in ancient funeral orations, including voluntary death in which soldiers choose death rather than to become captive slaves or in order to punish foes even though their own death is a certainty (cf. Thucydides, *Hist.* 2.42–43).

Jesus's audience dismisses his insult by discrediting its source. **Once more there arose a rift among the Jews concerning these words** (10:19). **Many of them were saying, "He has a demon and is crazed. Why do you listen to him?"** (10:20). **Others were saying, "These are not the words of one possessed of a demon. Surely a demon cannot open the eyes of a blind man [can it]?"** (10:21). The scene ends with a picture of Jesus's opponents impugning one another's common sense.

The Exegetical Puzzle and Rhetorical Trap (10:22–39)

Some time passes without narration before the dialogue resumes. **At that time, it happened to be the Feast of Dedication in Jerusalem** [presumably the festival of Hanukkah]; **it was winter** (10:22), **and Jesus was wandering about in the temple in Solomon's portico** (10:23). According to Josephus (*Ant.* 20.221), this colonnade was the single vestige of Solomon's Temple. On top of this scenic detail, John provides graphic description of the action. **Then the Jews encircled him [*ekyklōsan*] and were saying to him, "How long are you going to keep our life in suspense [*aireis*; perhaps a play on 10:18]? If you are the Christ, speak to us frankly [*parrhēsia*]"** (10:24). Here is an ironic stroke of Johannine genius. He has Jesus's opponents state bluntly that the proof of Jesus's status is frank speech, something that Jesus has consistently demonstrated. Jesus points this out: **"I told you and you don't believe. The deeds that I am doing in the name of my Father, these testify on my behalf"** (10:25). He then picks up the terms of the *paroimia* and uses them metaphorically: **"But you do not believe, because you are not from my sheepfold** (10:26). **My sheep listen to my voice, and I know them and they follow me** (10:27), **and I give them eternal life so that they should not perish, not ever** [the double negative followed by the aorist subjective is the most emphatic way in Greek to deny a future possibility], **and someone will not snatch them out of my hand** (10:28). **My Father who has given [my sheep] to me is greater than everything,** and no one is able to snatch out of the hand of the Father (10:29). I and the Father are one" (10:30). Jesus persists in referring to God as "the Father" or "my Father," but his meaning is clear to his narrative audience, with the result that the **Jews again picked up stones in order that they might stone him** (10:31). Jesus asks a question designed not to disarm but to delay them: **"I showed you many good deeds from the Father; for which deed of this sort are you stoning me?"** (10:32). Tom Thatcher (2000, 219–29) categorizes this as a "neck riddle" in that it "saves Jesus's neck by deflecting his opponent." The Jews' reply is appropriate to the defense that Jesus has offered for his violations of the Sabbath: **"We are not stoning you for a good deed, but for blasphemy, and because you, who are a man, make yourself a god"** (10:33). The charge once more is hubris.

> ### Rhetorical Trap
>
> Rhetorical traps are set when an argument is made that exploits ambiguity inherent in language, making it impossible to deny a premise without affirming a falsehood or strengthening one's opponent's claim. Cicero (*Phil.* 2.110) uses this strategy in an argument to discredit Anthony's piety by exploiting the semantic ambiguity of the word *pulvinar*, which can mean either a sacred couch or a *lectisternium*, a type of propitiatory ceremony.

Rather than returning to his habitual defense that he does not make himself equal to God but that God is the source of his authority, Jesus turns to an exegetical argument. Jerome Neyrey (1989) has laid out an elaborate argument to show that Jesus uses midrash on Ps. 82:6 to ally himself with Israel at Sinai and thereby to deny that he has sinned, but Jesus's exegesis also lays a rhetorical trap: **"Is it not written in your law that 'I said you are gods'** (10:34). **If God called those gods for whom the word of God came into being, and Scripture cannot be annulled** (10:35), **how can you say [that] you, whom the Father sanctifies and sends into the world, blaspheme because I said, 'I am a son of God'?"** (10:36). (This translation changes the Greek word order significantly to get it to work without changing cases.) Jesus's question is comparable to the logical fallacy of a complex question like "Are you still beating your spouse?" A reply of either yes or no confirms that one previously beat their spouse. To say that Jesus blasphemes by calling himself the Son of God is to admit that they annul Scripture. The only response that the opponents can give is silence.

Jesus reverts to his main argument, which he has repeated in many forms. **"If I do the deeds of my father, you should believe me"** (10:37). He then turns to the rhetorical strategy of recognizing that doubt in his word is a possibility and offering material evidence to corroborate its truth: **"But if I do, and you do not believe me, believe the deeds so that you will have known and might know that the Father is in me and I [am] in the Father"** (10:38). Jesus's argument, rather than persuading, provokes the resumption of physical hostility. **Therefore they were seeking again to seize him, and he slipped from their hands** (10:39).

Jesus Departs and Many Believe (10:40–42)

The extended episode ends with Jesus's exit. **And he went away again across the Jordan to the place where John was first baptizing and remained there** (10:40). The narrator leaves us with a parting glance at those who honor Jesus by comparing him to the Baptist. **And many came to him and were saying that "On the one hand, John did not perform a sign, and on the other hand, everything as great as John said about this [man] was true"** (10:41). **And many believed in him there** (10:42).

Theological Issues

Sin, Blindness, and Begging

The suggestion that God has inflicted the man with blindness so that Jesus can demonstrate his power by restoring his sight is avoided above by moving the full stop forward in 9:3. The first and earliest manuscripts appeared as *scriptio continua*, without spaces or punctuation marks between words. The narrative supports putting a period after the dismissal of the disciples' question. Jesus has not set out to find this man. In the course of a day of wandering through the streets of Jerusalem, Jesus would pass by scores of people with afflictions. What we would think of as a minor wound, infection, or parasite could easily result in major irreparable damage in antiquity. Jesus's healing of the man is prompted by the disciples' question. His response suggests that they are working with the wrong set of theological presuppositions. Set within the broad context of his ministry, Jesus has come to show that God is the God of life, not of death and affliction. As Judith Lieu (1988, 84) notes, Jesus's answer to the disciples' question is that "it is not the blind man who sinned but those who claim to have sight."

The disciples' question regarding whose sin caused the man's blindness can give the false impression that Jewish society always equated blindness with sin. As mentioned above, earlier and later Jewish traditions suggest otherwise. Tobit, whose fortune is confiscated as consequence for the good deeds he performs on behalf of the Jews of Nineveh (1:10–20), becomes blind for four years when he accidentally washes with water polluted by sparrow droppings after piously burying a murdered Jew (2:7–10). As a consequence of his malady, he becomes destitute and the recipient of others' charity (2:10–14). In the Mishnah (e.g., *m. Ḥag.* 1.1), the rabbis discuss whether the blind are exempt from fulfilling positive commands due to their disability and not because they are impure (see Abrams 1998, 190). They formulate rules to protect the blind from exploitation (e.g., *m. B. Qam.* 8.1). While Hebrew Scripture used the trope of physical blindness to signify obliviousness to the faults of others (Gen. 27:1–4; 1 Sam. 3:2) and as a metaphor for Israel's collective willful refusal to use eyes and ears to perceive the truth of God's message

(Isa. 6:9–10; 42:18–20; Lieu 1988, 88; Abrams 1998, 76), the blindness of the prophet Ahijah is balanced by his prophetic insight (1 Kings 14:1–18; Abrams 1998, 87). Rabbinic literature contains examples of the trope of the blind seer whose physical blindness signifies spiritual insight. For example, Rav Sheshet (AD 290–320) was able to sit in the presence of the *Shekinah* (*šĕkînâ*) precisely because he was blind (*b. Meg.* 29a). In the rabbinic literature, the blind, the ragged, or naked man and the child are treated as one category (*m. Meg.* 4.6; *m. B. Qam.* 8.1; see Abrams 1998, 36–37). It seems that rather than sin and blindness, poverty and blindness are the relevant paired concepts. Blindness is a cause of poverty and is an affliction that prevents one from seeing and, therefore, from being a reliable witness.

The details of the narrative suggest that the Gospel of John is more concerned with the consequences of the blindness than its cause. Since this Gospel is overtly concerned with Christology and theology, it becomes easy to overlook signs of concern for social and ethical issues. John presents a man twice afflicted. Not only is he blind; he also makes a living by supplication: he begs for food or small coins.

Ancient Greco-Roman authors often criticize the public support of the disabled and beggars. Aristotle writes that "there should certainly be a law to prevent the rearing of deformed children" (*Pol.* 7.16 [1335b]). Plutarch writes a positive account of the efforts of Gaius Gracchus (159–121 BC) to rid Rome of the poor by sending them to newly established colonies (*Ti. C. Gracch.* 8.3–8). In the comedy *Trinummus*, Plautus places platitudes of Roman virtues such as the following on the lips of Philto, the father of the protagonist: "You do a beggar bad service by giving him food and drink; you lose what you give and prolong his life for more misery" (*Trin.* 339, trans. Nixon 1938). Author after author advocates charity but only to the deserving, those who are good or capable of contributing to society (see Isocrates, *Demon.* 29; Cicero, *Off.* 2.54). As Seneca puts it, "To some I shall not give although they are in need, because, even if I should give, they would still be in need" (*Vit. beat.* 24.1, trans. Basore 1958). Later Christian attitudes were countercultural. John Chrysostom thought that Christians should give to any poor man who asked and let the poor determine if he needed it or not (*Quatr. Laz.* 2.5).

There is little mention of begging in Second Temple literature. Ethical texts that equate poverty with piety and encourage provision of necessities for the disenfranchised allow Bruce Malina (1987, 356–62) to imagine that Judean society knew no destitution and contend that poverty was a social rather than an economic distinction. Timothy Ling (2006, 105) takes issue with Malina and suggests that the NT authors would have been well acquainted with the distinction between *penēs*, those who could earn money and experience a temporary setback, and the *ptōchos*, those who were destitute. The man's begging suggests that the social distinction of being blind creates economic hardship. While John does not provide sufficient data with which to reconstruct the economic relationship between the man and his parents, two scenarios are logical: the parents have ceased to support their son, or the parents have set their son to begging. The contrast between the parent's fear of being *aposynagōgos* and the son's boldness in allying with Jesus makes the former scenario the more probable. They have much to lose; their son has little to lose. He is already at the margins of society. His unwillingness to cave into the Pharisees' pressure to denounce Jesus stands not only in counterpoint to his parents' fear but also to Nicodemus's silence.

In contrast to the synoptic Jesus, the Johannine Jesus does not preach about the virtues and piety of poverty. Instead, John weaves a fine thread through his narrative that points to the difficulty for those whose identity is derived from established social structures to ally themselves with a new identity in Christ, and the willingness of those at the margins to make Jesus central to their identity. Nevertheless, the Gospel contains sufficient evidence with which to construct a *fabula* in which Jesus's ministry includes gifts to the poor. Judas's critique of Mary of Bethany's extravagant gift (12:4–5) and the disciples' supposition that he goes to give alms to the poor (13:29) are indexes of habitual charitable giving.

Aposynagōgos

Aposynagōgos appears only three times in the written record of the ancient Greek language, and all are in this Gospel (9:22; 12:42; 16:2). Earlier commentaries treated the Pharisees as an organized body capable of promulgating and enforcing a ruling that whoever confessed Jesus to be the messiah would be expelled from the synagogue just as one is excommunicated or banned from the church (see, e.g., Filson 1963, 84). In the 1960s and 1970s, a hypothesis arose and gained near axiomatic status for Johannine scholarship that this word referred to the official expulsion of Jesus's followers after the rabbinic council at Yavneh (ca. AD 80). This understanding is central to both J. Louis Martyn (1968) and Raymond E. Brown's (1979) theories of the composition of the Gospel. The means of the expulsion was an addition, euphemistically called the *Birkat ha-Minim* (*mînîm*), "the blessing of the heretics," to the Shemoneh Esreh, a prayer of benediction in the synagogue liturgy. The "blessing" required participants in the liturgy to utter a curse on heretics, including the Nazarenes. Christians who wanted to avoid cursing themselves would supposedly have ceased to attend synagogue prayer services. Therefore, being cast out of the synagogue was understood to describe the experience of the Johannine community toward

> **The Birkat ha-Minim**
>
> "For the renegades let there be no hope, and may the arrogant kingdom soon be rooted out in our days, and the Nazarenes and the minim perish as in a moment and be blotted out from the book of life, and with the righteous may they not be inscribed." (trans. Jocz 1979, 51–57)

the end of the first century and not the experience of Jesus's followers during or shortly after his lifetime.

Questions about the hypothesis soon arose. In 1985, Wayne Meeks declared the *Birkat ha-Minim* "a red-herring in Johannine research" (Meeks 1985, 102–3). Jewish scholars such as Reuven Kimmelman (1981), Shaye Cohen (1999), Adele Reinhartz (2001), and Daniel Boyarin (2001) have provided insights into the history of the Yavneh tradition and the *Birkat ha-Minim* that call into question seeing the concept of *aposynagōgos* as an official policy of an organized Jewish synagogue. First of all, the institution that we know of as the synagogue was, in antiquity, much less formal, without an overarching administrative structure. Second, the *Birkat ha-Minim* is not in the Mishnah. Though there may be an allusion to it in the Tosefta (*t. Ber.* 3.25; ca. late third cent. AD), it appears much later in the Babylonian Talmud (fifth cent. AD). Third, the story of the Yavneh composition of the blessing does not point to its widespread adoption. The Talmud contains a story in which Rabban Gamaliel asks Samuel the Small to compose the blessing, but then Gamaliel forgets it and, a year later, has to think for a couple of hours in order to remember it (*b. Ber.* 28b–29a). The probability that there was a council at Yavneh that defined orthodox Judaism in the wake of the destruction of the temple has come under serious question. As Daniel Boyarin (2001, 427) puts it, the Yavneh tradition is an effect of the rise of new social practices that seek to claim "the authority . . . of hoary antiquity." Nevertheless, the *Birkat ha-Minim* hypothesis makes such good sense of the story that it tends to cling on tenaciously (see Burridge 2005, 153; Wedderburn 2004, 179). Many scholars continue to agree that *aposynagōgos* is a status that existed in the life of the later community rather than during Jesus's ministry, at a point when the church had begun to see itself as something apart from Jewish institutions. Some see John's references as evidence that some sort of centralized authority in a nascent rabbinic Judaism meted out the punishment of expulsion from the synagogue and that the Johannine community witnessed expulsions or experienced it directly (e.g., Blasi, Dumaime, and Turcotte 2002, 365). On the other side of the discussion, Adele Reinhartz has pointed out data—such as the presence of Jews who comfort Mary and Martha after Lazarus's death, and the description of Jews following Jesus in 12:10–11—as evidence that we cannot draw a sharp line between Christ's followers and Jews. She argues that, if anything, Jesus's followers are leaving the synagogue rather than being cast out (Reinhartz 2001, 40–41). Robert Kysar (2002, 24) steps in line with Reinhartz's observations: "The Gospel regards the separation as an 'expulsion,' but that may tell us more about how the Johannine Christians felt than what really happened" (for a longer treatment, see Kysar 2005, 237–45).

Even if *aposynagōgos* refers to the Johannine community's experience of exclusion or alienation, this would not necessarily be a formal excommunication. Ancient synagogues were not the modern institutions of church and

167

synagogue, with a membership list. Moreover, to be thrown out of the synagogue is not to be denied salvation through its mechanisms but to be denied the sort of support and facilitation that it offered. If it were access to worship of God that were being denied, then one would expect language of exclusion from the temple comparable to the Samaritan experience. Larry Hurtado (2005, 70–71) argues that *synagōgē* here "connotes the Jewish *community*," not a formal institutional organization, and that *aposynagōgos* could signify actions like those taken against Stephen or any of the punitive acts directed against Paul as described in 2 Cor. 11:22–29. Paul was often literally thrown out of synagogues (Acts 13:45, 50; 14:5, 19). The blind man is thrown out of the gathering in order to be publicly humiliated. John seems to be representing an action taken by local synagogue leaders on an occasion when they heard things that offended them—as part of the culture of honor and shame in which they lived and as part of the McCarthyesque mood of the Gospel.

Placed in the context of the synagogue in the first century AD, the term *aposynagōgos* may reify a general fear of social death into its most concrete form, exclusion from the security, benefits, and services provided by the organized community. In *The Anatomy of Criticism*, Northrop Frye (1957, 39) observes, "The root idea of pathos is the exclusion of an individual on our own level from a social group to which he is trying to belong." To be *aposynagōgos* is to suffer vulnerability and to be without status. *Aposynagōgos* may be John's way of saying persona non grata. Members of John's audience who risked exclusion from the benefits of pagan society would have recognized themselves in John's story. Once again, the point is that to ally with Jesus is to risk much but to gain even more.

The Johannine Son of Man

Compared to Jesus's occasional use of the term "the Son of Man" in the Synoptic Gospels, he uses it incessantly in the Gospel of John (1:51; 3:13, 14; 5:27; 6:27, 53, 62; 8:28; 9:35; 12:23, 34 [2x; the crowd echoing Jesus's use of the name]; 13:31). Within the OT, the term *ben-ādām* refers most often to a human being in its frailty (e.g., Ps. 8:4; Job 25:6; Ezek. 2:6; Dan. 8:17), but in Dan. 7:13, the Son of Man is a heavenly being. Delbert Burkett (1999, 120) points out that there is no shared or unified interpretation of Dan. 7:13 in Jewish intertestamental messianic or Son of Man texts or in the NT. In the Synoptic Gospels, Jesus both identifies himself as Daniel's Son of Man when asked if he is the Messiah (Mark 14:61–62; Matt. 26:63–64; Luke 22:67–69) and calls himself the Son of Man when describing his vulnerability (e.g., Matt. 8:20; par. Luke 9:58; Mark 10:32–34; par. Matt. 20:17–19 and Luke 18:31–34). The synoptic tradition seems to combine the figures of the Son of Man with Isaiah's Suffering Servant.

Johannine scholars continue to debate whether the Johannine Jesus's use of the term points to a human or a heavenly figure. Publications in the 1960s and 1970s tended to favor a human identification. Francis J. Moloney (1976, 208–20), using a diachronic approach, sees Jesus's use of the term as evidence that John represents Jesus during his life as a "perfect man" and notes that after Jesus's glorification on the cross, John ceases to use the title "Son of Man." Revisiting the topic three decades later and using a synchronic reading, Moloney (2005) arrives at the same conclusion. To do so, he distinguishes between the preexistent *logos* (1:1–2) or "the Son" in 17:1, 5 and Jesus (1:14, 17) and offers alternative readings of 3:13 and 6:62, in which the theme of heavenly origin is most prominent.

The absolute distinction between human and divine and the focus on ontology is less pronounced in more-recent examinations of the question. Instead, the unique role assigned to Jesus by God as the means of breaching the divide between heaven and the world comes into focus. Benjamin E. Reynolds (2008) makes a persuasive case for situating John's use of the Son of Man within the revelatory themes of the apocalyptic tradition and argues that John develops the salvific role apportioned to the messianic figure in *4 Ezra* (2 Esd.) 13.26, 49 and *2 Bar.* 40.1–3 and 72.2. The Johannine Jesus combines the figure of the Son of Man with a wide variety of OT images, such as Jacob's ladder (John 1:51) and the snake that Moses lifts up (John 3:14), to play on the homology of the verb *aireō*, with references to crucifixion and glorification. The association of the Son of Man with Jacob's ladder points to Jesus's identity as the means by which God communicates or reveals himself to humanity and the means by which humans enter into heaven, the gate to which Jesus refers in John 10:7. The Son of Man gives food that lasts forever (6:27); to have life, people need to eat the flesh of the Son of Man and drink his blood (6:53). The use of the Son of Man fits into the complex of passages in which Jesus serves as the new temple. In the exchange with the formerly blind man, John emphasizes that the human response to the authority of the Son of Man is to worship (*proskyneō*) him (see 9:38). In contrast to the synoptic tradition, John uses the tradition of the Son of Man to emphasize Jesus's heavenly connections rather than his humanity (Reynolds 2008, 223).

John 11:1–12:11

The Sweet Scent of Death

Introductory Matters

The episodes in this unit revolve around the family of Lazarus, Martha, and Mary. The principal action is a reversal—the dead one lives—but to the simplicity of this reversal, John adds the complexity of emotion, allusion, report, reaction, and counterreaction. Grief and censure turn to an expression of gratitude—the anointing of feet—that in turn comes to signify a funerary rite. Jesus raises Lazarus to life, and the authorities plot to take both their lives. John plays with epithets and allusions to underscore that Lazarus's story foreshadows Jesus's death and resurrection in a variety of ways. Table 5 lays out some of the intricacies in the action.

Table 5. Complexity of Action in John 11:1–12:11

Location	Report	Response	Sign	Plots	Reversal
across the Jordan	"Lazarus is ill"	Jesus delays departure			
Bethany: "the home of Mary, who anointed the Lord"	"Jesus is coming"; "Jesus calls for you"	regret at Jesus's delayed arrival			mourning
			Jesus raises Lazarus		
Jerusalem	"Jesus has raised Lazarus"			plot to kill Jesus	
Bethany: "the home of Lazarus, whom Jesus raised from the dead"		Mary anoints Jesus			celebration
Jerusalem		crowd seeks both Jesus and Lazarus		plot to kill Lazarus	

The epilogue with which the Gospel ends makes clear that what is narrated is not the whole story: "And there are many other things that Jesus did that if they were written down one at a time, I do not suppose the world to have room for all the books being written" (21:25). The story that is told is about the public man who speaks openly (cf. 18:2–21). The stories of the Bethany family suggest that another narrative could be told, the story of the private man, that of a friend. The liminality of both friendship, which bridges the private realm of the family and the public realm of the civic order, and mourning, which marks the passage from life to death, opens a gap in John's narrative that causes the steady stride of the Son of God to falter.

Lazarus bears the epithet, "the one whom you [Jesus] love [*phileis*]" (11:3). *Philia* in the Greco-Roman world signified, in the case of a man, that one had become an intimate not just of his friend but also of his household, so that the rules of honor and shame that restricted interaction with its women were relaxed (see Konstan 1997, 80–89). The liminal space before the tomb adds to this confusion between public and private because mourning women were released from the social structures that ruled the living. They could speak frankly in their grief, and the private sentiments of the home were put on public display. Mary and Martha treat Jesus as an intimate friend, and he responds in kind. John's rhetorical aim in his narrative is to present Jesus's death as an occasion for

Liminality

Anthropologists Arnold van Gennep in *Les rites de passage* (1909) and later Victor Turner (cf. 1969) use the term "liminality," derived from the Latin word for "threshold," *limen*, to describe psychological and social events characterized by ambiguity or indeterminacy. In these liminal states, individuals or groups no longer fit within the categories that define normalcy or social status. The period of betrothal in traditional societies, in which a woman is a member of two patriarchal families, and the period of mourning, in which family members straddle the realms of life and death, are two such liminal states. Rites of passage are designed to carry individuals or groups safely through liminal zones.

John 11:1–12:11 in the Narrative Flow

In the beginning (1:1–2:12)

Jesus's itinerant ministry (2:13–12:11)

Transforming sacred space (2:13–4:54)

God works on the Sabbath (5:1–47)

Bread and circuses (6:1–71)

Verbal sparring at the Festival of Sukkoth (7:1–8:59)

A second Sabbath violation at a second pool (9:1–10:42)

▶The sweet scent of death (11:1–12:11)

The reversal (11:1–44)

The report and reaction in Jerusalem (11:45–57)

The counterreaction in Bethany (12:1–8)

The Jerusalem reaction continued (12:9–11)

joy; yet in the story of Lazarus, he allows the grief over the death of a loved one to have a role as a plot element.

Tracing the Narrative Flow

The Reversal (11:1–44)

After healing two people who have suffered long-term afflictions without his being asked, Jesus responds with ennui to an implicit but clear request to come quickly. The narrator tells the story in such a way as to emphasize that Jesus acts contrary to expectations.

There was a certain man, Lazarus from Bethany, from the village of Mary and her sister Martha (11:1). **It was Mary, who soothed the Lord with ointment and wiped off his feet with her hair, whose brother Lazarus fell ill** (11:2). John uses a proleptic reference (a reference to something that has not yet happened) as an epithet with which to identify Mary. Moreover, contrary to cultural norms, Martha is referred to as the sister of Mary rather than of Lazarus. The epithet and the action to which it points then serve to frame the unit, and Mary more than Lazarus becomes the focus of the story. Jesus is presumably still in the region of Perea, within a day's journey of Bethany, when he receives a message from the sisters: **"Lord, take note, the one whom you love has fallen ill"** (11:3). The report of news is an important element in the unit and will be used in various ways (11:20, 28, 46). Once more John represents women making an indirect request (see John 2:3). The message is fraught with subtext. Faith in a friend is confidence in receiving their help when needed (Epicurus, *Gnom. vat.* 23, 34, 39). The frankness of the sisters in the following action points to the degree of friendship. Jesus responds to the report from the perspective of his relationship to God rather than Lazarus: **"This illness is not to death** [i.e., fatal] **but for the purpose of the glory of God, in order that the Son of God may be glorified through it"** (11:4). The narrator provides an apologetic aside that serves to accentuate the apparent tension between the competing loyalties: **But Jesus loved** [imperfect] **Martha and her sister and Lazarus** (11:5). **Nevertheless, when** [*hōs oun*] **he did hear that he is ill,** [*tote men*] **he remained in the place where he was two days** (11:6). The syntax of this verse and the affirmation of friendship underscore Jesus's lack of action. **After all this** [this seems to be a narrative convention denoting a surprising turn], **he says to the disciples, "Let's go to Judea again"** (11:7).

By this point in the narrative, Judea has come explicitly to signify a place of danger. **The disciples say to him, "Rabbi, the Jews were just now seeking to stone you, and are you going to go back there again?"** (11:8). **Jesus replied, "Are there not twelve hours** [of light] **in a day? If anyone walks about in the day, he** [or she] **does not stumble because he** [or she] **sees the light of this world"** (11:9). The verb for "stumble," *proskoptei*, is often used metaphorically to mean give offense, and in this context, Jesus's meaning may be a double entendre: Jesus does not violate his friendship, and if the disciples trust him, they will not go wrong. **"If, on the other hand, anyone walks about in the dark, he does stumble, because the light is not in him"** (11:10). In other words, Jesus says he knows what he is doing and that he is not making a misstep. **He said these things, and with this, he says to them, "Lazarus, our friend, has fallen asleep [*kekoimētai*], but I am going over [to Bethany] in order to wake him up"** (11:11). Jesus uses sleeping and waking as a common metaphor for death and resurrection (see Isa. 26:19; Dan. 12:2; 1 Cor. 15:6, 20), but the disciples take his words literally: **"Lord, if he has fallen asleep, he will be safe** [from death]" (11:12). The narrator's clarification of Jesus's meaning serves more to underscore the disciples' confusion than to inform the audience of Jesus's intent. **But Jesus had been talking about his death, but those** [disciples] **supposed that he speaks about the slumber of sleep** (11:13). **Therefore from that time he spoke to them frankly, "Lazarus is dead** (11:14). **But I rejoice for you that you may believe, because I was not there, but let us go to him"** (11:15). Jesus leaves more unsaid than said. He refers obliquely to the resurrection that he will perform by anticipating the belief that Lazarus's resurrection will produce in his disciples. The juxtaposition of death and joy bring into view the paradox at the center of Christian thought, that in dying one is born to eternal life.

> ### Sleep and Health in Antiquity
>
> In Greek iconography, Hypnos, the god of sleep, is often represented asleep at the feet of Hygieia (the goddess of health and daughter of Asclepius, the god of medicine and healing) or with his twin brother, Thanatos, the god of death. In the cult of Asclepius, practiced widely in the Mediterranean world, cures took place while the patient slept, in a process called *enkoimēsis*, or *incubatio*, in which Asclepius would appear to the patient in a dream and give the patient advice.

Figure 18. Hypnos and his brother Thanatos (death) vie for the body of Sarpedon (Greek Euphronios krater, ca. 515 BC).

© Jaime Ardiles-Arce

Then Thomas, the one called Twin [*Didymos*] by his fellow disciples, enters the dialogue for the first time and said, "Yes, do let *us* go so that we might die with him" (11:16). Thomas (Aramaic *Tě'ômā'*) means "twin" and is a nickname. In the *Acts of Thomas* and several Nag Hammadi texts (*Thom. Cont.* 142; *Gos. Thom.* 32), his given name is Judas. The *Acts of Thomas* calls him Jesus's twin brother (1, 29, 54). Thomas's speech can be delivered as a piece of sarcasm. As we shall see in 20:25, John represents Thomas as a killjoy or "agelast" (from Gk. *agelastos*, "gloomy"), a character type marked by the use of sarcasm and a propensity for pessimism. Of Theophrastus's character types, he most closely resembles the *mempsimoiria*, one who habitually finds cause not to rejoice (*Char.* 17). Mood rather than meaning is what is important here. While Jesus foresees the joy of life in the postresurrection community, Thomas envisions a community of death.

Upon arriving, Jesus found him [Lazarus] already entombed for four days (11:17). The four days signifies that Lazarus is really dead, but it also brings a degree of tension to the story that borders on the macabre when Lazarus is disinterred. John then underscores the proximity to Jerusalem. Bethany was near Jerusalem, approximately fifteen stadia away (11:18). One Ptolemaic stadium is 185 meters; Jerusalem is about 2.75 kilometer or 1.75 miles away. John's reasons for bringing Bethany's relation to Jerusalem in view is probably twofold: (1) to make it clear that Jesus is "dancing in the dragon's jaws" (an allusion to Bruce Cockburn's song "Hills of Morning," True North Productions, 1979) and (2) to bring the parallels between Lazarus and Jesus's death into view.

Many of the Jews [the implication seems to be that they have come from Jerusalem, because Bethany is a village with a small population] had come to Martha and Mary in order to console them over [the loss of] their brother (11:19). The death of an adult brother who is head of a family is a calamity for unmarried sisters. The number of mourners also gives the impression that Lazarus was an important, or well-respected, man. His entombment stands in contrast with that of Jesus, who receives only clandestine funeral rites. This group will serve as reporters of the event, thereby pushing Jesus's narrative to its precipice.

The report of Jesus's arrival precedes him. Then Martha, when she heard that Jesus is coming, went to meet him, while Mary stayed in the house (11:20). The act of going out to meet him is the first step in a suppliant act, but healing is no longer possible; therefore, Martha's words sound like a reproach because her request is cast in the tense and mood of the unreal conditional: "Lord, if you had been here, then my brother would not be dead" (11:21). Her resignation turns to hope when she says, "But even now I know that whatever you might request of God, God will give you" (11:22). Again, the woman's request is indirect. Within the context of Jewish mourning, a typical petition would include requests on behalf of the dead for forgiveness and inclusion in the book of life (see 2 Macc. 12:42–45; *1 En.* 47.4). There is no need to infer that she asks Jesus to resurrect Lazarus immediately. The Gospel's audience may anticipate Lazarus's prompt resurrection, but Martha understands Jesus's response, **"Your brother will rise again"** (11:23), within the confines of conventional future eschatology, in which all who are dead will be raised and then judged. **Martha says to him, "I know that he will rise in the resurrection on the last day"** (11:24). If Martha's petition is for intercession regarding judgment, Jesus's speech—**"I am the resurrection and the life; the one who believes in me, even though he [or she] dies, shall live"** (11:25)—indicates that he fulfills her request. Jesus then makes his oft-repeated claim that belief in him makes the future event a present reality: **"And all who live and believe in me, no, they shall never die."** In an unprecedented move, Jesus asks her bluntly, **"Do you believe this?"** (11:26). Martha makes the verbal gesture appropriate to supplication; belief is necessary for eternal life (cf. 6:29, 53): **"Yes, Lord, I have believed that you are the Christ, the Son of God, who is come into the world"** (11:27). The use of the perfect tense and the description of what she believes is an enthymeme that can be paraphrased as "Given that I have believed this about you, I now trust that the future will unfold as you have said." This is the clearest affirmation of belief so far in what Jesus has been saying about himself. Her words of caution in 11:39 indicate that she does not anticipate immediate fulfillment of her expectations.

Rather than following the Johannine pattern of private admission followed by public acclamation, John keeps the action within the realm of the family. **And having said this, she left and spoke to Mary her sister without being perceived, saying, "The teacher has arrived and calls [for] you"** (11:28). **Jesus had not yet come to the village, but was still in the place where Martha had met him** (11:30). John practices an economy of narrative by leaving out Jesus's request and providing only the private report.

The action that follows is marked by intimacy of friendship and calls for the addition of the "third man," someone with a credible reason for observing the private lives of the main characters. In literature, the servant often fulfills this role. John's eavesdroppers come in the form of mourners. **Then the Jews who were with her in the house and consoling her, after seeing that Mary quickly rose and left, followed her, supposing that she is going to the tomb so that she might lament there** (11:31). John now provides details of what they can see. Mary comes to Jesus and makes what looks like a gesture of supplication—**Then Mary, when she came there, seeing it was Jesus, fell at his feet**—but she makes no conditional request, she gives no indication of hope. Her words are a blunt reproach: **"If you had been here, then my brother would not be dead"** (11:32). The repetition of Martha's first words points to their shared grief, but the absence of the follow-up underscores both that these are two distinct people and John's dramatic purpose. As the Son of God, Jesus engages in theological discourse with Martha; as the friend of Lazarus, he reacts to Mary's sorrow with emotion and takes action. **Jesus then seeing her lamenting so, and the Jews coming with her lamenting, was deeply moved** [*enebrimēsato*] **in spirit and stirred himself** [*etaraxen heauton*] (11:33). Both verbs signify visible evidence of an emotional state, but John does not name the emotion (see "Jesus's Humanity and Commiseration" in the theological issues section below). Jesus's role is reversed in this encounter with Mary. He becomes the seeker and asks, **"Where have you put him?"** Mary Magdalene later asks the same question about Jesus's body (20:15). Their invitation, **"Lord, come and see"** (11:34), echoes Jesus's invitation to the disciples (1:39). Jesus is in a position in which he is not found elsewhere in the Gospel. He asks a question that is not polemical and for which he does not seem already to know the answer. Then comes the surprising sight: **Jesus wept** (as in, cried tears; 11:35). John focuses not on what Jesus feels but on how he appears to the Jewish mourners, who respond, **"See how he loved him"** (11:36). This observation creates dissonance: **"Would not this man who opened the eyes of the blind man have been able to do** [something] **so that this man would not be dead?"** (11:37). Jesus has appeared to violate his friendship with Lazarus. Whereas the previous narrated signs have been demonstrations of God's glory, what follows seems to be a demonstration of friendship. **Then Jesus again sighed deeply and goes to the tomb** (11:38a).

The description of the tomb emphasizes the barrier between life and death. **There was a grotto and a rock placed against it, sealing it shut** (11:38b). **Jesus says, "Lift and take away the stone." Martha, the sister of the deceased, says to him, "Lord, he smells already for it is** [the] **fourth** [day]**"** (11:39). According to the Mishnah, after three days a corpse may have decayed so badly that it can no longer be identified with certainty (*m. Yebam.* 16.3). The opening of the tomb would be an offense not just to the people outside the tomb but also to the body within. Defenseless bodies are placed in tombs or sealed in coffins to protect them from postmortem abuse and the indignity of being seen. What cannot be seen cannot bring shame. Jesus subverts cultural expectations: **"Did I not say to you that whoever believes shall see the glory of God?"** (11:40). Jesus's authority overrides their compunctions: **They then lifted up and took the stone away.**

Jesus then prays for the first of three times. All three prayers use the address Father (see 12:27–28; 17:1–25), a feature common to Jewish prayers in which the afflicted or persecuted appeal for mercy or forgiveness (e.g., *Jos. Asen.* 12.8–15; Sir. 23:1; Mark 14:36), but this is where similarities end. As Mary Rose D'Angelo (1999, 70) notes, "None of the prayers or references to prayer in the Gospel of John makes or commends petitions for forgiveness or divine mercy for the sinner." **Jesus lifted up his eyes upward and said, "Father, I thank you that you heard me** (11:41). **I have known that you always listen to me, but I have said this on account of the crowd standing around in order they might believe that you did send me"** (11:42). This is a prayer of thanks, not supplication. Moreover, its rhetorical purpose is not to address God but to be overhead addressing God so that Jesus's actions will be interpreted as the work of God. The volume with which Jesus speaks can be heard from the grave and dramatizes the story told in the *paroimia* of the Good Shepherd (10:3). **And saying this in a loud voice, he cried out, "Lazarus, come on out"** (11:43). John provides a piece of *ekphrasis*: **The one who had been dead came out, the feet and the hands bound in bandages** [swathing] **and his face with a kerchief tied round** [it]. Kerchiefs were typically tied around the head to prevent the mouth from falling open. **Jesus says to them, "Loosen him and set him free to go away"** (11:44). John shows no interest in Lazarus's response to the resurrection.

The Report and Reaction in Jerusalem (11:45–57)

John withholds Mary's response until the next chapter. Rather than continuing by narrating the fulfillment of his commands as he does in the sign at Cana (2:7–8) and the healing of the blind man (9:7), John cuts directly to the response in Jerusalem. **Then many of the Jews, those coming to Mary and watching what he did, believed in him** (11:45). Some of the witnesses to the Johannine signs become reporters who could be characterized as informants or worse: **But some of them went to the Pharisees and told them what Jesus had done** (11:46). The mourners who grieve the death of Jesus's friend become complicit in Jesus's death.

John then describes an official response that requires the collusion of two parties who, according to E. P. Sanders (1992, 388–407), probably were at odds with each other during the late Second Temple period. On the one hand, John may be collapsing the reality of the historical Jesus, when the priests were the chief authorities, with the post-70 Johannine community at a time when the heirs to the Pharisees had supposedly stepped into the leadership role left vacant after the destruction of the temple. On the other hand, he may be ignorant of the membership of the Sanhedrin. Or in the context of tyranny, he may be pointing to the degree of anxiety that Jesus generates for those in power. As the proverb goes, "The enemy of my enemy is my friend." **Then the high priests and Pharisees convened a Sanhedrin and were saying, "What are we going to do, for this man does many signs?** (11:47). **If we leave him alone this way, all will believe in him, and the Romans will come and will put an end to us, both the place** [i.e., the temple] **and the nation"** (11:48). John employs dramatic irony, for his audience knows that their fear is realized in AD 70, when Titus destroys the temple. Their conviction that the temple in Jerusalem and their leadership are necessary for the preservation of God's people is precisely the supposition that this Gospel refutes. Belief in Jesus allows God's children to have eternal life.

The high priest, the highest authority, comes into view for the first time and gives his only speech in this Gospel. The introduction draws attention to the limited nature of his authority. Caiaphas's words in turn underscore the self-serving nature of the Sanhedrin's limited powers of discernment. **But a certain one of them, Caiaphas, who was high priest that cycle, said to them, "You do not know a thing, not at all (11:49). Nor do you calculate that it is profitable for you that one man should die on behalf of the people lest all of the nation be utterly destroyed"** (11:50). When such a line is put in the mouth of the one who is willing to die so that others may live, it is laudatory (John 10:11; Euripides, *Iph. aul.* 1375–99). On the lips of the one seeking to kill, it is deliberative; it is concerned with what is expedient rather than what is honorable or just (see Quintilian. *Inst.* 3.4.16).

Once more, John makes use of dramatic irony. The audience knows that Caiaphas's words are truer than he thinks. Within the context of tense relations with Rome, Caiaphas plays the game of Roman diplomacy. Through war, Rome conquered those people whom it characterized as warmongering and saw itself as the bringer of peace. In order to sue for peace, the people who were subsumed into the empire were invited to offer up their king to die on behalf of the nation (see Livy, *Hist.* 29.3; 30.16). When the Jewish authorities finally hand Jesus over to Pilate, they offer him as one who claims to be king, and they deny Jesus's kingship over them.

The narrator then adds a puzzling aside: **He did not say this on his own, but as high priest for that cycle, he prophesied that Jesus was about to die on behalf of the nation** (11:51). The notion that priests were able to foretell the future has its roots in Scripture (see Num. 27:21) and is affirmed by Philo (*Spec.* 4.192) and Josephus (*J.W.* 3.352). That Caiaphas is conscious of having received a communication from God, however, is not evident. The aside seems to make possible an elaboration based on a prophetic tradition of the ingathering of the nations, which is most clearly articulated in Isa. 11:10–12 and Jer. 3:17–18 but is not within Caiaphas's field of vision: **And not on behalf of the nation alone, but also so that the children of God who were scattered should be gathered into one** (11:52). Once more, the imagery in the *paroimia* of the Good Shepherd (10:16) becomes a reality. Read in the context of John 3:16, this seems to be a reference to universal salvation and not just the Jewish Diaspora (see "Universalism" in the theological issues section of 12:12–50).

John ends the episode with the effect of Caiaphas's words upon the assembly: **Then from that day, they resolved to kill him** (11:53). This resolution leads to a tactical retreat by Jesus so that he can pick the time of his arrest. **Then Jesus no longer went about openly among the Jews, but he departed that** [place] **to the countryside near the wilderness, to Ephraim, a so-called city, and remained there with the disciples** (11:54). Geographers have not located Ephraim. Perhaps this is precisely the point. Jesus chooses a location so far off the beaten path that few have heard of it.

John is careful to set the stage for Jesus's final entry into Jerusalem. **The Passover of the Jews was drawing near, and many went up to Jerusalem from** the countryside for the Passover in order that they might purify themselves (11:55). John introduces a chord of tension that he will play throughout the Passion Narrative, signifying the constraint of time as the Passover approaches and the pressure to be ritually clean in preparation increases. With the use of double negatives, the crowd implicitly articulates what the political climate is: **Then they were looking for Jesus and standing about in the temple saying among one another, "What do you suppose? Because he surely will not come to the festival [will he]?"** (11:56). **But the high priest and the Pharisees had given an order that if anyone knew where he is, he disclose where they might apprehend him** (11:57). By forcing ordinary citizens to become informants, the Jerusalem authorities seek comprehensive surveillance comparable to that of twentieth-century totalitarian states.

The Counterreaction in Bethany (12:1–8)

The "warrant" for Jesus's arrest is placed between two Bethany episodes, making clear that both are harbingers of the crucifixion that will follow. **Then Jesus, six days prior to Passover, went to Bethany, where Lazarus was, whom Jesus raised from the dead** (12:1). Mary was introduced in 11:2 with a proleptic epithet to tie the first episode with the last, and now Lazarus is introduced with an analeptic epithet for the same purpose. But the reference to his resurrected status also constructs a ritual space. Lazarus's home is an abode of the dead. Rites of hospitality become funeral rites. **Then they made for him a banquet there, and Martha was serving while Lazarus was one among those lying at table with him** (12:2). Lazarus attends his own funeral banquet. Later rabbinic tradition describes the first meal after the burial as a *se'udat havra'ah* (*sĕ'ûdat habra'â*, meal of comfort) and a family occasion (*b. Šabb.* 105b). By the late Second Temple period, Jews in Palestine had adopted the habit of reclining at table as a statement of their status as free people. John sets the scene by painting a typical picture of gendered roles and prepares for Mary's break with convention (see Luke 10:38–42). **Then Mary, taking a liter of ointment, very costly liquid nard, soothed Jesus's feet and wiped off his feet with her hair** (12:3). John's representation of the scene prepares for Judas's objection.

Pliny (*Nat.* 12.26) describes nard, the foremost perfume in the Greco-Roman world, as a sweet-scented, lightweight oil, with a dark ruddy hue. The Song of Songs provides the only biblical references to nard. The bride declares, "Your anointing oils are fragrant, your name is perfume poured out; therefore the maidens love you. . . . While the king was on his couch, my nard gave forth its fragrance" (Song 1:3, 12). Washing feet is a preliminary act of hospitality, done when one is welcomed into the house, but this action occurs during the feast and so, at the very least, would appear to be an extravagant gesture. Martha is doing what is socially subscribed; Mary chooses to do something more.

John constructs the scene as a struggle over who will define the meaning of the action. Jesus says and does nothing to signify rejection of her offering. In a backbiting aside, **Judas the Iscariot, who is about to hand him over, says to his disciples** (12:4), **"Why was this ointment not sold for three hundred denarii and given to the poor?"** (12:5). Judas evaluates the worth of the nard at about one year's wages for a laborer (see Mark 14:3). Pliny (*Nat.* 12.26) gives a price of one hundred denarii for a pound of nard spikes. The prepared ointment would be more expensive per pound. Given the possible range of values, Judas chooses the highest in order to put the extravagance in the worst light. John's narrator then provides the following glimpse into the private world of Judas's intent: **But he said this, not because the poor concerned him, but because he was a thief and having the case** [*glōssokomon*, an odd choice to refer to a cash box; it more commonly refers to a coffin] **appropriated the deposits** (12:6). This is the most explicit negative assessment of Judas's character in the four Gospels.

In the Markan version of the story, the flask containing the oil is smashed, but Jesus implies that some oil remains, so that Mary's act becomes a prelude to the preparation of a body for burial, another and more socially acceptable expression of devotion assigned to women in antiquity. **"Leave her alone in order that she might keep it for the day of my entombment"** (12:7). Jesus then adds a line that has been subjected to abuse: **"For the poor you will always have with you, but you will not always have me"** (12:8). The accent ought to be on the foreshadowing of Jesus's death, not the deprecation of charitable deeds. William Klassen (1996, 146–47) explores how the church took advantage of John's vilification of Judas to silence those who criticized spending the church's wealth on expensive building projects to honor Jesus while neglecting the poor. Treating 12:8 as a divine sanction of a status quo in which there are people suffering from poverty is unwarranted. Jesus's response to Judas here should not be interpreted as contradicting the teaching elsewhere in the NT that if one serves the poor, one serves the Lord (e.g., Matt. 25:31–46).

The Jerusalem Reaction Continued (12:9–11)

Once more John turns attention to the broader political environment in order to show his audience what Jesus's words portend. **Then a great crowd of Jews realized that he is there and came not only on account of Jesus but also in order that they might see Lazarus, whom he raised from the dead** (12:9). Lazarus has become a spectacle, a wonder of the Judean world, and as is the case when one tries to control events through violence, the violence cannot be contained. Caiaphas's claim that it takes only one man's death to secure peace is shown to be a lie. **Meanwhile the high priests resolved to kill Lazarus** (12:10), **because many of the Jews were being drawn in on account of him and believing in Jesus** (12:11). The reference to high priests when there is technically only one high priest at a time fits into the picture of the office that John paints after Jesus's arrest. "High priest" becomes a title passed around six members of a family ruled by Annas from AD 6, when Judea comes under direct Roman rule, until AD 66, when Annas is assassinated by insurgents as a Roman collaborator.

Theological Issues

The issues that swirl around readings of the stories of Lazarus, Martha, and Mary tend to center on questions of identity. Jesus's divinity and humanity seem to collide, Judas emerges as "a Judas," and the prominence of the role of women becomes indisputable, but its significance remains debatable.

Jesus's Humanity and Commiseration

Much of the theological discussion generated by this section focuses on the questionable observation of mourning and hospitality rituals and the chinks in Jesus's divine armor exposed by his participation in them. In his treatment of the story of Lazarus, John Chrysostom (*Hom. Jo.* 62.4) joined early Christian leaders in the critique of most funerary observations, other than the funeral banquet, because mourning was a denial of the resurrection.

Many twentieth-century exegetes take the signs of emotion as indications of anger at Mary's lack of faith (see *embrimasthai* in Dan. 11:30; Mark 1:43; John 11:33, 38), as though anger were a more appropriate emotion for God than commiseration. But if Jesus were angry, one would expect a direct object, that at which he is angry rather than the indirect "in spirit." As Abraham Joshua Heschel has persuasively explained, God's pathos of sympathy stands at the center of the theology of the Hebrew Prophets:

> He does not simply command and expect obedience; He is also moved and affected by what happens in the world, and reacts accordingly. Events and human actions arouse in Him joy or sorrow, pleasure or wrath. He is not conceived as judging the world in detachment. He reacts in an intimate and subjective manner. (2001, 288–89)

In the Jewish context, Jesus's sorrow may be a sign of his divinity as much as his humanity.

Juvenal's comments on tears provide another context within the Greco-Roman world for understanding the narrative significance of Jesus's tears:

> By giving tears to the human race Nature revealed she was giving us also tender hearts; compassion is the finest part of our make-up. She therefore moves us to pity the accused, as he pleads his case unkempt in body and dress. . . . It is Nature who makes us cry when we meet the cortège of a girl on the eve of marriage, or a little child too small for the pyre is laid in a grave. (*Sat.* 15.132–45, trans. Rudd 1999)

There is no reason to deny Jesus a sense of commiseration with humanity because he knows the future. Rather, John seems to juxtapose the demands of obedience to God with those of friendship and then reconcile them through Jesus's death (see 15:13) and the resurrection he offers. The stories of Jesus's friendship with one Bethany family illustrate the implications of the pronouncement made in 3:16 that God is motivated by love when he grants humanity eternal life through Jesus.

Resurrection and Eternal Life

While John makes the moment of belief the gesture that accompanies the gift of eternal life, eschatological resurrection remains in view. When Martha refers to belief in the general resurrection in 11:24, Jesus does not challenge her convictions but rather confirms them and promises, "I am the resurrection and the life; the one who believes in me, even though he [or she] dies, shall live" (11:25). The significance of death is then so reduced that Jesus can say to Martha that "all who live and believe in me . . . shall never die" (11:26). Given the way that John draws attention to the unjust suffering of the community of believers (15:20), it seems safe to place the general resurrection in the same category as the Lord's Supper, something with which the audience is supposed to be so well acquainted that it need not be discussed explicitly. When Jesus says, "You have crushing pain in the world, but take courage, I have conquered the world" (16:33), it seems most likely that he is referring to the conquest of death and the door that he has opened to eternal life through his resurrection. When he alludes to Peter's death in 21:18–19 and invites him to "Follow me," the invitation is surely to be taken as a gesture toward both death and resurrection.

John's Vilification of Judas

John's narrator adds several pieces of retrospective reflection that support the indictment of Judas as a traitor. The Matthean account leaves room to suppose that Judas colludes with Jesus in arranging a location and time for the arrest in order to prevent a riot. When Judas arrives in Gethsemane, Jesus greets him and sanctions his act by saying, "Friend, do what you came for" (Matt. 26:50 NIV). Judas confesses his sin, returns the money paid to him, and then hangs himself in remorse (Matt. 27:3–5). The notion that suicide is sin enters Christian discourse only with Saint Augustine, in the early fifth century.

William Klassen suspects that John has a personal bias that informs his depiction. Judas becomes not simply the one who hands Jesus over but also one who has gone over to the side of Satan and acts as his agent (Klassen 1996, 142–43). Even though John's narrator echoes Luke 22:3 by saying that Satan enters into him during the Last Supper (John 13:26–27), he represents Judas as one in league with evil throughout the story. The narrator reveals that

Jesus knows that one of his disciples has a devil (John 6:70) and then makes it clear that Jesus refers to Judas (6:71). In the story of Lazarus, John reveals that Judas cares more about money than the poor and that he is an embezzler (12:6), an observation that smacks of the suspicions of hindsight rather than knowledge of fact, for who, knowing that Judas was stealing from the common purse, would allow him to keep it? At the final meal, the narrator explains that the devil has put the thought of handing Jesus over into Judas's mind (13:2). Although Jesus washes Judas's feet and Judas does not object, Jesus alludes to one of the Twelve who is not clean (13:10), and the narrator makes it clear that he refers to the one who will hand him over (13:11). Jesus suggests that Judas was destined to be lost so that Scripture would be fulfilled (17:12). Judas then leads the detachment sent to arrest Jesus, but he serves no real purpose at the arrest (18:1–11). Judas's actions are something apart from Jesus's plan to hand himself over.

In his study of Judas, Kim Paffenroth notices the correspondence between Judas and the Jews in John's Gospel. Both are associated with the devil (see 8:44), and the emphasis on the word *Ioudaioi* suggests that the homology with Judas's name becomes an opportune coincidence (Paffenroth 2001, 33). Beginning with the church fathers (e.g., Jerome, *Comm. Ps.* 108 [109]; John Chrysostom, *Hom. Act.* 3), the equating of the Jews with Judas becomes a prevalent theme in Christian literature, with the result that even Dietrich Bonhoeffer (1961, 412), who dies in 1945 as a Nazi resister, can write in a sermon in 1937:

> Who is Judas? Shouldn't we ask here also about the name which he carries? "Judas," doesn't it stand here for that deeply divided people of Jesus's origin, for the elect people, who had received the promise of the Messiah and yet rejected [him]? For the people of Judah, which loved the Messiah and yet could not love him thus? (trans. Klassen 1996, 31; see Paffenroth 2001, 51–56)

While John—who seems to have struggled with the question of how the Jews could reject Jesus and one of his own could betray him—could not anticipate the legacy of his treatment of Judas, those who inherit this tradition have the responsibility to recognize that Judas's depiction is a facet of Johannine storytelling and then to untangle the identity of Judas from that of an entire nation. Though Satan and demons are characters within the narrative of the Synoptic Gospels, John limits the presence of evil to its incarnation within human beings or activities. John does not provide enough material to construct a complete picture of evil, its origins, or its cosmology. He tells the story of how Jesus comprehends Judas's lack of fidelity from its beginning, and the story of Jesus's arrest shows that even the most malevolent intent succumbs to the irony that God intends Jesus's death on the cross and renders efforts to crucify Jesus almost comic. The Johannine Jesus presents the betrayal in a digression (13:31) rather than as the opening statement of his Farewell Address (in contrast to Mark 14:18; Matt. 26:21) and does not speak words of malediction against him comparable to those found in the synoptic account (Mark 14:21; par. Matt.26:24 and Luke 22:22).

Johannine Women

The prominent role that women play as Jesus's dialogue partners in John's Gospel and on occasion as witnesses (4:29; 20:18) gives rise to discussion in the context of modern debates about their status as disciples and women's role in ministry. Johannine women have a strong voice, which is articulate and heard. Women are all but silent in Mark, and the quoted speech of women in Matthew and Luke is limited for the most part to the birth narratives or a stray line (Matt. 15:27; 20:21; Luke 10:40; 11:27) or reported thought (Matt. 9:21). Their women are speechless in the resurrection scenes. In John, the Samaritan woman has nine lines of dialogue, and Martha's two conversations with Jesus and her private dialogue with Mary give her a total of six lines, including her confession. While the mother of Jesus has only two lines and Mary of Bethany has but one, both figure prominently in two episodes each. Mary Magdalene engages in dialogue with both the angels and Jesus at the empty tomb. All the Johannine women line up on the side of those who believe in Jesus. Consequently, Turid Karlsen Seim (1987, 56–73) calls the women paradigms for discipleship. Martin Scott (1992, 238–45) contends that they serve as "exemplary disciples" who replace the traditional male disciples. Robert Gordon Maccini (1996, 224) looks at the freedom with which Johannine women express their faith and concludes that the Gospel writer gives equal value to the testimony of either men or women as individuals. The similarity between Martha's confession in John and that of Peter in Matthew leads Elisabeth Schüssler Fiorenza (1986, 31) to pronounce Martha as the embodiment of "the full apostolic faith of the Johannine community."

If we consider John's use of women in his narrative in the context of Greco-Roman literature, it becomes evident that his purpose may be christological: he is saying more about Jesus than about women. In her study of Greek tragedy, Froma I. Zeitlin (1990, 68) concludes that the speech of women serves an exploration of male selfhood and that male, paternal structures of authority are reestablished at the ends of the plays. An examination of comparable elements in John's Gospel suggests that John also uses the tensions created when Jesus enters into women's space to explore Jesus's male identity. At the end of the Gospel, patriarchal structures remain intact: believers reside within the house of the Father, and Jesus remains God's obedient Son. During Jesus's ministry, his encounters with women happen in social locations that are liminal spaces, such as weddings and funerals, where men and women mix and the boundary between private and public are blurred. The conversations are filled with domestic concerns, such as provision of refreshments, marriages, and caring for corpses. In each of the scenes, Jesus's identity is threatened or challenged. At Cana, he must balance his mother's wish with the revelation of his Father's glory. In Samaria, Jesus violates a number of social taboos and juggles his identity as a Jewish man with his offer of the gift of living water. In the scene at the tomb, Jesus must meet friendship's demands while fulfilling his own purposes. Judas's criticism of Mary's use of expensive ointment on Jesus's feet is an indirect challenge to Jesus's authority insofar as he has failed to control the woman and her spending (see Sir. 25:21–22; 33:20–21). In the ancient Mediterranean world, honor was something that was given to men or families in the public realm. Women belonged to the private realm in which they guarded their family's honor by demonstrating a proper sense of shame. When women interacted with men beyond the confines of the household, they became potential sources of shame (see Moxnes 1996, 21–22). Jesus's forays into the private realm of women creates a new notion of glory that anticipates the reversal of the categories of honor and shame at Jesus's crucifixion (see Brant 2004, 212–24).

Although these observations suggest that John's concern is not to establish a precedent for women in ministry, they do not provide support for opposition to women's ministry. Many of the arguments against women's ordination are based on the precedent set by the temple priesthood—a form of authority that John seems to impugn—or on the lack of authority of a woman's witness, something that John's narrative does not support.

PART 3

John 12:12–19:42

Jesus's Triumphant Hour

Part 3 of this commentary contains the episodes that mark the last week of Jesus's life
and are commemorated in the church calendar
as Holy Week. In the synoptic tradition, the
entry into Jerusalem sets the stage for the action in the temple and marks the beginning of
the Passion Narrative. In John, the entry is a
denouement following the raising of Lazarus.
There are several additional reasons why the
entry into Jerusalem could be counted as the
final episode in the previous section. Many
exegetes treat it as the conclusion to the Book
of Signs. The argument with which Jesus ends
chapter 12 provides the conclusion to an argument that he begins in chapter 5 and sustains
through chapter 10. The speech in 12:44–50
pulls threads of earlier discourses together and
uses them to emphasize that Jesus's death is exaltation rather than humiliation. The decision

to include 12:12–50 in the section that includes his death is based on its emphasis on triumph. Jesus proclaims his arrival in Jerusalem as his hour (12:27) and "the critical moment of this world" when "the ruler of this world will be expelled" (12:31). He will go on to proclaim that he has conquered the world (16:33), and he will be raised on the cross as a victorious king rather than a defeated pretender.

John 12:12–50

Jesus the Triumphator

Introductory Matters

John presents the crowd as going out to meet Jesus and receiving him into the city as the parousia (arrival in person) of the king, in imitation of the Hellenistic and Roman traditions of welcoming the returning victor from battle. The word "triumph" (*thriambos*) does not appear in the text, but Paul uses a related verb to refer to Jesus's victory. Paul writes, "To God be thanks, who always leads us triumphing [*thriambeuonti*, in the act of a triumphal procession] in Christ" (2 Cor. 2:14). The image of a victory parade is even clearer in

---

The Triumph

In Hellenistic and Roman traditions, the general returning to his city from a military victory was awarded a form of parade called a "triumph" (Latin *triumphus*). The triumphator, riding in a chariot, drove the most illustrious of his captives ahead of him and paraded the spoils of war before the crowd. Awarded the privilege of wearing purple and crowned with a laurel wreath, the Roman triumphator played the role of Jupiter, the god who blesses the warrior with victory (see Polybius, *Hist.* 30.25; Pliny, *Nat.* 33.11; Josephus, *J.W.* 7.132–57, describes Titus's triumph in AD 70; see fig. 19). The Roman senate granted Julius Caesar the privilege of wearing the purple robe and crown all the time (Suetonius, *Jul.* 76), and eventually the emperors granted themselves the exclusive right to wear the dress of the triumphator.

Figure 19. Frieze on Titus's triumph arch commemorating victory in the Judean War (AD 70).

Col. 2:15: "Having stripped the rulers and authorities, he made a show of their appearance, having triumphed [*thriambeusas*] over them." Tertullian (*Cor.* 13) provides the first known use of "triumph" to refer to the last entry into Jerusalem: "He would enter Jerusalem in triumph without even an ass of his own."

The various subunits of this exegetical unit form one main action, in which the crowd reverses itself. In the Synoptic Gospels, Jesus is seen to consciously enact Zech. 9:9 and proclaim himself king, but in John, the crowd proclaims him king, and he responds by getting on a donkey. He accepts their acknowledgment, not as a king who will kill to save them, but as a king who will die for their salvation. The action of the entry opens out into the future by having it end with the naive prophecy of the Pharisees, "See, the world has gone after him" (12:19), which is quickly fulfilled by several Greeks who wish to see Jesus. When Jesus speaks of the necessity of his death, the crowd slips back into confusion and is unable to recognize Jesus for who he is. Consequently Jesus withdraws to wait his time.

The chapter ends with a short speech by Jesus (12:44–50), which is disconnected from the narrative as though Jesus speaks directly to the Gospel's audience. In this speech, he provides the conclusion of the argument begun in John 5, that he acts as God's life-giving agent. He ends by proclaiming that he has come "to save the world" (12:47).

Tracing the Narrative Flow

Jesus's Reception in Jerusalem (12:12–19)

The crowd that greets Jesus is composed of pilgrims. As we shall see, John makes it clear that Jesus's reputation has spread to the Diaspora.

The next day, when the great crowd that came to the festival heard that Jesus is coming to Jerusalem (12:12), they took fronds of date palm and went out to a rendezvous with him and were crying out, "Hosanna; blessed is the one who comes in the name of the Lord, the king of Israel" (12:13). Jerome Neyrey (2007a, 212) notes, "The citations from Zechariah and Psalm 118 are shaved to emphasize the acclamation of Jesus as 'King'" (see also John 12:15). The first part of their song is from Ps. 118:25–26, one of the Hallel psalms sung at festivals, to which they add their own epithet, "king of Israel." "Hosanna" is generally not translated. It is the Hebrew petition "Please, save!" The Greek word *hypantēsis*, translated above as "rendezvous," is a technical term for a civic reception of a ruler (see Josephus, *Ant*. 11.329). The crowd's actions prompt Jesus to make a gesture that fulfills the prophecy of Zech. 9:9 and accepts his kingship. **Jesus, finding a small donkey, mounted it, just as it is written (12:14), "Fear not, daughter of Zion. Behold, your king comes, sitting upon a foal of a donkey"** (12:15).

While Jesus and the crowd act in consort, the disciples are represented as out of step with the action. Only in retrospect can they make sense of what is happening: **At first his disciples did not understand these things, but when Jesus was glorified, then they remembered that these things were written about him and they did these things to him** (12:16). It seems odd that the disciples would not associate this event with Zech. 9:9 and conclude immediately that Jesus is accepting the throne that the crowd offers. This editorial aside links the final entry into Jerusalem with Jesus's prediction of his resurrection during the temple event (2:20), which the disciples similarly recalled only after he had risen from the dead (2:22).

The narrative resumes with a picture of a crowd that is swelling. **Then the crowd that was with him testified that he had called Lazarus from the tomb and raised him from the dead (12:17). On account of this, the crowd also went out to meet him, because they heard this about his having done the sign** (12:18). One of the puzzling features of the synoptic account is that the entry does not provoke Jesus's arrest or Roman opposition. Luke has some Pharisees in the crowd protest (19:39), but there is no official response. John provides a more logical account, first, by making it clear that a plan is already in motion to arrest Jesus, and second, by capturing the surveillance of the event by the Pharisees with their words to each other: **"Watch, because you are helpless; see, the world has gone after him"** (12:19). At this point all they can do is stand and watch the spectacle if they do not want to risk a riot. Their exaggerated reference to the crowd as "the world" is a piece of dramatic irony that anticipates what happens next, the approach of some Greeks, as well as Jesus's summary remark, "I will save the world" (12:47).

Jesus Delivers the World (12:20–33)

The fulfillment of the Pharisees' prophetic words begins immediately: **Some of the Greeks who had come up in order to worship in the festival were there**

(12:20). The term Greek (*Hellēnes*) can signify that these are either Greek-speaking Jews from the Diaspora, like the *Hellēnistai* of Acts 6:1, or that these are non-Jews like Paul's *Hellēn* in Gal. 3:28. The crowd's use of the term *Hellēnes* in John 7:35 and Jesus's words suggest that these are people whom the disciples treat as a world apart from their own, that is, not Jews.

Travelers in the Greco-Roman era moved through a sacred landscape filled with sanctuaries and shrines, and to ignore the sanctity of a place by refraining from worship ran the risk of offending at least the residents if not the local deity. Jerusalem stood apart from this norm. Josephus describes a temple inhospitable to pagan "religious tourists." He makes the refusal of sacrifices offered on behalf of the emperor a cause of the First Revolt (Josephus, *J.W.* 2.409). In *Ant.* 3.318–19, where Josephus tries to demonstrate that veneration of Moses was widespread, he tells the story of a group that comes from beyond the Euphrates. After a journey of four months, they arrive only to find that they are not allowed to make sacrifices. Out of reverence for Moses, even though some had already begun the rituals, they refrain from trying to complete their offering.

John's *Hellēnes* need not be people who have come to believe exclusively in the God of the Israelites, but they do present themselves as having deference toward Jesus's status by approaching him indirectly through an attendant. **These then approached Philip, who was from Bethsaida of Galilee, and petitioned him, saying, "Sir [*Kyrie*], we wish to see Jesus"** (12:21). John may be dramatizing the ironic fulfillment of the crowd's confused speculation that Jesus was planning to go to the Diaspora to teach the Greeks (7:35). Jerome Neyrey (2007a, 213) points to a pattern established in chapter 1: "Jesus never calls anyone to be a disciple; they are all brought to him by others, whose association he then confirms." Philip is the one disciple who has only a Greek name and comes from a city close to the Decapolis; thus he seems to be a suitable candidate to serve as a translator as well as a courier of the travelers' request. His agency also recalls his role as Jesus's front man in the story of the feeding of the five thousand (6:5–7). Once more, John depicts Philip as lacking confidence in his capacity to fulfill his role when he stops for backup, as though the request will carry more weight if delivered in tandem or by a disciple with more seniority or influence. **Philip comes and speaks to Andrew, Andrew comes along with Philip, and they speak to Jesus** (12:22). John does not provide their direct speech, and Jesus's response is not a direct answer to the request. Neyrey (2007b, 108) argues that Jesus discourages volunteers (see Matt. 8:19–22; Luke 9:57–62) and that his words signify a dismissal. His declaration—**"The hour has come for the Son of Man to be glorified"** (12:23)—could also suggest that the disciples have framed the request in a way that anticipates his refusal, because he seems to provide a rationale for receiving the Greeks. Jesus begins by referring obliquely to his death. Then he explains why his death is necessary for geometric growth of his followers through an analogy that may be a known proverb (see Keener 2003, 873): **"Truly, truly, I say to you, unless the seed of grain has fallen to the earth and dies, it alone remains. If it should die, it bears much fruit"** (12:24). He then adds another proverb: **"The one who loves his life loses it; and the one who hates his life in this world preserves it forever"** (12:25). This last axiom closely resembles a synoptic saying, "Those who find their life will lose it, and those who lose their life for my sake will find it" (Matt. 10:39; see also Luke 17:33). In this context, Jesus seems to suggest that the Greeks' request signifies a total break with their former life. They cannot simply be religious tourists: they must become part of the divine household. He then issues a broad invitation to discipleship. **"Whoever would serve me, follow me! And wherever I am, there also is my servant. Whoever should serve me, the Father will honor him"** (12:26).

Jesus digresses with a piece of reportage in which he imagines what he might pray: **"Now my soul quakes, and what should I say, 'Father, save me from this hour!'?"** Jesus then answers his own question: **"But for this purpose** [to save the world] **I came to this hour"** (12:27). John recasts the Gethsemane prayer found in the synoptic tradition, in which Jesus struggles with his task (Mark 14:35–36), as a rhetorical strategy of reasoning aloud. By asking and then immediately answering his own question (*anthypophora*), Jesus underscores his certitude. He follows with an actual prayer—**"Father, glorify your name!"**—answered by a second party. **Then a voice came from heaven, "I have glorified** [it], **and indeed I shall glorify** [it] **again"** (12:28). Jesus's claim in John 5:37 that the Father who sent him has testified on his behalf is now confirmed by the narrative.

Whatever message the disciples carry back to the Greek petitioners or whether there is an interview is not narrated. Attention turns to the bystanders who hear the voice, but not with the same clarity as the Gospel's audience. Once more the sign that ought to point to Jesus's identity sends the crowd into its endless debate. **Then the crowd that was standing** [there] **and listening was saying that it was thunder; others were saying, "An angel has spoken to him"** (12:29)—a logical deduction given the tradition that angels' voices sound like thunder (Rev. 6:1; 10:3–4; 14:2; 19:6). Whether thunder or an angel, in the ancient mind the sonorous voice would portend either death or judgment or both (see Gen. 19:1; 2 Chron. 32:21; Acts 12:7–11, 23; Sophocles, *Oed. col.* 1463). Jesus then clarifies whose end has come: **"The voice did not happen for my sake but for your sake** (12:30). **Now is the critical moment of this world, now the ruler of this world will be expelled** [*ekblēthēsetai*]" (12:31; see 14:30; 16:11).

In the political drama that is unfolding in the minds of the crowd and the Jewish authorities, Jesus seems to sound a battle cry for the overthrow of Roman occupation. Set within the narrative that Jesus has been telling, his pronouncement takes on a different meaning. *Ekblēthēsetai* can also mean

193

"be exposed." In light of the crucifixion, the ruler of this world will be shown to be powerless. Even death will not prevent the world from being drawn to God's Son. **"And I, at such time as I am lifted up from the ground, will draw all** [the world] **to myself"** (12:32). The very act intended to prevent the world from going after Jesus will make that event possible. In case the Gospel's audience does not understand Jesus's allusion, the narrator provides an aside: **But he was saying this to signify** [*sēmainōn*] **the sort of death he was about to die** (12:33). The use of the verb form of *sēmeia* underscores the way that Jesus's demonstrations of his divine power function as signs; they point beyond themselves, generally in anticipation of the crucifixion and resurrection.

Jesus's Rejection (12:34–43)

The narrative audience recognizes that "lifted up" is an allusion to either death or ascension to heaven in the same way that Enoch and Elijah ascended (Gen. 5:24; 2 Kings 2:1–12). The Son of Man in Dan. 7:13 descends from heaven rather than ascends; therefore, the predictions of departure prompt them to reply, **"We have heard from the Law** [the choice of verb is appropriate to an aural reception of Scripture] **that the Christ remains forever, so how** [can] **you say that it is necessary for the Son of Man to be lifted up? Who is this Son of Man?"** (12:34). Law is a metonymy for Scripture. The crowd perhaps refers to the divine promise that the throne of David's kingdom will be established forever (2 Sam. 7:13). Jesus has not mentioned "the Son of Man" since 12:23, after which he refers to himself in the first person. The crowd seems to have put two and two together and realizes that Jesus calls himself "the Son of Man" and that he uses the phrase to refer to the messiah. This means that the question "Who is this Son of Man?" is not about picking him out of a lineup but about his role. Their expectations for the messiah do not line up with Jesus's announcement.

Jesus issues one last invitation, which echoes language found in the prologue: **"For a little while the light is in you. Walk about while you have the light, lest darkness overtake you. And the one walking about in the darkness does not know where he is going** [*hypagei*]**"** (12:35). The verb *hypagō* suggests that one is not simply stumbling about in the dark, but that one ends up in the wrong place. **"While you have the light, believe in the light, in order that you may become sons** [children] **of light"** (12:36a). Jesus's final words open to an undetermined and hopeful future rather than condemning the crowd for its lack of belief in him. Time is not a fixed past but an emerging event and a realm of becoming.

John closes the scene with an exit. After **Jesus spoke these things, he departed, hidden from them** (12:36b). The manner of his exit stands in contrast to his entry.

The narrator provides a comment that marks the crowd's return to dismissal of Jesus after their brief period of enthusiasm and signifies a closed past.

Despite his doing so many signs in front of them, they did not believe in him (12:37). As though an apology is needed, the narrator recites two quotations from Isaiah that demonstrate, first, that the crowd's rejection of Jesus fulfills prophecy, and second, that God has caused their confusion so that they will turn to God for answers: "Lord, who has believed our report? And the arm of the Lord, to whom has it been revealed?" (12:38; Isa. 53:1 LXX). "He has blinded their eyes and hardened their heart, so that they should not see with the eyes nor apprehend with the heart, and they should turn and I will cure them" (12:40; Isa. 6:9–10, a fusion of the MT and LXX). Isaiah's vision of the heavenly throne (Isa. 6:1–13) becomes a prophecy about Jesus's crucifixion: Isaiah said this because he saw his glory, and he spoke about him (12:41). John then adds a surprising exception to the general incomprehension: Yet all the same [*homōs mentoi*], many of the leaders believed in him, but on account of the Pharisees they did not avow [their belief] lest they become *aposynagōgoi* (12:42). For they loved the glory [given to them by] men even more than the glory of God (12:43). In John's diagnosis of the problem, fear of losing social status is as much a factor as disbelief. John seems to resonate with 1 Corinthians, in which Paul observes that believers look like fools to the world (1:18–31; 3:18–20; 4:10).

Jesus Concludes His Argument (12:44–50)

The narrator provides no context for Jesus's closing speech, no narrative entrance, no temporal or physical setting. Without a narrative frame for this speech, Jesus's reference to the words that he has spoken point not to an immediate context but to everything said in his speeches. By going over many of the main themes of arguments that dominate chapters 5, 6, 8, and 10, Jesus provides the *conclusio*, or *peroratio*, for his principal argument that he acts as God's obedient Son (see Quintilian, *Inst.* 6.1.1). Jesus called out and said, "The one believing in me does not believe in me but in the one who sent me" (12:44). Jesus reasserts his role as savior rather than judge: "I, light [itself], have come into the world, in order that everyone who believes in me shall not remain in the darkness (12:46; see 8:12). Even so, whoever should hear my words yet does not keep [them], I do not condemn him [see 5:24]. For I did not come so that I pass sentence upon the world [see 8:16], but so that I will save the world" (12:47). Jesus reiterates an assertion he makes in 3:17, but now he stands in the place of God as agent of salvation. The work his Father does, he does (see 5:19). Jesus affirms the petition "hosanna" (please save) made by those who go out to meet him when he arrives in Jerusalem (12:13), but if they hope for a royal messiah who will vindicate them and condemn their enemies to death, Jesus confounds expectations by offering to save both Israel and the world.

The next line seems to contradict what Jesus has just said: "The one who refuses me and who does not receive my words has his judge; the word that I have spoken, this will judge him on the last day" (12:48; the antithesis of 5:24). To the modern reader, Jesus may seem to be splitting hairs, but in the ancient context in which speech acts serve a more vital role in the socioeconomic order, the distinction makes more sense. To refuse (*athetōn*) is used in the context of treaties and other sorts of contractual or political interactions. To refuse Jesus is to break faith with or cancel a treaty or promise. Those who do not believe are represented as turning down an offer or nullifying a covenant. God has sent them a champion as promised, and they have refused him.

For a final time, Jesus reiterates that he speaks as a son on behalf of a father: **"Because I have not spoken from myself** [out of my own inclinations], **but the Father who sent me, he has given me a command as to what I may say and what I may speak"** (12:49; see 8:27). The distinction between "say" (*legō*) and "speak" (*laleō*) is perhaps a way of saying what and how I should speak. **"And I know that his command is eternal life. Therefore these things I speak, just as the Father has ordered me, I speak"** (12:50). Given this final public statement, it now becomes appropriate to translate the clauses *En archē ēn ho logos, kai ho logos ēn pros ton theon* as "In the beginning was the word, and the word was from God" (1:1).

The significance of what Jesus has said in his conclusion depends on whether the plot is tragic or epic and whether the rhetoric is forensic (an argument to accuse or defend an individual or group) or epideictic (to praise Jesus and show that his words and actions indeed glorify God). If the plot is tragic and the rhetoric forensic, the accent falls upon both the narrator's conclusion and the failure of those who do not recognize Jesus and their fate. Jerome Neyrey (2007b) supports this reading and argues that chapter 12 functions as the part of a *peroratio* that arouses emotions of hatred toward those who reject Jesus. If the plot is epic and the rhetoric epideictic, the accent falls on the truth of Jesus's words that he will vanquish the ruler of this world and as a result draw all people to himself, even though some have denied both his authority to act as God's agent and his ability to fulfill his boast. Jesus's words are then analogous to the vaunting of a Homeric hero who speaks as though victory is won before he enters the battle (see Hector's speech in Homer, *Il.* 8.161–83) and even if he dies (see Achilles's speech in Homer, *Il.* 20.178–98).

Theological Issues

Universalism

The arrival of the Greeks on the eve of Jesus's passion brings the world to the foot of the cross. One might even say that John dramatizes Gal. 3:28. Whether one is a man from the Galilee or a woman from Samaria, whether one is an elite royal official or a blind beggar, whether one is a Jew or Greek—Jesus issues the same invitation to believe in him and the same promise of eternal life. The narrative substantiates Jesus's assertions that when he is lifted up, he will draw all to him (12:32) and that he comes to save the world (12:47). As Peder Borgen (1996, 112) observes, this positive use of the term "Greeks" suggests "a more positive and open attitude, a more universal perspective, than that of a sect." Jesus's presence in the world radically alters the nature of the sacred landscape. Standing in Jerusalem, at the threshold of the temple, traditional barriers that limit the access of some to the God of the Israelites become irrelevant.

These claims that Jesus makes about the inclusive implications of his mission become a foothold in Scripture for theologians who articulate a truly universal salvation.

John 12:32 is one of the key texts (see also 1 Cor. 15:28) used by Jacques Ellul (1989, 189–90); in building upon the work of Karl Barth, he argues that God "cannot send to hell the creation which he so loved that he gave his only Son for it. He cannot reject it because it is his creation. This would be to cut off himself." Ellul (1989, 191) argues against the notion that God offers universal salvation that people can reject or accept:

> We have often said that God wants free people. He undoubtedly does, except in relation to this last and definitive decision. We are not free to decide and choose to be damned. To say that God presents us with the good news of the gospel and then leaves the final issue to our free choice either to accept it and be saved or to reject it and be lost is foolish. To take this point of view is to make us arbiters of the situation. In this case it is we who finally decide our own salvation. This view reverses a well-known thesis and would have it that God proposes and man disposes.

Ellul's argument is logical, but it does not address statements in the Gospel of John that suggest the contrary.

John's Gospel provides us with a picture of the human predicament with its conflicting traditions and fear of ostracism and humiliation, which makes it clear why some reject Jesus's invitation. The equation of salvation with eternal life, and eternal life with knowledge of the Father through the Son—all this stands in tension with Ellul's picture of salvation without acceptance of Jesus. In John, those who refuse Jesus stand under indictment and before a judge (12:48; cf. 5:29). The question that remains open is whether John anticipates a mission to the world that will draw all people to Jesus (12:32), including those who currently reject him, and whether he allows for repentance by those who refuse Jesus after the parousia and the general resurrection.

The Ruler of This World

This commentary treats "the ruler of this world" (12:31) as a reference to its political rulers and Jesus's act of salvation as the defeat of their deadly tactics to prevent God from realizing his goal of drawing all people to him. This makes sense within the context of a world in which who and where one worships contributes to the stability of the social fabric of society. But another reading of this text ought to be entertained.

Judith L. Kovacs (1995, 231) contends that the ruler of this world refers to Satan and that "the Fourth Evangelist sees the death, resurrection, and ascent of Jesus as the turning point in the conflict between God and the forces of evil." Jesus refers to the ruler of this world two more times in his Farewell Address, first, as "one who is coming" (14:30), presumably as an agent in his arrest, and again, when he explains that the Paraclete will make clear that the world has been wrong about judgment: "The ruler of this world has been judged" (16:11). Given that Jesus does not specify who the ruler of this world is, J. Kovacs (1995, 233) relies on the dualistic tendencies of the prologue and Jesus's discourse and Jesus's words in 8:44, in which he accuses the Jews of being children of the devil, to substantiate that the Gospel tells the story of a "battle between God and Satan—a battle acted out in the sphere of human history." Kovacs's case may seem to hang by thin threads when considered within the light of modern rational sensibilities, but J. Kovacs (1995, 235–44) contends that there are sufficient connections between John's Gospel and Jewish apocalyptic texts that clearly depict a cosmic battle between God and Satan to argue that John's audience would have set Jesus's reference to the ruler of this world within this context.

If Kovacs is correct, the absence of demonic exorcisms in the Gospel of John becomes more puzzling. An exorcism would allow Jesus to make a statement comparable to Mark 3:27: "No one is able into the house of the strong one to enter, his equipment to spoil, unless first the strong one he binds."

The problem that many theologians have with setting Jesus's reference to the ruler of this world within the context of a cosmic battle is that this grants too much salvific import to the crucifixion and not enough to the revelation of the truth. Kovacs's reading tends to ignore the stress that John places on Jesus's glorification and the power that human glory holds over those who resist seeing the revelation of God's love in Jesus's death. Believers are not released from the power of Satan by his defeat; they are drawn to Jesus by the revelation of God's love on the cross. This does not mean that the ruler of this world cannot be a reference to Satan. In John, Satan is the father of lies (8:44). Jesus's victory, however, lies not in a cosmic battle but in the revelation that he dies an honorable death, putting to rest the lie that crucifixion is humiliation. As Sigve Tonstad (2008, 201–6) concludes, Jesus's claim to triumph is theodicy, not soteriology.

John 13:1–30, 36–38

After the Last Supper

Introductory Matters

In chapters 13–19, John gives almost half of his Gospel to the last twenty-four hours of Jesus's life, more narrative space than the other three Gospel accounts combined. Chapters 13–17 record the events of Jesus's last evening with his disciples: the introduction of the ritual of footwashing, predictions of Judas's betrayal and Peter's denial, and Jesus's parting words and prayer. The unity of time in these seven chapters (13–19) invites giving them a sustained reading, but to make the task less formidable, the Farewell Address will be treated separately from the narrative that introduces it and the action that follows. The Farewell Address begins in 13:31, but the prediction of Peter's denial (13:36–38) interrupts the speech. In order not to sever the beginning of the speech from the body, 13:31–35 will be reiterated at the beginning of the next chapter of this commentary and will be translated without comment in this chapter.

The action begins in medias res: the meal has already begun. John provides no information about the location of the meal or the time other than that it is before the Passover. Here is a place where an argument from silence seems warranted. John seems to play with the expectations of an audience informed by something like the synoptic account. The Synoptic Gospels provide careful delineation of the time and preparation appropriate to the celebration of a Passover meal (Mark 14:12–16; Matt. 26:17–19; Luke 22:7–13). John makes it clear that this is not that meal. The reader approaches the scene disoriented and perhaps more attentive to the details that will be shared and sensitive to the actions, such as the institution of the Eucharist, that do not happen. John uses rhetorical techniques that appeal to the sense of sight so that the scene unfolds before the audience's mind's eye.

Tracing the Narrative Flow

The Footwashing (13:1–17)

John begins the narrative of Jesus's last hours with his disciples with a one-verse summary of its major themes: Jesus's departure from the world, his relation to God, and his love for his disciples. **Before the festival of the Passover, Jesus, knowing that his hour was come in order that he depart from this world to the Father, loving his own who were in the world, until the end he loved them** (13:1).

In 13:2–4, John constructs a very long sentence, with multiple participial and subjunctive clauses that precede the main clause and that are often translated with finite verbs (e.g., NIV). The sentence begins, **And dinner having been served, the devil already having put into the heart** [*beblēkotos eis tēn kardian*; fig., resolved] **that Judas Simon of Iscariot would hand him over** (13:2). Many translations change the word order to make it explicit that the heart belongs to Judas, but the Greek permits ambiguity. The next two clauses juxtapose God's intentions with those of the devil: [all the while Jesus] **knowing that the Father gave all to him into the hands and that he came from God and departs to God** (13:3). The sentence now moves to a series of finite verbs, some in the present tense, the effect of which is to produce a vivid piece of narration focalized from the perspective of the disciples. Jesus **rises from the dinner and lays down the outer garment** [*himatia*] **and taking a cloth** [*lention*; from the Latin *linteum*] **he girded himself** (13:4). It appears that he is still wearing his inner tunic or loincloth and that he is tying the *lention* around his waist. **Then he puts water into the washbasin and began to wash the feet of the disciples and to wipe** [them] **off with the cloth with which he was girded** (13:5). The narration underscores the methodical and deliberate nature of Jesus's actions.

The action happens in silence, with no explanation. Given the cultural context in which female servants normally perform this servile task and the placement of the gesture after the meal rather than before, it ought to startle all the disciples, but John focuses only on Simon Peter's resistance and about-turn. Peter's reversals figure prominently in the remainder of the Gospel (see table 6). In the context of the suspenseful silence of Jesus's gesture and the narrative frame that casts the shadow of Jesus's imminent arrest over the action, Peter provides relief from the tension. The other disciples may have been disturbed but are not bold enough to object, but Simon Peter protests, **"Lord, are *you my* feet going to wash?"** (13:6). The pronouns "you" (*sy*) and "my" (*mou*) appear back-to-back to underscore his opposition. The dialogue proceeds without conjunctions (asyndeton), rendering each response more emphatic. Jesus's reply—**"What I am doing you do not know [*oidas*] yet, but you will understand [*gnōsē*] after these things"** (13:7)—emphasizes through verbs of cognition that Peter cannot appreciate what Jesus is doing until after the passion. Peter's hyperbolic **"No, you shall not wash my feet for all eternity"** reflects his habit of making absolute pledges that he later compromises. Jesus counters, **"Unless I wash you, you do not have a part [*meros*] with me"** (13:8), as in either no role to play in Jesus's life or share in Jesus's legacy. Without hesitation, **Simon Peter says to him, "Lord, not only my feet but also the hands and head"** (13:9). **Jesus says to him, "One having bathed has no need to be washed except the feet, but is wholly spotless [*katharos*;** the word can have ritual connotations as in 'free of defilement'] **and you** [pl.] **are spotless, but not all"** (13:10). Jesus may be referring to the disciples' having visited a *miqweh* in preparation for the Passover. In 13:29 the disciples make an assumption about a traditional gift to the destitute on the occasion of the Passover—something done to ensure that all can celebrate it. If John paints a picture here of Jewish activities, then he does not reject all things Jewish. The narrator now provides an aside, making clear that Jesus has prescience of what Judas will do. **For he knew who was handing him over; on account of this, he said that not all are spotless** (13:11). There is no indication, however, that Jesus excludes Judas from the footwashing.

Table 6. The Good Shepherd and Peter's Reversals

Jesus: A Good Shepherd lays down his life for his sheep. (10:11)	Peter: I will lay my life down for you. (13:37)	⤬	Peter is willing to kill for Jesus. (18:10) Peter denies being a disciple. (3x; 18:17, 25–27)	⤬	Jesus: Do you love me? Peter: I do. Jesus: Feed my sheep! (3x; 21:15–19)

In the account of his actions, Jesus makes it clear that the footwashing affects and even changes relationships. **Therefore when he washed their feet and he took his *himaton* and reclined again, he said to them, "Do you understand what I have done to you? (13:12). You call me 'the teacher' and 'the Lord,' and you speak correctly, for I am** (13:13). **If then I washed [your] feet—[I who am] the Lord and the teacher, you are also obliged to wash each other's feet"** (13:14). Jesus invokes the cultural assumption that a service rendered to a

Figure 20. Christ washing Peter's feet (detail of portion of frieze forming lintel of central portal, west facade of the Abbey Church of St.-Gilles-du-Gard, ca. 1140–80).

client by a patron requires a form of reciprocity to honor the service—in this case, by imitating the action and washing the feet of others. **"For I gave you a pattern so that just as I did to you, you too should do"** (13:15). "Pattern" (*hypodeigma*) found here and in Heb. 4:11; 8:6; 9:23; James 5:10; and 2 Pet. 2:6 is used consistently to refer to models of humility. R. Alan Culpepper (1991, 143–44) notes the association in the Septuagint of *hypodeigma* with martyrs' deaths (see, e.g., 2 Macc. 6:28; 4 Macc. 17:22–23; Sir. 44:16). Jesus's next words resemble sayings from the synoptic tradition: **"Truly, truly, I say to you, a slave is not greater than his Lord nor is one who is sent [*apostolos*] greater than the one sending him"** (13:16; see Matt. 10:24 and esp. Luke 6:40). Once more John dramatizes a synoptic teaching. The footwashing is a gesture that illustrates what Jesus teaches during the meal in Luke 22:25–30: he comes as one who serves. Jesus has turned the social order on its head.

His final words, **"If you know these things, you are blessed if ever you should do them"** (13:17), are the first of two Johannine beatitudes (see 20:29).

Jesus's Prediction of Judas's Betrayal (13:18–30)

John presents Jesus's prediction of Judas's betrayal as a digression or a clarification: **"I do not speak about all of you; I know those I picked out, but in order that the writing be fulfilled, 'The one eating with me the bread lifted up against me his heel'"** (13:18). Jesus leaves the thought to be completed by his audience. Luke contains no prediction, and Matthew and Mark present it as Jesus's first order of business once they have reclined to eat (Mark 14:17–18; Matt. 26:20–21). The synoptic account includes a curse on one who betrays the Son of Man at the end of Jesus's speech (Mark 14:21; par. Matt. 26:24 and Luke 22:22). While the Gospel of John emphasizes Judas's league with Satan, Jesus also makes it clear that events are unfolding by God's mandate.

The quotation from Ps. 41:9—"Even my bosom friend in whom I trusted, who ate of my bread, has lifted the heel against me"—refers to what is still an extremely rude gesture in many Mediterranean cultures. The disciples have reluctantly had to make this gesture as Jesus washed their feet. Whereas Jesus's words to the disciples have nullified the offense, he does not grant the same pardon to Judas. Judas will continue to dishonor Jesus by his actions. **"From now on I tell you [something] before it comes about in order that you should believe when it happens that I am"** (13:19). Jesus's prescience is a sign of his identity, but one that can be understood only in retrospect.

As Jesus continues to speak about his betrayal, his speech and actions turn elements of the Jesus tradition on their head. **"Truly, truly, I say to you, the one receiving [*lambanōn*] anyone I will send, receives [*lambanei*] me; the one receiving receives the one sending me"** (13:20) resembles the statement about hospitality in Matt. 10:40. In its immediate context, however, being received refers to accepting Jesus when he is handed over. The narrator marks Jesus's visceral reaction to his own words: **Having said these things, Jesus trembled in the spirit and testified and said, "Truly, truly, I say to you that one of you will hand me over"** (13:21). John describes the disciples' response to Jesus's startling but incomplete revelation through a series of actions characteristic of their portrayal elsewhere in this Gospel. **The disciples were looking at each other, being at a loss about what he says** (13:22). **There was lying close one of the disciples to the breast of Jesus whom Jesus loved** (13:23). John's syntax, awkward when rendered in English, delays the identification of the disciple to the final clause. **Then Simon Peter nods to this one to inquire about whom he might be speaking** (13:24). Simon Peter, who is normally eager to take the lead, is reticent to ask. Peter's gesture dramatizes the anxiety expressed verbally in the Markan and Matthean accounts where the disciples each ask, "Surely not I?" (Mark 14:19; Matt 26:22). The Beloved Disciple's question—**"Lord, who is it?"** (13:25)—expresses no anxiety that he himself is the one. In Matthew and Mark, Jesus simply indicates that the one who will hand him over has been dipping bread into a common bowl (Matt. 26:23; Mark 14:20). In John, Jesus's words **"That one is the one for whom I will dip the morsel and will give [it] to him"** anticipate the action: **Then having dipped the morsel, he gave [it] to Judas Simon of Iscariot** (13:26). **And with the morsel, Satan then entered into that one. Then Jesus says to him, "What you are going to do, do it quickly"** (13:27). By handing the bread to Judas, Jesus delegates the task of being handed over to him. Jesus is in complete control of the means and the moment at which to unleash the malevolent intentions that govern the world. Eating the wine-soaked bread becomes a form of parody of the Eucharist by signaling Jesus's departure rather than his presence.

John continues to balance the tension of the betrayal with the disciples' obtuseness. **No one of those reclining understood this, with reference to what he said to him** (13:28). **For some were supposing since Judas was holding the [money] case, that Jesus says to him, go, purchase what we have need for the feast or [go] to the beggars in order that they might give something to them to participate in the feast** (13:29). In contrast, he portrays Judas as acting with full comprehension of the import of the words. **Then receiving the morsel that one went out immediately. And it was night** (13:30). The reference to night serves multiple purposes. It points back to the words with which Jesus ends his last public discourse: "the one walking about in the darkness does not know where he is going" (12:35). Judas walks into the darkness and out of the domain of Jesus's light. Moreover, Judas's betrayal and Peter's denial at morning's first light frame the darkness.

Jesus's Prediction of Peter's Denial (13:36–38)

The urgency with which Jesus directs Judas stands in contrast to the length of his final speech. The character and meaning of that speech will be explored in the next chapter of this commentary. Jesus's opening lines are cited here in order to provide a context for the prediction of Peter's denial. Like the prediction of Judas's betrayal, John treats the prediction as an unpremeditated announcement that arises when Peter interrupts Jesus's speech. In the Markan account, Jesus introduces the general topic of the disciples' defection, and when Peter argues that he will never fall away, Jesus counters with the prediction. Luke's account similarly has Jesus raise the subject (Luke 22:31–34). Mark allows Peter and the disciples' protest to be the last word (Mark 14:27–31; par. Matt. 26:31–35). Jesus begins his address as follows:

> Now the Son of Man has been glorified, and God has been glorified in him. If God is glorified in him, and God will glorify him in himself, and he will glorify him immediately. Children, I am still with you briefly. You will search for me, just as I said to the Jews that "Where I am going you are not able to go," I now say to you. A new commandment I give to you, that you love one another, just as I have loved you so that you also love one another. In this [way] all shall realize that you are my disciples, insofar as you have love for one another. (13:31–35)

Simon Peter's question—**"Lord, where are you going?"**—interrupts Jesus's speech and reveals his lack of understanding about both what is to come and the significance of the footwashing. Jesus replies with a veiled allusion to Peter's own death: **"Where I go you are not able to follow now, but you will follow later"** (13:36). Peter's reply implies that he has some idea that Jesus will follow a perilous path: **"Lord, on account of what am I not able to follow you now? I will lay down my very soul on your behalf"** (13:37). His overblown sense of his own capacities forces Jesus to confront him with his limitations via a sarcastic question: **"Will you** [indeed] **lay down your very being on my behalf?"** He then answers his own question, accenting the speed with which Peter will betray his own words: **"Truly, truly,** *I* **say to** *you*, **a cock will not sound** [its call] **before you will disown me thrice"** (13:38). The night that begins with Judas's betrayal ends with Peter's denial.

John picks up the prediction of the disciples' desertion again at the end of his Farewell Address (16:32) before he concludes with a prayer. If John is dependent upon Mark, as many contend (see Smith 2001, 196–98), the address to the disciples (14:1–16:28) can be treated as a lengthy insertion into the prediction of their desertion as it is found in Mark 12:27–31 (see table 7).

Table 7. The Farewell Address Compared with Mark's Narrative

Mark 14:27, 29–31b NRSV	John 13:37–16:32
[27]"You will all become deserters; for it is written, 'I will strike the shepherd, and the sheep will be scattered.'"	
[29]Peter said to him, "... I will not."	[13:37]Peter said to him, "Lord ... I will lay down my very soul on your behalf."
[30]Jesus said to him, "Very truly ... before the cock crows twice, you will deny me three times."	[38]Jesus answered, "Will you lay down your very being for me? Truly, truly, I say to you, before the cock crows, you will have denied me three times."
[31a]But he said vehemently, "Even though I must die with you, I will not deny you."	
	(Farewell Address to Disciples [14:1–16:28])
[31b]And all of them said the same.	[16:29]His disciples said, "Yes, now you are speaking in frankness ... [30]in this we believe that you came from God."
	[31]Jesus answered them, "Do you now believe? [32]Look, an hour is coming and has come, so that you will be scattered. ..."

Theological Issues

Footwashing

Footwashing was a common gesture of hospitality in ancient Mediterranean cultures and took place when a guest was welcomed into a home. In the hierarchy of honor and shame inscribed on the human body, the feet are at the bottom and, therefore, footwashing is the task of a servant, usually a female servant. On occasion a man will wash another man's feet as an act of extreme humility or an extraordinary gesture by a client to a patron. In his study of footwashing, John Christopher Thomas (1991, 40) cites only three other cases in which a man undertakes the task: *T. Ab.* 3.6–9; Plutarch, *Pomp.* 73.6–7; and Petronius, *Satyr.* 31 (in this case, the youth are clearly assuming female roles). In the other references to footwashing in the NT, women perform the act (Luke 7:36–50; 1 Tim. 5:9–10; see also John 12:3).

The language of cleansing and necessity leads to an ongoing discussion about whether the Gospel writer considered footwashing to be a symbolic act of humility, a purification ritual, a rite of passage, or simply a commemorative ceremony. Thomas (1991, 94) stresses the way that Jesus's act of humility prepares the disciples for the shame of the cross, which they also must overcome as they undertake their own acts of service. Some see it as an act of purification in preparation to receive the forgiveness made possible by Jesus's expiatory self-sacrificial death (e.g., Dunn 1970). Jerome Neyrey (1995) draws a distinction between the ritual of footwashing that the disciples undergo and the ceremony of footwashing that they are commanded to perform regularly (13:12–20). He treats Jesus's footwashing as a transformative ritual akin to baptism and the disciple's subsequent performance of the act as a way of confirming the group's identity and their role as leaders. These readings tend to focus on the humility associated with the act rather than its cultural associations. Mary Coloe (2004) takes into account the narrative and cultural setting and concludes that the footwashing is the act of welcoming the disciples into God's household. Footwashing is a way to receive the stranger as a friend who can sit at the table as though he were a member of the family. In this case, Jesus acts as host and changes his relationship to his disciples. They have crossed the threshold into Jesus's Father's house. They are no longer servants but are friends. The discourse that follows reflects this change.

Jesus commands that his disciples wash each other's feet, but very few denominations follow this commandment. References in the early patristic material make it clear that footwashing was normative in the early church (Thomas 1991, 174). In the Roman Catholic, Eastern Orthodox, and Byzantine Catholic traditions, clergy wash the feet of twelve men as a symbolic reenactment indicating that they construe the commandment as limited to the twelve apostles. Protestant denominations that practice footwashing appear to have two things in common: (1) they stress humility in their ethic, and (2) they construe the concept of discipleship as inclusive of all members of the church. Many denominations and congregations have let the practice lapse. The cultural context that gave rise to footwashing as a gesture of hospitality has vanished, and all that remains is the sense of degradation that no longer fits with their ethos.

The Significance of the Last Supper

While the Bread of Life discourse seems to anticipate the practice of the Eucharist, John does not describe its institution. That John did not know the ritual seems impossible given the centrality of the practice in the heated disputes of the early church recorded in the Acts of the Apostles and Paul's Epistles. Of the possible motives one might imagine for its omission, most exegetes favor one of the following: John chose to ignore it in order to give attention to the footwashing that was omitted in the Synoptic Gospels or because he has dealt with it implicitly in the Bread of Life discourse. The institution of the Lord's Supper is then just another of Jesus's signs not written in this book (John 20:30). A few scholars put forward the more-extreme position that John was trying to counter a quasi-magical view of the sacraments in order to emphasize the life-giving role of the Spirit (see Barrett 1978, 82–85), or rejecting a sacramental theology that made salvation the result of participating in a ritual rather than faith (see Bultmann 1941, 485–86). In order to sustain either of these last two arguments, one must dismiss John 6:53–56 as not original to the Gospel.

Insofar as John moves the setting of the meal back a day so that Jesus's death is timed with the slaying of the Passover lambs, the final meal loses any association with a holy day. Recently scholars have placed the Johannine account of the Last Supper within the context of Greco-Roman dining events: the *cena* or *deipnon*, an evening meal followed by entertainment, or the *symposion*, a meal followed by a long evening of conversation, fueled by too much wine, about topics such as love, piety, and courage (see Moloney 1998; Parsenios 2005, 31–34; Athenaeus, *Deipnosophistae*; Plutarch, *Quaest. conv.* 697e). The symposium provides the setting for several major literary works (see Plato, *Symposium*; Xenophon the Historian, *Symposium*) and ensemble scenes within Greco-Roman drama (e.g., Plautus, *Pers.* 753–857; *Stic.* 670–772). On top of the wine served at the meal, into which Jesus dipped the bread, Jesus's emphasis on the imagery of the vine provides an abundance of metaphorical wine. The meal then becomes the occasion for the speech at the center of the narrative.

The ancient reader who understood the dining culture of the Greco-Roman world would recognize that the meal and the speech that follows make a statement about the role of Jesus's disciples. Meals were not family times. If a man did not dine alone, he dined with friends. Plutarch expresses the joy of the company of friends at table: "The most truly godlike seasoning at the dining-table is the presence of a friend or companion or intimate acquaintance—not because of his eating and drinking with us, but because he participates in the give-and-take of conversation, at least if there is something profitable and probable and relevant in what is said" (*Quaest. conv.* 697d, trans. Bradley 2001, 38). The pleasure of the dinner party does not stop at its conclusion. Keith Bradley explains that its participants were expected to disseminate the themes of the conversation and the nature of the entertainments in order to enhance the reputation of the host. As guests at Jesus's dinner and as the audience for the Farewell Address, the disciples step into the role of "the interpreters of the host's reputation to a wider social group" (see Bradley 2001, 50).

John 13:31–35; 14:1–17:26

The Farewell Address

Introductory Matters

A sustained reading of Jesus's parting words to his disciples and final prayer presents a challenge to even the hardiest of Johannine scholars. The following preliminary comments are designed to provide a modern reader with a mental picture of the action and a grasp of the rhetorical norms that will make a reading from beginning to end a more meaningful experience.

The presence of a farewell address is yet another element that sets the Gospel of John apart from the Synoptic Gospels. In the synoptic tradition the institution of the Eucharist, something missing in John, fulfills the role of Jesus's major, albeit short, farewell speech that is framed by the prediction of Judas's betrayal and the disciples' abandonment of Jesus at his arrest. Though there is insufficient evidence to prove that John was familiar with the synoptic tradition, it is helpful to consider what he adds to Mark and Luke's telling of the story. In Mark, Jesus's final words to the disciples are a plea to remain (*meinate*) with him and keep watch (14:34; par. Matt. 26:38). *Meinate* in the Johannine Farewell Address becomes a call to fidelity for the remainder of the disciples' lives. In Luke, Jesus admonishes the sleeping disciples to pray so as not to fall into temptation (22:40, 46). The disciples' failures add to the poignancy of the synoptic account. The Johannine speech is framed between the prediction of Peter's denial and the disciples' denial that they will desert Jesus. John does not allow Jesus's final words to be a grim picture of infidelity. Jesus's words are, in effect, an antithetical rejoinder. Although the disciples will initially fall away, Jesus will remain with them; Jesus will provide the assistance that they need to remain bound to him. Jesus promises that whatever they request in his name will be granted, and he prays on their behalf. John, in effect, provides the uplifting speech that ancient readers expected to hear before a hero departed to death.

Studies by George A. Kennedy (1984) and George Parsenios (2005) demonstrate that the form and content of the speech bears all the hallmarks of classical, as well as modern, farewell addresses. It assures the following:

1. The parting is necessary and for the best (14:1–4; 15:13)
2. It takes place only after careful consideration and at the appropriate time (16:6–7)
3. Those who are present have been one community (15:1–8)
4. The relationship that has been forged will be sustained (14:15–21, 23–26; 15:15; 16:15)
5. The purpose or work of the community has been noble (15:8, 10)
6. Its purpose or work will be an enduring venture (14:11–14)

One would do well either to reflect on retirement speeches that one has heard or to read historical examples such as George Washington's announcement in 1796, in which he declared his intent not to seek reelection. Washington assured his audience that his departure was the result of careful consideration and did not signify a loss of zeal for America's future. He praised what the citizens of the United States had accomplished because of their unity and warned of dangers ahead that threaten that unity. He prayed on the country's behalf and concluded by assuring his audience that by resigning he would partake more fully in the society of "my fellow Americans." Jesus's address bears comparison.

When such a farewell address is given in anticipation of the death of the one who delivers it, the speech assumes the role of a funeral oration by consoling the audience for its loss prior to the actual and inevitable event. Jesus's speech invites comparison with Socrates's final words (Plato, *Apol.* 40c–42a; *Phaed.* 115c–e) or Seneca's farewell (Tacitus,

---

Classic Advice on Grief

In his advice on how to write letters of consolation, Cicero (*Tusc.* 3.31–32) summarizes the teachings of his predecessors:

Peripatetics minimize the evil of death.

Cleanthus explains that death is not an evil (cf. John 14:28; 15:13; 16:10; 18:11; 21:19).

Epicureans turn attention away from the evil of death to good things (cf. John 14:2–4; 16:6–7; 16:20–24).

Cyreniac reminds that death is an expected event (cf. John 16:3–4a).

Chrysippus explains that mourning should be a welcomed duty because it speeds the process of grieving.

Cicero teaches that time will make even the most acute grief more tolerable (*Fam.* 4.5.6; cf. John 16:20–22).

The Rhetoric of Exhortation
(*Paraklēsis* or *Paraenesis*)

Posidonius (ca. 135–51 BC) seems to have delineated three broad categories of exhortations: advice for actions, instruction on character or habits, and consolation of passion (cited by Seneca, *Ep*. 94.64–66), but a much longer list—including such things as scolding, praising, and warning—can be constructed from the various discussions of *paraklēsis* (Greek) and *paraenesis* (Latin, English) by classical rhetoricians. The goal of giving advice, according to Seneca, is to tighten the grip of memory on familiar teachings (see Seneca, *Ep*. 94.25). New Testament scholars have treated *paraenesis* as a genre, but Troels Engberg-Pedersen (2004, 52–53) recommends that it be viewed as "an activity" or "a traditional system of popular ethics."

Ann. 15.62; see Parsenios 2005, 22–34). The teachers of classical rhetoric give significant attention to the task of consolatory speech and how to sooth not by sharing expressions of grief but by exhortations against grieving. Jesus's speech contains similar arguments.

While the speech contains argumentation, its rhetoric is not focused on a logical progression to prove a point. Here, perhaps more than in any other speech in the Gospel, the epideictic nature of Johannine rhetoric is clear. Its purpose is to bolster the beliefs and values of the audience by circling around, elaborating on, and interlacing four assertions about Jesus's death. (1) While his death is a departure from the disciples, it is also a return to the Father. (2) His death is an act of love that exemplifies his parting command to love one another. (3) He lives on within the community if they honor his death by fulfilling the love commandment through the agency of the Paraclete. (4) His death is a revelation of God's glory. As Jesus proceeds through his words of comfort he intersperses a series of repeated exhortations and pieces of advice. Exhortations are frequently accompanied by a promise that provides comfort and motivation to act on Jesus's advice.

The disciples' occasional interruptions provide an opportunity for reiteration of ideas. The interruptions also serve to keep the address grounded in its narrative setting by providing inappropriate reactions to Jesus's words. Readers familiar with the comedy routines of Abbott and Costello, George Burns and Gracie Allen, or Dick and Tom Smothers will recognize the comic form of the interruptions and how they both temper the gravity of Jesus's speech with the disciples' humorous lack of understanding and arrest its speed by preventing Jesus from moving too quickly through his points.

Outline of the Farewell Address

Announcement: The Son of Man has been glorified; the time of departure has come (13:31–33)
Issuance of a love commandment (13:34–35)
Peter interrupts—Jesus predicts denial (13:36–38)

Consolation: I return to the Father to prepare a place (14:1–4)
    Thomas interrupts—Jesus reiterates his divine agency (14:6–7)
    Philip interrupts—Jesus reiterates his relations to God (14:8–10)
  Assurance that God's work of love will be done with the help of a
    paraklētos (14:11–21)
    Judas's interruption (14:22)
  Promise of a *paraklētos* reiterated (14:23–26)
Consolation: Rejoice because I am returning to the Father (14:27–28)
  Exhortation to abide: Provision of the vine metaphor (15:1–8)
  Clarification on Jesus's love or friendship (15:9–17)
  Warning about the world's hatred (15:18–25)
  Admonition to testify to what they have witnessed (15:26–27)
  Warning about persecution (16:1–4a)
Consolation: I leave so that the *paraklētos* can come (16:4b–7)
  Repetition assuring the help of the *paraklētos* (16:8–16)
    Disciples interrupt (16:17–18)
  Repetition assuring God's work of love will be done (16:19–28)
    Disciples interrupt—Jesus predicts desertion (16:29–33)

Jesus's Petitionary Prayer

1. Glorify the Son (17:1–5)
2. Protect the disciples (17:6–16)
3. Sanctify the disciples (17:17–19)
4. Let all believers know God's love (17:20–26)

For modern readers who no longer delight in repetition, the speech can seem monotonous, but if one listens for the poetic language and looks for action and reaction, the momentum of the speech can help hold one's attention through its four chapters. This speech, with a few digressions, makes use of a grand style and includes a wide variety of figures of speech. The following translation sacrifices the elegance of English prose to preserve word order and distinctions in vocabulary, but interpretation ought not make too much of the meaning of these features. Their purpose is to render Jesus's speech stirring (see Quintilian, *Inst.* 12.10.61–62).

Tracing the Narrative Flow

Jesus's Farewell Address to the Disciples (13:31–35; 14:1–16:33)

Announcement: The time of departure has come. Jesus charges Judas to act quickly, and while he speaks he keeps one eye on the time, but as Edmund L. Epstein observes, "the persuasive balance of the rhetoric itself conveys the steady tranquility to which the content refers" (2001, 88). Jesus begins with a statement that subverts the outrage of Judas's betrayal. Jesus's death does not call for revenge in order to restore his honor: **"Now the Son of Man has been glorified, and God has been glorified in him"** (13:31). Judas's departure sets the crucifixion in motion and, as a result, Jesus can speak retrospectively about his death. The next line makes odd use of a conditional conjunction in the protasis: **"If God is glorified in him, and God will glorify him in himself, and he will glorify him immediately"** (13:32). Usually this construction expresses mere possibility, but this cannot be the sense here. Given this grammatical difficulty and its shaky manuscript attestation, some translations ignore the conditional clause (e.g., ASV). Within context, the repetition dispels doubt about God's approval of Jesus's death.

Jesus turns to his disciples and for the first time in the Gospel uses an intimate address: **"Children, I am still with you briefly. You will search for me; just as I said to the Jews that where I am going you are not able to go, I now say to you"** (13:33). This verse reaches back and encapsulates the action of the first twelve chapters of the Gospel and then proceeds to the imperative that summarizes the remaining chapters.

Issuance of love command. Jesus uses repetition to reinforce the need for reciprocation or imitation of divine love through the commandment's balanced clauses and memorable language (13:34–35):

"A new commandment I	give to	you,	that	you love one another,
just as	I have loved	you	so that	you also love one another.
In this [way] all shall realize			that	you are my disciples,
			insofar as	you have love for one another."

Jesus repeatedly returns to the implications and fulfillment of this commandment as he proceeds through his speech. (In the church calendar, the Latin for "new commandment," *mandatum novum*, provides the name Maundy Thursday to the day before Good Friday.) Simon Peter then interrupts the speech, and Jesus predicts his disavowal (see table 7 in the preceding chapter).

Consolation against grieving. After this prediction and confusing allusions to what is to come (13:36–38), Jesus turns to words of comfort, beginning with an exhortation appropriate to the consolatory address: **"Do not let your hearts be troubled. Trust in God and in me trust"** (14:1). This use of *epanalēpsis* (repetition of a word at the beginning and end of a line, phrase, or clause) lends the line force (Quintilian, *Inst.* 9.3.29). To show that death is a good rather than an evil, Jesus then treats his demise as analogous to a journey of a bridegroom to his home, where he prepares a place for his bride and future children. **"In my Father's house there are many rooms** [*monai* has the sense in Attic Greek of resting places and is the root for the word "monastery"]. **If there were not, would I have said to you that I cross over** [*poreuomai*, a euphemism for death; e.g., Julianus Aegyptius, *Ep.* 14] **to prepare you a place?"** (14:2). The negative hypothetical conditional implies incontrovertible logic to invite his audience to affirm that Jesus goes to prepare a place. The next line duplicates Jesus's words in an elegant construction that completes the analogy of the marriage: **"And when it is that I have crossed over and have prepared you a place, I come again and will take you for my own** [*paralēmpsomai hymas pros emauton*; this is the language used for taking a wife, adopting a child, or taking a partner or ally], **so that where I am, you also should be** (14:3). **And whither I go, you know the way"** (14:4). Jesus is not contradicting himself but speaks proleptically, anticipating a future reality. Once he has been crucified, they will know the way.

Interruptions and digression. Thomas, ever the killjoy, sees only impossibility and immediately **says to him, "Lord, we do not know where you are going. How are we able to know the way?"** (14:5). In summary form, Jesus then reiterates the description of his role as divine agent, which he has provided in the first half of the Gospel. He begins with his characteristic use of "I am" and augments his habitual pattern of speech by using polysyndeton (repetition of a conjunction between clauses): **"I am the way and the truth and the life."** This assertion is followed by an absolute conditional rendered adamant by the use of the negative. **"No one comes to the father unless through me"** (14:6). He then asserts his claim in the positive form by using a material conditional (a conditional in the indicative mood) that expresses certainty: **"If you have come to know** [*egnōkate*] **me, you will also come to know** [*gnōsesthe*] **my Father."** (Some translations follow alternate manuscripts that have pluperfects: "If you had really known me, you would also have known my father," suggesting a condition contrary to fact; e.g., KJV, ISV.) **"And from now on you know** [*ginōskete*] **him and you have seen him"** (14:7). The English translation cannot capture the elegant variations of the verb *ginōskō*.

Philip's interruption—**"Lord, point out the Father to us, and it will satisfy us"** (14:8)—leads Jesus further away from the task at hand and reveals Philip's lack of comprehension of both what Jesus has just said and his previous speeches. Once more, John uses a disciple as a foil. The foolishness of the disciples' questions invites the audience to receive Jesus's words without question. The doubling of foolish interruptions provokes Jesus to ask a series of questions that serve to underscore how inappropriate the disciples' lack of comprehension is and to reiterate Jesus's teachings about his relationship to God. Jesus's questions that include allo-repetition encode his exasperation or disappointment: **"Am I with you** [all] **this time, and you have not come to know me, Philip? One who has seen me has also seen the Father. How can you say, 'Point out the Father to us'?"** (14:9). Jesus continues to speak directly to Philip. **"Do you not trust that I am in the Father and the Father is in me? The words that I say to you, I am not speaking from myself."** The contemporary idiom "I don't talk to hear my own voice" perhaps captures the tone of the previous line. **"Given that the Father abides in me, I do his works"** (14:10).

God's work will be done. Turning to all of the disciples, Jesus returns to the task of the Farewell Address by issuing an exhortation in the form of *antimetabolē* (repetition of words in successive clauses in reverse grammatical order):

> **"Trust** [*pisteuete*] **me** [*moi*] **because I am in** [*en*] **the Father** [*patēr*]
> **and the Father** [*patēr*] **is in** [*en*] **me** [*moi*]**. If not, then on account of
> the works themselves trust** [*pisteuete*]**."** (14:11)

The exhortation to trust is followed appropriately by a promise: **"Truly, truly, I say to you, the one who believes in me, that person will also do the works that I do and will do even greater than these, because I am crossing over to the Father"** (14:12). Jesus clarifies how his death makes another good possible. From his position at the side of the Father, he acts so that his followers will become true disciples, who not only serve but also imitate their teacher. Death does not mark the end of his work but its furtherance. His vehemence is captured first with an unrestricted promise: **"Whatever you might ask in my name, this I will do, so that the Father may be glorified in the Son"** (14:13). For reassurance, the promise is then repeated with a material conditional that is more emphatic: **"If you should ask me for something in my name, I will do** [it]**"** (14:14).

One ought not to take the hyperbolic use of "whatever" in 14:13 to mean "anything whatsoever," as those who preach a gospel of prosperity are wont to do. Jesus sets the requests of those who ask in the context of the language associated with righteous obedience to God's will: **"If you** [pl.] **love me, you will keep my commandments"** (14:15). This reference probably comprehends the love commandment, but the use of the plural points to the Johannine habit of opening windows to other events and teachings not narrated in the Gospel. The fulfillment of commandments as an expression of love evokes the Shema (Deut. 6:4–9). Covenantal fidelity, or the notion of being God's people, is in view.

The repetition of the command to demonstrate love of Jesus by fulfilling his commandments here and in 14:15 and 14:21 form a frame for a special feature of Jesus's reassuring promise: **"And I will entreat the Father, and another** *paraklēton* **he will give to you, so as to be with you to the end of time"** (14:16). To whom or what the Paraclete refers will be addressed in the theological issues section below. In the rhetorical context of a farewell address, the accent should be placed on the Paraclete as a helper. Jesus provides a long clause that modifies the word *paraklētos*: **"the Spirit of truth, which the world is not able to receive because it neither observes it nor perceives it."** The Paraclete acts to reinforce the disciples' confidence in the verity that Jesus's commandments are God's will. Given the dullness of the disciples, Jesus's next statement seems to be contrary to fact—**"You perceive it; because it abides with you and it is in you"** (14:17)—but it is appropriate to a consolatory discourse, in which the presence rather than the absence of the departed is stressed. Jesus's next line follows in the same vein of consolation, rejecting the notion that death is loss by emphasizing his continued presence: **"I will not leave you orphans; I am coming to you (14:18). Yet a short time and the world no longer observes me, but you observe me, because I live and you will live (14:19). On that day, you will perceive that I am in my Father and you are in me and I am in you"** (14:20). He makes clear that his presence is made possible through fulfillment of the command to love him, yet the rhetorical accent falls not on the admonition to love but on the assurance that the one who loves is loved. **"The one having my commandments and keeping them, that one is one who loves me. Moreover the one loving me will be loved by my Father, and I will love him** [or her] **and I will show myself to him** [or her]**"** (14:21).

Judas's interruption. Once more a disciple interrupts the flow of Jesus's speech in a way that indicates lack of comprehension. **Judas (not the Iscariot),** possibly Thomas (see 11:16), jumps in at this point to ask a question about Jesus's statement in 14:17 and thereby suggest that he thinks Jesus plans to retire into a more private life: **"Lord, what has happened that you are going to show yourself to us and not to the world?"** (14:22). Judas is focused on what has passed rather than Jesus's speech about what will happen.

Jesus reiterates promise of a paraklētos. Jesus does not provide a direct answer to Judas's question until 15:19–20. Instead, he elaborates on his point from 14:21: **"If someone loves me, he will keep my word, and my Father will love him, and we will come to him and we will make ourselves a dwelling in his presence"** (14:23). Whereas in 14:2–4, Jesus's words suggest a transcendent dwelling to which the disciples will be taken, he now describes an immanent residence made possible by love. Jesus then expresses the same thought in antithetical form, thereby providing a partial answer to Judas's question. The world presumably does not love Jesus and as a result cannot be consoled by his presence. **"The one who does not love me does not keep my words, and the word that you hear is not mine but of the Father who sent me"** (14:24).

He then adds another aspect to his description of the role of the Paraclete: "These [words] I have spoken to you while I remain in your presence (14:25). Whereas the *parakletos*, the spirit of holiness, whom the Father will send in my name, that one will teach you all and will make you remember all that I said to you" (14:26). The Paraclete is the agent of recollection: insofar as memories are a means by which the dead continue to be present in the lives of those left behind, the Paraclete serves as a comforter and a reminder to do God's work just as Jesus has done his Father's work.

Consolation against grief. Jesus prefaces the repetition of his exhortation not to grieve over his departure with a farewell gift of peace. His death, unlike the death of most leaders, does not leave them in a state in which their well-being is in jeopardy. The contrast with the peace of the world is probably with its transitory nature. Jesus gives an abiding peace. "Peace I leave with you, my peace I give to you; not as the world gives, I give to you. Do not let your heart be troubled, do not be afraid" (14:27). He then makes a point typical to consolatory rhetoric. If one properly understands death, one ought to feel joy rather than grief or fear. "You have listened because I spoke to you [that] I am leaving and I am coming [back] to you. If you loved me, you would rejoice because I am crossing over to the Father, because the Father is greater than me" (14:28). Many Christian funeral meditations and condolence cards make the same argument: the departed have gone to a better place.

The next three verses seem to draw the speech to a close, first by turning attention to the passage of time and to Jesus's imminent arrest, and then by telling the disciples to leave. "And now I have told you before it happens, so that when it happens, you trust (14:29). I will no longer talk at length with you for the ruler of the world comes; and in me, he has no part, none [whatsoever] (14:30). But in order that the world should know that I love the Father, and just as the Father authorizes me, so I act." Jesus echoes a contrast that he draws in 12:31–32. The ruler of this world acts without love for Jesus, but as a result, Jesus's love is revealed to the world according to God's plan. Jesus then tells his disciples, "Rise up, let us go from here" (14:31). John does not narrate any action that fulfills Jesus's command, and Jesus continues to speak in a leisurely fashion.

Some commentators (see Carson 1991, 479) imagine that the command is fulfilled and that Jesus delivers the remainder of his speech while walking from a house in the city to the garden where he is arrested. The abrupt command serves as a reminder to the Gospel's audience that Jesus speaks to a narrative audience. The convention of frozen action, in which a command is made but not fulfilled for a prolonged period, occurs several times in Greek tragedy (Sophocles, *Ant.* 805–928; Euripides, *Herc. fur.* 520; *Tro.* 1285). In the tragedies, the delay allows for the repetition of themes. The command signals that what will be said next is an elaboration of what has just been said rather than new thoughts. Jesus will continue to speak without interruption until 16:17, but

John employs techniques that keep the speech grounded in the dramatic here and now (see 16:1–6).

Exhortation to abide in Jesus. Jesus uses a conventional metaphor to describe the close relationship of members of the community and extends the metaphor through use of antithetical constructions. **"I am the true grapevine, and my Father is the gardener (15:1). Every branch [*klēma*] in me not bearing fruit [*karpon*] he removes [*airei*; lit., 'lifts'] it."** It is perhaps ironic that Jesus uses the verb *airō*, when elsewhere it means to exalt. **"And every [branch] bearing fruit he cuts it back [*kathairei*; lit., 'brings it down'] in order that it bear more fruit"** (15:2). The two verbs *airei* and *kathairei* indicate contrasting motion. **"Already you are without blemish [*katharoi*] on account of the word that I have spoken to you"** (15:3). *Katharoi* appears in 13:10 to refer to purity, but in the context of this metaphor, it refers to bruising. In this sentence and in 15:4, Jesus uses *paronomasis* (paronomasia: the use of similar-sounding words) in the language of pruning and blemish and significant alliteration using the Greek letter *kappa*, the sounds of which are difficult to replicate in English translation. The metaphor provides an image that informs the exhortation: **"Remain in me, and I too [will remain] in you. Just as the branch is not able to bear fruit from itself unless it remain on the grapevine, thus neither [are] you [able to bear fruit] unless you remain in me (15:4). I am the grapevine, you are the branches. The one remaining in me, I also [remain] in him [or her] whereby he [or she] will bear much fruit, because apart from me you are able to do nothing, not[hing at all] (15:5). If [*ean mē*] someone should not remain in me, he [or she] is thrown out like the branch and dried out, and they gather**

Figure 21. Christian sarcophagus (ca. AD 370–380) from the cemetery of Pretestao, depicting grape harvest (Museo Pio Cristiano, Vatican). Many early Christian sarcophagi were decorated with imagery from the Gospel of John, including the two healing stories, the resurrection of Lazarus, the Good Shepherd, and the vine metaphor.

[*synagousin*] it together with other dried branches and they throw [*ballousin*] it into the fire and it kindles [*kaietai*]" (15:6). There is, perhaps, a play on the word "synagogue" in this speech. Rather than Jesus's followers being thrown out of the synagogue, those who reject Jesus are thrown onto the fire.

The *ean mē* at the beginning of 15:6 builds in force to anaphora (a series of clauses that begin with similar sounds), bringing the figure to a crescendo in order to amplify the promise made in 14:13–14. "But if [*ean meinēte*] you remain in me and my words remain in you, whatever you might want [*ean thelēte*], ask and it will happen for you (15:7). In this [way] my Father is glorified in order that you bear much fruit, and you will become disciples to me" (15:8). As noted earlier (1:19–2:12; 6:3–13), John does not begin by characterizing Jesus's followers as interns but as servants. Jesus's death and their acknowledgment of its honorable or righteous nature serve as an initiation into full-fledged discipleship, in which one does the work of the master.

Clarification on love. The figure of the vine provides language with which to elaborate on the love commandment. Jesus now makes clear first how one shows one's love for God and himself by loving those whom they love, and then what constitutes an act of love. Next he repeats the encouragement to feel joy: "Just as the Father [has] loved me, I also [have] loved you. Remain in my love (15:9). If you keep my commandment, you will remain in my love, just as I have kept my Father's commandment and I remain his in love (15:10). I have spoken these things to you so that my joy be in you and your joy may be complete" (15:11). The word "complete" (*plērōthē*), often used to signify being satiated with food, complements the promise of living water and the bread of life.

The repetition of the commandment with which Jesus begins his address—"This is my commandment, that you love one another just as I [have] loved you" (15:12)—prepares for amplification on what constitutes love and friendship. "Greater than this love no one has, that someone his very being [*psychē*] would lay down [*thē*] on behalf of his friends" (15:13). Love is not a sentiment; it is an action. The verb "lay down" (*tithēmi*) needs to be located in a cultural setting in order to grasp the degree of dedication for which Jesus calls. One can lay down one's arms as an act of fealty or lay down an offering on an altar. Jesus certainly alludes to his own death, but the demonstration of love lies in the act of surrender that leaves one vulnerable to death. Jesus's words do not sanction Peter's potentially suicidal attempt to defend Jesus with his sword (18:10). "You are my friends if you do what I command you" (15:14). We must be wary about imposing upon these passages a notion of friendship as principally a category of affection. Simon Goldhill (1986, 82) explains that in the Greco-Roman world, friendship comprehends "a series of complex obligations, duties and claims."

Once more, Jesus returns to his point that his death brings a new intimacy to his relationship with the disciples: "I no longer call you servants [the act of washing their feet ends this relationship], **because a servant does not know what the master does; I have said friends, because all that you heard concerning my Father, I made known to you"** (15:15). Within the Greco-Roman ethos, Jesus's openness or frank speech about his death is a hallmark of friendship. Seneca writes, "Speak boldly with him [a friend] as with yourself; . . . share with a friend all your worries, all your thoughts. . . . Treat him as loyal and he will be loyal. Why should I hold back any words in the presence of my friend?" (*Ep.* 3.2–3, trans. Konstan 1997). Jesus now retells the story of their call to discipleship, using this new language of friendship. **"You did not choose me for yourself, but rather I chose you for myself, and I planted you so that you grow [*hypagēte*; lit., 'ascend'] and bear fruit and your fruit may remain, so that whatever you ask the Father in my name, he may give to you (15:16). This is my commandment, that you love one another"** (15:17). Jesus calls the disciples to dedicate their lives to one another so that what they ask is not for their own gain but on behalf of others.

Warning about the world's hatred. What follows brings into view the context in which dedication to one another is a necessity and in which death may be the outcome of such an alliance. **"If the world hates you, you know that it first has hated me"** (15:18). Jesus now addresses Judas's question from 14:22 about the distinction between the disciples and the world: **"If I were from the world, the world would love its own, in that it is from the world, but I chose you for myself out of the world; on account of this the world hates you** (15:19). **Remember the word that I said to you, 'A slave is not greater than his [or her] master' [see 13:16]. If they persecute me, they will also persecute you. If they scrutinized my word, they will also scrutinize yours"** (15:20). Within the hierarchical culture of patronage and honor and shame, Jesus's humiliation extends down to his disciples. Moreover, abuse of servants or agents constitutes abuse of the head of the household. **"But they will do all these things to you on account of my name,"** which comes to signify to the world one who has been crucified. Jesus then points out their error by broadening the scope of his social reality and representing himself as an intermediate figure and God as the paterfamilias. The world can treat that name with derision only **"because they do not know the one sending me"** (15:21).

Now Jesus characterizes their error by using the concept of sin (*hamartia*) in a way that resonates with Aristotle's (*Poet.* 1453a.13–16) coining of the term to signify a tragic error. This reference to sin must be contextualized within a system of honor and shame. Observe that sin is not used as a verb but as an object that one can possess: **"If I had not come and spoken to them, they would not have sin,"** meaning the shame that comes from failing to honor God's agent. Jesus explains that their violation is without basis **"but now they do not have an excuse for their sin"** (15:22), and as a result they have dishonored both Jesus and God. **"The one who hates [*misōn*] me also hates my Father"** (15:23). Jerome Neyrey (2007b, 109–10) explains that hatred in the classical context is the opposite of friendliness and signified distancing oneself from a person or disavowing an allegiance to them (see Aristotle, *Rhet.* 2.4.30–32 [1382a]). John emphasizes that following Jesus stands in continuity with past revelation and that those who deny that Jesus does God's work reject their relationship with God. The next verse reiterates the point made in 15:22–23, while magnifying their error by using polysyndeton (repetition of a conjunction between clauses): **"If I did not do the works among them that no one else has done, they would not have sin. But now** [I have done these works] **and** [*kai*] **they have seen and** [*kai*] **they have hated both** [*kai*] **me and** [*kai*] **my Father"** (15:24). In the immediate context, Jesus's purpose is not to explore the criteria for salvation but to demonstrate that what happens to him is part of a divine plan. Though those who hate Jesus have shamed themselves, Jesus is not shamed by their persecution of him. John treats enmity as a sign of scriptural fulfillment: **"But in order that the word written in their law be fulfilled that they hated me gratuitously** [*dōrean*]**"** (15:25). In its immediate context, *dōrean* means without cause, but within the broader context of Jesus's case, it underscores the paradox of their actions. *Dōrean* comes from the same root as *dōrea* (a gift), something that one gives to bestow honor. Their hatred that dishonors God results in a gift, the crucifixion, that signifies God's glory.

Admonition to testify. Jesus turns the warning into words of encouragement by returning to the theme of the gift of a Paraclete who will expose the world's error. **"When the *paraklētos* should come whom I will send to you from the Father, the Spirit of Truth who proceeds from the Father, that one will testify concerning me"** (15:26). The Paraclete's testimony sets off a chain reaction: **"And you too testify, because you are with me from the beginning"** (15:27).

Warning about persecution. In the next verses, Jesus's style shifts suddenly to the simple patterns of ordinary speech, in which he seems to misspeak or struggles to make his purpose clear to his disciples. The effect is so dramatic that thirteenth-century authorities assigned the break to a new chapter, but no new topic is introduced. The move is more about the drama of the narrative than development of ideas. Jesus returns to his immediate task: he is preparing his disciples to respond to his death and its consequences appropriately. **"I have told these things to you lest you be made to stumble** [*skandalisthēte*]**"** (16:1), presumably by the crucifixion (cf. 1 Cor. 1:23). The disciples themselves will become a scandal or something at which others take offense, the result of which will be ostracism. **"[At first] they will make you *aposynagōgous*** [out of the synagogue], **but an hour comes when killing you will be thought a service to present to God"** (16:2). Note the continued play on the concept of gift giving in a system of patronage. Jesus's consolatory speech extends beyond comfort for the grief caused by his death to offer comfort in the face of their own persecution. **"And they will do these things because they know neither the Father nor me** (16:3). **But I have said these things to you so that when their hour should come** [i.e., the hour of persecution] **you may remember**

them because I said [them] **to you."** This is an argument found elsewhere in consolatory rhetoric. Death or tribulation ought not to be distressful when one expects it.

Consolation against grief. Jesus anticipates the question of why he has not warned the disciples of their fate earlier. **"I have not said these things to you from the beginning, because I was being with you (16:4). Now I withdraw to the one who sent me, and no one of you puts the question to me, 'Where are you going?'"** (16:5). Given that the disciples have asked this question (13:36; 14:5–8), Jesus's remark seems inappropriate or an aporia, but Jesus may be referring to the immediate effect of his words. Jesus's prediction of persecution has left them speechless: **"But because I have said these things to you, the grief has filled your hearts"** (16:6). John often lets Jesus describe the reaction to his words in order to ground the speech within its narrative setting without having the narrator interrupt the speech (e.g., 3:7; 6:43, 61). **"But I tell you the truth, it is to your benefit that I go away"** (*apeltho* is a common poetic reference to death; see Euripides, *Alc.* 379; Sophocles, *Ant.* 818). In 16:7 Jesus begins to slip back into grand style with the use of antithesis (two contrasting ideas juxtaposed in a parallel structure):

> **"For unless** [*ean gar mē*] **I go away, the** *paraklētos* **will not come to you; if** [*ean de*] **I cross over, I will send him to you."** (16:7)

Jesus's death makes it possible, with the assistance of the Paraclete, for the disciples to step into his role.

Repetition of assurance in 14:11–21. The next two verses enumerate the parts of the Paraclete's role by using the slow rhythm of polysyndeton (repeated clauses beginning with a conjunction), augmented with anaphora (a series of clauses that begin with similar sounds), and then sustaining the rhythm to explicate the parts but increasing its speed by using asyndeton (omission of conjunctions). **"And when that one comes, he will confute the world concerning** [*peri*] **error and concerning** [*kai peri*] **justice and concerning** [*kai peri*] **judgment (16:8). Concerning** [*peri*] **error, because they do not believe in me"** (16:9). The implication seems to be that the Paraclete proves that Jesus is the Son of God. **"Concerning** [*peri*] **justice, because I go to the Father and you will no longer observe me"** (16:10). The implication seems to be that Jesus's restoration to the Father is an expression of God's righteousness. **"Concerning** [*peri*] **judgment, because the ruler of this world has been judged"** (16:11). Jesus refers to the notion that his death is a victory over the ruler of this world.

The word "confute" (*elenxei*) in 16:8 has many nuances, including putting to shame or confounding, but in the immediate context in which Jesus speaks of false witnesses and punishment, the Paraclete serves as an advocate (a legal defender), who decisively refutes the arguments of the accuser. John uses a

221

forensic term that is hard to capture without picturing a courtroom drama in which forensic evidence like DNA and bloody knives and gloves and footprints play no role, but where rhetoric wins the case. For fans of the television series *Boston Legal*, this line might call to mind the closing arguments presented by attorney Alan Shore (James Spader), in which he makes ethical arguments that upset what seems to be a closed case.

Jesus returns to speaking in the moment: **"I still have much to say to you, but you cannot bear it now"** (16:12), either the full implications or the emotional weight of the speech. **"When that one comes, the Spirit of Truth, he will guide you in the whole truth,"** in the sense that he will show you the way through everything that will happen so that it makes sense and you will not stumble. **"For he will not speak for himself, but what he hears he will speak, and what is to come he will report to you** (16:13). **That one will glorify me, because from me he will receive and he will report** [it] **to you"** (16:14). Jesus introduces another element of the consolatory speech: the praise of the deceased raises up the spirits of those who are left behind. The Paraclete's reports of Jesus's glory provide solace. **"All that the Father has is mine; on account of this I said that he receives from me and will report to you"** (16:15). Jesus reassures his audience that his death does not sever relations. Given that it is not clear to whom Jesus refers when he speaks of the Paraclete—at times it seems to be the Holy Spirit and at other times, himself—the next sentence may be either a new idea or a continuation of what Jesus has just said. **"In a little while you shall no longer look on me, and in a little while you shall see me again"** (16:16).

Disciples' interruption. Jesus's veiled promise of the resurrection serves only to bewilder the disciples, who turn to one another for clarification: **"What is he saying to us, 'In a little while you shall not look on me and in a little while you will see me again' and 'Because I depart to the Father'?"** (16:17). Their allo-repetition points to their lack of comprehension: **"What is this 'little while' to which he refers? We do not know what he is talking about"** (16:18).

Repetition of assurance from 14:11–21. The narrator provides an aside—**Jesus knew that they wanted to ask him**—to underscore Jesus's intimate knowledge, and Jesus comments accordingly on their behavior. **"Concerning this do you inquire with one another that I said, 'In a little while you shall no longer look on me, and in a little while you shall see me again'?** (16:19). **Truly, truly, I say to you that you will weep and wail** [as in sing a dirge] **while the world will rejoice; you will grieve but your grief will turn into joy"** (16:20). Jesus describes the reversal of crucifixion and resurrection in terms of the disciples' emotions. This reversal will be the major action of the resurrection appearances in chapter 20.

Jesus then turns to an analogy, an extended implicit comparison, to describe the true nature of their grief. The Greek language of grief denotes mental and physical pain true to the actual experience of grief. It is not simply a cognitive event. The arguments about how one should understand grief are about changing the cognitive understanding of the sorts of pain that they will experience at the loss of Jesus and in their own experience of persecution. **"While a woman is bringing forth, she has pain, because her hour has come, but when she has given birth to the child, she no longer remembers the contractions for the joy because she has brought a human being into the world (16:21). And so you now have pain. I shall see you again, and you shall rejoice in your heart, and no one takes away from you your joy"** (16:22; see Rom. 8:19–22, where Paul also uses images of childbirth to describe eschatological events). Jesus then reiterates the promise made several times already: **"And on that day you shall not see me, not one of you. Truly, truly, I say to you, whatever you shall ask the Father in my name, he will give you (16:23). Until now you have not asked for anything at all in my name; ask and you will receive in order that your joy may be complete"** (16:24). Jesus does not expect his disciples to endure what is about to happen without feeling pain, but he does seek to help them understand that this pain is not without purpose.

Jesus then acknowledges that he has been speaking in a manner designed to comfort more than clarify. **"I have spoken these things to you in proverbs [*paroimiais*]; an hour is coming when I will no longer speak in proverbs [*paroimiais*]; but in frankness [*parrhēsia*] I will report [*apangelō*] to you concerning the Father [*peri tou patros*]"** (16:25). The pronounced alliteration in 16:25 is sustained throughout verses 26–28. The act of reporting is the same task that he assigns to the Paraclete in 16:14. Frankness is a virtue associated with the intimacy of friendship, which will mark Jesus's new relationship with his disciples. Then with a rhetorical flourish, Jesus reveals that the disciples will be free to speak frankly to the Father. **"On that day, in my name, you shall ask and, I say to you, that I will not petition the Father [*patera*] concerning [*peri*] you (16:26), for the Father [*patēr*] himself loves you, because you have loved [*pephilēkate*] me and have believed [*pepisteukate*] that I came from [*para*] God"** (16:27). In other words, God will respond directly to their petitions in Jesus's name. Rather than negating the Christology of agency of which he has spoken so often by eliminating his role, this clarification serves as a guarantee of his promise. The reiteration of the assurance **"I came from the Father [*para tou patros*] and I have come into the world, again [*palin*] I leave [*aphiēmi*; cf. 14:18] the world and cross over to the Father [*poreuomai pros ton patera*]"** (16:28) now serves as proof that his promise is good. John's long insertion of a speech between the prediction of Peter's denial and the prediction of the disciple's desertion now comes to an end.

Disciples' interruption and Jesus's prediction of desertion. The disciples' interjection ignores the future timing for speaking in clear terms: **"Look, now you are speaking in frankness, and you are saying not one riddle (16:29). Now we see that you know everything and you do not have need for one to inquire of you; in this we believe that you came from God"** (16:30). They protest: "We understand; therefore, you need not leave." Jesus recognizes this as dissembling or self-deception rather than true comprehension by asking a wry question: **"Do you now believe?"** (16:31). The true state of their understanding will be revealed by their actions: **"Look, an hour is coming and has come so that you be scattered each one for himself, and I will be left alone; but I am not alone, because the Father is with me"** (16:32; see Mark 14:27–31; Matt. 26:31–35). The language of frank warning continues to serve a consolatory purpose. While the disciples will have cause for self-recrimination, Jesus minimizes the consequences of their actions in order to diminish their remorse. **"I have said these things to you in order that you may have peace in me. You have crushing [pain] in the world** [referring back to the birth metaphor], **but take courage, I have conquered [*nenikēka*] the world"** (16:33). The speech builds to the dramatic pronouncement that the condition that makes their pain signify a joyful event is already in place. At the point in the Markan tradition when Jesus refers to his own emotional distress and sorrow and prays to be spared the crucifixion (Mark 14:34–36; par. Matt. 26:38–39), John has Jesus describe the disciples' agony, and he prays on their behalf.

Jesus's Prayer (17:1–26)

The petition for glorification. Jesus now turns from addressing the disciples to addressing God. The petition "Keep my disciples" summarizes the entire prayer. Jesus violates the principle set forth in Matt. 6:7–8 regarding prayer: keep it simple because God knows what you need before you ask for it. Clearly the rhetoric of the prayer is designed not to persuade God but to lay out, before the audience of the Gospel, Jesus's concern for his disciples and how he conceives of his relationship with them. By praying, Jesus shows his concern.

Farewell speeches often contain allusions to prayer on behalf of those left behind (see, e.g., Moses's prayer in Deut. 32; *4 Ezra* [2 Esd.] 8.19b–36; Hector's parting words to his family in Homer, *Il.* 6.476–81; or Dwight D. Eisenhower's farewell address given on January 17, 1961). John chooses to dramatize this aspect of such a speech. George A. Kennedy calls the prayer "a larger epilogue to the entire rhetorical unit. It is the actualization of the potential inherent in . . . Jesus's claim of a unique relationship to the Father, and its objective is the actualization of the potential in . . . the special relationship of the disciples to Jesus" (1984, 84).

Jesus makes a gesture that signifies prayer—**Lifting up his eyes to heaven**— and addresses God, **"Father, the hour has come; glorify your Son, so that [*hina*] the Son may glorify you"** (17:1). He then ties this glory to Jesus's ongoing creative work of giving life by summarizing his assertions about his divine origins and work. **"Just as you gave to him authority over all flesh, so that [*hina*] all that you have given to him, he might give to them life eternal (17:2). This is eternal life that [*hina*] they might know you [are] the only true God and the one you sent [is] Jesus Christ (17:3). I have glorified you on earth,** accomplishing the works that you have given me [*hina*] to do (17:4). **And now glorify me, Father, in your presence [with] the glory that I had in your presence before the world [came] to be"** (17:5). The repetition of subjunctive *hina* clauses gives the prayer a rhythm that gets lost by rendering it into sensible English. One might infer from this speech that the incarnation was a *kenōsis*, a self-emptying, and that Jesus's glory needs to be restored (see Phil. 2:6–11), but in the context of the Gospel, the line invites the audience to look back to the prologue and understand that the glory comes from being commissioned to do God's work. The act of submitting to crucifixion is then equivalent in status to the act of creation. Jesus is saying, "I am given the honor of performing a task. I honor those who give me this honor by performing it well."

Petition for protection. Jesus now turns his attention to the witnesses to that glory. **"I make your name manifest to the people whom you gave me from the world."** Again the language of name is associated with honor or reputation. Jesus turns from a description of what he has done, his bona fides, to a description of the faithfulness of the disciples: **"They were yours and you have given them to me and they have kept your word"** (17:6). The bar is not set high at this point. The disciples have accompanied and served Jesus and have been open to the truth, but they have demonstrated very little understanding of the truth. Jesus speaks proleptically. **"Now they have come to know that whatsoever you have given me is from you (17:7). Because the words you have given me, I have given to them, and they have received [them] and have come truly to know that they came from you, and they trusted that you sent me"** (17:8). Now that Jesus has established the merits of the disciples, he is ready to present his petition: **"I am requesting on their behalf, I am not requesting on behalf of the world, but on behalf of those whom you have given me, because they are yours (17:9); and all that is mine is yours and that which is yours is mine, and I have been glorified in them"** (17:10). This language is perhaps best described as boasting. Jesus praises the disciples. He does not describe the service he will provide them as something that he does even though they are unworthy. His words exalt them. The audience of the prayer shares in Jesus's name and thus in his glory.

The petition begins to take on more specificity when Jesus prays for the unity of the community. Again, this is a theme common to farewell and consolatory addresses. **"And no longer am I in the world, and they are in the world, and I am coming to you; Holy Father, keep them in your name that you have given me, in order that they may be one, just as we [are one] (17:11). When I was being with them, I kept them in your name that you have given me, and have guarded [them], and not one of them perished [*apōleto*; middle aorist] except the son of perdition [*apōleias*] so that the writing be fulfilled"** (17:12). This translation preserves the *adnominatio* (repeating a word using cognates) at the risk of imposing a meaning on the text. The word perdition has come to mean damnation, but *apōleias* in this context may refer to something that is lost (see Lev. 5:22 LXX [6:3]). If Jesus refers to the laws of lost property, hope for Judas's redemption becomes possible. The next line refers to the joy of unity: **"Now I am coming to you, and these things I am speaking in the world in order that they might have my joy having been fulfilled in them"** (17:13).

In the next three verses the phrase *ek tou kosmou/ponērou* appears six times. This form of repetition (*conduplicatio*) usually expresses emotion. Translation requires the use of different English prepositions for *ek*. As a result, the rhythm of the repetition is lost. **"I have given them your word and the world hated them, because they are not of the world [*ek tou kosmou*] just as I am not of the world [*ek tou kosmou*]"** (17:14), harkening back to what he said in 15:19. **"I am not requesting in order that you might lift them up out of the world [*ek tou kosmou*], but in order that you might keep them from the evil one [*ek tou ponērou*]** (17:15). **They are not of the world [*ek tou kosmou*] just as I am not of the world [*ek tou kosmou*]"** (17:16). The repeated sound emphasizes the wish that the disciples be shielded from the world and the evil one.

Petition for sanctification. Jesus now introduces holiness language, which leads some to call this a priestly prayer: **"Sanctify [them] in the truth; the word is your truth"** (17:17). One has a distinct sense that John has returned to the language of the prologue and that the word is now a reference to Jesus. The repetition in 17:14–16 continues, but the preposition *ek* is replaced with *eis* to mark a change in the petition from protection to commission: **"Just as you sent me into the world [*eis ton kosmon*], I sent them into the world"** (17:18). This commissioning of the disciples is an indication that the Gospel envisions some sort of universal mission rather than narrow sectarianism. Jesus speaks as though this has been accomplished even though there is nothing in the Gospel like the commissioning that appears in Matt. 10:1–42 or Luke 9:1–6. **"And on their behalf I sanctify myself, in order that they might also be sanctified in the truth"** (17:19). How and when this sanctification happens is ambiguous. It seems logical to assume that Jesus is referring to his death as a consecration but also as an act that makes the truth known. To what truth he refers then becomes the question. Perhaps everything points back to 3:16. The truth is that Jesus's death is an expression of God's love for the world rather than the judgment of the world against Jesus. God does not condemn the world for killing Jesus. Accordingly, the prayer now moves in a more-inclusive direction.

Petition for the world. The next petition points to the success of their mission in creating more disciples who will also be in need of God's protection. **"Not on behalf of these alone do I make my request, but also concerning those believing on account of their word in me"** (17:20), that is, those who believe in me on account of what they say, **"so that all are one, just as you, Father, are in me and I am in you, so that they may also be in us, so that the world may believe that you have sent me"** (17:21). The request continues in a similar set of convoluted parallel clauses that reiterate numerous themes from the Gospel, the primary purpose of which seems to be to end the prayer with a rhetorical flourish. Sadly, the effect is diminished in my translation. **"And I—the glory that you have given to me—give to them so that they might be one just as we are one** (17:22). **I am in them and you are in me so that they might be complete in one, in order that the world should know that you sent me and you loved them just as you loved me"** (17:23). The disciples are charged with taking the message of God's love for the world to the world. The petition is really a commission. **"Father, I wish that where I am, those that you gave to me may also be with me, so that they may look upon my glory, which you have given me because you loved me before the foundation of the world"** (17:24). Once again, the force of Jesus's petition should be contextualized in the rhetoric of consolation. These words express the degree to which Jesus loved his disciples, leaving no room for regret. At the same time, the repetition of the words "in" (*en*), "have given" (*dedōkas*), "glory" (*doxa*), and "loved" (*ēgapēsas*), and the pronouns "you" and "me"—all express the depth of Jesus's feelings.

The prayer ends with a petition that God make the unity described in the metaphor of the vine a reality. The word order of pronouns and the epistrophe (repetition of the same word or words at the end of a series of phrases or clauses) makes for awkward English but are preserved here for emphasis:

> **"Righteous Father,**
> **even though the world [nom.] you [acc.] did not acknowledge [*egnō*],**
> **I [nom.] you [acc.] acknowledged [*egnōn*],**
> **and these [the disciples] acknowledged [*egnōsan*]**
> **that you [nom.] me [acc.] sent."** (17:25)

The final verse ends with a promise to God that sums up Jesus's mission by referring to the past and the future: **"And I made known to them your name and I will make [it] known, so that the love with which you have loved me may be in them and I [may be] in them"** (17:26).

Theological Issues

Although the design of the Farewell Address is rhetorical, its content is substantial. The speech contains expressions that give shape to the identity of an emerging social reality that we know as the church.

Community and Friendship

John, like other NT writers, draws from the tradition, no doubt established by the historical Jesus, thus considering the community of followers as a family or household, with God as the father and members as brothers and sisters, but John also draws from the language of friendship. Jesus construes this gathering to be one of friends. The footwashing is a ceremony that happens

227

between host and guests—receiving the stranger as a friend. Friendship is not an exclusive category as is family; one can be a friend with one's wife or siblings, but one does not have to be family to be a friend.

In American discourse, the term "friend" is freely used to describe both casual and intimate long-term relationships. The concept of friendship in antiquity is more circumscribed. A client in a patronage relationship could be called a friend of the patron. For example, a member of the social and political elite who received the Roman emperor's favors was called a "friend of Caesar" (*amicus Caesaris*; cf. John 19:12). Political supporters were called *amici* and political factions, *amicitia*. What friendship signifies was a principal topic of discussion in Greco-Roman ethical philosophy (e.g., Aristotle, *Eth. nic.* 8). Jesus's call to love one another acknowledges that at the heart of friendship is a need for reciprocity. The events that follow—Judas's handing Jesus over and Peter's denials—point to the vulnerability that comes with this sort of intimate mutual reliance. When Jesus states that the greatest expression of friendship is a demonstration of selflessness, he in effect is weighing in on the question of the relationship of altruism and self-interest in friendship.

Some argue that the Johannine ethic is exclusive or sectarian because it is defined in terms of friendship and lacks the language of loving enemies (e.g., Meeks 1996, 324). I, in contrast, situate Jesus's use of friendship within the objectives of the Farewell Discourse. The Synoptic Gospels make it clear that neighborhoods and kinship determine the basis for one's security or well-being in Galilean and Judean societies. These Gospels stress the importance of creating fictive family relations to replace the ties that are broken by the disciples' itinerancy and violation of family responsibilities when they fulfill Jesus's call to participate in his mission. Jesus's call for loyalty and steadfastness, two qualities that characterize a friend (Epictetus, *Diatr.* 2.22; Cicero, *Amic.* 19, 65) in the face of the world's murderous hatred, is not about forming exclusive relationships but about virtue and courage. The discussion of love for one another on the eve of Jesus's death does not preclude performing acts that benefit those who are not yet one's friends.

The virtues of friendship described in Greco-Roman literature line up with the "virtues" extolled in the Gospel of John. According to David Konstan (1997, 21), *parrhēsia* (frankness), once a term used in a democratic polis to denote a political right, came to signify a moral virtue. The friend who was faithful or trustworthy demonstrated the virtue of *pistos* (loyalty). *Philos* and *pistos* were used metrically as complementary terms in the formulaic epithets attached to heroes (Konstan 1997, 33).

Aristotle contends that a friend would not seek to become a god since the distance would sever the bonds of friendship (*Eth. nic.* 8.7.6). Jesus's use of the metaphor of the vine, as well as the promise of the Paraclete and his return, provide a counter to Aristotle's assertion. His return to his Father makes possible the sort of reciprocity and service that define true friendship. In the context of adversity and the derision of the world that will come with his arrest and follow his crucifixion, the disciples are provided with an opportunity to demonstrate that they are true friends (cf. Rensberger 1992, 305–9).

Swedish theologian Anders Nygren's *Den kristna kärlekstanken genom tiderna: Eros och Agape* (1930–36; ET: *Agape and Eros*, 1953) introduced the misconception into Christian discourse that the biblical authors worked with a particular Christian concept of love as unconditional and something distinct from the passion associated with *erōs* or the reciprocity of *philia*. The verb *agapaō* appears frequently within Jesus's Farewell Address, but it is used either as a synonym for *philia* or as an expression of concern or affection. Jesus makes clear that both forms of love require obedience to his command and to God (14:15, 23, 31; 15:14).

If one focuses narrowly on the love command as the performative act that constitutes the community of believers, one may miss that the Farewell Address as a whole defines community. In his study of the rhetoric of Greco-Roman consolation, Donovon J. Ochs concludes that their funeral orations sought to restore or redefine social relationships when they are torn apart by death. The oration assures the audience that life will continue and that the legacy left by the departed will benefit the family or community. Though the context of the speech may be about the past, the speech is really oriented toward the future. When that death is done in order to ensure the survival of the community, death is not merely to be accepted but commemorated and even celebrated (Ochs 1993, 74). The identity of the community is shaped by their commemoration of Jesus's death as an act of friendship and by their joy as the appropriate response to the concern that Jesus has shown them. This unity and joy are not ends in themselves, but serve as a visible presence by which the world can come to know Jesus (17:23).

The Paraclete

On the one hand, John's use of the term *paraklētos* to identify the heavenly agent described elsewhere in the NT as the Holy Spirit suggests to many that John's treatment of the Paraclete as a person points to a trinitarian theology. On the other hand, John's reference to the Paraclete as one among others and its superfluity, given Jesus's own imminent return, suggests that the Paraclete is Jesus's agent, or even a reference to Jesus himself, rather than the third member of the Trinity. Though Jesus states that the Spirit of Truth goes out from the Father (15:26b), Jesus is the one who sends the Paraclete (15:26a; 16:7). In his resurrection appearance, Jesus breathes the Holy Spirit upon the disciples (20:22). The Paraclete will glorify Jesus, not by being his own person, but by repeating what Jesus says to him (16:14).

Paraklētos appears too infrequently in earlier Greek texts to fix a precise technical meaning. Some of the earliest occurrences suggest that Paraclete could be used to refer to an advocate in a trial setting (see Demosthenes, *Fals. leg.*

1); more often, as Kenneth Grayston (1981) finds after an extensive survey, the term *paraklētos* is largely absent in texts that discuss legal cases and elsewhere simply means a supporter. If the Paraclete has a role within the trial motif of the Gospel, it is as a prosecuting attorney who indicts the world, but this may be imposing too much of a forensic context on the task described in 16:8–11. The Paraclete convinces the world that the ruler of this world is wrong when it comes to righteousness, sin, and judgment.

Leon Morris (1971, 662, 665) finds that when one looks at the sort of support that a *paraklētos* offers, the *paraklētos* acts as a friend. Grayston (1981, 72) situates the role of a *paraklētos* within an ancient social reality in which one uses influential supporters or a group of supporters in order to negotiate political structures. Jesus's Paraclete is not visible to the world but stands behind the disciples, assuring them that what they believe and testify about Jesus is true (14:16–17; 15:26–27). The gift of the Spirit will transform the speech of the disciples into something akin to the frankness of Jesus's speech. The Paraclete will teach the disciples and remind them of what Jesus has said (14:26). Within the context of ancient understandings of inspiration, this may be an allusion to the oral traditions that inform the Gospel or to the Gospel itself. The Spirit of Truth is the living memory of the community, passed down through the recitation of Jesus's teachings and stories. Insofar as the Spirit speaks only what the Spirit receives from Jesus, the Spirit is a guarantor of the authority of the tradition, either as the words of Jesus while he was on earth or the words of the resurrected Jesus from above (16:13–14).

John 18:1–19:42

Behold the Man

Introductory Matters

The story of Jesus's arrest, interrogation by the priests, trial before Pilate, and crucifixion is traditionally called the Passion Narrative. The word "passion" comes from the Greek word *pathos*. Aristotle describes *pathos* as "an action resulting in destruction or distress such as death on stage, agony, or other forms of affliction" (*Poet.* 1452b.12), and tragic *pathos* as an action that arouses pity and fear (1453b.32). The Gospel of John contains a Passion Narrative only insofar as it ends in Jesus's death since Jesus expresses no distress. The story is told in a way that prevents the audience from pitying Jesus or fearing and thus seeking to avoid a similar fate.

John's narrative unfolds in a series of discrete scenes marked by entrances and exits and changes in characters. The strong staccato rhythm produced by the stops and starts of the action places stress on the indecisive folly of those who seek to be agents of the action and the constancy of Jesus as he stands stoically at the center of the text, the object of the action. The minor characters who debate Jesus's fate before the praetorium continue their quarrel while he hangs on the cross. Consequently, rather than taking advantage of the transition from trial to execution and breaking the reading into two sections, this presentation will follow Jesus from his arrest to his death.

The section begins in the garden in which Jesus is arrested and ends in the garden in which he is buried. This suggests to some the presence of a chiastic pattern, with the garden scenes as a frame, but delineation of the pattern tends to be determined by where one locates its center. For example, Peter F.

Ellis (1984, 254–55) places it at the rejection of Jesus at his trial, whereas Jeffrey L. Staley (2002, 96–97) sees the questions about divine sonship (19:7–11) as the center of an ideological code. Other organizing principles also govern the narrative, the first of which is the unity of time. The action takes place over the course of one day, the day that the Passover lamb is prepared for the Passover meal, culminating in the preparation of Jesus's body for death. Another clear organizing principle of these episodes is an action represented by the word *paradidōmi* (to hand over). English translation often obscures its eight occurrences (18:2, 5, 30, 35, 36; 19:11, 16, 30), particularly when used with reference to Judas. Jesus is handed over from one agent to another, but John makes clear to the reader that Jesus controls the action and that it fulfills Jesus's and Scripture's prophetic pronouncements. In the end, it is Jesus who hands himself over to death as he had declared he would (10:17–18). The action of the narrative also centers on what would normally be physical humiliation of a prisoner, beginning with being restrained and including being slapped and flogged, being forced to carry the instrument of one's execution through the crowd-lined streets, culminating in being nailed to a cross, and ending with the piercing of his corpse. The burial scene brings to a close the action of handing Jesus's body over and makes a new beginning by shifting to the honorable treatment of Jesus's body.

John's Passion Narrative differs from that of the synoptic account in significant ways. There is no agony in the garden and no Jewish trial. John moves the scourging and mocking by the soldiers ahead in the action, and he includes a dialogue about the *titulus* (the sign on the cross) and an adoption scene at the foot of the cross. These distinctive features, as well as many other nuances and details, point to one thematic principle that determines what is included and how it is included. In the Roman theater of cruelty, crucifixion served both to humiliate opponents of Roman authority—insurgents against Rome's political power and slaves who failed to obey or please their masters—and to reassure those who advocated the execution that the condemned indeed deserved their status. The victim's body was on display so that observers could jeer and supporters of the one crucified would feel the humiliation. (For a detailed treatment of crucifixion, consult Hengel 1977.) For Jews, crucifixion brought an added stigma since the law reads, "Anyone hung on a tree is under God's curse" and will "defile the land" if left there overnight (Deut. 21:23). Crucifixion was the subject of comedy and satire and not of "serious" Roman literature (see Catullus's mime *Laureolus*, referred to in Juvenal, *Sat.* 8.183–93; and Suetonius, *Cal.* 57.4; Plautus, *Mil. glor.* 372; see also Josephus, *Ant.* 19.94); hence it would have startled a Greco-Roman audience that the first Christians made the account of Jesus's execution central to their liturgies. The earliest graphic representation of the crucifixion, reproduced in figure 22, mocks Christian worship of a crucified lord. John makes clear that Jesus is in no way dishonored or humiliated by what happens: Jesus's death is heroic.

Figure 22. Reproduction of a piece of graffito depicting the crucifixion of a man with an ass's head and the words "Alexamenos worships his god" scratched underneath (ca. AD 200, located near the Circus Maximus in Rome).

In contrast to the depiction of Jesus, John takes great care to present the actions of those who inflict suffering as that of fools. Jesus does not dominate the dialogue in the Passion Narrative, and when others get the chance to speak, feet end up in mouths. Familiarity with the traits of stock characters in Greek comic literature brings into sharp relief the techniques that the Gospel writer uses to draw his characters. According to Aristotle (*Eth. nic.* 2.7.12), the *eirōn* is a self-deprecating character who instigates action but claims to be powerless and seeks the assistance of an *alazōn*, a character who claims to have power to fulfill the goal of the *eirōn*. In the dialogues that lead to the plan to have Jesus executed, the priests, like an *eirōn*, use self-referential language that points to their incapacity to act, see, and understand (7:45–52; 11:45–53), and in the trial scene, they point to themselves as fettered by law and external powers (18:31; 19:7, 15). In contrast, Pilate is the *alazōn*, who represents himself in his verbal posturing as having power (18:38b–39; 19:4, 6, 10, 14–15). His movement from inside the praetorium, where he speaks with Jesus, to outside, where he speaks with the Jews—this shuttling dramatizes his attempt to control the action. The Gospel's audience, allowed to see into the interior space of the praetorium, witnesses Pilate's lack of control over Jesus. His repeated movement through the door of the praetorium comes to signify vacillation and manipulation that is at odds with his claim to absolute power. Peter manifests traits of the *mōros*, who is deficient in intellect or understanding and so commits rash and impulsive or absurd acts. In Greco-Roman comic theater, the *mōros* is

233

the secondary character who imitates the actions of the principal character and misunderstands or reacts inappropriately (see Welborn 2005, 37–48). In the resurrection scene, Thomas fulfills the role of a fourth kind of fool, the killjoy.

Tracing the Narrative Flow

Time and place continue to be important to John. The Synoptic Gospels characterize the last meal that Jesus shares with his disciples as a Passover meal, but John sets it one night before the festival begins so that Jesus's death occurs at the time that the Passover lambs are ritually slaughtered in the temple. Some background information about the late Second Temple celebration of Passover helps make sense of the action. Pilate and his soldiers were in the city to deal with any disruptions, but they maintained a low profile to avoid creating disruptions; therefore, they would not choose to arrest Jesus during the day in a public place. The priests would have purified themselves in advance of their busy day, sacrificing lambs in the temple. Any defilement that they incurred ran the risk of delaying the Passover by an entire lunar month (Num. 9:6–12). Because Jesus controls the timing of his arrest, he puts the priests under pressure to complete both their objective of having him crucified before the Passover and their responsibilities for the Passover. In short, John's timing adds to the suspense of the narrative.

Jesus Hands Himself Over to the Arrest Party (18:1–12)

In the darkest hours of the night, **having said these things** [presumably everything said in 13:1–17:26], **Jesus went out with his disciples across the winter runoff channel of Kidron, where an** [enclosed] **garden was into which he entered and** [also] **his disciples** (18:1). Although John does not name the Mount of Olives, this is where the garden would be located. Jesus chooses the time for his arrest (13:27) and the place to await his arrest, **the place Judas also knew** because Jesus gathered there many times with his disciples (cf. 8:1). The location would have offered him an easy escape if he so chose: he does not.

Attention then shifts to Judas and the entourage that he guides. The narrator introduces Judas with the epithet **the one handing him over** [*ho paradidous auton*] (18:2), used again in 18:5, drawing attention to the central action of the narrative. Knowing where Jesus would be, **Judas then, taking the cohort** [*speiran*] **and the attendants** [*hypēretas*] **from the chief priests and Pharisees, comes there with torches and lamps and weapons** (18:3). John uses the words *speiran*—the term usually denoting six hundred Roman soldiers—and *hypēretas*—a term often translated as "officers" or "police" but that denotes a servant or weapons bearer, one who does the physical labor, or in this case the dirty work, of others (Xenophon the Historian, *Cyr.* 2.1.31; Pollux, *Onom.* 6.31). That it is a term used to describe the role of Christian leaders (e.g., 1 Cor. 4:1) does not signify that it is an honorable role in Greco-Roman cultures. This collusion of three parties—Rome, the Jewish authorities, and Judas, who is both the residence of evil and Jesus's own (6:70; 13:18)—signify the three constituencies that will, one after the other, hand Jesus over. This excessive show of force points only to the arrest party's own impotence. Their efforts to illuminate the darkness with artificial light so that they can work evil (see 3:19) stands in counterpoint to the unfolding divine action of the true light, revealing its full glory. The verb *labōn* suggests that Judas guides the force, but when the moment comes for him to perform the critical action of identifying Jesus, he becomes redundant. John contains no kiss, no greeting. Jesus identifies himself.

Jesus, knowing all things coming upon him, stepping forward and assuming control of the arrest, **said, "Whom do you seek?"** (18:4). **They answered him, "Jesus of Nazareth"** (18:5a). "Jesus of Nazareth" may simply be a way of distinguishing this Jesus from the many others of that name, but given the use of Nazareth as a signifier of derision elsewhere in the Gospel (1:46; 19:19), their choice of words may be a sign of contempt. Jesus's response, "I am he [*egō eimi*]," serves both as a straightforward acknowledgment that he is Jesus and also as a theological statement. In Jesus's day, uttering the name of God was prohibited (see Josephus, *Ant.* 2.275–76; 1QS 6.27–7.2). The Septuagint does not translate the name YHWH (a first-person form of the verb "to be") but instead uses Lord (*Kyrios*). In Greek, Jesus's words *egō eimi* alone do not necessarily signify the divine name YHWH, but the arrest party's response points to their theological significance. Josephus (*J.W.* 5.438) describes the name as *to phrikton onoma*, something that causes one to shudder in religious awe. **Judas, the one handing him over, was also with them** (18:5b), **and when he** [Jesus] **then told them, "I am," they reared back,** as though the words had a physical force, **and fell to the ground** (18:6), in a posture of submission to a divine being and an indication of their weakness.

Now that the troops are effectively neutralized, Jesus demonstrates his control of the action by repeating—**"Whom do you seek?"**—and calling the troops back to their task. **They then said, "Jesus of Nazareth"** (18:7). **Jesus** [immediately] **responded, "I told you that I am. So if you seek me, let these** [*toutous*] **retreat"** (18:8). *Toutous* may refer to the soldiers, in which case he is indicating that they do not need to constrain him—or Jesus may refer to the disciples, in which case he is asking that they be free to go. If the latter, the specific location and timing of the arrest limit the violence to one man, as Caiaphas wishes and as Jesus intends. The narrator then substantiates that Jesus intends the latter interpretation **in order that the word might be fulfilled, which said that "from those whom you gave me, I have not lost, not one"** (18:9). This prophecy does not appear verbatim in the Gospel, but it seems to refer back to 17:12 or perhaps 6:39. Whatever the antecedent, Thomas's prediction (11:16) that they will go to Judea and die with Jesus is not realized.

It is now Peter's turn to play the *mōros*, the impulsive and naive fool. **Simon Peter, having a sword, drew it and struck the high priest's slave and lopped off his right ear** (18:10a). In Mark 14:47 and Luke 22:50, Jesus is arrested and then an unidentified disciple attacks an unnamed servant. John identifies Simon Peter as the perpetrator who acts out his intention to lay down his life for Jesus (13:37). This seems like a quixotic act if one supposes that Peter intends to rescue Jesus. It makes better sense within a context that views death at the point of a sword as heroic and death on a cross ignoble. Martial calls "death inflicted by a sharp weapon" a "Roman death" (*Epig.* 1.78). To die during an arrest is much less shameful than to be convicted and executed. Valerius Maximus (*Fact.* 9.12.4–7) tells numerous tales to illustrate this point: one former Praetor throws himself from a balcony while votes at his trial are being counted, thereby preventing his property from being confiscated and his family from the reproach caused by a conviction for extortion (9.12.7). Peter seems to be provoking a lethal conflict to protect Jesus's honor.

John is the only evangelist to name the sword's victim: **Malchus** (18:10b). While we cannot know John's purpose, the inclusion of the name reminds us that we cannot reduce the people in this story to symbols. Someone is really hurt. Luke narrates how Jesus restores the servant's ear. John provides no such resolution. The wound is left open. Perhaps Thornton Wilder, in his one-act play *Now the Servant's Name Was Malchus*, provides appropriate insight. The setting is heaven. Malchus asks Jesus to delete the Johannine addition because whenever his name is read, the reader thinks him ridiculous, and Malchus is distracted from whatever game he is playing. Jesus responds with the invitation, "Come, be ridiculous with me." In the ancient world, deformities were the stuff of humor (Aristotle, *Poet.* 1449a.33–38; Cicero, *De or.* 2.236–39; Quintilian, *Inst.* 6.3.8). In the context of the Gospel, those who serve as the men at arms either for Jesus or the priests are rendered laughable. What may be more puzzling is that Peter suffers no consequences for his aggression. It seems that Jesus's words continue to exert control over those who arrest him.

The petition that Jesus puts to God in prayer in the synoptic tradition, "take away this cup" (Mark 14:36; par. Matt. 26:39; Luke 22:42), becomes a rhetorical question. **Jesus then said to Peter, "Put your sword into the sheath; the cup that the Father has given me, should I not drink it?"** (18:11). The association of the cup with immortality belongs to later holy-grail legends. In the biblical tradition, the cup like the sword signifies judgment and death (Jer. 25:15–27; cf., Deut. 32:32–35; Pss. 11:6; 75:8; Lam. 4:21; Isa. 51:17, 22; Jer. 51:7; Ezek. 23:31–33; Obad. 16; Hab. 2:15–16; Zech. 12:2, 9; Rev. 14:10; 16:19; 17:4; 18:6). John uses Peter's vain attempt to defend Jesus as an opportunity to underscore that Jesus's resolve is unwavering.

The narrator proceeds to the main action, which now seems like a scene out of a slapstick silent film in which a band of incompetent police officers act as though the harmless hero is a dangerous criminal (e.g., Buster Keaton in *Cops*, First National Pictures, 1922). **Then the cohort and the commanding officer** [*chiliarchos*], who stands out at this point for having done no commanding, **and the attendants of the Jews together seized Jesus and bound him** (18:12).

Jesus Is Handed Over to the High Priest (18:13–27)

The action proceeds on an unexpected course. **They led him away first** not to Caiaphas, the only authority to be named so far, but **to Annas.** The narrator suggests that this makes sense, **for he was the father-in-law of Caiaphas, who was high priest that year** (18:13). Annas appears at this point as a power to whom Caiaphas is answerable, but nevertheless one obliged to Roman authorities. Quirinius, governor of Syria, appointed Annas as high priest in AD 6, and then Procurator Gratus dismissed him in AD 15. Although Caiaphas is the acting high priest at this time, Num. 35:25–28 suggests that high priests served for life, and therefore Annas, who still lives, seems to legitimately retain the title. Moreover, Annas continued to wield influence at least over the candidates: five of the next high priests who serve until AD 63 were his sons, and Joseph Caiaphas, who served from AD 18–36, was his son-in-law (Josephus, *Ant* 18.34; 20.198). Rabbinic literature characterizes the family as extremely wealthy and powerful and as a target of the zealots (*b. Pesaḥ.* 57a; *t. Menaḥ.* 13.21–22). The Gospel seems to presuppose that the reader knows about the tense alliance between the house of Annas and Rome and their mutual anxiety about opposition to their authority.

The narrator reminds the reader that **Caiaphas was the one who advised the Jews that it is expedient for one man to be slain on behalf of the people** (18:14). From the onset, even though the Jewish authorities appeal to the law, Jewish law plays no role in the action. John contains no Jewish trial.

The scene is divided between two settings: the interior of the high priest Annas's house, where Jesus questions his interrogator, and the courtyard of the house, where Peter is questioned by the high priest's servants. In Matthew and Mark's account, the Sanhedrin examines Jesus, and the action comes to a climax with the accusation of blasphemy and the sentence of death (Matt. 26:59–67; Mark 14:55–65). Peter's denial follows as a discrete action (Matt.

237

Simultaneous Action in Ancient Narrative

According to the "Zielinksi Law," there is no true simultaneous action in Homer, who treats time as a ticking clock. Nevertheless, scholars must find some language to describe departures from the progression of time in Homer. Irene De Jong (2001, 589–90) coins the phrase the "interlace technique" to describe how, in the *Odyssey*, Homer switches back and forth between the stories of Odysseus, Telemachus, and Ithaca. Ruth Scodal likens Homer's habit of cutting to side stories in the *Iliad* to the modern cinematographic technique of reaction shots. In the *Iliad*, Homer on occasion cuts to a side story, such as the tale of Patroclus sitting on the beach and tending the wounded Eurypylos while the Achaians fight the Trojans (*Il.* 15.390–97; Scodal 2008, 110). Hebrew narrators seem to be more adept at handling action on two narrative planes. First Samuel 2:11–3:4 cuts back and forth between the stories of Samuel and Eli's sons to create perspective by which the audience can see the tension between background and foreground (see Kawashima 2004, 137–38). In his study of simultaneous action in Tobit, Ryan S. Schellenberg notes how for "ancient readers simultaneity suggested providential interweaving of fates" (2009, 7–9).

26:68–75; Mark 14:66–72). In Luke, Peter's denial precedes the trial before the Sanhedrin (Luke 22:55–62, 63–71). John's sandwiching of the interrogation between two stages in Peter's denial represents interlacing or simultaneous action and juxtaposes the false witness that Peter gives outside with the request for witnesses that Jesus makes inside. John sets up a contrast between Jesus's constancy and Peter's inconstancy and then brings the action together so that Peter denies Jesus just as Jesus is leaving Annas's chambers. The reader is left to imagine both Jesus's and Peter's reactions.

The narration focuses first on **Simon Peter and another disciple who followed after Jesus** (18:15a). John sets up Peter's denial with care. The contrast between interior space and exterior space that is so pronounced in the scenes with Pilate is no less important here. In the interior space of the Last Supper, Peter is frank and speaks his mind. In the exterior space, he no longer finds the courage to speak with such virtue. The anonymity of the other disciple raises the question of whether he is the Beloved Disciple, who is paired frequently with Peter (13:23–25; 20:2–10; 21:7, 20–21). The second disciple provides a foil for Peter's inconstancy. The two arrive at the house together, **but that disciple was known to the high priest and entered together with Jesus into the court of the high priest** (18:15b), **while Peter stood outside at the door. Then the disciple, the other one,** who, we are told once more, **was known to the high priest, came out and spoke to the woman doorkeeper and brought in Peter** (18:16). This little hiccup in the action prepares for what will follow. Peter seems to have lost his resolve and is no longer the agent of his own destiny, as he has presented himself thus far. John periodically uses the historic present to lay out the action of the denial as though it unfolds before the audience's eyes. **The young girl, the doorkeeper, then says to Peter, "Are you not also one of this man's disciples?"** (18:17a). The maidservant in the synoptic tradition is a doorkeeper in John.

John's scene is comparable to other doorkeeper scenes in ancient literature (e.g., Aristophanes, *Ach.* 393–406) as well as the doorkeeper scene in Shakespeare's *Macbeth* and in modern comedies. Doorkeepers were the lowest of domestic servants, often female, and the first member of the household whom a visitor would encounter. The disparity between the intent of the visitor, often a person of rank, to enter and the aim of the servant to keep unwanted elements from doing so sets up the conditions for comic conflict. Movie fans might think of scenes such as the one in *Keeping the Faith* (Edward Norton, dir., Spyglass, Touchstone, 2000), in which the character played by Ben Stiller is repeatedly kept from entering his girlfriend's office building by a burley doorman. The purpose of the comic scene, especially in a tragedy, is not to provide relief but rather to heighten the tension. For example, the porter (doorkeeper) in Macbeth responds to Macduff's knock (Shakespeare, *Macbeth*, act 2, scene 3):

> Here's a knocking indeed! If a
> man were porter of hell-gate, he should have
> old turning the key.
>
> *(Knocking within)*
>
> Knock,
> knock, knock! Who's there, i' the name of
> Beelzebub?

The porter's words, drawn from the Townley cycle of the medieval passion play in which Jesus knocks on hell's gate in order to gain entrance in the harrowing-of-hell story, unwittingly point to the hell that Macbeth's castle has become. The king lies murdered within. Similarly, inside Annas's palace lies danger for those who are friends of the true king.

The Johannine doorkeeper's question ("Are you not also one of this man's disciples?") seems to anticipate a "yes" answer by implying that she knows the unnamed disciple follows Jesus. Whoever the unnamed disciple is, he seems to have taken to heart Jesus's promise that none of his followers will fall, whereas Peter has not. Although saying yes would not necessarily prevent his entering, Peter **answers** [abruptly], **"I am not"** (18:17b). He enters the courtyard an unreliable witness not simply to Jesus but also to his own identity. His next act adds to the poignancy of his defection. The narrator provides some

Figure 23. This relief
by Arrigo da Campione
(fourteenth cent.) on the
pulpit in the Cathedral
of Modena, Italy, depicts
Peter warming his hands
by the fire as he denies
that he is one of Jesus's
disciples.

scenic detail: **And the slaves and the attendants,** presumably members of the
arrest party, **had been standing there, having made a charcoal fire because it
was cold, and were getting warm.** Our attention is then called to the fact that
there with them was Peter standing and getting warm (18:18). The intent of
his actions has shifted from loyalty to Jesus to his own comfort and security.
Note: Peter will be invited to a second charcoal fire in 21:9–10.

Not only is John's account striking for its lack of a formal Jewish trial; the
interrogation before Annas also is puzzling because Caiaphas takes no part in
it, and John does not narrate the particular questions that the (former) high
priest (Annas) puts to Jesus about his teaching. Moreover, when he writes,
**Then the high priest questioned Jesus about his disciples and about his teach-
ing** (18:19), he does not specify which high priest is asking the questions. One
might easily think that Caiaphas conducts the inquiry and then be caught off
guard when, at the end of the scene, one learns that Annas sends Jesus on to
Caiaphas. Jeffery L. Staley (1993) treats this as a case of entrapment of the
reader, but this confusion of personalities may also point to John's lack of
interest in distinguishing which Jewish authority speaks (see 1:19, 24). John
underscores the perfunctory nature of Jesus's arrest and the total absence of
due process. The course of events is set long before at the festival of Sukkoth,
when the Pharisees and chief priests make their first attempt at an arrest (7:32)
or when they draw conclusions about Jesus without a trial (7:45–52) or when
Caiaphas speaks his blind prophecy (11:50).

Jesus does not comply by answering Annas's questions. **"I spoke openly
to the world; I always taught in the synagogue and in the temple, where Jews
always gather, and I spoke nothing in secret"** (18:20). His time to speak is
over. Jesus's description of his openness should not be confused with the sort

of transparency that is named as a value in modern political rhetoric. In the ancient context, this sort of frankness and absence of dissimulating courtesy is normally reserved for circles of friends. Jesus is acknowledging that he spoke dangerously, without regard for his personal safety. So his present situation does not catch him off guard. He seems to anticipate the accusation that he has spoken sedition, an act that usually occurs behind closed doors. At one level, Jesus is the one who calls for witnesses and a trial: **"Why question me? Question those having heard what I spoke to them. Look, these know what I said"** (18:21). His words seem to point to the attendants and perhaps their presence at his speeches at Sukkoth. At another level, Jesus's words signify that the time for dialogue has passed: Jesus's eye is on the cross, and the task of recounting his teachings now passes to others. Jesus makes no claims about his identity; he does not refer to himself as the Son of Man, but his defiance of the high priest provokes a response. **Upon Jesus's speaking this way, one of the attendants standing nearby gave [him] a slap on the face, saying to Jesus, "Do you answer the high priest this way?"** (18:22). The slap is a serious challenge to Jesus's dignity, which Jesus repairs by questioning the righteousness of his interrogators. **"If I spoke wrongly [*kakōs*], testify [*martyrēson*] to the wrong [*kakou*]; but if well [*kalōs*], why strike me?"** (18:23).

When the narrator mentions that **Annas therefore sent him [Jesus] bound to Caiaphas the high priest** (18:24), he sets the stage for a second interrogation, perhaps a more-formal hearing, but he skips over the event as inconsequential to the action. As Jesus leaves, the narrator turns to the action that has been taking place outside. **Simon Peter was standing and getting warm.** True to Jesus's prediction, Peter denies Jesus two more times, first when **they said to him, "Are you not also one of his disciples?"** Peter, identified as **that one** as though he stands in contrast with the other disciple, **denied this and said, "I am not"** (18:25), and then **one of the slaves of the high priest, who is a relative of the one whose ear Peter cut off, says, "Did I not see you in the garden with him?"** (18:26). As a witness to the events in the garden and Malchus's relative, this man would possess a motive and legitimate basis for turning Peter over to the authorities. In Matthew and Mark, Peter ends the discussion by denying knowing Jesus and fortifying his words with oaths (Matt. 26:74; Mark 14:71). John writes simply that **Peter again denied, and at once a cock crowed** (18:27). In the Synoptic Gospels, the crow serves to remind the reader and Peter of Jesus's prediction, so that Peter breaks down in tears. With his clipped language, John makes the sound of the cock more ominous; this is Peter's catastrophe. His declaration *ouk eimi* (I am not) stands in counterpoint to Jesus's *egō eimi* (I am). This is perhaps John's finest example of enthymematic narrative. When the audience must supply Peter's and Jesus's reaction to the denial, its own reaction becomes more central in the storytelling. The omission of reference to Peter's horror at his own words leaves his story unfinished, making the restoration narrated in chapter 21 important to the unity of the Gospel.

Jesus Is Handed Over to Pilate; Pilate Tries to Hand Him Back (18:28–19:16)

John provides no introduction to Pilate and seems to presuppose that his audience is well acquainted with him and his situation. The narrator picks up the main action again as it moves on to the next setting: **They then led Jesus from Caiaphas to the praetorium** (18:28a) at Antonia, Pilate's fortress headquarters attached to the northwest corner of the temple. The scene at the praetorium is one of the most carefully crafted in the Gospel and, as such, is clearly central to the evangelist's objectives. It is divided into seven discrete subscenes demarcated by Pilate's movement back and forth between the interior and exterior of the building. (See 9:1–41 for a discussion of a similar dramatic structure.) The seven scenes form a chiasm:

A Exterior: Priests demand Jesus's death; Pilate refuses (18:29–32)
B Interior: Pilate inquires about Jesus's status as king (18:33–38a)
C Exterior: Pilate finds no harm in Jesus; priests choose Barabbas (18:38b–40)
D Interior: Soldiers scourge Jesus, mock him as king (19:1–3)
C' Exterior: Pilate finds no harm; priests make capital charge (19:4–8)
B' Interior: Pilate inquires about Jesus's origins (19:9–11)
A' Exterior: Priests demand Jesus's crucifixion; Pilate concedes (19:12–15)

Scene 1. John begins by noting the time constraints that add to the tension of the scene. **It was early and they did not enter the praetorium, so as not to be defiled and still eat the Passover** (18:28b). The praetorium would have been littered with idolatrous images and implements that would make it subject to various forms of impurity, including corpse impurity. The priests have no time to purify themselves again prior to the Passover. John uses a *hina mē* clause, his substitute for the infinitive, to add an element of apprehension because it connotes warding off something undesired. The fear of defilement or delay determines the action. This anxiety is ironic given that they seek the crucifixion of Jesus, an act that on one level defiles and on another level is the slaughter of the Passover lamb. John refers to Jesus's accusers as *hoi Ioudaioi* throughout the praetorium scene, perhaps to heighten the juxtaposition of Jewish and Roman political interests. **Pilate came out to them.** By conceding to the Jews, Pilate places himself at a disadvantage in the power struggle that will ensue, but he takes charge by demanding an account of why Jesus has been brought to him: **"What charge do you bring against this man?"** (18:29). The priests resist giving way to Pilate's authority by suggesting that arrest equals guilt: **"If this were not a wrongdoer, we would not have handed him over to you"** (18:30). Pilate is not prepared to be the agent of the Jewish authorities: **"You take him, and judge him according to your law!"** The Jews make it clear that they are demanding that Jesus be put to death: **"For us it is not allowed to put anyone to death"** (18:31). As a result, Pilate is forced to respond to their request, but he takes his time in an effort to show that he

---

Pontius Pilate, "Friend of Caesar"

Pilate governed Judea from AD 26 to 36. Tiberius had withdrawn to Capri in 26, and Lucius Aelius Sejanus, who bore the official title of "friend of Caesar" and was Pilate's patron, served as regent. Sejanus was executed in AD 31 on the charge of *maiestas* (sedition) after conspiring to take the throne. The people of Rome expressed their hatred for him by tearing his corpse into pieces and throwing them into the Tiber (Tacitus, *Ann.* 3.7, 72–73; 4.1–3, 34–35; 6.51). Jesus's trial takes place shortly before or after these events; therefore, Pilate may be anxious to avoid the attention of his Roman superiors. During the early years of his rule, whenever the people of Jerusalem objected to his actions, he threatened or responded with lethal force (Josephus, *J.W.* 2.169–74, 175–77; *Ant.* 18.55–59, 60–62). In the final years of his power, the Jews learned to appeal to Tiberias, who reproached Pilate (Philo, *Legat.* 301). When the Samaritans brought charges of brutality against him to Vitellius, governor of Syria, Vitellius appointed a new administrator in Judea and ordered Pilate to return to Rome to give an account of his actions to Tiberius. Pilate dawdled on his way to Rome, and Tiberias died before he arrived (Josephus, *Ant.* 18.88–89). History does not record what fate befell Pilate.

---

acts according to his own inclination rather than that of the Jewish authorities. Pilate's independent inquest and alternative actions exacerbate the Jews' sense of urgency and make them impulsive in their choice of words.

The scene ends with a fulfillment formula—**in order that the words of Jesus might be fulfilled that he said signifying [*semainōn*] the sort of death he was about to die** (18:32)—that points back to Jesus's prescience in 12:32–33. The passage underscores that while the Jewish authorities think that they act to fulfill their own intents, the action is unfolding according to Jesus's purpose and divine foresight. While crucifixion has not explicitly been requested, it is understood, given that Rome will be the executioner.

Scene 2. The action moves inside—**Pilate then entered the praetorium again, and summoned Jesus**—where Pilate adopts the guise of a governor on top of his game. Pilate's initial interaction with the Jews suggests that he has no knowledge of the case, but inside his first question, **"Are you the King of the Jews?"** (18:33), suggests that he knows what happened when Jesus entered Jerusalem (12:13–15) and that he is seeking grounds for accusing Jesus of *Lex Iulia de maiestate*, sedition against the imperial authority of Rome. In the dialogue that follows, two things happen: (1) Pilate is persuaded that he need not comply with the priest's demand, and (2) Jesus indirectly impugns Pilate's integrity without consequence.

Jesus avoids answering Pilate's question by asking one of his own: **"Do you speak for yourself, or did others tell you about me?"** (18:34). Jesus comes very

243

close to naming what Pilate fears: he is being made the servant of the Jewish authorities. Pilate acknowledges the slight with the rhetorical question **"I am not a Jew, am I?"** and then asks an open question, **"Your people and the chief priests handed you over to me. What did you do?"** (18:35). Once again, Jesus does not honor Pilate with a direct answer but instead delivers a heavily nuanced response: **"My kingdom is not from this world. If my kingdom were from this world, my attendants** [hypēretai] **would have contended** [ēgōnizonto] **so that I would not have been handed over to the Jews. But as it is, my kingdom is not from that source"** (18:36). Rather than seeing this as a reference to a future eschatological kingdom or to a spiritual transcendent kingdom, Reimund Bieringer (2000) makes the case that Jesus rejects kingship conferred by human agents, the kind that the crowd seeks to thrust upon him in 6:15 or 12:13 or that the Romans mock in 19:2–3, 19. Jesus's speech is remarkable for its frankness. The choice of the term hypēretai, the term used to denote the chief priests' strong men, and the verb ēgōnizonto characterize the conflict as a contest. Pilate seems to treat the refusal to enter into armed conflict as a denial of kingship: **"So you [really] are not a king [are you]?"** Jesus rhetorically points his finger at Pilate by answering, **"You say that I am king"** (18:37a), as though the very act of conducting an inquiry is an acknowledgment that Jesus is a threat. It seems unlikely that a prisoner could get away with speaking to Pilate the way Jesus has, especially when similar responses earned him a slap from Annas's man. Pilate's imperviousness indicates that he continues to view the Jewish authorities as a greater challenge to his demonstration of power than any challenge that Jesus poses.

Jesus then identifies himself as a witness rather than the accused: **"For this I was born, and for this I have come into the world, so that that I may testify to the truth. All who are from the truth hear my voice"** (18:37b). Pilate then demonstrates that he is not one who listens by countering: **"What is truth?"** (18:38a). The question is rhetorical and dismissive. His abrupt departure signifies that he wants no reply.

While the question "What is truth?" may be an index of Pilate's cynical character, it also points to the contrast between how Pilate, as a Roman authority, views what is happening compared to what Jesus sees. At this point, Jesus's implicit claim to a heavenly dominion seems not to concern Pilate. Jesus's purpose in coming into the world is to serve as God's agent of redemption; therefore the truth to which he testifies is God's faithfulness. When a Roman speaks of truth, it is matter of fact, what has happened (see Keener 2003, 2:1113). Pilate's rhetorical question underscores the view of power and authority that differentiates him, and indirectly Caesar, from Jesus.

Scene 3. Pilate's movement to the exterior resumes the conflict with the Jews. **And having said this, he again came out to the Jews, and he tells them, "I find not a single charge [to lay] on him"** (18:38b). His words seem designed to slight the Jews, from whom he has heard no specific charge. What follows is part of the traditional passion material, but John handles it with a purpose. Matthew and Mark treat the release of a prisoner at Passover as Pilate's personal custom, which the crowd asks Pilate to fulfill. Though there is no source other than the Gospels with which to corroborate either the story of Barabbas or a tradition of releasing a prisoner at Passover, Roman rulers did use the power of clemency as an indication of their supreme power (see Seneca, *Clem.* 1.21.2–3). John has Pilate state that the custom is Jewish: "**But there is a custom among you that I should release one to you on the Passover.**" His words point to an inconsistency in the Jews' demand to execute rather than release Jesus. Whereas Matthew has Pilate present the crowd with the choice between Jesus and Barabbas (27:15–17), John's Pilate makes an offer, "**Do you wish therefore I release to you the king of the Jews?**" (18:39), that mocks Jewish nationalistic hopes and demonstrates that he knows what charge the priests are anticipating. John's Pilate seems not to consider the possibility that the Jews will name an alternate choice; therefore, his strategy backfires when they say, "**Not this one but Barabbas.**" The narrator makes the irony clear by adding **only Barabbas was a bandit** (18:40). Rather than demonstrating his power to release Jesus, Pilate is confronted with having to release someone who satisfies his definition of truth. Barabbas has demonstrated that he is a threat to law and order. While tradition provides John with the name Barabbas, that the Jews choose a violent revolutionary whose Aramaic name means "son of a father" is no less ironic. They fear that Jesus's following will bring Roman wrath upon the nation, but they choose to have released the sort of man who will incite the uprising that leads to the Roman destruction of the temple in AD 70. Luke presents a similar chain of events and has Pilate follow through by releasing Barabbas. John makes no mention of what Pilate does. Releasing Barabbas is not his agenda.

Scene 4. The choice of Barabbas necessitates that Pilate deal with Jesus and pushes the action back into the interior for the fourth scene: **So then Pilate took and scourged** [*emastigōsen*; Greek for the Latin *excoriare*] **Jesus** (19:1): Pilate had the soldiers scourge him. John places the mocking of Jesus at the center of the trial and the chiasm. The Synoptic Gospels handle this event very differently. Luke has Pilate offer to have Jesus chastised (*paideusas*) as an alternative to crucifixion; therefore, there is no flogging (23:22), and Luke places the mocking in the context of the audience with Herod (23:11). In Matthew and Mark, the flogging (*phragellōsas*) and the mocking occur after Jesus is sentenced to die (Matt. 27:26–30; Mark 15:15–20), as a preliminary stage in Roman capital punishment. John's Pilate has Jesus flogged in an effort to either satisfy the temple authorities' desire for punishment or to solicit a confession through torture (see Glancy 2005). If the former is the case, Pilate compromises his resolve not to bow to the Jews' wishes without doing exactly what they have demanded. If he is torturing him, Pilate stays on the same course of action he pursued in his first interrogation of Jesus. He is not

Roman Corporal Punishment

The *virga* (the rod) was the symbol of a magistrate's authority; therefore, the act of flogging Jesus is above all a demonstration of Pilate's authority. *Excoriare* was the form of punishment used for patricide, so it seems that death could be an expected outcome of the flogging. In Roman culture, physical pain was not the primary intended outcome of corporal punishment. Romans distinguished bodies that were protected by their honor and bodies that had no protective honor and hence could be abused; therefore corporal punishment was normally reserved for the lower classes, the *humiliores* (Saller 1994, 133–42). Cato described being whipped (with *verbera*) as "extreme ignominy," which brought the victim to the level of a slave (cited in Aulus Gellius, *Noct. att.* 10.3.17).

opposed to crucifying Jesus as long as he does so based on evidence, in this case Jesus's confession, rather than the demands of the priests.

John presents a detailed picture of the mocking: **the soldiers braided a crown out of a thorny plant, placed [it] on his head, and they threw around him a purple robe (19:2), and they kept coming up to him and saying, "Hail, the king of the Jews," and giving him slaps on the face (19:3).** John uses imperfect verbs to emphasize the repetition of this action. The soldiers are imitating the spectacle of Roman public executions, which took the form of dramatic performances: the condemned were dressed to reenact historical events or to represent a defeated king (Coleman 1990). Tertullian (*Apol.* 15.4) describes one criminal who was dressed as Attis and then castrated, and another who was burned alive in the role of Hercules. Clement of Rome (*1 Clem.* 6.2) describes women martyrs dressed as either the daughters of King Danaus (who were condemned in Hades to forever fill water jugs with holes in their bottoms for having stabbed their husbands on their wedding night) or Circe the enchantress. The *Passion of Perpetua and Felicitas* 6.1 recounts how men were dressed as the priests of Saturn and the women as the priestesses of Ceres before their execution. John (and Mark) describes a purple robe (himation porphyroun), the garb of a Hellenistic king. Such cruelty strikes the modern audience as unprovoked, but we must contextualize this in the world of the Roman soldiers, the ones whose lives are at stake in the conflict with insurrectionists. The point is not simply to punish the offender but to alter his status. By virtue of being scourged, Jesus supposedly can no longer become the king that the crowd has twice tried to proclaim him (John 6:15; 12:13).

Scene 5. The movement to the exterior and the resumption of the dialogue between Pilate and the Jews opens up rhetorical space so that the humiliation can point to Jesus's glory. In this fifth scene, John depicts Pilate as presenting Jesus to the Jews in an attempt to control what Jesus's appearance signifies: **"Behold, I am bringing him out to you so that you should know** [gnōte; aorist subjunctive] **that I find not one charge** [to lay] **on him"** (19:4). The presentation follows: **Jesus then came out, bearing the thorny crown and the purple**

robe. Pilate then points to Jesus: **"Behold, the man!"** (19:5). The word "man" (*anthrōpos*) has multiple significations, all of which the evangelist could be exploiting. The intended readers of the Gospel are certainly meant to recognize that, with reference to Jesus, "man" no longer signifies mortality but echoes Jesus's own use of the term "Son of Man" (*huios tou anthrōpou*). A Jewish audience might recognize this phrase as an echo of God's pronouncement about Saul, "Here is the man of whom I spoke to you. He it is who shall rule over my people" (1 Sam. 9:17). In this case, they would see the robe and the crown as the soldiers intended them, as a mocking of Jewish hopes of sovereignty. What Pilate could mean by these words is less clear. Could he be reiterating the soldiers' mocking or, as Ernst Haenchen (1984, 2:181) concludes, is he saying that Jesus is just a pitiable man and not a king? The Gospel presents a third choice that stands in continuity with its emphasis on Jesus's victory over death. Jesus's silent endurance of torture is analogous to the trial by combat in the arena, in which the gladiator wins his life (Wiedemann 1992, 9). For a Roman, the word *virtus*, "manliness," meant exhibiting no fear at death and no hope of evading death (Cicero, *Tusc.* 2.17; Pliny the Younger, *Pan.* 33.1). This is the meaning that Martin Luther takes in his translation "Sehet, welch ein Mensch!" (See, what a man!). Colleen Conway (2008, 143–51) demonstrates that John consistently represents Jesus in word and deed in ways that confirm his masculinity within the norms of the broader context of the Greco-Roman Mediterranean world. An epigram from Martial provides a glimpse of the satisfaction that Romans felt when they could admire the deportment of the condemned in the arena. He describes the crowds' delight when on one occasion a man who was condemned to have his hand burned "grasps the flame and delights in its punishing pain," and then holding it up, became himself a spectator admiring "his right hand's gallant death" (Martial, *Epig.* 8.30). With the words "Behold, the man," Pilate does not proclaim Jesus's innocence: he proclaims his worth. What he intends them to see—a body covered in red, crowned with thorns, and draped in purple—is then the image of the triumphator, the victor who earns the privilege to wear the *corona* and the *toga purpura*, and not necessarily a king.

Whatever Pilate's intended sense of the words "Behold, the man," his purpose is to bend the crowd to his will, but his efforts seem only to heighten their sense of urgency. **When they then saw him, the high priests and their attendants howled** [*ekraugasan*], **saying "Crucify! Crucify!"** John uses the verb *kraugazein*, the verb used to describe the baying of dogs. Pilate's exasperation is captured by the illogic of his response: **"Take him yourselves and crucify** [him]," and he repeats for a third time **"for I do not find a charge** [to lay] **on him"** (19:6). The seeming impasse is broken when **the Jews** finally comply with his initial request for a charge: **"We have a law and according to the law he must die, because he has made himself the Son of God"** (19:7). That to proclaim oneself the Son of God is not self-evidently blasphemy or a violation of Jewish or Roman law renders this an excited utterance rather than a calculated effort to move the case forward.

Scene 6. John then tells us that **upon hearing this speech, Pilate became more afraid** [*mallon ephobēthē*] (19:8) **and went into the praetorium again** (19:9a). What in particular compels Pilate to retreat for a second dialogue with Jesus is not clear. Does this mean that Pilate has been afraid and at this point grows more afraid, or does it signify that he becomes very afraid? Moreover, what in particular does he fear? Is it Jesus, or is it his own failure to gain control of the situation, or both? John does not provide sufficient data to posit certainty. As a Roman, Pilate would be inclined to believe in the presence of divine men of various sorts and would be prepared to consider the possibility that he is dealing with one now. Certainly Jesus's endurance of the scourging would provide corroboration of this conclusion. He might also understand the title Son of God to be an imperial title and thus a direct challenge to Caesar's supremacy and authority, in which case he would be forced to reconsider the charge of *Lex Iulia de maiestate*.

Why Pilate would ask **Jesus, "Where are you from?"** (19:9b) is also not clear. This might represent an attempt comparable to that described in Luke 23:6–7, to send Jesus, the Galilean, to Herod. The effect on his characterization is clearer. In his first interrogation of Jesus, Pilate asks questions anticipating the conclusion that he has already drawn. Now he seeks information that points to his want of understanding. His vulnerability is showing. Jesus now moves from indirect insult to a direct challenge of Pilate's authority: **Jesus did not give him an answer** (19:9c). Pilate is forced to acknowledge the offense— **"Do you not speak to me?"**—and to assert his authority—**"Don't you know that I have authority to release you, and I have the authority to crucify you?"** (19:10). Jesus challenges Pilate directly: **"You do not have authority, not over me, if it was not given to you from above."** The syntax emphasizes that Pilate's authority does not extend to Jesus without divine sanction. This is not a claim that government in general is divinely ordained. Jesus then reverses roles, placing Pilate in the position of the one on trial by partially exonerating him: **"accordingly, the one handing me over to you has greater fault"** (19:11). Jesus seems to refer either to the Jewish authorities who have been granted some authority by God and as a result make a greater error, or to Judas, who is disloyal.

What follows is an odd construction that juxtaposes Pilate's continuing actions with those of the Jewish authorities. **In consequence of** [*ek toutou*] **Pilate's continuing to try to release him, the Jews howled, saying, "If you release this** [man], **you are not a friend of Caesar"** (19:12a). As voices from outside intrude on the interior space, the distinction between the exterior and interior begins to collapse. "Friend of Caesar" (*amicus Caesaris*) is a technical term signifying that Caesar's patronage is direct. Pilate's patron, not Pilate himself, bore this title. The cessation of this relationship meant the end of the client's public career, confiscation of property, and the choice of exile or suicide (Rogers 1959; Cicero, *Att.* 10.8b). The phrase *ek toutous* need not signify that Jesus's words cause Pilate to seek to release him because he believes Jesus. Rather, Jesus's challenge that Pilate has no power would have fixed Pilate's resolve to show that he is in charge.

The syntax that juxtaposes Pilate's intent and the sound of the Jewish voices outside serves to accentuate the growing tension between Pilate's desire and the forces causing him to act against his own inclinations. The sound of the crowd's voices bring an accusation that he cannot ignore: **"Everyone who makes himself a king challenges [*antilegei*] Caesar"** (19:12b). The verb *antilegei* suggests that Jesus makes a counterclaim to Caesar's rule. The charge is then sedition. The Jews' words imply that Pilate opens himself to the charge of *Lex Iulia de maiestate*. Given the historical circumstances of Pilate's rule, this veiled threat is real and a sufficient cause to move him to convict.

Scene 7. The narrator indicates that Pilate moves the action outside again for the seventh and final scene, **when Pilate comprehends these words**, when he understands the full implications of what they are saying. The wording of what happens next forces the reader to make a choice. Pilate **brought Jesus out and sat [*ekathisen*] on the seat [*bēmatos*] in a place called Stone Pavement, in Hebrew, Gabbatha** (19:13), a word suggesting an elevation. The location may be symbolically pointing to another action constitutive of the narrative, the exaltation of Jesus. John then emphasizes that time is wasting for the priests: **It was the preparation of Passover and about the sixth hour** (either midmorning or noon). If *ekathisen* is transitive and the *bēmatos* is simply a seat, Jesus is the one being seated, and when Pilate says, **"Behold, your king!"** (19:14), he enacts a mock enthronement. The howl of the crowd, **"Away, away, crucify him,"** is then a protest. If *ekathisen* is intransitive and Pilate takes the judgment seat, the audience would be prepared for the finality of a verdict, and the pronouncement signifies that he has found Jesus guilty of a capital crime. The cry, "Away, away, crucify him," now becomes a call for immediate execution. Scholars provide support for either reading. Perhaps John intends his audience to entertain both.

Pilate resists the crowd's urgency by asking, **"Shall I crucify your king?"** The high priests' response is impulsive and betrays desperation to be done with the banter: **"We haven't a king if not Caesar"** (19:15). The duplication of a negative—usually reduced to one in translation (e.g., NIV, NRSV)—points to a lack of attention to the implication of their words. Without thinking, they have denied the principal theological claim of Judaism: God is sovereign. Something like the statement "Our father, our king, we have no king but you," a line from the *Abinu Malkenu* from the Yom Kippur liturgy (*b. Ta'an.* 25b is the earliest attestation), was probably proclaimed in the Sabbath liturgy to confess that God's sovereignty gives life to Israel or Jewish national identity. By denying God's sovereignty, the Jews would cease to exist as a people. At this point, Pilate can publicly concede to the Jewish authorities' demand without risk of relinquishing his own authority. **He then handed Jesus over** [*paredōken*] **in order that he might be crucified.** The Roman soldiers **then took Jesus and led** [him] **away** (19:16).

The Crucifixion: Jesus Hands Himself Over to Death (19:17–42)

A quick comparison with the synoptic treatments makes it clear that the action in John's crucifixion account is represented as a series of seven discrete acts. Each is comparable to a dramatic vignette that captures one action. Some bear comparison to Roman mime, comic sketches that mock human pretensions. Together, with the exception of the fourth and fifth vignette, they form a montage in which each party is absorbed in its own little drama and misses the important action, the glorification of God's Son. This technique of contrasting montage is used frequently in modern film, especially suspense dramas. For example, in the film *Pearl Harbor* (Michael Bay, dir.; Touchstone; Jerry Bruckheimer, producer, 2001) a montage of short scenes showing sailors sleeping in their berths, fishing and playing at dice, a woman hanging laundry, and boys playing baseball—all are spliced into the footage of the Japanese bombers arriving over the island of Oahu, to accentuate the unexpected and unprovoked nature of the violence about to happen. Mark's account, in contrast, collapses the various activities in one breathless sequence (Mark 15:22–37).

Sequence of Events in John 19:16b–42

1. Crucifixion (19:16b–18)
2. Debate over titulus (19:19–22)
3. Gambling over cloth (19:23–25a)
4. Adoption enacted (19:25b–27)
5. Jesus gives up spirit (19:28–30)
6. Piercing of body (19:31–37)
7. Entombment (19:38–42)

1. *Jesus is crucified.* John's account of the story of the journey to the cross and the crucifixion itself is brief, but it contains a couple of notable features. First, he emphasizes that **Jesus, carrying the cross for himself, came out to the place called the skull, which is called in Hebrew, Golgotha** (19:17). Tradition provides John with the sinister name. In Roman practice, the condemned were flogged in preparation for crucifixion and then carried the *patibulum*, the transverse beam, to the site of execution (Plautus, *Mil. glor.* 359–60). The synoptic accounts reflect this practice and include a piece of verisimilitude: the flogging renders him incapable of carrying the cross, and so Simon of Cyrene is conscripted to carry it (Mark 15:21; Matt. 27:32; Luke 23:26). If John chooses not to include the story of Simon of Cyrene, his intent may be

twofold: (1) no one else suffers directly as a consequence of Jesus's arrest and crucifixion, and (2) Jesus moves forward at every step, sustained by his resolve. The second feature is that John controls the mind's eye so that it moves back and forth before resting on Jesus: **They crucified him there and two others with him on this side** [*enteuthen*] **and on that side** [*enteuthen*]**, then in the center** [*meson*] **Jesus** (19:18). In contrast to the synoptic accounts, the others' offenses go without mention, perhaps underscoring the arbitrary nature of Roman justice.

2. *The titulus.* At the end of the trial scene, the high priests emerge as the winner of the trial insofar as they secure Jesus's death sentence, but the audience knows that they have condemned themselves. Like the dupe of Roman comedy, the priests think that they have manipulated Pilate to work on their behalf. The *titulus* scene (19:19–22) functions as a recognition scene in which they become aware of their own foolishness.

John writes that **Pilate then wrote a placard** [*titlon*] **and placed it on the cross, and what was written was** [*ēn de gegrammenon*] **"Jesus the Nazarene, the king of the Jews"** (19:19). This probably means that he ordered the act rather than performed it himself. *Titlos* is the Greek form of the Latin world *titulus.* Such a placard was a common feature in Roman punishment. Suetonius describes a public banquet in Rome at which Caligula had the hands of a slave cut off and hung around his neck and had a placard describing his offense carried before him as he was led among the guests before being handed over to the executioners (*Cal.* 32.2; see also *Dom.* 10.1; Cassius Dio, *Hist.* 54.3.6–7; 73.16.5). The sign served to inform the public as well as to ridicule the offender. The crowd that gathers around the cross would have expected a term such as *lēstēs* to be placed above the cross or around his neck.

John emphasizes a number of the placard's features that provoke the chief priests to object. First, the idea that somebody from Nazareth could be king of the Jews would be seen as an intended insult. Second, **many of the Jews, therefore, read this placard because the place where Jesus was crucified was near the city. And** third, **what was written was in Hebrew, in Roman** [Latin], **and in Greek** (19:20); therefore, everyone present could understand its meaning. People would not be reading the placard as though they were all literate, silent readers. Those who were literate would read it aloud, and in doing so, play into Pilate's hands by proclaiming Jesus of Nazareth (Jesus here crucified) the Jewish king. Pilate has created a scene, and the chief priests are compelled to protest: **"Do not write, 'The King of the Jews,' but that 'this** [man] **said, "I am king of the Jews"'"** (19:21); they try to get the sign to point directly to Jesus rather than to Jewish political pretensions. **Pilate replied, "What I have written, I have written"** (19:22), and so acts the part of the *alazōn*, thinking that he can determine the significance of the crucifixion, but he does not control the significance of his own text. As Craig Keener (2003, 2:1138) observes, every other appearance of the word "written" in the Gospel thus far refers to

Scripture (see 2:17; 6:31, 45; 8:17; 10:34–35; 12:14, 16; 15:25). For the audience of the Gospel, the three languages and the content of the superscription point to the universality of Jesus's reign. Ironically, Pilate is the first gospel writer.

3. *Gambling as a diversion.* The gambling vignette (19:23–25), in which **the soldiers, when they crucified Jesus, took his outer garments [*himatia*] and made four parts, a part for each soldier** (19:23a), comes from the tradition shared with the Synoptic Gospels. Roman law allowed those performing an execution to confiscate the victim's minor possessions as an act analogous to stripping the bodies of those defeated in battle (*Dig.* 48.20.6). Christian apologists have resisted picturing Jesus naked upon the cross because they deem it too humiliating, but this was precisely the soldiers' objective.

John describes a second garment, **a tunic [*chitōna*], and the tunic was seamless, woven from the top throughout** (19:23b). Speculation about the significance of the seamless cloth may distract the reader from the course that the narrative follows. In Cyprian's allegorical reading, the cloth was the unity of the church (*Unit. eccl.* 7). Many exegetes have suggested that the cloth represents the high priest's garment (see Lev. 21:10), but the LXX does not use the noun *chitōn*. Its significance may lie less in its symbolic value and more in what role it serves in the story. The effect of the additional tunic in the Fourth Gospel is to turn attention away from Jesus's naked body to the soldiers' preoccupation with Jesus's clothing. **They then said to one another, "Let's not divide it, but let's cast lots to see whose it will be"** (19:24a). This simple line has multiple significations. In their greed, a trivial object easily distracts the soldiers from attending to the important task of executing a supposed threat to their power. The action turns away from one entertainment—the spectacle of the crucifixion—to another entertainment, one designed to satisfy greed and to allay boredom, and from Jesus as the object of ridicule to the ridiculous soldiers.

John inserts a quotation from Ps. 22:18 (21:19 LXX) in between the words of the soldiers and their actions **that Scripture might be fulfilled which said, "They divided my outer garments [*himatia*] among themselves, and over my apparel [*himatismon*] they cast a lot"** (19:24b). Psalm 22 is also the source of Jesus's words of lament in Matt. 27:46 and Mark 15:34. He then writes, **the soldiers then did this** (19:25a). While the soldiers think they are following their own agenda, their actions are actually scripted.

4. *Jesus hands over his mother.* In the next vignette, eyes are turned toward the women. The Synoptic Gospels emphasize that many women stood at a distance, perhaps to separate themselves from the crowd that mocks Jesus and views the crucifixion as a spectacle (Matt. 27:55; Mark 15:40–41; Luke 23:48–49). John brings the women so close that Jesus can speak to them. **They had been standing beside the cross, his mother and the sister of his mother, Mary the [wife] of Klopas, and Mary the Magdalene** (19:25b). They appear to be neither wailing nor beating their breasts in the traditional role given to

women mourners (cf. Luke 23:27). All three women present are named Mary. The paring down of the women to three cannot be limited to the dictates of the dramatic dialogue or action, for the second two women serve no overt role in the narrative. In his commentary, Raymond Brown (1970, 904) notes that a count of four women (treating the sister and wife as two different women) would provide symmetry with the four soldiers, but in a later work he argues that John simply draws from an established tradition (Brown 1994, 1013–19). Once again, the reader ought not to be derailed by speculation about the symbolic significance of a detail for which the Gospel provides insufficient information to draw any conclusions. The mother of Jesus is the significant figure, and it would be culturally inappropriate for her to be standing alone in this setting. His mother's presence serves a literary purpose. This crucifixion scene is tied with numerous threads, including the elements of water and wine, to the wedding of Cana, when Jesus's hour had not yet come. Moreover, Jesus undercuts the pathos of a mother, supported in her loss by two women, by the establishment of a new relationship with a young man.

Jesus then, seeing the mother and the disciple standing nearby whom he loved, says to the mother, "Woman, behold your son" (19:26). **Then he says to the disciple, "Behold your mother." And from that day, the disciple took this** [woman] **into his own** [home] (19:27). The Beloved Disciple appears for the only time not in the company of Peter. The Fourth Gospel's unique contribution to the Passion Narrative seems to subvert the pathos of the story by enacting the sort of happy ending that Aristotle associates with comedy (*Poet.* 1453a.13). At the moment of death, Jesus celebrates a birth: the fictive birth of the Beloved Disciple as the son of his mother.

5. *Jesus hands himself over to death.* The story then proceeds to Jesus's death with a line confirming that Jesus is in charge of a process normally characterized by loss of control. **After this Jesus, knowing that all things have been now accomplished** [*tetelestai*] **in order that Scripture be completed** [*teleiōthē*], **says, "I thirst"** (19:28), as though it were a line in a script rather than a prophecy to be fulfilled. Jesus speaks as one of the righteous who suffers thirst (Pss. 22:15; 69:3) and is given vinegar by his tormentors (69:21). **Then a vessel full of vinegar was set** [there], **and having filled a sponge with vinegar and putting it around** [some] **hyssop, they bought** [it] **to his mouth** (19:29). However ironic Jesus's thirst may be given that he is the living water who satisfies all thirst (cf. Moore 1993), in this vignette the Gospel writer seems intent on the symbolic associations of the hyssop dipped in blood and used to touch the lintel and doorposts in Exod. 12:22. Jesus's death is that of the Passover lamb. Jesus's thirst is connected with his desire to drink from the cup: he wills his own death. He has no need to recite a psalm of lament to mark the distance that he feels from God (see Matt. 27:46; Mark 15:34). Instead, **when he then took the vinegar, Jesus said, "It has been completed** [*tetelestai*]**,"** recalling both the words at the end of the creation account ("and

God completed [*synetelesen*] his work on the seventh day"; Gen. 2:2 LXX) and Jesus's unity with God. **And resting the head he handed the spirit over** [*paredōken to pneuma*] (19:30). In the end, it is neither Judas nor the chief priests nor Pilate but Jesus who hands himself over to death.

6. *Making sure that he is truly dead.* The crucifixion account ends with a denouement (19:31–37) that stands in surprising contrast with what follows Jesus's death in the Synoptic Gospels, where their reader's attention turns immediately to environmental events (Matt. 27:51–53) or the reaction of on-lookers (Matt. 27:54–55; Mark 15:40; Luke 23:47–49). John marks the contrast between the knowledge of the Gospel's audience that Jesus has died with the uncertainty of the narrative audience, and he allows all eyes to dwell on Jesus's corpse even though the lifeless body on the cross is an offense according to the law (Deut. 21:23). The foolishness of the request that Jesus be crucified is underscored by anxiety about purity. **Therefore the Jews, since it was the day of preparation, lest the bodies remain on the cross on the Sabbath, for the day of that Sabbath was important, solicited Pilate so that their legs might be shattered,** presumably to hasten their death, **and** the bodies **might be lifted off** (19:31). Here is more Johannine irony: the ones charged with preparing for the Passover by slaughtering the lambs, the unbroken shank bone of which will be eaten at the Passover meal (Exod. 12:46; Num. 9:12), order the defilement of the true Passover lamb. The action then seesaws between suspense and relief. First, Jesus's body is threatened with bone breakage. **So the soldiers came and shattered the legs of the first and the other crucified with him** (19:32). **But upon coming to Jesus,** there is reprieve, **when they saw he was already dead, they did not shatter his legs** (19:33). No sooner said, **but one of the soldiers with his lance pierced the side, and** to his surprise, and surely to that of the first audience, **out came a flow of blood and water** (19:34). This issue of fluid invites investigation of its surplus of symbolic meaning and ironic significance. The solider, who seems to imitate the humiliation of a defeated combative enemy, is showered with life-giving elements. Mary Coloe points out that this is temple imagery. Jesus dies at the same time as the blood from the Passover lamb flows from the temple. The water signifies that Jesus is the eschatological temple, from which the water of the spirit of life flows (Coloe 2001, 208; for a treatment of various symbolic values, see Keener 2003, 1152–54).

The voice of the narrator intrudes at this point with three distinct editorial comments. First, he provides a reliable source: **the one seeing this has witnessed, and his witness is true.** Second, he provides a motive: **that one knows the true he speaks in order that you,** the audience of the Gospel, **may believe** (19:35). This seems to be in preparation for a more-developed statement of purpose in 20:30–31. Third, he provides a prophecy: **for these things happened so that the Scripture might be fulfilled, "Not a bone of his was splintered"** [19:36; a combination of Ps. 34:20 (a reference to God's protecting the bones of the righteous from breakage) and Exod. 12:46 and Num. 9:12 (references to the

Passover lamb)], **and again another Scripture says, "They will look at one whom they have stabbed"** (19:37; see Zech. 12:10). The clear purpose of the fulfillment formula is to end with the chord that has been struck throughout the crucifixion narrative (18:9, 32; 19:24, 28). While the agents of the particular events may have their own motives and think that they act according to their own intent, events unfold according to a divine plan.

7. *The entombment.* With the phrase **after these events,** John signals a turn in the action from the attempts to humiliate Jesus's body to the attempt to honor his corpse. This scene can be read either as the end of the crucifixion narrative or the beginning of the resurrection account. John introduces a new character, **Joseph from Arimathea, being a disciple of Jesus but** [with] **concealed** [identity] **on account of fear of the Jews.** Rather than representing Joseph as a rich man (cf. Matt. 27:57), John identifies Joseph as a closeted follower of Jesus and later as an associate of Nicodemus. The precise nature of his fear is not clear, but given Nicodemus's experience (7:50–52) and earlier comments about the fear of being put out of the synagogue (9:22; 12:42), anxiety about the social costs of his actions and, perhaps, exclusion from festival activities are the logical motives for furtiveness.

Bryon R. McCane (2003, 56) suggests that Joseph acts as an agent of the Jewish authorities when he **petitioned Pilate so that he might lift and take away** [the verb *arē* needs two English verbs to capture the action] **Jesus's body,** because it is they who do not want to violate Jewish law by leaving him on the cross. Josephus (*J.W.* 4.314–17) describes the scruples of Jews to bury even those crucified before sunset, in accord with biblical law (Deut. 21:22–23; Ezek. 39:14, 16), and Philo (*Flacc.* 83) provides evidence for the release of such bodies to family members. John the Baptist's body was released to his disciples (Mark 6:14–29). The startling aspect of the story is that Joseph is not a relative. The absence of family members may point to Jesus's status as a criminal in the eyes of Jewish authorities, who did not permit the family to honor the dead, but disposed of the corpses themselves. If John's reader is expected to know this fact, here is an added piece of irony. The two delegates of the authorities are covertly allied with the criminal. **He then came and lifted and took away his body** (19:38).

The narrator now reveals that **there came also Nicodemus, the one who came to him at night for the first time,** as if this is a surprise. Nicodemus's presence and actions invite speculation about the status of his faith. With little to go on, it seems safest to say he is heading in the right direction. Nicodemus comes **bearing a mixture of myrrh and aloes, around one hundred liters** (19:39). The presence of so much superfluous and expensive cosmetics demands attention, even though it is of no real consequence. Why would a Pharisee such as Nicodemus think that this mixture is necessary? Perfumes were used primarily to mask the stench of death and were especially important if some delay in final preparation or burial was anticipated. The myrrh prevented desiccation of the body. The amount, however, far exceeds anything approximating typical. If we treat this as symbolic, we might conclude, as Raymond Brown does, that John has "transformed the crucifixion into the triumph of Jesus. One who reigned as a king on the cross receives a burial worthy of his status" (1994, 1268). Josephus (*J.W.* 1.670–73; *Ant.* 17.199) provides a description of Herod's funeral, in which five hundred servants were required to carry the burial spices. If we shift the focus to Joseph and Nicodemus, John paints a poignant but absurd picture of two distinguished men trying to give Jesus an honorable burial in a context in which honor is to be denied Jesus. But the audience also knows that such efforts are not necessary because Jesus's death is not humiliating and that the normal concerns about long-term internment of his body are misguided.

Then they took the body of Jesus and bound it in linen cloths with aromatics, just as custom is for the Jews to prepare for burial (19:40). The customs to which John refers include the use of spices, the binding with strips of cloth, and the internment in a tomb (a room with ledges for bodies). John's choice of words draws attention to what is absent from the customary—the family and women or other mourners—and deviations from custom—burial in other than a family tomb. **And there was in the place where he was crucified a garden, and in the garden a new tomb [*mnēmeion*] in which not a single person had as yet been laid** (19:41). The word for tomb points to its purpose as a place of memorial. McCane (2003, 56) suggests that its being new signifies this to be a shameful burial, and this shameful corpse should not be allowed to bring shame to other corpses. Yet John's language points not to the indignity of this location but rather to the haste with which Jesus is buried by noting **there then, on account of the day of preparation of the Jews, because the tomb was handy, they laid Jesus** (19:42). John takes one more opportunity to remind his audience that these events unfold in preparation for the Passover.

Theological Issues

Mother, Behold Your Son

Throughout exegetical history, two different interpretations for Jesus's words to his mother and the Beloved Disciple have been presented as exclusive of each other. The first presents this as a simple act of filial piety, in which Jesus makes sure that he meets his obligations to his mother by appointing a surrogate son. The other is theological. Mary is the new Eve, giving birth to a redeemed humanity; she is the church, giving new life through baptism (see Brown 1994, 1021–23).

Recent attention to the language of fictive family that pervades the Synoptic Gospels and the Pauline Epistles leans toward an interpretation that draws from both of the above. Jesus's death brings into being new social relationships for his followers, which replace the biological families that defined the socio-economic order of the Greco-Roman world. As he does with his allusions to the Lord's Supper, John uses the defining features of the early church as plot elements. The context for this act is significant. At the point in which the power of Roman law seems to quash Jesus's proclamations about life, Jesus uses a procedure enshrined in Roman law, and not evident in the Jewish tradition, to signify the continuation of his identity. Under Roman law, adoptions provided for the continuation of upper-class families through the creation of a relationship that allowed a man to pass on his name and family property and maintain the family's sacred rituals (Gardner 1998, 155–59). In the imperial family, adoptions served dynastic political purposes. Jesus's enactment of an adoption between a woman and man is a tacit claim to imperial authority and status but also the provision of a model of life in Christ, where one cares for members of the community the way one cares for one's own family, especially if they have been robbed of that family through their baptism into the church (see the widows of Acts 6:1–3; 1 Tim. 5:5–10).

These words can also be contextualized within the rhetoric of Jesus's last discourse. This is the last testament of a virtuous man. Jesus's actions resemble a practice to which Plutarch bears witness: "It was a custom with the Romans of that time, when they were going into action, and were about to gird up their cloaks and take up their bucklers, to make at the same time an unwritten will [*diathēkas agraphous*], naming their heirs in the hearing of three or four witnesses" (*Cor.* 9.3, trans. Perrin 1916). His last thoughts are for others: he does not die intestate.

Jesus's Suffering

John clearly represents the mortality of Jesus; Jesus comes in the flesh and as a result dies in the flesh. Nevertheless, the Johannine portrait of Jesus's prescience and unshakable resolve about his immanent, painful death might be construed as evidence to support a conclusion, such as that reached by Ernst Käsemann (1968, 19–20, 25–26), that this portrayal is "naïvely docetic." "Docetist" is a name that Bishop Serapion of Antioch, in the late second century, gave to those who had a tendency to treat the humanity and suffering of Jesus as an illusion. To say that Jesus does not suffer misses John's point that Jesus is not humiliated by his suffering. In the ancient world, pain was a constant. The sources for pain were plentiful—tooth absences, skin irritations, physically backbreaking work—and the remedies were limited. The punishment of crucifixion was not just the pain itself, but the infliction of pain upon a body rendered completely helpless. John makes it possible to gaze on Jesus's body upon the cross without feeling his humiliation or needing to look away. The Romans intended crucifixion to be a deterrent to anyone who might wish to continue to identify with or step into the role of the one crucified. John treats the crucifixion as the epitome of the good death.

257

The Meaning of Jesus's Death

Christian confessions have tended to reduce the significance of Jesus's death to a sacrifice through which sins are forgiven, but one would be hard pressed to develop such a doctrine from what John provides. The Baptist provides the witness, "Look, the Lamb of God who takes up the sin of the world" (1:29). This line, made to stand alone, might suggest that Jesus is the *tamid*, the daily sin offering of the temple. But when we get to the passion, it becomes clear that Jesus is not the *tamid* but the Passover lamb, something quite different. Bruce H. Grigsby (1982, 53–57) puts forward a case for a "Johannized" "expiatory rationale" that bestows "a state of existence wherein sin is eliminated and judgment is escaped," based largely on the argument that in Jesus's day the paschal sacrifice was understood to have atoning value (see also de Boer 1996, 253–309). While this may be the case, the accent in John is on Jesus's triumph over the powers that bring death. He is the Passover lamb who causes death to skip over the Israelites in Egypt who have painted its blood upon their doorposts (Exod. 12:23) and, in doing so, makes possible the birth of a new people, the children of God. Throughout the Gospel, Jesus characterizes his death as an event that makes possible the formation of a community in which his spirit dwells (12:24; 14:16–17; 16:20–21).

The Gospel resists reducing the meaning of Jesus's death to one paradigm. Jesus is the Good Shepherd who lays down his life for his sheep (10:11). He is the best of friends, the kind who dies for his friends (15:13). These passages make it clear that Jesus's death is a selfless act on behalf of others (Matera 1988). Jesus's death not only reveals the depths of his love; it also reveals his confidence in the power of God's love to defeat death through resurrection. The Gospel characterizes this victory over death as the overthrow of "the ruler of this world" (see the theological issues section of 12:12–50) by painting a vivid picture of how the political forces of this world conspire to kill Jesus in order to maintain their hold. Whether one construes the power of this world as satanic or political, the most powerful weapon in its arsenal is death or the fear thereof. By moving Jesus's glorification back to the cross and not limiting it to the resurrection, John makes clear that the powers of the world are defeated when their weapon is met, not with resistance, but with knowledge of its limits.

How one understands the crucifixion narrative depends to a great extent on the rhetorical purpose that one ascribes to it. If one treats it as a piece of prose designed to persuade one to adopt a particular theory of how Jesus's death works, then one seeks the bits and pieces that can be paraphrased into a creed. But if one treats it as a piece of rhetoric that seeks to commemorate Jesus's death in a way that leads its audience to praise Jesus, then one considers what it gives its audience: a sense of the irony of the events, confidence that God is in charge and is motivated by love for the world, comfort in knowing that Jesus was not a reluctant party to God's plan or a humiliated victim, and a model of love with which to articulate a community ethic.

Who Is Responsible for Jesus's Death?

Church doctrine—informed by Scripture, in particular Paul's Letters—makes all humanity responsible for Jesus's death because Jesus dies for its sins (e.g., 1 Cor. 15:3). The Johannine narrative, however, suggests that there are degrees of culpability when Jesus says to Pilate that "the one handing me over to you has greater fault [*hamartian*]" (19:11b). Given that Pilate has earlier disavowed being responsible for Jesus's accusation by pointing out, "Your people and the chief priests handed you over to me" (18:35), Jesus seems to be pointing, in general, to those people who have rejected him and to the priesthood in particular.

When the Jewish authorities hand Jesus over, they state that they cannot put a man to death. Given that biblical law names death as a punishment, the implication is that under Roman rule, they cannot execute a person. We have no direct corroboration of this limitation, but given that the few known executions at the hands of Jews during this period are all under particular circumstances, this seems to be a fact. Stephen dies at the hands of a mob (Acts 7:58) and the stoning of an adulteress (John 8:1–5) would be seen as an appropriate discipline by the *paterfamilias* under the Roman law of *Lex Iulia de Adulteriis Coercendis* (17 BC), and the execution of James, Jesus's brother, takes place during a transition in Roman procurators and brings Roman reprisal upon the high priest who ordered it (Josephus, *Ant.* 20.197–203).

We have good cause to resist faulting the Jews, given the retribution brought upon their descendents by those who have thought of them as Christ's killers. Once again, it is important to read this as if we were much closer to the event. John presents a picture of the institutional powers of Jerusalem, those associated with the temple, acting to preserve their institution rather than to fulfill its mission to preserve the worship of the true God. In the Farewell Address, Jesus represents the actions of those who kill his followers as a wrong-headed attempt to worship God (16:2). John depicts the Jewish authorities ignoring the law in order to preserve their authority under the law (7:45–52). He shows them making Jesus into a scapegoat against whom to direct Rome's need to exercise its authority, so that Rome will not destroy their nation (11:50), and with it, their temple, the central marker of their relationship with God. He shows the trap of thinking that one can tap into Rome's power without denying God's sovereignty (19:15). The story unfolds in the context of Jewish history, and so those who hand Jesus over are Jews, but John's story points to an action that is far from unique. History is littered with the bodies of those who were innocent but whose death seemed expedient in order to preserve an institution or an ideology. Jesus's death as God's Son proves as clearly as possible that the world is wrong in its self-righteousness (see 16:7–8).

While John may expose the Jews' error in judgment in handing Jesus over, he does not exonerate Pilate or Rome. Taken out of context, Jesus's claim that "my kingdom is not from this world" (18:36) and that Pilate's authority has been given from above (19:11) could be paired with Paul's comments in Rom. 13:1–7 to suggest that Rome is ordained by God and the Christian movement is somehow apolitical and not a challenge to Rome. This is an overreading of the text. Pilate can exercise his power in this instance, not because God ordains his office, but because Jesus's death is God's will. Pilate's fixation on Jesus's status as king and condemnation of Jesus for sedition against Caesar point to the role that human pretensions to sovereignty play in seeking to humiliate and crucify Jesus. In choosing crucifixion, Jesus makes the conflict one between Caesar in Rome and God in heaven (see Rensberger 1988, 69–98).

A casual reader of the Gospel might take Pilate's resistance to comply with the Jewish authorities' request to execute Jesus as evidence of his concern for justice. Understanding Roman legal procedures and habits and Pilate's background renders a reader much more sensitive to the tensions within the Gospel's trial scene and the complexity of Pilate's motives. The scene before Pilate is labeled a trial in the exegetical tradition, but judgment is a better term. Roman trials were for Roman citizens. The Gospel presents a picture of a recognizable Roman legal process. An informant (*index*), someone directly involved in the alleged crime, served as a *delator*, who denounced an associate privately to an authority, who then served as an *accusator*. The *accusator* brought the accusation to the prosecutor, who, according to Quintilian, needed to proceed with the case with the appearance of reluctance (*Inst.* 11.1.57; 12.7.1–3), as though he disdained the *accusator* as some sort of necessary evil. Roman law handed Pilate absolute power over people such as Jesus and afforded him a set of harsh penalties that he was expected to apply, but if the occasion allowed, he could choose a lesser penalty in order to demonstrate Roman clemency (see Wiedemann 1992, 69). Tertullian, in a letter to the proconsul of Africa (*Scap.* 4.3), provides us with a picture of how later Roman governors could operate when confronted with the unwanted demand to execute a Christian. Governors took the accused aside and coached them on how to answer questions so they could go free, or they simply dismissed them, saying that to give in to one crowd would enrage another crowd, or they had them flogged and then released. Pilate's actions seem to follow comparable tactics to avoid being embroiled in a dispute among Jews. Without formal charges, in order for Jesus to be executed under Roman law, Pilate must find some offense under Roman law. From Pilate's first question put to Jesus to the nailing of the *titulus* on the cross, the Gospel implies that the charge in mind is *Lex Iulia de maiestate*, a charge that under Augustus had come to cover any sort of threat of treason against the state from out-and-out rebellion, to unauthorized troop movement, to slander against the person of Caesar. Roman provincial rulers faced a double-edged sword. On the one hand, executions demonstrated their power, but if coerced by the crowd to condemn someone, their authority could be undermined. On the other hand, if the local authorities objected to the actions of the Roman administrator, they could seek justice from a higher Roman power (Weidemann 1992, 166–67). John captures Pilate's struggle to maintain the appearance of absolute power, when he actually is dependent on the goodwill of the people he rules and the tenuous patronage of Tiberius Caesar.

PART 4

John 20:1–21:25

Jesus's Resurrection: Endings and Epilogues

As anyone who has written a paper, a poem, or any other piece of prose knows, deciding how to end and where to end is as difficult as deciding where and how to begin. Like Jesus's final words on the cross, "It is finished" (19:30), the conclusion of John's Gospel is marked by finality, surety, and coherence. Jesus delivers on his promise of joy, peace, and the Spirit. There is clarity, no ambiguity, that Jesus has done what he was sent by his Father to do. But as if reluctant to stop, after the Fourth Evangelist provides a conclusion to his account of Jesus's resurrection in which the narrator ad-

> **John 20:1–21:25 in Context**
>
> In the beginning (1:1–2:12)
>
> Jesus's itinerant ministry (2:13–12:11)
>
> Jesus's triumphant hour (12:12–19:42)
>
> ▶ Jesus's resurrection: Endings and epilogues (20:1–21:25)
>
> Recognition and reversal (20:1–31)
>
> Out of the past and into the future (21:1–25)

dresses the audience (20:30–31), he turns the page and adds another episode and ends with an epilogue that reveals the future fate of Simon Peter and the Beloved Disciple (21:15–23) and then a final conclusion in which the narrator again turns and addresses the audience (21:24–25). Upon inspection, it appears that John includes only what is needed to satisfy the demands of the complexity of his plot.

In a detailed study of the discourse of food in ancient Greek comedy, John Wilkens observes, "Greeks imagined certain foods to be extraordinarily desirable, fish above all. Fish belonged to a category of *opson*, a supplement to the staple diet of cereals" (2000, xviii). A final meal of fish and bread, a breakfast at the break of dawn, is an appropriate end to a Gospel promising that one's desire for bread will be met and one's thirst for water can be quenched and ending with the suggestion that even an insatiable desire for stories about Jesus can be satisfied.

John 20:1–31

Recognition and Reversal

Introductory Matters

Given that, in the Gospel of John, the crucifixion is Jesus's exaltation, one might anticipate a treatment of the resurrection that warrants the following observation made by Rudolf Bultmann (1955, 56):

> If Jesus's death on the cross is already his exaltation and glorification, *his resurrection* cannot be an event of special significance. No resurrection is needed to destroy the triumph which death might be supposed to have gained in the crucifixion.

Instead, the Gospel contains a polished literary treatment that hones attention on the significance of resurrection for a believing community. The cross is Jesus's exaltation. The resurrection is the exaltation of the believer from grief to joy, from despairing doubt to exuberant confession, from loss to blessing.

Whether a character recognizes Jesus as one sent by God is important to the action of the entire Gospel; yet in the resurrection scenes, John draws on the conventions of classical Greek literature in order to achieve what Aristotle (*Poet.* 1452a.18) judged the *telos* of superior tragedy, the synchronization of *anagnōrisis*, recognition, and the *peripeteia*, a sudden reversal in the circumstances of a main character. The chapter contains a series of moments of recognition. Readers who focus on Christology tend to look for some sort of progression in understanding. The following commentary will focus on the differences in the reversals that together constitute the nature of Johannine faith.

Tracing the Narrative Flow

The Discovery of the Empty Tomb (20:1–10)

John continues to emphasize the haste that characterizes Joseph of Arimathea and Nicodemus's actions by beginning **On the first [day] of the week, Mary Magdalene came early, [it] still being dark, to the tomb.** Matthew and Luke's women come at first light (Matt. 28:1; Luke 24:1). The early hour captures Mary's desolation. A woman who comes alone in darkness to such a place abandons propriety and safety in order to commemorate Jesus with her grief. John represents her anxiety by focalizing the setting through her eyes: she **sees the stone has been removed from the tomb** (20:1). The narrator flips back and forth between past tenses and the historic present and begins almost every sentence with *oun* as a way of telling the story breathlessly and to help the audience see the action unfolding in the mind's eye. Mary misinterprets the implications of what she sees and begins the action that delays recognition of the resurrected Jesus. **She runs then and comes to Simon Peter and to the other disciple whom Jesus loved and says to them, "Someone has removed the Lord from the tomb, and we do not know where they have put him"** (20:2). In a diachronic reading, the plural pronoun becomes an aporia that produces hypotheses, such as surmising that John has edited an account including several women. In a synchronic reading, one looks for logic and examines such things as the reaction to her words. The plural pronoun implicates the disciples in her anxiety, and her words provoke the disciples to imitate her frantic pace: **Then Peter and the other disciple went out and were going to the tomb** (20:3). **The two ran together, and the other disciple quickly ran ahead of Peter, and he arrived first to the tomb** (20:4). The narrator describes a sort of tag-team race in which they begin in tandem; however, Peter is outstripped, but then the Beloved Disciple ("the other disciple whom Jesus loved") pauses at the entrance of the tomb, and **stooping to peer sees the linens [just] lying [there]** [the participle *keimena* suggests that they were left behind as Jesus rose], **yet he did not enter** (20:5).

If this verse leaves some people anxious about Jesus's state of undress, they will not be the first to think such thoughts. The Talmud (*b. Sanh.* 90b) contains a dialogue between Rabbi Meir and Queen Cleopatra in which she asks, "Will the dead rise naked or with clothes?" to which Rabbi Meir responds that just as a seed of wheat is resurrected with manifold clothing, so will the righteous be resurrected.

The Beloved Disciple's reticence adds suspense to the narrative. It stands in contrast to his willingness to follow Jesus in advance of Peter to Annas's house and to witness Jesus's crucifixion. **Then Simon Peter came, following him, and he entered the tomb [first] and beheld [*theōrei*] the lying linens (20:6), and the kerchief that was upon his head not with the lying linens but apart, having been rolled up into one place (20:7).** John writes a "detective narrative" in which the audience looks through the eyes of various characters at the evidence with which to construct what has happened. Quintilian (*Inst.* 4.2.63) uses the (Latin) term *energia* to describe storytelling that makes things self-evident without telling the audience explicitly what has happened. The verb for "rolled up" (*entetyligmenon*) is in the passive voice and stands in contrast with the verb used for the linens. Someone has performed the action. The placement of the cloth speaks against body snatchers. One imagines the linens being left in place as Jesus rises. Jesus then calmly rolls up the headcloth and sets it down

Anagnōrisis

Aristotle (*Poet.* 1452a.30) defines *anagnōrisis* not just as a moment of change from ignorance to knowledge but as a change in disposition toward the person recognized, either to friendship or enmity, either for good or misfortune. Kasper Bro Larsen (2008, 63–71) treats the motif of recognition in the Gospel of John in detail and provides the following breakdown of its constitutive elements:

> An encounter or meeting
> A delay in recognition caused by resistance, doubt, or distrust
> Presentation of the tokens or signs of identity
> The moment of recognition
> Reaction and reunion

> "In order to be convincing, the moment of recognition must be made visible to the audience through the language and gestures of the character that proceed from natural emotions and logical inference." (Aristotle, *Poet.* 1455a.20–1455b.12)

before leaving the tomb. Lazarus, in contrast, comes stumbling from the tomb, bound in his linens and with the cloth over his face. Jesus is as fully in command of his resurrection as he is of his death. John's account also exonerates the disciples from allegations that they stole the body (Matt. 27:64; 28:13–15; *Gos. Pet.* 30; Justin Martyr, *Dial.* 108.2; Tertullian, *Spect.* 30; *Apol.* 23). The focalization creates so strong a sense of realism that earlier commentators used this passage to argue for the historicity of the event (see Kennard 1955, 227).

In describing what occurs next, John provides a glimpse into the mental state of a character but does not describe precise thoughts: **Then the other disciple entered who came to the tomb first and saw and believed (20:8).** Either the Beloved Disciple has come to the correct empirical conclusion that Jesus has risen from the dead, or he has previously doubted Mary's testimony and now believes that someone has taken Jesus's body. Rudolf Bultmann (1971, 685–87) doubts that John would have introduced the Beloved Disciple to the scene for so trite a reason as the latter and points to the combination of seeing and believing in 20:29 as evidence that the Beloved Disciple's faith is mature and complete. At a narrative level, it seems odd that the Beloved Disciple would remain silent about what he has witnessed and not influence the action that follows if he believes that Jesus has been raised from the dead (see Lee 1995, 39–40). The next aside—**For they had not yet known** [*ēdeisan*] **the Scripture that it was necessary for him from** [the] **dead to rise** (20:9)—if it includes the Beloved Disciple, suggests that he simply believes that Jesus's body has been taken. The pluperfect tense of the verb *oida* can also signify that up to this moment the Beloved Disciple has not considered the tradition of the resurrection, but now he has and so believes. Given that no particular piece of Scripture is cited, John may refer to a number of passages, including Dan. 12:2–3 and Ps. 16:11 (see Acts 2:25–28), that were understood by many in the late Second Temple period to signify resurrection (see 1 Cor. 15:4). John ends the scene by noting, **Then the disciples went away again to the same** [places] (20:10) without providing clarity to the puzzle of the state of the Beloved Disciple's belief. The scene begins and ends with Mary alone at the tomb.

Mary's Recognition Scene (20:11–18)

The encounter. John now makes it clear that Mary has followed the disciples back to the tomb, **but** that while they went into the tomb, **Mary had been standing in front of the tomb, lamenting** [*klaiousa*] **outside.** Translating the Greek *klaiousa* with the word "weeping" risks filling the action with behaviors normative to a culture that is not Mary's. This is not silent weeping but wailing aloud, with streaming tears as a sign of the depth of her sorrow and respect for the dead as well as the added grief over the possible disrespect done to Jesus's body. **Then as she lamented, she stooped to peer into the tomb** (20:11), in an action that mimics that of Peter, **and** she **beholds two angels in white, sitting one at the head and one at the feet, where the body of Jesus has been lying** (20:12). The image may be an allusion to the ark of the covenant, especially the mercy seat (Gk. *hilastērion*; Heb. *kappōret*) flanked by two golden cherubim, facing each other with spread wings touching (Exod. 25:10–22). The mercy seat is the place where God meets Moses in order to convey his commands to the Israelites. Philo (*Cher.* 25; *Mos.* 2.95, 97; *Fug.* 100) treats the *hilastērion* as a symbol of God's beneficent power.

Mary seems strangely unperturbed by the angels' sudden appearance. In sharp contrast to the women in Luke who are terrified and bow their heads to the ground (24:4–5), or the guards in Matthew who are paralyzed with fear (28:4), Mary is so bent on her mission to attend to Jesus's body that she seems oblivious to the fact that she is talking to heavenly creatures. The dialogue begins with the angels' question: **"Woman, why are you lamenting?"** In Greek tragedies, such questions typically provide the means of obscuring true identity, delaying recognition, and naming or dramatizing emotions (e.g., Sophocles, *El.* 1176–81). In a theatrical production, questions allow actors to speak about and through their grief. Mary's response—**"They have removed my Lord, and I do not know where they have put him"** (20:13)—begins a set of her short speeches, organized in a balanced pattern:

A They have removed my Lord,
   B and I do not know where they have put him.
      C Lord, if you carried him off,
  B′ tell me where you have put him,
A′ and I will remove him. (20:13–15)

In dramatic speeches, such constructions bear the weight of strong emotions so that the display of emotions that normally render one inarticulate is not diminished by the character's ability to continue to speak.

The delay. John describes Mary's next action with a variety of verb tenses that capture the dynamic tension between action and cognition. **Saying these things, she turned back and beholds Jesus standing** [there] **and had not known that he is Jesus** (20:14). **Jesus** repeats the angels' question, **"Woman, why do you lament?"** By echoing the words of the angels, Jesus allies himself with them and presents himself as someone whom she ought not to recognize. To add to his disguise, he follows with the question **"Whom do you seek?"** to distinguish himself from the object of her weeping. **Supposing that he is the gardener, she says to him, "Lord."** It is ironic that she addresses a stranger with the honorific title that he has just used in 20:13 to identify Jesus. The confusion of Jesus with a gardener is logical, given that they are standing in a garden. The misidentification points to the degree to which Jesus's appearance is unexpected. That Jesus has left his burial clothes in the tomb might provoke fanciful speculation that Jesus has borrowed the gardener's clothes. Rembrandt depicts this possibility in his painting *The Resurrected Lord Appears to Mary Magdalene* (1651).

Mary's next words—**"If you** [*sy*] **carried him off, tell me** [*moi*] **where you have put him, and I** [*kagō*] **will remove him"** (20:15)—with the use of deictic pronouns places the two dialogue partners in an antagonistic relationship and is more of an accusation and a demand than a polite request. The idea that she would be able to bear Jesus's body herself points to her desperation, but it also evokes recollections of other women who in mourning become guardians of the dead. Rizpah, Saul's concubine, watches over the corpses of her two sons and five of Saul's grandchildren for five months so that they will not be desecrated by scavenging birds until David is moved to bury their bones

Figure 24. Electra's recognition of Orestes was a popular decorative motif in the Greco-Roman world (krater, ca. 340 BC).

(2 Sam. 21:10–14). Antigone disobeys her uncle's edict that her brother Polynices be denied burial rites and attempts twice to give him a shallow grave (Sophocles, *Ant.*)

The token. When **Jesus says to her "Mariam,"** he provides the sign or token identified in the Good Shepherd *paroimia* by which a follower of Jesus will recognize him (10:4). The power of the voice to correct her mistake may also work in a fashion comparable to other recognition scenes. In Sophocles's *Electra*, when Electra begins to understand that the stranger with whom she has been speaking is her twin brother, Orestes, whom she has been mourning, she says, "Voice, have you come?" (*El.* 1225). The eyes filled with tears cannot perceive what the ears can understand.

The moment of recognition. The narrator marks her reaction first by noting her movement—**being turned**—suggesting that she has looked away after making her demand and Jesus's words cause her to turn about suddenly. The double turn puzzles exegetes, but Ernst Haenchen's observation—"for reasons of rhythm, one hesitates to dispense with it" (1984, 2:209)—may point to the importance of the phrase for the oration of the story. John marks the moment of recognition with a word, **"Rabbouni,"** the familiar form of address used by Jesus's disciples throughout the Gospel, to which Mary appends the first-person possessive suffix: "my Rabbi." The narrator provides the translation **Teacher** (20:16), which ignores the suffix. With dramatic economy and without the interjections by an omniscient narrator, the Gospel represents the private experience of recognition through public displays of emotion. Her choice of address is not the language of faith but of reunion (Larsen 2008, 190). The personal address "Mariam" calls for a more personal response. She has not been prepared to see Jesus by any prior witness. The response is a pure outpouring of joy.

Reaction and reunion. The act of recognition in the Gospel ends, as many recognition scenes do in Greek literature (Sophocles, *El.* 1226; Euripides, *Iph. taur.* 798–99, 827–31), with an embrace made evident to the audience by a character's words rather than the narrator's description. Jesus tells Mary, **"Do not cling on me** [the verb *haptou* suggests that she has flung her arms around him] **for I have not yet gone up to the Father.**" This narrative moment is often referred to with the Latin phrase *Noli me tangere* and becomes the title for many classical paintings. Once more, Jesus's choice of words can spin the reader off in the direction of speculation, especially since he will later invite Thomas to touch his wounds. Do his words signify that it is inappropriate for a woman to touch the risen Lord (see Spicq 1948)? Does something change in the status of his body between this moment and his encounter with Thomas (see D'Angelo 1990)? Do his words point to the inadequacy of Mary's reaction or understanding (see Lincoln 2005, 493)? Or is this part of John's dramatic economy that needs to be read in tandem with Jesus's instructions **"Go to my brothers [and sisters] and say to them, 'I am going up to my Father and your Father, to my God and your God'"** (20:17)? The command "Do not cling" then forms an antithetical parallelism with the command "Go." He reorients Mary's joy away from reunion to proclamation. Too much attention to Jesus's physical status or Mary's faith can lead one to overlook the important language that Jesus has introduced into his discourse. Jesus refers to his followers as brothers and sisters; the God, to whom Jesus has referred as exclusively "my Father," has now become "our Father." John then presents her response to Jesus's command: **Mary Magdalene came to the disciples, proclaiming that "I have seen the Lord" and these thing he said to her** (20:18). Once more the word "Lord" intends its appropriate referent.

The Disciples' Recognition Scene (20:19–23)

The progression of time marks a change of scene: **It being then evening of that day, the first of the week;** and a series of participle phrases describes the physical setting and mood: **and the doors having been barred shut where the disciples were on account of fear of the Jews.** The narrator does not give an account of the disciples' reception of Mary's testimony, but it is clear that news of the resurrection has not dispelled the fear generated by his execution. The encounter with Jesus juxtaposes their fear and the peace that he offers: **Jesus came and stood in the middle and says to them, "Peace to you"** (20:19). This is not an unusual greeting, but it may be significant insofar as it echoes Jesus's intent that the disciples have peace (14:27; 16:33). His words also serve to dispel their fear. The angel of the Lord greets Gideon: "Peace be to you; do not fear, you shall not die" (Judg. 6:23).

The scene proceeds without delay to the display of the token by which Jesus can be recognized. Jesus's token invites comparison to Eurycleia's recognition of Odysseus's scar (Homer, *Od.* 19.393–466). Given the disciples' fear, Jesus's demonstration of the token—**And [while] saying this, he showed them the hands and the side**—serves a second purpose. The gesture enacts his words. Rather than showing a weapon, Jesus shows his commitment to nonviolence. John then narrates rather than dramatizes the moment of recognition and their reaction: **And the disciples then rejoiced [at] seeing the Lord** (20:20).

John continues the pattern introduced in Mary's recognition scene of adding mission to reunion. **Jesus then said to them again, "Peace to you,"** reiterating the effect that his appearance should have on their cognitive state in preparation for an act of sending—**"As the Father has sent me, I also send you"** (20:21)—of greater ecclesiological significance than the sending that ends Mary's recognition scene. **And having said this, he blew** [as one blows into a flute] **and he says to them, "Receive** [the] **Holy Spirit"** (20:22). The verb "receive" (*labete*) captures the twofold action: Jesus offers, but the disciples must take or accept.

What Jesus says next—**"Whosoever sins** [*tas hamartias*] **you forgive, have been forgiven them; whosoever you hold fast, they have been held fast"** (20:23)— requires care in translation. Many have read this as an antithetical parallelism and translated it as the NRSV does by repeating the noun *hamartias* in the second line, "If you forgive the sins of any, they are forgiven them; if you retain the sins of any, they are retained." The line can also be read as a synthetic parallelism, signifying that forgiveness binds the forgiven into close community (see "The Postresurrection Community and the Holy Spirit" in the theological issues section below).

Thomas's Recognition Scene (20:24–29)

By withholding the information—**Thomas one of the Twelve, the one called Didymos, was not with them when Jesus came** (20:24)—the narrator prepares for the necessity of another delayed recognition scene and then jumps ahead without narrating Jesus's departure or Thomas's arrival. The disciples echo Mary's pronouncement, **We have seen the Lord.** In the next verse, the direct article *ho* to refer to Thomas registers the contrast between the disciples' testimony and Thomas's reception. **But this one** [*ho*] **said to them, "Unless I see in his hands the mark of the nails and I stick** [*balō*] **my finger into the mark of the nails and I stick** [*balō*] **my hand into his side, I will not believe"** (20:25). Thomas has only three lines in the Gospel, but each time he speaks his words suggest a degree of pessimism or skepticism. He seems to be a man not inclined toward joy. He is the *agelast*, or killjoy, in this story. His choice of language, scandalous in its disrespect for Jesus's body, living or dead, should also convey a sense of the unreal condition: Thomas does not think that Jesus will appear. The forceful verbs help mark the turn that he will take not simply from disbelief to belief but from cynicism to exuberant belief.

Thomas is left to stew in his miserable state longer than the others before his encounter with Jesus sets him right. **And after eight days his disciples were again inside and Thomas with them. Jesus comes,** [although] **the door had been barred, and stood in the middle and he said, "Peace to you** [pl.]**"** (20:26). Jesus now turns from greeting the disciples to address Thomas. The narrator begins the sentence with the word *eita*, which denotes either surprise at Jesus's actions or contempt for Thomas. **Then** [*eita*] **he says to Thomas, "Bring your finger here and see my hands and bring your hand and stick it** into my side, and be not an unbeliever but a believer" (20:27). The audience ought not immediately to conclude that Thomas does what Jesus tells him to do. John does not describe Thomas's actions but rather focuses on his words of recognition: "O my Lord and my God" (20:28). Mary's turn was from grief to joy, and the disciples from fear to joy; Thomas's turn must be from doubt to belief, and therefore it is appropriate that the words he speaks signify a conviction about Jesus's identity. The declaration that Jesus is not only his Lord but also his God is a confession unbounded by convention and points to his abandonment of all qualifications. The words also call for relief for the audience that he does not follow through on his stated conditions for belief.

Many take Jesus's next words as a critique of Thomas's need for proof— "Because you have seen me, do you believe? Blessed [*makarioi*] [are] those not seeing and [yet] believing" (20:29)—and couple it with the thought that Jesus begins in 4:48: "Unless you see signs and wonders, you will not believe" (see "The Role of Signs" in the theological issues section of 2:13–4:54). While a rhetorical question can be a means of chiding (*epiplēxis*), it can also be a way of summing up an argument against one's adversary's case (*erōtēma*; Lat. *interrogatio*; *Rhet. Her.* 4.15.22). Jesus has just proved Thomas's skepticism to be unfounded in a dramatic and grim manner. English idiom would put the question "So, now do you believe?" The progression from rhetorical question to blessing can be compared to a moment in theater when a character violates the imaginary fourth wall that separates the stage and the audience by turning and speaking to the audience. The audience of the Gospel is the recipient of Jesus's words. The contrast between Thomas and a believing audience need not lie in the quality of their belief but in the nature of their experience. They have been spared the horror of looking on Jesus's wounds. Jesus's words can also be translated as "Happy are those who believe without having seen."

First Epilogue (20:30–31)

Just as Jesus seems to turn to the audience, the narrator now addresses the audience. John employs a convention used by many ancient authors in which the selective nature of storytelling is described. **Many, then, and other signs Jesus performed in the sight of his disciples that are not having been written in this book** (20:30). **But these have been written in order that you believe** [*pisteuēte*, present subjunctive; see below] **that Jesus is the Christ the Son of God, and in order that** [while] **believing you may have life in his name** (20:31). These two verses follow logically from 20:29. The Gospel does not suggest that faith is possible without Jesus's signs, but the Gospel does suggest that people can come to faith through the witness of a story rather than relying on their own direct experience of an event. Craig Keener (2003, 1214–15) provides a long list of comparable endings. Just one example will suffice here to illustrate the convention. Plutarch warns his reader that he is leaving out many celebrated parts of the story because he is writing not a history but a life. He compares himself to a portrait painter who selects particular parts to point to Alexander's character (*Alex.* 1.1).

The two manuscript traditions for the tense of the verb *pisteuō* in 20:31 require translators to make a choice that affects meaning: the present subjunctive (*pisteuēte*) suggests that the audience continues in its belief; the aorist subjective (*pisteusēte*), that they come to belief. Set within the rhetoric of the entire Gospel with its reliance on dramatic irony that assumes an audience in the know, the former makes the most sense. It is also possible that the accent falls not on belief but on the correct designation of Jesus's identity (see Carson 1991, 662). Throughout the Gospel, people have asserted that Jesus is the Messiah; the Gospel asserts that the Messiah is the Son of God.

This seems like the end of the Gospel, but it is not. Scholars looking for evidence of use of sources and editing take this as a closing line and argue that what follows is the hand of a later redactor, but acquaintance with ancient narratives may render it the beginning of an ending, a feign that prepares the reader for a final round. This is not the first "false ending" in John. Jesus's words in 14:31 suggest that he will stop talking, but he continues. Paul's words, "Finally, my brothers and sister, rejoice in the Lord" (Phil. 3:1), also sound like a conclusion but are followed by many more thoughts. When the chorus begins a lament in Aeschylus's *Seven against Thebes* (986), the audience could reasonably conclude that the action has ended, but after the lament ends, a herald enters with the announcement that Cadmus has prohibited the burial of his nephews (1015–30), and dialogue resumes until the Chorus begins its second closing song (1060–80). That the Good Shepherd motif comes to conclusion in chapter 21 suggests that the next chapter is a part of the original design.

Theological Issues

Jesus's Physical Presence

While the narrative contains the appearances that provide the basis for testimony to the fact of the resurrection, the resurrection itself is an event without witnesses. We see only the proof that it has occurred. Like the Corinthians, we can easily get caught up in technical questions by asking, "How are the dead raised? What is the nature of the body in which they come?" (1 Cor. 15:35). The signs of the resurrection in the tomb, Jesus's admonition to Mary not to touch him, Jesus's appearance in the middle of a locked room, and his invitation to Thomas to touch him—all draw a great deal of attention to the physicality of the resurrection. Jesus is no apparition (*phantasma*; cf. Plutarch, *Dion* 2) or spirit (*psychē*; cf. Josephus, *Ant.* 6.333–34). John, like Paul, affirms the reality of the resurrection as a physical event. John's emphasis is not on a change in Jesus's ontological status either from humiliation to exaltation, or from a mortal to a glorified body. The body that appears in the middle of the room seems to be the same body that appeared as walking on the water (6:16–21). Sandra M. Schneiders (2005) lays out the semantic fields for all of John's language related to the self in the context of Semitic understanding of a person's identity and body. She comes to the conclusion that in the Johannine view, "unless he is alive in the full integrity of his humanity symbolized in his body, he is not present, either as the presence of humanity in God or as God's divinely human presence to us" (2005, 173). John's interest is in not the physics of the resurrection but the continuation of a relationship made possible by Jesus's eternal life.

The new intimacy promised in the Farewell Address is encoded with the new language that Jesus introduces in the resurrection accounts for the believing community. The first hint of change occurs when Jesus calls Mary by name. Not only does this fulfill the expectations of the Good Shepherd discourse (10:3); this also is the first time in this Gospel that Jesus addresses anyone by name other than when he says to Simon Peter "You are Simon son of John" (1:42) and when he calls Lazarus out of his tomb (11:43). He then refers to the disciples as *adelphoi mou*, "my brothers [and sisters]," a familial term that has not figured in his discourse before. This is promptly followed by the statement, "I am going up to my Father and your Father, to my God and your God" (20:17). Prior to this, Jesus has referred to God as though he were exclusively his Father, or as "the Father" without a possessive pronoun. Mary Coloe (2001, 218–19) describes the resurrection as "the process of building the new Temple (household) of God" predicted by Jesus in John 2:20, which fulfills the promise made in the prologue that believers will become children of God. Jesus's death is the journey in which he prepares a place for his disciples in his Father's house, and his resurrection is the promised return (14:3, 28), the fulfillment of the promise not to leave the disciples orphans (14:18).

The way that the disciples refer to Jesus also changes after his resurrection. Before the passion, characters typically addressed Jesus as "rabbi" or "teacher" or "Lord." In her excitement, Mary adds the possessive suffix and calls Jesus "my rabbi." Thomas now calls Jesus "my Lord" and "my God." In chapter 21, Peter three times affirms his friendship or love for Jesus.

The Postresurrection Community and the Holy Spirit

In a very few verses, John tells us a great deal about this community that requires some unpacking. Jesus proclaims, "As the Father has sent me, I also send you" (20:21). Then he breathes on them and says, "Receive the Holy Spirit. Whosoever sins you forgive have been forgiven them; whosoever you hold fast, they have been held fast" (20:22–23).

There are a number of doctrinal questions related to the Holy Spirit with which to grapple. The debate over the question of whether the Holy Spirit proceeds from the Father, or from the Father and the Son, led to a split in the liturgical practices of the church in AD 589, when the Roman church changed the Nicene Creed, "We believe in the Holy Spirit, . . . who proceeds from the Father," so that it read "We believe in the Holy Spirit, . . . who proceeds from the Father *and the Son* [*filioque*]." This insertion was largely responsible for the AD 1054 schism between the Roman Catholic and the Eastern Orthodox churches. The Eastern Orthodox churches insist that the Holy Spirit comes from the Father *through* the Son.

A question raised by the church fathers that still occupies modern readers' thoughts is whether John presents an account of the gift of the Holy Spirit that is in tension with that found in Acts. Theodore of Mopsuestia (sixth cent.) suggested that Jesus promises the Spirit but does not actually give the Spirit. John Chrysostom (*Hom. Jo.* 86.3) split the gift of the Spirit in two by having Jesus grant his followers that part of the Spirit's work that makes possible the forgiveness of sins at Easter, and then impart the Spirit's miraculous powers at Pentecost. If we approach the Gospel from the perspective of its poetics, John's streamlining of events achieves a unity of action by including within its narration the fulfillment of the promises that Jesus's death brings eternal life and makes possible the coming of the Paraclete (see 16:7). John's Gospel begins and ends with Jesus, and there is no room for the narration of the fulfillment of Jesus's promise of the Paraclete in the absence of Jesus. The community arises with Jesus's resurrection, and Jesus breathes life into it on the day of its conception. The differences between the Acts and Johannine accounts can also be treated as exegetical. The account of the coming of the Spirit in Acts fulfills God's promise in Joel that he will dwell in Israel's midst (Joel 2:28; cited in Acts 2:17) and reverses God's dispersal of humanity through language confusion at Babel (Gen. 11:7–9). John's imagery links the event to creation and God's animating spirit (Gen. 2:7).

Forgiveness in the Johannine Community

The concept of forgiveness, so central to Jesus's proclamation in the synoptic tradition, is all but absent in John. As a result, it is startling to read how Jesus imparts the power of forgiveness to the disciples, along with the gift of the Spirit. The possible tension with the synoptic demand for excessive forgiveness arrests attention.

The translation of 20:23 found above—"Whosever sins you forgive [*aphēte*] have been forgiven [*apheōntai*] them, whosever you hold fast [*kratēte*] they have been held fast [*kekratēntai*]"—differs from many English translations:

If you forgive the sins of any, they are forgiven them; if you retain the sins of any, they are retained. (NRSV)

Whose soever sins ye remit, they are remitted unto them; and whose soever sins ye retain, they are retained. (KJV)

The NRSV and KJV translations have treated the Greek passage as an example of antithetical parallelism, in which the second line expresses the opposite idea found in the first line.

If one treats 20:23 as an example of antithetical parallelism, several approaches to its significance are possible. This may be a Johannine version of the authority given to the church in Matt. 16:19—"Whatever you bind [*dēsēs*] on earth will be bound [*dedemenon*] in heaven, and whatever you release [*lysēs*] on earth will be released [*lelymenon*] in heaven"—that construes this power narrowly by applying it only to forgiveness (cf. Matt. 18:18). Bruce J. Malina and Richard L. Rohrbaugh contextualize John 20:23 within what they call John's antisociety so that the disciples are given the "choice to forgive or not forgive offenses against their in-group" (1998, 281). Charles Talbert (2005) looks at it as the choice to forgive offenses committed by members of the community against each other. He observes that the gift that Jesus imparts elsewhere in the Gospel signifies the unity of the community. For example, "The glory that you have given me I have given them, so that they may be one, as we are one" (17:22). Talbert treats the encouragement to forgive as a continuation of the act of foot washing: "His washing of feet symbolizes forgiveness of daily post-baptismal sins. So if the disciples do as he has done, they will forgive one another as he forgives them" (2005, 263–64). The failure to forgive is then a warning rather than a condoned power. "If disciples forgive other disciples' sins against them, the sins are removed as an obstacle to community oneness; if they continue to hold on to the sins against them, the sins remain as obstacles to community harmony" (Talbert 2005, 264).

Because the word "sins" (*hamartias*) does not appear in the second line of the structure, it is possible to treat the saying as an example of synthetic parallelism in which two ideas have a cause-and-effect relationship (e.g., Ps. 119:11). Sandra M. Schneiders (1999, 186) provides one such possible reading by contextualizing the saying within the missionary activity of the community. Given that the named sin in the Gospel is unbelief, forgiveness of sins entails "bringing people to belief." The consequence of this is then to hold the forgiven fast, to bind them into the community. This reading lines up with passages where Jesus describes holding on and keeping his followers (6:37, 39; 10:27–29; 17:12; 18:9).

John 21:1–25

Out of the Past and into the Future

Introductory Matters

The last chapter of the Gospel of John is commonly called an epilogue, words that stand apart from the story because the plot elements have come to closure. For much of the twentieth century, redaction critics looked at chapter 21 as a later addition to the Gospel even though there is no version of John in the manuscript tradition without chapter 21. However, toward the close of that century, scholars such as Paul S. Minear (1983) began to attend to literary features of the chapter that point to one author and that help account for the double ending. The literary style, grammar, and vocabulary are consistent with the first twenty chapters; the chapter brings a number of motifs to a conclusion, and it ties up loose ends in the plot. In particular, the matrix of texts comprising the Good Shepherd motif is completed (see table 6 at John 13:1–17).

The chapter unfolds in three parts: (1) the theophany of the miraculous catch, followed by the meal of fish and bread; (2) the dialogue with Peter, in which his fate and that of the Beloved Disciple are disclosed (21:15–22); and (3) the final closing words, addressed to the audience (21:23–25). The term "epilogue" best describes the second and third part. Epilogue generally refers to additional narration at the end of a story that serves to bring closure to a work by having the narrator address the audience directly and reveal the fates of the characters. Plutarch ends a number of his biographies by using one or both conventions. The story of Demosthenes concludes with Plutarch's personal recollection about a soldier who puts a gold coin into the hands of a statue of Demosthenes; the sad fate of Demades, Demosthenes's rival; and these closing words to the audience, "There you have regarding Demosthenes, Sosius, the life from what has been published or supplied" (*Dem.* 31; see *Phoc.* 38; *Alex.* 77; *Demetr.* 53). Modern readers may be more familiar with epilogues in film than in ancient literature, with films offering a montage of images, often accompanied by text, describing what happens to each character (e.g., George Lucas, dir., *American Graffiti*, Universal, Lucasfilm, 1973; David O. Russell, dir., *Three Kings*, Warner Bros., Village Roadshow, 1999).

Tracing the Narrative Flow

The Galilee Theophany (21:1–14)

This episode begins with the stock transition **After these things** (also in 3:22; 5:1; 6:1; 7:1), marking an undetermined lapse of time. The phrase **Jesus showed himself again to the disciples** forms an inclusio with the line "This was now the third time Jesus showed [himself] to the disciples" in 21:14, thereby demarcating 20:1–14 as the theophany to which the next verse refers: **on the sea[shore] of Tiberias, and he showed [himself] in this way** (21:1). John repeats the verb *ephanerōsen*, a form of the verb *phaneroō*, used throughout the Gospel to signify the manifestation of Jesus's glory as the Son of God (1:31; 2:11; 3:21; 7:4; 9:3; 17:6).

The next sentence qualifies who is meant by the disciples by providing a list: **Simon Peter and Thomas, the one called Didymos, and Nathanael from Cana of Galilee** [last mentioned in 1:49–50 without reference to his hometown], **and the [sons] of Zebedee and two others out of the disciples were together** (21:2). John mentions twelve disciples who remain with him after the Bread of Life discourse (6:70–71), but here the list is limited to seven. The number seven suggests to some an intertextual relation to the seven *diakonia*, those who serve at table in Acts 6:2–6. Seven is also the number of fulfillment or completion. The reduction to seven may be a realistic detail, signifying that of the disciples, these are all fishermen or residents of the region. Limiting the number to seven may also be an artful way to avoid the number twelve, reduced by the defection of Judas. It serves neither John's purpose nor style to add to the action and tell of nominating a replacement disciple.

John 21:1–25 in the Narrative Flow

In the beginning (1:1–2:12)

Jesus's itinerant ministry (2:13–12:11)

Jesus's triumphant hour (12:12–19:42)

Jesus's resurrection: Endings and epilogues (20:1–21:25)

  Recognition and reversal (20:1–31)

▶ Out of the past and into the future (21:1–25)

    The Galilee theophany (21:1–14)

    Peter's reversal and fate (21:15–19)

    The Beloved Disciple's fate (21:20–23)

    The end (21:24–25)

The named disciples include the two sons of Zebedee. John withholds their personal names, James and John. This is the only time that the trio of James, John, and Peter, so prominent in the synoptic accounts (see Mark 1:29; 5:37; 9:2; 13:3; 14:33), is mentioned in the Gospel of John. On the one hand, this could be an intentional invitation to the reader to put the pieces together and come to the conclusion that John is the Beloved Disciple. On the other hand, by leaving two additional disciples unnamed, the author could continue to protect the Beloved Disciple's anonymity (see Keener 2003, 1228–29).

The action, heavily marked by asyndeton, begins when **Simon Peter** [suddenly] **says to them, "I am going out to fish."** The lack of explanatory detail about what the disciples are doing in the Galilee and the abruptness of his announcement may suggest that fishing is not their primary intent and that Peter is restless and needs activity or even income. **They** [immediately] **say to him, "We also are coming with you"** (*erchometha kai hēmeis syn soi*). In the Greek, the emphatic use of the pronoun and the word order suggest that the less-literal translation "You are not going alone" might capture the import of their words. Peter will need their help. Maneuvering the boat and casting a net are not activities that one can handle on one's own.

They [at once] **went off and boarded the boat, and that night they caught nothing** (21:3). The word "nothing" (*oudeis*) occurs fifty-three times in the Gospel, frequently with reference to humanity and Jesus's incapacity to accomplish anything without God (see, e.g., 5:19; 9:33; and esp. 15:5), and thus it anticipates the action that will follow. The next sentence continues to emphasize

The Hero on the Beach

D. K. Crowne (1960, 371) coined the phrase "the hero on the beach" to identify a trope in Anglo-Saxon literature in which the hero meets his retainers on a beach, at the point of departure or return from a journey. Though it would be a fallacy to impose this trope on John's narrative, affinity with the trope draws attention to the significance of John's setting as a liminal space that presents two fates. In the *Iliad*, Achilles stands on a beach to make a decision between two paths:

> "I carry two sorts of destiny toward the day of my death. Either, if I stay here and fight beside the city of the Trojans, my return home is gone, but my glory shall be everlasting; but if I return home to the beloved land of my fathers, the excellence of my glory is gone, but there will be a long life left to me, and my end in death will not come to me quickly." (*Il.* 9.411–16, trans. Lattimore 1951)

In the Gospel of John, Simon Peter stands on the threshold of a fate comparable to the one chosen by Achilles. He follows Jesus to a death that earns him the glory of a martyr. By contrast, the Beloved Disciple follows a fate that leads to a quieter death and anonymity.

the limitations of the disciples. **By this time [*prōias de ēdē*] it was becoming early [morning]—Jesus stood on the beach—however [*ou mentoi*], the disciples did not know [*ēdeisan hoi mathētai*] that it is Jesus** (21:4). The various verb tenses and the carefully balanced diction of the first and last clause make this a difficult sentence to render verbatim in sound English. The sense of the *de/ men* construction is that the dawning light does not facilitate clarity of sight for the disciples. The omission of a conjunction in the statement about Jesus signals to a reader to voice excitement when reading the inserted Jesus clause.

When Jesus says to them, "Children [*Paidia*], do you not have food [*prosphagion*]?" They answered him, "No" (21:5). The absence of a reciprocal title of polite address captures the irritation in the disciples' reply. This is the only time that Jesus addresses the disciples with the term "children." Given the movement to familial language, it seems sensible to treat the use of *paidia* within the context of the fictive family that Jesus establishes rather than as a rebuke. The word that Jesus uses for fish (*prosphagion*) can simply mean food, but it also carries the connotation of relish, the savory morsels that make staples such as bread or porridge more appetizing.

Given that Jesus earlier states that the sheep will recognize their shepherd's voice (10:4) and that Mary Magdalene knows Jesus when he calls her by name (20:16), it seems odd that the disciples continue to fail to recognize him. If they have been waiting for him, their slowness is all the more puzzling. Once more John seems to be playing with the conventions of supplication by making their answer fail to anticipate the boon that Jesus will grant. **Then he told them, "Cast the net on the right side of the boat** [right as opposed to left was considered more auspicious in antiquity]**, and you will find [fish]."** In the Lucan story of the miraculous draught, Peter meets Jesus's command to let down the net in the deep water with protest (Luke 5:4–5). The prompt obedience to the command of a stranger on the beach might suggest that they respond to Jesus like sheep follow the shepherd, without taking time to reflect on why they obey. **So they cast, and they had insufficient force [*ischyon*] to draw it because of the abundance of fish [*ichthyōn*]** (21:6). This translation sacrifices the choice of a noun better suited to the action of drawing for a noun that captures the alliteration of *ischyon* and *ichthyōn*. Given that this is the only time that John uses *ischyō*—he prefers *dynamai*, which he uses thirty-six times—the alliteration is certainly intentional. Andrew Lincoln (2005, 511) suggests that the abundance of the catch may be the fulfillment of Ezekiel's eschatological image of a prolific fishery on the Dead Sea comparable to the Great Sea (Ezek. 47:7–10).

The act of recognition falls to the Beloved Disciple, but he shares the realization, **"It is the Lord,"** with only Peter. This is one of two pieces of direct speech uttered by the Beloved Disciple in the Gospel. The first speech is the question "Lord, who is it?" that Peter directs him to ask (13:25). Now the Beloved Disciple takes the lead, and Peter responds to his words. **So Simon**

Peter, hearing that it is the Lord, girded around the middle [of his waist] the outer garment, for he was [practically] naked [*gymnos*], and threw himself into the sea (21:7). Peter appears to have stripped down to his loincloth to work. *Gymnos* can mean completely naked but usually means some state of undress or even that one is unarmed. Peter takes at least one moment to consider that it would be shameful to present himself to the Lord in his present state before he impetuously dives into the water.

At this point there is a minor gap in the narration. The text does not make it clear if Peter arrives first, or if he is sitting with Jesus when the other disciples arrive, or if his efforts are in vain because they all arrive together.

Although they are prepared to follow Peter fishing, **the other disciples** do not follow him into the water but **came in the skiff.** John substitutes *ploiarion* for *ploion* in this third reference to the boat. Unlike the substitution of *ischyō* for *dynamai* above, this seems to be a change in vocabulary for variety's sake, a pattern that marks much of this chapter. The disciples' reasons for not following Peter are sound, **for they were not far from the land but about two hundred forearms** [cubits] **away, dragging the net of fish** (21:8). **As soon as they disembarked on the land, they saw a charcoal fire untended and small fish** [*opsarion*] **placed on it and bread** (21:9). The use of the diminutive *opsarion* here and in 21:10 ties this meal to the one provided by the boy in 6:9. The size of the fish points even more clearly to a meal of delicacies.

Jesus [immediately] **says to them, "Bring some of** [*apo*] **the small fish that you caught now"** (21:10). This is the only time that John makes use of *apo* as a partitive; otherwise he uses *ek* for this purpose. Given that he has provided fish, this command is most likely symbolic. Jerome Neyrey (2007a, 336) suggests that Jesus shows them that they are now able to provide the food that they could not provide in the story of the Samaritan woman (4:31–32). If the small fish represent delicacies, Jesus seems to be encouraging them to eat the best of the catch themselves.

Simon Peter, true to his tendency to act first, **accordingly went aboard** [*anebē*—could also signify that he got up, or went up a bank, but the selected meaning fits the action that follows] **and hauled onto the land the net stuffed full of fish** [*meston icthyōn megalōn* signifies beyond capacity], **one hundred and fifty-three, and though there were so many, the net did not split** (21:11). Many readers have sought ways to make this number signify the unity of the church. Jerome (*Comm. Ezech.* 595) cites a poet, Oppianus Cilix, to support his claim that there are one hundred and fifty-three varieties of fish. Augustine (*Tract. Ev. Jo.* 122) points out that it is a triangular number, that is, if one adds 1 plus 2, plus 3, . . . plus 17, the total is 153. An alternative to this symbolic reading is to see this as a piece of narrative realism, in which case knowledge of the precise number points to the authority of the Beloved Disciple's witness as one who was there and would know such details. Ancient sensibilities might have led the first audience to draw connections between the net and the seamless robe that fit it into the pattern of marvels that run throughout the Gospel.

The meal begins with an invitation: **"Come here! Take breakfast!"** Rather than describing how the disciples react to the invitation, John describes what they do not say. **No one of the disciples were venturing to question him closely, "Who are you?" knowing that it is the Lord** (21:12). Unlike their speechlessness when they found Jesus with the Samaritan woman (4:27), this silence does not signify shame. Gone is the need for the question that characterizes the dialogues of the Gospel: "Who are you?" Jesus then proceeds to serve the meal in silence. The description—**Jesus comes and takes the bread and gives** [it] **to them, and the small fish likewise** (21:13)—echoes the description of the feeding of the multitude (6:11). No reported speech substantiates whether this can be treated as a eucharistic meal.

The first third of the chapter ends with a characteristic Johannine enumeration. **This was now the third time Jesus was made manifest to the disciples since being raised from the dead** (21:14). The exclusion of Mary from this count need not signify that the appearance to her is dismissed. She might be excluded because John is counting appearances to the group that is present.

Peter's Reversal and Fate (21:15–19)

The dialogue in John 21:15–22 has been described in terms of rehabilitation, reinstatement as leader, and redemption. Within the framework of Aristotle's (*Poet.* 1452a.23–1452b.14) plot elements, the dialogue enacts Peter's reversal of his relationship with Jesus (*peripeteia*). Peter has denied his role as a disciple in acts of self-preservation (18:17, 25, 27). Now he acknowledges his attachment to Jesus and completes his identification with the Good Shepherd (see table 6 at 13:11).

After they had taken breakfast, the heart of the action begins when **Jesus says to Simon Peter, "Simon** [son] **of John, do you love** [*agapas*] **me more than these** [*toutōn*]**?"** (21:15a). *Toutōn* could refer to the disciples or to the fish, which signify his occupation. Jesus may be preparing Peter to leave the solidarity of the disciples for a solitary path, or he may be preparing Peter for the choice to leave his old way of life and follow a path to a martyr's death. The fish may also signify a life of comfort: recall that Peter's physical comfort is linked with his denials in 18:17–27. Jesus uses Peter's given name (Simon) rather than his nickname (Cephas/Peter; see 1:42), suggesting that Peter is indeed starting over.

In the give-and-take that follows, John alternates words for love (*agapaō* and *phileō*), sheep (*arnia* and *probata*), and tend (*boskō* and *poimainō*) so that no combination is repeated. Nineteenth-century scholars tend to argue for the superiority of *agapaō* over *phileō* and insist that Peter persists in misunderstanding the nature of divine love when he says, **"Yes, Lord, you know that I love** [*philō*] **you."** The current consensus is that the words *agapaō* and *phileō* are synonyms (see also Augustine, *Tract. Ev. Jo.* 123.5); therefore, when Jesus says, "**Graze** [*boske*] **my lambs** [*arnia*]" (21:15b), he is clarifying what that love entails and reiterating the love commandment (13:34; 14:15). A more-elegant translation would be "See that my lambs can graze." The process of canceling out Peter's threefold denial continues when Jesus repeats the question: "**Simon** [son] **of John, do you love** [*agapas*] **me?**" Peter replies, "**Yes, Lord, you know that I love** [*philō*] **you,**" and Jesus instructs, "**Shepherd** [*poimaine*] **my flock** [*probata*]**!**" (21:16). With Jesus's third repetition of the question, "**Simon** [son] **of John, do you love** [*phileis*] **me?**" the narrator registers Peter's emotional response: **Peter was pained that he said to him a third time,** "**Do you love** [*phileis*] **me?**" The narrator's glimpse into Peter's interiority at this point, after he has withheld it at the time of his denial, perhaps suggests that Peter continues to suffer for what he has done. Peter's longer response is then not simply an expression of his convictions about Jesus's omniscience; it is a confession: "**Lord, you know** [*oidas*] **everything; you know** [*ginōskeis*] **that I love** [*philō*] **you.**" Jesus's repeated instruction, "**Graze** [*boske*] **my flock** [*probata*]**!**" (21:17), becomes an acknowledgment of Peter's past failure and present contrition as well as a commission. Besides negating Peter's threefold denial and substantiating Peter's sincerity, the exchange draws on the storytelling "rule of three," the phenomenon that things that come in three are more satisfying, be it three wishes, three musketeers, or "life, liberty, and the pursuit of happiness."

Jesus then clarifies the significance of Peter's reversal: "**Truly, truly, I say to you that when you were younger, you girded yourself** [*ezōnnyes seauton*; a metaphor for preparing for battle or work; see, e.g., Job 38:3; 40:7; 1 Pet. 1:13] **and walked about** [*peripateis*; figurative for lived] **wherever you wished.**" Jesus's choice of words may recall God's call to Jeremiah: "But you, gird up your loins [*perizōsai tēn osphyn*]; stand up and tell them everything that I command you" (Jer. 1:17 LXX); as such, it continues the theme of commissioning. The language also reflects Peter's previous habits as well as the action of jumping out of the boat that we have just witnessed. "**When you grow old, you will stretch out your hand, and another will gird** [*zōsei*] **you and take you wherever they wish**" (21:18). Rudolf Bultmann, supposing that Jesus quotes a proverb known to his ancient audience but lost to us, reconstructs it as follows: "In youth a man is free to go where he wills; in old age a man must let himself be taken where he does not will" (1971, 713). In the ancient context the transition is not simply from independence to dependence but from manliness to the emasculation of dependence. A woman was taken by the hand in marriage as a gesture of the man's authority over her. The narrator then clarifies Jesus's intent: **He said this signifying** [with] **what sort of death he will glorify God.** Peter's death is presented as a future event, but for those who know the story of Peter's execution (see *Acts Pet.* 37; Tertullian, *Praescr.* 36; Eusebius, *Hist. eccl.* 3.1), Jesus's words anticipate the image of Peter's arms stretched over the

Figure 25. This fourteenth-century French ivory panel (17.0 x 9.5 cm) depicts the apostle Peter preaching and crucified (photo by Gérard Blot, Musee National du Moyen Age, Thermes de Cluny, Paris, France, inv. Cl.395d).

patibulum as he is led to his crucifixion (see fig. 25). Many ancient Christian authors treat "stretched out hands" as a circumlocution for crucifixion, but they may be dependent on the Gospel of John (e.g., Justin Martyr, *1 Apol.* 35; Cyprian, *Test.* 2.20). The narrator's aside stresses that an act seen by the world as humiliation is God's glorification. **And having said this, he says to him, "Follow me!"** (21:19). The invitation at the beginning of Mark, "Follow me and I will make you fish for people" (1:17), signifies a life of activity. In John, the invitation is to follow a path to death.

The Beloved Disciple's Fate (21:20–23)

The dialogue then follows Peter's focalization as the narrator prepares to bring the story to a close. **Then turning, Peter sees the disciple whom Jesus loved following, [the one] who also reclined upon his breast in the supper and said, "Lord, who is the one handing you over?"** (21:20). Given that Jesus has just invited Peter to follow him, the Beloved Disciple's action might naturally suggest that he shares Peter's commission. The narrator's reminder of the intimacy shared with Jesus reinforces this possibility and prompts the question. **Seeing this one then Peter says to Jesus, "Lord, what about this one?"** (21:21). Jerome Neyrey (2007a, 341) contends that the question would have constituted a challenge in antiquity and points to a rivalry between Peter and the Beloved Disciple. Given the close association of the two disciples throughout the Gospel, Peter's question may also indicate a desire for their partnership to continue. Jesus's response seems to chide Peter: **"If I wish him to remain until I come, what is it to you? You are to follow me"** (21:22).

The narrator jumps from the progression of the narration forward through time to a retrospective perspective that begins the movement out of narrative

© Réunion des Musées Nationaux / Art Resource, NY.

time and space, into the present of the audience. **Therefore this word went out to the brothers** [and sisters] **that that disciple would not die, but Jesus did not say to him that he would not die but, "If I wish him to remain until I come, what is it to you?"** (21:23). This verse suggests that Jesus's words about the Beloved Disciple became part of the oral tradition and that they were understood to signify that the Beloved Disciple would not die, but he has died. The clarification also emphasizes that the Beloved Disciple's fate is also chosen for him by Jesus and, therefore, also glorifies God. As Charles H. Talbert puts it, "If Peter's death as crucified martyr is appropriate for him in his role as good shepherd, the beloved disciple's death in old age is appropriate for one who functioned in his lifetime as witness and interpreter of Jesus's life" (2005, 273).

The End (21:24–25)

The narrator completes the movement from narrative time to the present by acknowledging his debt to the Beloved Disciple. **This is the disciple, the witness concerning these things, and the one who has caused these things to be written.** The narrator moves from the past association with the Beloved Disciple to his present relationship to his audience and the affirmation **We know that his witness is true** (21:24). If one works within the methodology of source or redaction criticism, the plural first-person pronoun would appear to be evidence of an editor's hand or even an editorial committee. If one studies this text while working within the newer methodology of performance criticism, it seems analogous to the sort of liturgical closing that a reader may add to an oral presentation of the Gospels, "The Gospel of the Lord," to prompt the congregation to respond, "Praise be to you, Lord Jesus Christ." The book of Revelation ends with a comparable responsive litany (22:20–21 NRSV):

> The one who testifies to these things says, "Surely I am coming soon."
> Amen. Come, Lord Jesus!
> The grace of the Lord Jesus be with all the saints.
> Amen.

Anyone who reads John 21:24a aloud confesses to belief in the truth of what is read. The use of the plural first-person voice in 21:24b invites a response of affirmation from the audience.

John then closes with the same convention used at the end of chapter 20: **And there are many other things that Jesus did that, if they were written down one at a time, I do not suppose the world itself to have room for all the books being written. Amen** (21:25). The image is not simply of volumes of books but the continuous writing of books. Besides the world not affording enough space, it does not afford enough time. The ending short-circuits objections that some familiar story or another has been neglected and implicitly praises Jesus for having exploits too numerous to name.

Theological Issues

Two Models of Discipleship

The way that the Gospel pairs Peter and the Beloved Disciple has prompted considerable discourse and debate about whether one form of discipleship is preferred over another. Ernst Käsemann (1968, 28–29) argues that the rhetorical aim of the Gospel is to show the superior authority of the Beloved Disciple and to discredit Peter. Andrew Lincoln (2005, 522) contends that chapter 21 is an apology for the Beloved Disciple, who does not die a martyr's death. The Gospel then holds up two forms of discipleship as equally important.

If we set this Gospel in the stage of the early church, when the martyr narratives are beginning to take shape and a violent death in imitation of Christ is beginning to be extolled, the rhetorical aim of the Gospel is to provide an alternative role. The anonymity of the Beloved Disciple makes him the archetype of a typical follower of Jesus who takes the path of obscurity. He leads the life of the householder, the one who cares for Jesus's mother, whose task it is to remember the glory, to memorialize it, and by doing so to be no less ideal a disciple. The task of the audience is to participate in the applauding of Jesus's name, a name that they share, just as brothers and sisters share the name of their father, and in which they have life. The community is called to the task of recollection by preserving what the Beloved Disciple has remembered about Jesus.

Peter's discipleship is more active and public and, as a result, dangerous, but also occasion for receiving honor. Augustine (*Tract. Ev. Jo.* 123.5) treats the repetition in 21:15–17 as a warning against the vices of leadership, such as the desire for adoration and the pursuit of pleasure. If the implicit commissioning of Peter as pastor is the Johannine equivalent to the commissioning of Peter found in Matt. 16:18–19, then the reminder that the leader of the flock loves Jesus's sheep and follows a path seen by those in power as humiliating is the Johannine equivalent of Jesus's telling Peter, "Get behind me, Satan," when Peter reprimands Jesus for speaking of his death (Matt. 16:22–23). Peter requires a lesson in what it means to serve Jesus.

The absence of ethical teachings in the Gospel of John leads scholars to focus on the role of leader rather than the action to which Peter is called. Certainly teaching about Jesus is a principal task intended in the metaphor of feeding, and serving the bread and wine at the Lord's Supper should also be considered. There is a subtle pattern that runs throughout the Gospel that might also inform the metaphor and point to a broader concept of service. Jesus's followers are attentive to Jesus's physical realities. The disciples want to know where Jesus is staying (1:38). They go to get him food, leaving him to rest at a well (4:8), and then they encourage him to eat something (4:31). After the Samaritan woman initially rebuffs Jesus's request for minimal hospitality (a drink), the town invites him to stay with them (4:40). The disciples try to save

287

him by bringing him into the boat (6:21). Martha is concerned that the smell of Lazarus's body will offend Jesus (11:39). Mary soothes his feet (12:3), and Nicodemus provides an excessive amount of myrrh with which to bury him (19:39). Though their concern may be naive, it is poignant. Disciples showed their devotion to their teachers in antiquity by serving them, and John distills discipleship to these expressions of fidelity. Given that Jesus is no longer physically present in the community, how to express devotion to him becomes a question. In the charge to Peter, John perhaps presents the synoptic teaching that service done for the afflicted or vulnerable is service done for Jesus and in imitation of Jesus (e.g., Matt. 25:31–46).

If we treat the Gospel as an ancient biography, it is important not to impose upon it the form of a modern biography. John presents Jesus with no crisis. The Johannine story of Jesus belongs to Bakhtin's category of the rhetorical biography that is based on the encomium, the memorial speech that replaces lament as the way to honor the dead. The rhetorical biography praises civic-political acts or provides a full disclosure of the identity of its subject (Bakhtin 1981, 131). John tells an account of the events in Jesus's life that mark the progression from obscurity to notoriety to execution, and then ends with the fulfillment of trust in Jesus's name by narrating the stories of the resurrection—but Jesus is unchanged. Each story discloses another aspect of who he is and what he has always been. In this sense, chapter 20 is the conclusion to Jesus's story.

The account of Peter's life in chapter 21 is a biography within the biography of Jesus, but of a different order. Bakhtin describes the form of biography that entails a crisis the Platonic biography as "the life course of one seeking true knowledge" through a path that "passes from self-confident ignorance, through self-critical skepticism, to self-knowledge and ultimately to authentic knowing." The Platonic biography identifies isolated moments of crisis and rebirth (Bakhtin 1981, 130). This is Peter's story. The representation of the unity of a person's life is an expression of the "fullness of time," a term that Bakhtin prefers to fatedness. In the fullness of time, Peter becomes the good shepherd: he lives a life marked by love for the world and trusts in the name of Jesus.

The Sense of Ending

As John brings his Gospel to a close in 21:23–25, he changes the time of the narrative from the continuous flow of the present to reflection on an event long past; he does this by referring to unnarrated events and addressing the audience directly. The Beloved Disciple ceases to be a character in the action and becomes the witness to the events narrated. The last line of the Gospel borrows from a literary convention used commonly in a diverse range of ancient prose (for lists, see Talbert 2005, 274; Keener 2003, 1241). Here are two examples to illustrate the point, one from a Euripidean tragedy and one from Philo's treatise on laws peculiar to the Jews:

There are many shapes of divinity, and many things the gods accomplish against our expectations. What men look for is not brought to pass, but a god finds a way to achieve the unexpected. Such was the outcome of this story. (Euripides, *Alc*. 1159–63, trans. D. Kovacs 1994, 279–81; see *Bacch*. 1388–92; *Med*. 1415–19; *Hel*. 1689–90; *Andr*. 1284–88)

[T]he existence of the longest lived man of the human race would fail, if he were to attempt to enumerate all the praiseworthy qualities of equality, and of its offspring, justice. In consequence of which it seems to me to be best to be satisfied with what has already been said, which may be sufficient to rouse up the recollection of those persons who are fond of learning, and to leave the remaining circumstances unwritten in their souls, as divine images in a most sacred place. (Philo, *Spec*. 4.238, trans. Yonge 1993, 639)

This convention makes several aspects of the work to which it is appended clear: (1) the action of the drama or presentation of argument now lies in the past; (2) there is the need to be selective about which events are dramatized or arguments articulated; and (3) the selection is purposeful. John 21:24–25 achieves the first two of these objectives. The epilogue from the previous chapter (20:31) achieves the second and third.

Knowing that the ending follows a convention might lead a modern reader to think of it as banal or contrived, but to do so is to miss the importance of the use of a convention. In the context of a public reading, the audience must be made aware that the narration has come to an end. Using a convention is then an unmistakable signal that the storytelling is over. Conventions can also invoke a particular view of reality. The way that John handles time in this final chapter tends to anchor his soteriology in the past. The action of the Gospel is complete. Jesus has returned. The Holy Spirit has been given. The disciples have completed their tasks and are dead. Paradoxically, the Gospel that promises everlasting life (3:36; 6:47; 8:51–52) ends with reference to two deaths. In contrast, the Gospel of Matthew opens up into an untold future when Jesus says, "Remember, I am with you always, to the end of the age" (Matt. 28:20 NRSV). The Gospels of Mark and Luke end in the middle of affairs by providing a summary of the ongoing story. Mark describes an evangelical mission (16:9, 19–20), and Luke prepares for the continuation of his story in Acts by moving the disciples to Jerusalem (24:52–53).

The sense of closure at the end of John's Gospel helps to foster the hypothesis that the Johannine community is sectarian and not engaged in a mission to the world (see Rensberger 1988, 28). This conclusion ignores John's tendency to adhere to conventions of storytelling that, in this case, call for an ending that is complete and does not prompt the audience to wonder what happens next. While the Gospel of John contains references to future eschatology, the weight of its discourses and its form tips the balance toward realized eschatology. Mikhail Bakhtin (1981, 147) calls this a "historical inversion." The things that humans habitually look to find in the future, such things as purpose, justice, and perfection, are found in the past. The future in the Gospel of John is subsumed within the past that is the story of Jesus.

According to Bakhtin (1981, 148), when future time is presented as something "out of the past," the present ceases to be oriented toward the future and instead takes on a more spatial quality:

> There is a greater readiness to build a superstructure for reality [the present] along a vertical axis of upper and lower than to move forward along the horizontal axis of time. Should these vertical structures turn out as well to be other-worldly, idealistic, eternal, outside time, then this extratemporal and eternal quality is perceived as something simultaneous with a given moment in the present; it is something contemporaneous, and that which already exists is perceived as better than the future (which does not yet exist and which never did exist).

The form of the Gospel of John takes a shape appropriate to the gospel it proclaims. The Gospel gives its audience mere hints of a mission to the world, because the story it tells is not about what will be but about what is a present reality. We can see this shift in orientation toward a heavenly reality and away from the horizontal axis of historic time and movement of the word through the proclamation of the gospel in the Mediterranean world. Jesus is a heaven-sent gift: the bread from heaven, the living water, and the resurrection. Jesus is the gift of life itself. Whoever trusts in Jesus abides in him, even though Jesus has returned to the Father in heaven. Those who abide in the word of the Gospel and witness to Jesus's glory by reading it or hearing it read live in time commemorated as eternal in all its fullness. Joy is no longer an intermittent experience in varying degrees. Joy is the constant assurance of God's love for the world. Joy is complete.

Bibliography

Abrams, Judith Z. 1998. *Judaism and Disability: Portrayals in Ancient Texts from the Tanach through the Bavli.* Washington, DC: Gallaudet University Press.

Anderson, Paul N. 1997. *The Christology of the Fourth Gospel: Its Unity and Disunity in the Light of John 6.* Valley Forge, PA: Trinity.

Bakhtin, Mikhail. 1981. "Forms of Time and of the Chronotope in the Novel: Notes towards a Historical Poetics." In *The Dialogic Imagination: Four Essays*, edited by Michael Holquist, translated by Caryl Emerson and Michael Holquist, 84–258. Austin: University of Texas Press. Russian original, 1937–38.

Bal, Meike. 1997. *Narratology: Introduction to the Theory of Narrative.* Toronto: University of Toronto Press.

Barker, Elton T. E. 2009. *Entering the Agon: Dissent and Authority in Homer, Historiography and Tragedy.* Oxford: Oxford University Press.

Barrett, C. K. 1955. *The Gospel according to John.* London: SPCK.

———. 1971. *The Prologue of St John's Gospel: The Ethel M. Wood Lecture Delivered before the University of London on 19 February 1970.* London: Athlone.

———. 1978. *The Gospel according to St. John.* Philadelphia: Westminster.

———. 1982. *Essays on John.* London: SPCK.

Barthes, Roland. 1977. "The Death of the Author." In *Image, Music, Text*, edited and translated by Stephen Heath, 142–48. New York: Hill & Wang.

Basore, John W., trans. 1958. *Seneca*, vol. 2, *Moral Essays II.* Loeb Classical Library 254. Cambridge, MA: Harvard University Press.

Bauckham, Richard. 2006. "Messianism according to the Gospel of John." In *Challenging Perspectives on the Gospel of John*, edited by John Lierman, 34–58. Tübingen: Mohr Siebeck.

Baumgarten, Joseph, and Daniel Schwartz. 1995. "Damascus Document (CD)." In *Damascus Document, War Scroll, and Related Documents.* Vol. 2 of *The Dead Sea*

Scrolls: Hebrew, Aramaic, and Greek Texts with English Translations, edited by James Charlesworth, 4–57. Tübingen: Mohr; Louisville: Westminster John Knox.

Bieringer, Reimund. 2000. "'My Kingship Is Not of This World' (John 18,36): The Kingship of Jesus and Politics." In *The Myriad Christ: Plurality and the Quest for Unity in Contemporary Christology*, edited by Terrence Merrigan and Jacques Haers, 159–75. Leuven: Leuven University Press.

Bieringer, Reimund, Didier Pollefeyt, and Frederique Vandecasteele-Vanneuville, eds. 2001. *Anti-Judaism and the Fourth Gospel*. Louisville: Westminister John Knox.

Blasi, Anthony J., Jean Dumaime, and Paul-André Turcotte. 2002. *Handbook of Early Christianity: Social Science Approaches*. Landham, MD: Altamira.

Boer, Martinus C. de. 1996. *Johannine Perspectives on the Death of Jesus*. Kampen: Kok Pharos.

Bonhoeffer, Dietrich. 1961. "Predigt am Sonntag Judika über Judas." In *Gesammelte Schriften*, edited by E. Bethge, 406–13. Munich: Chr. Kaiser Verlag.

Borgen, Peder. 1981. *Bread from Heaven: Exegetical Study of the Concept of Manna in the Gospel of John and the Writings of Philo*. Supplements to Novum Testamentum 10. Leiden: Brill.

———. 1987. "Creation, Logos and the Son: Observations on John 1:1–18 and 5:17–18." *Ex auditu* 3:88–97.

———. 1996. "The Gospel of John and Hellenism." In *Exploring the Gospel of John*, edited by Dwight Moody Smith, R. Alan Culpepper, and Carl Clifton Black, 98–123. Louisville: Westminster John Knox.

———. 2003. "Philo of Alexandria as Exegete." In *The Ancient Period: A History of Biblical Interpretation*, edited by Alan J. Hauser and Duane F. Watson, 114–43. Grand Rapids: Eerdmans.

Boyarin, Daniel. 2001. "Justin Martyr Invents Judaism." *Church History* 79:427–61.

Bradley, Keith R. 2001. "The Roman Family at Dinner." In *Meals in a Social Context*, edited by Inge Nielsen and Hanne Sigismund Nielsen, 36–55. Aarhus: Aarhus University Press.

Brant, Jo-Ann A. 1996. "Husband Hunting: Characterization and Narrative Art in the Gospel of John." *Biblical Interpretation* 4:205–23.

———. 2004. *Dialogue and Drama: Elements of Greek Tragedy in the Fourth Gospel*. Peabody, MA: Hendrickson.

Brodie, Thomas L. 1997. *The Gospel according to John: A Literary and Theological Commentary*. New York: Oxford University Press.

Brown, Raymond E. 1966. *The Gospel according to John I–XII*. Anchor Bible 29. New York: Doubleday.

———. 1970. *The Gospel according to John XIII–XXI*. Anchor Bible 29A. New York: Doubleday.

———. 1979. *The Community of the Beloved Disciple*. New York: Paulist Press.

———. 1994. *Death of the Messiah: From Gethsemane to the Grave; Commentary on the Passion Narrative in the Four Gospels*. 2 vols. New York: Doubleday.

Bultmann, Rudolf. 1941. *Das Evangelium des Johannes*. Göttingen: Vandenhoeck & Ruprecht.

———. 1951. *Theology of the New Testament*. Vol. 1. Translated by Kendrick Grobel. New York: Charles Scribner's Sons.

———. 1955. *Theology of the New Testament*. Vol. 2. Translated by Kendrick Grobel. New York: Charles Scribner's Sons.

———. 1971. *The Gospel of John: A Commentary*. Translated by G. R. Beasley-Murray. Philadelphia: Westminster.

Burge, Gary M. 1987. *The Anointed Community: The Holy Spirit in the Johannine Tradition*. Grand Rapids: Eerdmans.

Burkett, Delbert. 1999. *The Son of Man Debate: A History and Evaluation*. Society for New Testament Studies Monograph Series 107. Cambridge: Cambridge University Press.

Burridge, Richard A. 2005. *Four Gospels, One Jesus? A Symbolic Reading*. 2nd ed. Grand Rapids: Eerdmans.

Calvin, John. 1997. *Concerning the Eternal Predestination of God*. Translated by J. K. Reid. Louisville: Westminster John Knox.

Carson, D. A. 1991. *The Gospel according to John: An Introduction and Commentary*. Grand Rapids: Eerdmans.

Casey, Maurice. 1996. *Is John's Gospel True?* London: Routledge.

Catchpole, David. 1998. "The Beloved Disciple and Nathanael." In *Understanding, Studying, Reading: New Testament Essays in Honour of John Ashton*, edited by Christopher Rowland et al., 69–92. Sheffield: Sheffield Academic Press.

Charlesworth, James H. 1985. "Odes of Solomon." In *The Old Testament Pseudepigrapha*, edited by James H. Charlesworth, 2:725–71. New York: Doubleday.

———. 1995. *The Beloved Disciple: Whose Witness Validates the Gospel of John?* Valley Forge, PA: Trinity.

Cohen, Shaye J. D. 1999. *The Beginnings of Jewishness: Boundaries, Varieties, Uncertainties*. Berkeley: University of California Press.

Coleman, K. M. 1990. "Fatal Charades: Roman Executions Staged as Mythological Enactments." *Journal of Roman Studies* 80:44–73.

Collins, Raymond. 1976. "Representative Figures in the Fourth Gospel." *Downside Review* 94:26–46, 118–32.

Coloe, Mary L. 2001. *God Dwells with Us: Temple Symbolism in the Fourth Gospel*. Collegeville, MN: Liturgical Press.

———. 2004. "Welcome into the Household of God: The Footwashing in John 13." *Catholic Biblical Quarterly* 66:400–415.

Conway, Colleen M. 2008. *Behold the Man: Jesus and Greco-Roman Masculinity*. Oxford: Oxford University Press.

Cotter, Wendy. 1999. *Miracles in Greco-Roman Antiquity: A Sourcebook*. London: Routledge.

Crossan, John Dominic. 1991. *The Historical Jesus: The Life of a Mediterranean Peasant*. San Francisco: Harper Collins.

Crowne, D. K. 1960. "The Hero on the Beach: An Example of Composition by Theme in Anglo-Saxon Poetry." *Neuphilologische Mitteilungen* 61:362–72.

Cullmann, Oscar. 1953. *Early Christian Worship*. Louisville: Westminster John Knox.

Culpepper, R. Alan. 1983. *The Anatomy of the Fourth Gospel*. Minneapolis: Fortress.

———. 1991. "The Johannine *Hypodeigma*: A Reading of John 13:1–38." In *The Fourth Gospel from a Literary Perspective*, edited by R. Alan Culpepper, 133–52. Society of Biblical Literature Semeia Series 53. Atlanta: Scholars Press.

———. 2000. *John, the Son of Zebedee: The Life of a Legend*. Minneapolis: Fortress.

Dalby, Andrew. 1996. *Siren Feasts: A History of Food and Gastronomy in Greece*. London: Routledge.

D'Angelo, Mary Rose. 1990. "A Critical Note: John 20:17 and Apocalypse of Moses 31." *Journal of Theological Studies* 41:481–503.

———. 1999. "Imitating Deity in the Gospel of John: Theological Language and 'Father' in 'Prayers of Jesus.'" In *God the Father in the Gospel of John*, edited by Adele Reinhartz, 59–82. Society of Biblical Literature Semeia Series 85. Atlanta: Scholars Press.

Daube, David. 1944. "Three Questions of Form in Matthew V." *Journal of Theological Studies* 45:21–31.

Day, Janeth Norfleete. 2002. *The Woman at the Well: Interpretation of John 4:1–42 in Retrospect and Prospect*. Biblical Interpretation Series 61. Leiden: Brill.

de Boer, Martinus C. *See* Boer, Martinus C. de

Destro, Adriana, and Mauro Pesce. 1995. "Kinship, Discipleship, and Movement: An Anthropological Study of John's Gospel." *Biblical Interpretation* 3:266–84.

Dodd, C. H. 1953. *The Interpretation of the Fourth Gospel*. Cambridge: Cambridge University Press.

Dunn, J. D. G. 1970. "The Washing of the Disciples' Feet in John 13:1–20." *Zeitschrift für die neutestamentliche Wissenschaft und die Kunde der älteren Kirche* 61:247–52.

Egan, Kieran. 1992. *Imagination in Teaching and Learning*. London: Routledge.

Eliade, Mircea. 1957. *The Sacred and the Profane: The Nature of Religion*. Edinburgh: T&T Clark.

Ellis, Peter F. 1984. *The Genius of John: A Composition-Critical Commentary on the Fourth Gospel*. Collegeville, MN: Liturgical Press.

Ellul, Jacques. 1989. *What I Believe*. Translated by Geoffrey W. Bromiley. Grand Rapids: Eerdmans.

Engberg-Pedersen, Troels. 2004. "The Concept of Paraenesis." In *Early Christian Paraenesis in Context*, edited by Troels Engberg-Pedersen and James M. Starr, 47–72. Berlin: de Gruyter.

Epstein, Edmund L. 2001. "The Words That You Gave to Me I Have Given to Them." In *The Rhetoric of the Gospel: Theological Artistry in the Gospels and Acts*, edited by Carl Clifton Black, 75–94. St. Louis: Chalice.

Filson, Floyd V. 1963. *The Gospel of John: The Layman's Bible Commentary*. Atlanta: John Knox.

Fredriksen, Paula. 2000. *From Jesus to Christ: The Origins of the New Testament Images of Christ*. New Haven: Yale University Press.

Frey, Jörg. 2005. "Eschatology in the Johannine Circle." In *Theology and Christology in the Fourth Gospel*, edited by G. Van Belle, J.G. van der Watt, and P. Maritz, 47–82. Leuven: Leuven University Press.

Freyne, Seán. 2004. *Jesus, a Jewish Galilean: A New Reading of the Jesus Story*. Edinburgh: T&T Clark.

Frye, Northrop. 1957. *The Anatomy of Criticism*. Princeton, NJ: Princeton University Press.

Gadamer, Hans-Georg. 1960. *Wahrheit und Methode: Grundzüge einer philosophischen Hermeneutik*. Tübingen: Mohr Siebeck. ET: *Truth and Method*. Translation edited by Garrett Barden and John Cumming. New York: Seabury, 1975.

Gardner, Jane F. 1998. *Family and Familia in Roman Law and Life*. Oxford: Clarendon.

Gaventa, Beverly Roberts. 1999. *Mary: Glimpses of the Mother of God*. Minneapolis: Fortress.

Gennep, Arnold van. 1909. *Les rites de passage*. Paris: Nourry.

———. 1960. *The Rites of Passage*. Translated by Monika B. Vizedom and Gabrielle L. Caffee. Chicago: University of Chicago Press.

Gerhardsson, Birger. 1998. *Memory and Manuscript: Oral Tradition and Written Transmission in Rabbinic Judaism and Early Christianity*. Grand Rapids: Eerdmans.

Gerrig, Richard J. 1996. "The Resilience of Suspense." In *Suspense: Conceptualization, Theoretical Analyses, and Empirical Explorations*, edited by Peter Vorderer et al., 93–106. Hillsdale, NJ: Lawrence Erlbaum.

Gide, André. 1954. *Journal 1889–1939: Souvenirs*. Paris: Gallimard.

Glancy, Jennifer A. 2005. "Torture: Flesh, Truth, and the Fourth Gospel." *Biblical Interpretation* 13:107–36.

Goldhill, Simon. 1986. *Reading Greek Tragedy*. Cambridge: Cambridge University Press.

Grassi, Joseph A. 1986. "The Role of Jesus' Mother in John's Gospel: A Reappraisal." *Catholic Biblical Quarterly* 48:67–80.

Graves, Robert, trans. 1957. *Suetonius: The Twelve Caesars*. Harmondsworth, England: Penguin.

Grayston, Kenneth. 1981. "The Meaning of *Paraklētos*." *Journal for the Study of the New Testament* 13:67–82.

Grigsby, Bruce H. 1982. "The Cross as an Expiatory Sacrifice in the Fourth Gospel." *Journal for the Study of the New Testament* 15:51–80.

Guilding, Aileen. 1960. *The Fourth Gospel and Jewish Worship*. Oxford: Clarendon.

Haenchen, Ernst. 1984. *A Commentary on the Gospel of John*. Translated by Robert W. Funk. 2 vols. Philadelphia: Fortress.

Halliday, M. A. K. 1975. "Anti-Languages." *American Anthropologist* 78:570–84.

Hammer, Reuven. 1995. *The Classic Midrash: Tannaitic Commentaries on the Bible*. Mahwah, NJ: Paulist Press.

Harvey, A. E. 1976. *Jesus on Trial: A Study in the Fourth Gospel*. London: SPCK.

Hawkin, David J. 1996. *The Johannine World: Reflections on the Theology of the Fourth Gospel and Contemporary Society*. New York: SUNY Press.

Hengel, Martin. 1977. *Crucifixion in the Ancient World and the Folly of the Message of the Cross*. Minneapolis: Augsburg Fortress.

———. 1993. *Die johanneische Frage: Ein Lösungsversuch*. Tübingen: Mohr Siebeck.

Heschel, Abraham J. 2001. *The Prophets*. Harper Perennial Modern Classics. New York: Perennial.

Hezser, Catherine. 2001. *Jewish Literacy in Roman Palestine*. Tübingen: Mohr Siebeck.

Hogan, Larry P. 1992. *Healing in the Second Temple Period*. Göttingen: Vandenhoeck & Ruprecht.

Horsley, Richard. 1995. *Galilee: History, Politics, People*. New York: Continuum.

Hunn, Debbie. 2004. "Who Are 'They' in John 8:33?" *Catholic Biblical Quarterly* 66:387–99.

Hurtado, Larry. 2005. *How on Earth Did Jesus Become a God? Historical Questions about Earliest Devotion to Jesus*. Grand Rapids: Eerdmans.

Hylen, Susan. 2005. *Allusion and Meaning in John 6*. Beihefte zur Zeitschrift für die neutestamentliche Wissenschaft und die Kunde der älteren Kirche 6. Berlin: de Gruyter.

Jensen, Robin Margaret. 2000. *Understanding Early Christian Art*. London: Routledge.

Jocz, Jacób. 1979. *The Jewish People and Jesus Christ*. Grand Rapids: Baker Books.

Jong, Irene J. F. de. 2001. *A Narratological Commentary on the Odyssey*. Cambridge: Cambridge University Press.

———. 2004. "Herodotus." In *Narrators, Narratees, and Narratives in Ancient Greek Literature*, edited by Irene J. F. de Jong, René Nünlist, and Angus M. Bowie, 101–14. Leiden: Brill.

Jonge, Marinus de. 1972. "Jewish Expectations about the 'Messiah' according to the Fourth Gospel." *New Testament Studies* 19:246–70.

Käsemann, Ernst. 1968. *The Testament of Jesus: A Study of the Gospel of John in the Light of Chapter 17*. London: SCM.

———. 1969. *New Testament Questions of Today*. Translated by W. J. Montague. London: SCM.

Kawashima, Robert S. 2004. *Biblical Narrative and the Death of the Rhapsode*. Bloomington: Indiana University Press.

Keener, Craig S. 1999. "Is Subordination within the Trinity Really Heresy? A Study of John 5:18 in Context." *Trinity Journal* 20:39–51.

———. 2003. *The Gospel of John: A Commentary*. 2 vols. Peabody, MA: Hendrickson.

Kennard, J. Spencer, Jr. 1955. "The Burial of Jesus." *Journal of Biblical Literature* 74:227–38.

Kennedy, George A. 1984. *New Testament Interpretation through Rhetorical Criticism*. Chapel Hill: University of North Carolina Press.

———. 2003. *Progymnasmata: Greek Textbooks of Prose Composition and Rhetoric*. Atlanta: Society of Biblical Literature.

Kimmelman, Reuven. 1981. "Birkat ha-Minim and the Lack of Evidence for an Anti-Christian Jewish Prayer in Late Antiquity." In *Jewish and Christian Self-Definition*, edited by E. P. Sanders, 2:226–44. London: SCM.

Kinneavy, James L. 1996. "Homiletics." In *Encyclopedia of Rhetoric and Composition: Communication from Ancient Times to the Information Age*, edited by Theresa Enos, 326–27. London: Routledge.

Klassen, William. 1996. *Judas: Betrayer or Friend of Jesus?* Minneapolis: Fortress.

Koester, Craig. 1989. "Hearing, Seeing, and Believing in the Gospel of John." *Biblica* 70:327–48.

———. 1995. *Symbolism in the Fourth Gospel: Meaning, Mystery, Community*. Minneapolis: Augburg Fortress.

Konstan, David. 1966. "Problems in the History of Christian Friendship." *Journal of Early Christian Studies* 4:87–113.

———. 1997. *Friendship in the Classical World*. Cambridge: Cambridge University Press.

Kovacs, David, trans. 1994. *Euripides*. Loeb Classical Library 12. Cambridge, MA and London: Harvard University Press.

Kovacs, Judith L. 1995. "'Now Shall the Ruler of This World Be Driven Out': Jesus' Death as Cosmic Battle in John 12.20–36." *Journal of Biblical Literature* 114:227–47.

Kysar, Robert. 1993. *John, the Maverick Gospel*. Louisville: Westminster John Knox.

———. 2002. *Preaching John*. Minneapolis: Fortress.

———. 2005. *Voyages with John: Charting the Fourth Gospel*. Waco: Baylor University Press.

Larsen, Kasper Bro. 2008. *Recognizing the Stranger: Recognition Scenes in the Gospel of John*. Biblical Interpretation Series 93. Leiden: Brill.

Lataire, Bianca. 2000. "Jesus' Equality with God: A Critical Reflection on John 5,18." In *The Myriad Christ: Plurality and the Quest for Unity in Contemporary Christology*, edited by Terrence Merrigan and Jacques Haers, 177–87. Leuven: Leuven University Press.

Lattimore, Richmond, trans. 1951. *The Iliad of Homer*. Chicago: University of Chicago Press.

———. 1979. *The Four Gospels and the Revelation*. New York: Farrar, Straus and Giroux.

Lee, D. A. 1995. "Partnership in Easter Faith: The Role of Mary Magdalene and Thomas in John 20." *Journal for the Study of the New Testament* 58:37–49.

Lessing, Gotthold Ephraim. 1777. *Das Testament Johannis*. Braunschweig: [Buchhandlung des Waisenhauses].

———. 1784. "Neue Hypothese über die Evangelisten als blos menschliche Geschichtschreiber betrachtet." In *Theologischer Nachlass*, 42–75. Berlin: Voss.

———. 1957. "The Testament of John." In *Lessing's Theological Writings: Selections in Translation*, edited and translated by Henry Chadwick, 57–61. Stanford, CA: Stanford University Press.

Lieu, Judith M. 1988. "Blindness in the Johannine Tradition." *New Testament Studies* 34:83–95.

———. 1999. "Temple and Synagogue in John." *New Testament Studies* 45:51–69.

Lincoln, Andrew. 2000. *Truth on Trial: The Lawsuit Motif in the Fourth Gospel.* Peabody, MA: Hendrickson.

———. 2005. *The Gospel according to John.* Black's New Testament Commentaries 4. Peabody, MA: Hendrickson.

Lindars, Barnabas. 1970. "Two Parables in John." *New Testament Studies* 16:318–29.

———. 1972. *The Gospel of John.* New Century Bible Commentary. Grand Rapids: Eerdmans.

Ling, Timothy J. M. 2006. *The Judaean Poor and the Fourth Gospel.* Cambridge: Cambridge University Press.

Loisy, Alfred. 1903. *Le quatrième Évangile.* Paris: Vrin.

Maccini, Robert Gordon. 1996. *Her Testimony Is True: Women as Witnesses according to John.* Journal for the Study of the New Testament: Supplement Series 125. Sheffield: JSOT Press.

Mack, Burton L. 1973. *Logos und Sophia: Untersuchungen zur Weisheitstheologie im hellenistischen Judentum.* Göttingen: Vandenhoeck & Ruprecht.

Malina, Bruce J. 1987. "Wealth and Poverty in the New Testament and Its World." *Interpretation* 41:354–67.

Malina, Bruce J., and Richard L. Rohrbaugh. 1998. *Social-Science Commentary on the Gospel of John.* Minneapolis: Fortress.

Marcus, Joel. 1998. "Rivers of Living Water from Jesus' Belly (John 7:38)." *Journal of Biblical Literature* 117:328–30.

Martyn, J. Louis. 1968. *History and Theology in the Fourth Gospel.* New York: Harper & Row.

———. 1979. *History and Theology in the Fourth Gospel.* 2nd ed., rev. and enlarged. Nashville: Abingdon.

Matera, Frank J. 1988. "'On Behalf of Others,' 'Cleansing,' and 'Return': Johannine Images for Jesus' Death." *Louvain Studies* 13:161–78.

McCane, Bryon R. 2003. *Roll Back the Stone: Death and Burial in the World of Jesus.* Harrisburg, PA: Trinity.

Meeks, Wayne A. 1967. *The Prophet-King: Moses Traditions and the Johannine Christology.* Leiden: Brill.

———. 1985. "Breaking Away: Three New Testament Pictures of Christianity's Separation from the Jewish Communities." In *To See Ourselves as Others See Us: Christians, Jews, "Others" in Late Antiquity,* edited by Jacob Neusner and Ernest S. Frerichs, 93–115. Chico: Scholars Press. Reprinted in *In Search of the Early Christians: Selected Essays,* edited by Wayne A. Meeks, Allen R. Hilton, and H. Gregory Snyder, 155–66. New Haven: Yale University Press.

———. 1990. "Equal to God." In *The Conversation Continues: Studies in Paul and John in Honor of J. Louis Martyn,* edited by Robert T. Fortna and Beverly R. Gaventa, 309–21. Nashville: Abingdon.

————. 1996. "The Ethics of the Fourth Gospel." In *Exploring the Gospel of John: In Honor of D. Moody Smith*, edited by R. Alan Culpepper and C. Clifton Black, 317–26. Louisville: Westminster John Knox.

Menken, Maarten J. J. 1996. "The Origins of the Old Testament Quotations in John 7:38." *Novum Testamentum* 38:160–75.

Minear, Paul Sevier. 1983. "The Original Functions of John 21." *Journal of Biblical Literature* 102:85–98.

Moloney, Francis J. 1976. *The Johannine Son of Man*. Rome: Libreria Ateneo Salesiano.

————. 1998. "The Function of John 13–17 within the Johannine Narrative." In *What Is John?* vol. 2, *Literary and Social Readings of the Fourth Gospel*, edited by Fernando F. Segovia, 43–66. Society of Biblical Literature Symposium Series 7. Atlanta: Scholars Press.

————. 2005. "The Johannine Son of Man Revisited." In *Theology and Christology in the Fourth Gospel*, edited by G. Van Belle, J. G. van der Watt, and P. Maritz, 177–202. Leuven: Leuven University Press.

Moore, Stephen D. 1993. "Are There Impurities in the Living Water That the Johannine Jesus Dispenses? Deconstruction, Feminism, and the Samaritan Woman." *Biblical Interpretation* 1:207–27.

Morris, Leon. 1971. *The Gospel according to John*. Grand Rapids: Eerdmans.

Moxnes, Halvor. 1996. "Honor and Shame." In *The Social Sciences and New Testament Interpretation*, edited by Richard L. Rohrbaugh, 19–40. Peabody, MA: Hendrickson.

Munro, Winsome. 1995. "The Pharisee and the Samaritan in John: Polar or Parallel?" *Catholic Biblical Quarterly* 57:710–38.

Myers, Alicia. 2009. "Prosopoetics and Conflict: Speech and Expectations in John 8." Paper presented at the annual meeting of the Society of Biblical Literature to the Johannine Literature Section, Atlanta, November 22.

Naiden, F. S. 2006. *Ancient Supplication*. Oxford: Oxford University Press.

Neyrey, Jerome H. 1989. "'I Said: You Are Gods': Psalm 82:6 and John 10." *Journal of Biblical Literature* 108:647–63.

————. 1995. "The Footwashing in John 13:6–11: Transformation Ritual or Ceremony?" In *The Social World of the First Christians: Essays in Honor of Wayne A. Meeks*, edited by L. Michael White and O. Larry Yarbrough, 198–213. Minneapolis: Fortress.

————. 2004. *Render to God: New Testament Understandings of the Divine*. Minneapolis: Fortress.

————. 2007a. *The Gospel of John*. Cambridge: Cambridge University Press.

————. 2007b. "In Conclusion. . . . John 12 as a Rhetorical Peroratio." *Biblical Theology Bulletin* 37:101–13.

Neyrey, Jerome H., and Richard L. Rohrbaugh. 2001. "He Must Increase, I Must Decrease." *Catholic Biblical Quarterly* 63:468–76.

Nielsen, Jesper Tang. 2006. "The Lamb of God: The Cognitive Structures of a Johannine Metaphor." In *Imagery in the Gospel of John*, edited by Jörg Frey et al., 217–58. Tübingen: Mohr Siebeck.

Nixon, Paul, trans. 1938. *Plautus*. Vol. 5. Loeb Classical Library 328. Cambridge, MA: Harvard University Press.

Nygren, Anders. 1930–36. *Den kristna kärlekstanken genom tiderna: Eros och Agape*. 2 vols. Stockholm: SKD.

———. 1953. *Agape and Eros*. Translated by Philip S. Watson. London: SPCK.

Ochs, Donovan J. 1993. *Consolatory Rhetoric: Grief, Symbol, and Ritual in the Greco-Roman Era*. Columbia: University of South Carolina Press.

O'Day, Gail. 1992. "John 7:53–8:11: A Study in Misreading." *Journal of Biblical Literature* 111:631–40.

O'Donnell, Tim. 2008. "Complementary Eschatologies in John 5:19–30." *Catholic Biblical Quarterly* 70:750–65.

Paffenroth, Kim. 2001. *Judas: Images of the Lost Disciple*. Louisville: Westminster John Knox.

Parsenios, George L. 2005. *Departure and Consolation: The Johannine Farewell Discourse in Light of Greco-Roman Literature*. Novum Testamentum Supplement 117. Leiden: Brill.

Perrin, Bernadotte. 1916. *Plutarch's Lives*. Vol. 4. London: Heinemann.

Petersen, Norman. 1993. *The Gospel of John and the Sociology of Light: Language and Characterization in the Gospel of John*. Valley Forge, PA: Trinity.

Phillips, Peter M. 2006. *The Prologue of the Fourth Gospel: A Sequential Reading*. Library of New Testament Studies 294. London: T&T Clark.

Poirier, John C. 1996. "'Day and Night' and the Punctuation of John 9.3." *New Testament Studies* 42:288–94.

Qimron, Elisha, and James H. Charlesworth. 1994. "Rule of the Community." In *Rule of the Community and Related Documents*. Vol. 1 of *The Dead Sea Scrolls: Hebrew, Aramaic, and Greek Texts with English Translations*, edited by James Charlesworth, 1–52. Tübingen: Mohr; Louisville: Westminster John Knox.

Reif, Stefan C. 2006. *Problems with Prayers: Studies in the Textual History of Early Rabbinic Liturgy*. Studia Judaica/Forschungen zur Wissenschaft des Judentums 37. Berlin: de Gruyter.

Reinhartz, Adele. 1999. "'And the Word Was Begotten': Divine Epigenesis in the Gospel of John." In *God the Father in the Gospel of John*, edited by Adele Reinhartz, 83–103. Society of Biblical Studies Semeia Series 85. Atlanta: Scholars Press.

———. 2001. *Befriending the Beloved Disciple: A Jewish Reading of the Gospel of John*. New York and London: Continuum.

Rensberger, David. 1988. *Johannine Faith and Liberating Community*. Philadelphia: Westminister Press.

———. 1992. "Love for One Another and Love for Enemies in the Gospel of John." In *The Love of Enemy and Nonretaliation in the New Testament*, edited by Willard M. Swartley, 287–96. Studies in Peace and Scripture 3. Louisville: Westminster John Knox.

———. 1999. "Anti-Judaism and the Gospel of John." In *Anti-Judaism and the Gospels*, edited by William Reuben Farmer, 120–57. Harrisburg, PA: Trinity.

————. 2002. "Spirituality and Christology in Johannine Sectarianism." In *Word, Theology, and Community in John*, edited by R. Alan Culpepper and Fernando F. Segovia, 173–88. St. Louis: Chalice.

Reynolds, Benjamin E. 2008. *The Apocalyptic Son of Man in the Gospel of John.* Tübingen: Mohr Siebeck.

Richards, E. Randolph. 2004. *Paul and First-Century Letter Writing: Secretaries, Composition and Collection.* Downers Grove, IL: InterVarsity.

Ricoeur, Paul. 1992. "The Self and Narrative Identity." In *Oneself as Another*, translated by Kathleen Blamey, 140–68. Chicago: University of Chicago Press.

Rogers, R. S. 1959. "The Emperor's Displeasure—*amicitiam renuntiare.*" *Transactions of the American Philological Association* 90:224–37.

Rudd, Niall, trans. 1999. *Juvenal: The Satires.* Oxford: Oxford University Press.

Salier, Willis Hedley. 2004. *The Rhetorical Impact of the Semeia in the Gospel of John: A Historical and Hermeneutical Perspective.* Wissenschaftliche Untersuchungen zum Neuen Testament 2.186. Tübingen: Mohr Siebeck.

Saller, Richard. 1994. *Patriarchy, Property, and Death in the Roman Family.* Cambridge: Cambridge University Press.

Sanders, E. P. 1992. *Judaism: Practice and Belief, 63 BCE–66 CE.* Philadelphia: Trinity.

Satlow, Michael L. 2001. *Jewish Marriage in Antiquity.* Princeton, NJ: Princeton University Press.

Schellenberg, Ryan S. 2009. "Suspense, Simultaneity, and the Providence of God: Theology and Narrative Structure in the Book of Tobit." Paper presented at the annual meeting of the Society of Biblical Literature to the Ancient Fiction and Early Christian and Jewish Narrative Section, Atlanta, November 23.

Schlatter, Adolf. 1930. *Der Evangelist Johannes wie er spricht, denkt und glaubt: Ein Kommentar zum vierten Evangelium.* Stuttgart: Calwer.

Schneiders, Sandra M. 1999. *Written That You May Believe: Encountering Jesus in the Fourth Gospel.* New York: Herder & Herder.

————. 2005. "The Resurrection (of the Body) in the Fourth Gospel: A Key to Johannine Spirituality." In *Life in Abundance: Studies of John's Gospel in Tribute to Raymond E. Brown, S.S.*, edited by John R. Donahue, 168–98. Collegeville, MN: Liturgical Press.

Schüssler Fiorenza, Elisabeth. 1986. "A Feminist Critical Interpretation for Liberation: Martha and Mary; Luke 10:38–42." *Religion and Intellectual Life* 3:16–36.

Scodal, Ruth. 2008. "Zielinski's Law Reconsidered." *Transactions of the American Philological Association* 138:107–25.

Scott, Martin. 1992. *Sophia and the Johannine Jesus.* Journal for the Study of the Old Testament: Supplement Series 212. Sheffield: Sheffield Academic Press.

Seim, Turid Karlsen. 1987. "Roles of Women in the Gospel of John." In *Aspects on the Johannine Literature: Papers Presented at a Conference of Scandinavian New Testament Exegesis at Uppsala, June 16–19, 1986*, edited by Lars Hartman and Birger Olsson, 56–73. Coniectanea biblica: New Testament Series 18. Uppsala: Almqvist & Wiksell.

Smith, Dwight Moody. 2001. *John among the Gospels*. 2nd ed. Columbia: University of South Carolina Press.

Spicq, Ceslas. 1948. "Noli me tangere." *Revue des sciences philosophiques et théologiques* 32:226–27.

Staley, Jeffrey Lloyd. 1988. *The Print's First Kiss: A Rhetorical Investigation of the Implied Reader in the Fourth Gospel*. Society of Biblical Literature Dissertation Series 82. Atlanta: Scholars Press.

———. 1991. "Stumbling in the Dark, Reaching for the Light: Reading Characters in John 5 and 9." In *The Fourth Gospel from a Literary Perspective*, edited by R. Alan Culpepper, 55–80. Society of Biblical Literature Semeia Series 53. Atlanta: Scholars Press.

———. 1993. "Subversive Narrator/Victimized Reader: A Reader Response Assessment of Text-Critical Problems, John 18:12–24." *Journal for the Study of the New Testament* 51:79–98.

———. 2002. *Reading with a Passion: Rhetoric, Autobiography, and the American West in the Gospel of John*. New York: Continuum.

Sternberg, Meir. 1985. *The Poetics of Biblical Narrative*. Bloomington: University of Indiana Press.

Stibbe, Mark W. G. 1992. *John as Storyteller: Narrative Criticism and the Fourth Gospel*. Cambridge: Cambridge University Press.

———.1993. *John*. Sheffield: Sheffield Academic Press.

Sutton, E. W., trans. 1942. *Cicero: On the Orator, Books I–II*. Loeb Classical Library 348. Cambridge, MA: Harvard University Press.

Talbert, Charles H. 2005. *Reading John: A Literary and Theological Commentary on the Fourth Gospel and the Johannine Epistles*. Macon, GA: Smyth & Helwys.

Thatcher, Tom. 2000. *The Riddles of Jesus in John*. Society of Biblical Literature Monograph Series 53. Atlanta: Scholars Press.

Thomas, John Christopher. 1991. *Footwashing in John 13 and the Johannine Community*. Journal for the Study of the New Testament: Supplement Series 61. Sheffield: JSOT Press.

———. 1995. "'Stop Sinning Lest Something Worse Come upon You': The Man at the Pool in John 5." *Journal for the Study of the New Testament* 59:3–20.

Thompson, James W. 2008. *Hebrews*. Paideia: Commentaries on the New Testament. Grand Rapids: Baker Academic.

Thompson, Marianne Meye. 2001. *The God of the Gospel of John*. Grand Rapids: Eerdmans.

Tonstad, Sigve K. 2008. "'The Father of Lies,' 'the Mother of Lies,' and the Death of Jesus." In *The Gospel of John and Christian Theology*, edited by Richard Bauckham and Carl Mosser, 193–210. Grand Rapids: Eerdmans.

Trites, Allison A. 1977. *The New Testament Concept of Witness*. Society of New Testament Studies Monograph Series 31. Cambridge: Cambridge University Press.

Trumbower, Jeffrey A. 1992. *Born from Above: The Anthropology of the Gospel of John*. Hermeneutische Untersuchungen zur Theologie 29. Tübingen: Mohr Siebeck.

Turner, Victor. 1969. *The Ritual Process: Structure and Anti-structure*. Ithaca, NY: Cornell University Press.

Vermès, Géza. 2001. *The Changing Faces of Jesus*. New York: Viking.

Waetjen, Herman C. 2005. *The Gospel of the Beloved Disciple: A Work in Two Editions*. Edinburgh: T&T Clark.

Wallace, D. B. 1996. *Greek Grammar beyond the Basics*. Grand Rapids: Zondervan.

Wedderburn, Alexander J. M. 2004. *A History of the First Christians*. London and New York: T&T Clark.

Welborn, L. L. 2005. *Paul, The Fool of Christ: A Study of 1 Corinthians 1–4 in the Comic-Philosophic Tradition*. Journal for the Study of the New Testament: Supplement Series 293. London: T&T Clark.

Wiedemann, Thomas. 1992. *Emperors and Gladiators*. London: Routledge.

Wilkens, John. 2000. *The Boastful Chef: The Discourse of Food in Ancient Greek Comedy*. Oxford: Oxford University Press.

Williams, P. J. 2007. "Not the Prologue of the Gospel of John." Paper presented at the annual meeting of the Society of Biblical Literature, San Diego, November 17.

Wimsatt, W. K., and Monroe Beardsley. 1946. "The Intentional Fallacy." *Sewanee Review* 54:468–88.

Yee, Gail. 1989. *Jewish Feasts and the Gospel of John*. Wilmington, DE: Michael Glazier.

Yonge, C. D., trans. 1993. *The Works of Philo*. Peabody, MA: Hendrickson.

Zeitlin, Froma I. 1990. "Playing the Other: Theater, Theatricality, and the Feminine in Greek Drama." In *Nothing to Do with Dionysos*, edited by John Winkler and Froma Zeitlin, 63–96. Princeton, NJ: Princeton University Press.

Index of Subjects

Index of Modern Authors

Index of Scripture and Ancient Sources

315

Pro Sestio
103 113

Tusculanae disputationes
2.17 247
3.31–32 209

Clement of Alexandria

Paedagogus
1.6.46–47 127

Stromata
5.12 36

Cyprian

Ad Quirinum testimonia adversus Judaeos
2.20 285

De catholicae ecclesiae unitate
7 252

Demosthenes

De falsa legatione
1 229–30

De Halonneso
7.1 134

Dio Chrysostom

De regno iii (Or. 3)
3.30–31 118

Dionysius of Halicarnassus

Antiquitates romanae
7.31.2 134

Epictetus

Diatribai (Dissertationes)
2.22 228
2.22.29–30 141
3.16.11 89

Epicurus

Gnomologium vaticanum
23 172
34 172
39 172

Euripides

Alcestis
379 221
781 53
1159–63 289

Andromache
1284–88 289

Bacchae
465 53
1388–92 289

Helena
1689–90 289

Hercules furens
520 216

Iphigenia aulindensis
1375–99 178

Iphigenia taurica
798–99 270
827–31 270

Medea
1323–60 133
1415–19 289

Phoenissae
391 134
1619–20 53

Troades
1285 216

Eusebius

Historia ecclesiastica
3.1 284
5.8.4 5
6.14.7 10

Heliodorus

Aethiopica
6.7 161

Hermogenes

Progymnasmata
15 25
22–23 69
68 69

Herodotus

Historiae
2.38 121
4.65 124
7.213 80
7.221 35
8.144 33

Hesiod

Theogonia
426 35

Hippolytus

Refutatio omnium haeresium
7.10 4

Homer

Ilias
6.187–89 53
6.476–81 224
8.161–83 196
9.411–16 280
15.390–97 238
18.578–608 69
19.150 79
20.178–98 196
20.242–44 81
21.157–60 99
21.187–93 105

Odyssea
1.298–302 156
3.193–200 156
8.494 53
11.409–56 156
13.429–38 135

19.137 53
19.221 57
19.393–466 271

Irenaeus

Adversus haereses
1.8.5 26
3.1.1 5, 8
3.11.6 36

Isocrates

Ad Demonicum (Or. 1)
29 165

Jerome

Commentariorum in Ezechielem libri XVI
595 282

Commentarioli in Psalmos
108 [109] 183

John Chrysostom

Homiliae in Acta apostolorum
3 183

Homiliae in Joannem
22 56
23 59
62.4 181
86.3 276

In quatriduanum Lazarum
2.5 165

John of Sardis

Progymnasmata
139.5 30

Josephus

Against Apion
2.204 8